# Managing New Product Development and Innovation

NEW HORIZONS IN THE ECONOMICS OF INNOVATION

**General Editor:** Christopher Freeman, *Emeritus Professor of Science Policy, SPRU – Science and Technology Policy Research, University of Sussex, UK*

Technical innovation is vital to the competitive performance of firms and of nations and for the sustained growth of the world economy. The economics of innovation is an area that has expanded dramatically in recent years and this major series, edited by one of the most distinguished scholars in the field, contributes to the debate and advances in research in this most important area.

The main emphasis is on the development and application of new ideas. The series provides a forum for original research in technology, innovation systems and management, industrial organization, technological collaboration, knowledge and innovation, research and development, evolutionary theory and industrial strategy. International in its approach, the series includes some of the best theoretical and empirical work from both well-established researchers and the new generation of scholars.

Titles in the series include:

# Managing New Product Development and Innovation

## A Microeconomic Toolbox

**Hariolf Grupp**

*Fraunhofer Institute for Systems and Innovation Research (Fraunhofer ISI), Karlsruhe, Germany*

**Shlomo Maital**

*The Samuel Neaman Institute for Advanced Studies in Science and Technology, Technion, Israel Institute of Technology, Haifa, Israel*

*with contributions from*
*Amnon Frenkel and Knut Koschatzky*
*as well as Asaf Ben Arieh, Galit Dopelt, Irit Gillath,*
*Mel Horwitch, Guy Levy, Thomas Reiss, Avi Shoham,*
*Galit Sobel, Han Smit and Alexander Vaninsky*

NEW HORIZONS IN THE ECONOMICS OF INNOVATION

**Edward Elgar**

Cheltenham, UK • Northampton, MA, USA

Published by
Edward Elgar Publishing Limited
Glensanda House
Montpellier Parade
Cheltenham
Glos GL50 1UA
UK

Edward Elgar Publishing, Inc.
136 West Street
Suite 202
Northampton
Massachusetts 01060
USA

A catalogue record for this book
is available from the British Library

**Library of Congress Cataloguing in Publication Data**
Grupp, Hariolf.
    Managing new product development and innovation : a microeconomic toolbox / Hariolf Grupp and Shlomo Maital.
        p. cm.– (New horizons in the economics of innovation)
    Includes bibliographical references and index.
    1. New products. 2. Technological innovations–Economic aspects. I. Maital, Shlomo. II. Title. III. Series.

HF5415.153.G784 2001                            00-065447
658.5'75–dc21

ISBN 1 84064 571 7                        .

Printed and bound in Great Britain by MPG Books Ltd, Bodmin, Cornwall

# Contents

## PART I: TOOLS FOR DECISIONS

## PART II: LINKING INNOVATION AND PERFORMANCE

# Figures

# Tables

# Introduction: A Feature-Based Approach to Innovation

Innovation, however it is defined (see Chapters 1 and 2), is a complex process in which chaos and order coexist and cooperate. Chaos generates new ideas. Disorder encourages creative individuals and teams to disassemble old ways of doing things and recombine them in new and better ways, often adding entirely new concepts and technologies.

Order helps new ideas grow into major markets. Good organization designs prototypes, raises money, builds factories, integrates suppliers, runs logistics, builds sales forces, markets, advertises and promotes. Without order, there is no innovation. But without the chaotic process, there is no core of value around which order and organization can be structured.

The essence of managing new product development and innovation lies in managing the tension between chaos and order, finding an appropriate balance between the two, allowing each to thrive without damaging its fractious neighbour, and ultimately causing each to join forces with the other.

Consider an activity many of us do daily: swallowing a pill, often several times a day. It is a basic that medicine should be taken daily, at least, in order to ensure appropriate, steady levels of the drug in the blood stream. This is burdensome. It requires us to remember to carry the pills with us, and to take them at the appropriate intervals. Clever inventions – like musical pill boxes with built-in timers – exist to remind us.

Merck, a leading US pharmaceutical company, developed a drug known as Fosamax, which helps prevent loss of calcium and bone mass, especially among older women. A creative researcher challenged the once-a-day assumption and found that for this particular drug, a once-a-week regimen with seven times the daily dose was as good as once-a-day. For those taking Fosamax, the once-a-week idea was a true innovation. It arose from chaos – the ability to challenge even the most basic of principles – and from order – the skill to test new ideas rigorously (as in the clinical trials necessary to validate the new regimen).

The order and chaos of innovation are part of what has been called the Third Industrial Revolution – a revolution now unfolding around the world, at whose core is the process of creating new products.

## The Third Industrial Revolution

The First Industrial Revolution was the result of steam power. James Watt's steam engine (1769) provided a massive new source of power, far beyond existing ones. It radically altered the way people lived and worked. The Second Industrial Revolution was caused by the invention of the dynamo and electricity. Life without electricity is unimaginable – the true acid test of a revolution, compared to a major innovation. The Second Industrial Revolution created large national markets for mass-produced products like automobiles.

Thinkers like MIT's Lester Thurow (1999) and Harvard's David Moss (1996) claim we are now in a Third Industrial Revolution, characterized by rapid advances in robotics, computers, software, biotechnology, new materials and microelectronics. In this Revolution, markets are global, rather than national. Nations grow wealthy by successfully competing in world markets. Take, for example, Singapore. This small nation of only 3.3 million persons, with a land area of a few hundred square miles, has soared from $1,060 per capita GNP in 1970 to $32,810 in 1997 – five doublings of living standards in a single generation (World Bank, 1999). In the Second Industrial Revolution, small countries without land, population or resources found it hard to grow wealthy. But in the Third, small innovative countries flexible enough to reinvent their core activities in line with world demand can grow rich very quickly. In 1980, Singapore made no disk drives. In 1982 it was the world's leading producer of them. Singapore now focuses on its service sectors, seeking to become Asia's financial, communications and shipping capital.

Just as countries grow rich by innovation, so do companies. It is widely known that on average, fully one-quarter of all corporate profits come from only 10 per cent of companies' products – the innovative 10 per cent. The link between innovation, growth and profitability has been demonstrated empirically by Cooper (1993), Cooper and Kleinschmidt (1996), and Kim and Mauborgne (1997) (see Chapter 6).

In 1998, out of 59 industries in the USA, the most profitable was pharmaceuticals, with highest return on revenues (18.5 per cent), highest return on assets (16.6 per cent) and highest return on equity (39.4 per cent) (Fortune, 1999a). A major cause is the rapid pace of innovation in this industry. Merck, the largest US pharmaceutical company, earned $5.2 billion in net profits on $27 billion in sales in 1998, a 41 per cent rate of return on shareholders' equity. Over the past decade, Merck shareholders have enjoyed a 25 per cent average annual rate of return on their investment. While many protest the high price of innovative new drugs, few would choose the cash value of $2,500 a year in savings, in return for giving up all new drugs developed since 1960.

## Arithmetic of Innovation-Driven Profits

Companies that excel at innovation have, in this Third Industrial Revolution, become phenomenal engines for generating wealth, income and jobs. Consider, for instance, the US firm Cisco Systems, headquartered in San Jose, CA, a leading supplier of networking equipment and software. Over its entire life, Cisco has collected a total sum of $9.5 billion from its shareholders and lenders. It used that money for its R&D, labs, and innovations. By January 1, 1999, the market value of Cisco shares was $145 billion. Currently that number has now doubled itself. This means that Cisco has created $290 billion minus $9.5 billion = $280.5 billion in wealth for its shareholders (Fortune, 1999b), placing it close to the top wealth creators, Microsoft and General Electric.

A recent issue of Forbes magazine (1999) lists 50 US high-tech innovators, whose personal wealth (arising from stock ownership of innovative companies) is at least half a billion dollars each.

## Economics of Speed

Skill at innovation alone is no longer sufficient. As Harvard business historian Alfred Chandler has noted, it is now the economics of speed that drives global markets, not the economics of scale. Where once new technologies took two generations to reach a quarter of all households (see Table I.1) today they take less than a decade. It is worth recalling that the Internet was born only in 1991; in less than eight years market penetration in the USA reached the level it took the automobile 55 years to attain. Managers of companies seeking to become innovative must therefore not only foster innovation but must also know how to get innovations 'out the door' and into the marketplace quickly – another instance of how chaos and order must work closely together. We believe that despite the creative, chaotic nature of the innovation process, order – and speed – can be brought to decision-making by thoughtful efforts to supply quantitative decision-support methods.

*Table I.1:  Years required for technologies to spread to 50 per cent of the US population*

| Technology | Year of invention | Time needed to reach 25% of the population |
|---|---|---|
| Household Electricity | 1873 | 46 years |
| Telephone | 1875 | 35 years |
| Automobile | 1885 | 55 years |
| Airplane | 1903 | 54 years* |
| Radio | 1906 | 22 years |
| Television | 1925 | 26 years |
| VCR | 1952 | 34 years |
| Microwave oven | 1953 | 30 years |
| PC | 1975 | 15 years |
| Cellular phone | 1983 | 13 years |
| Internet | 1991 | 7 years |

*Note:* * Airplane: 25 per cent of the 1996 level of air miles travelled per capita.

*Source*: Wall Street Journal Almanac 1998: Dow-Jones, New York, NY, 1998, p. 476; for Internet: authors' estimates.

**Management and Measurement**

We believe that management begins with measurement. What you cannot measure, you cannot properly manage. Our objective, therefore, has been to develop a set of microeconomic tools that bring order to the chaotic innovation process, by supplying a system of metrics useful for benchmarking innovations and guiding them strategically to the marketplace.[1] The basis of our approach is a framework developed by one of the authors in 1985–6 and known as 'technometrics' – literally, the metrics of technology (for the most updated version see Grupp, 1998).

In the mid–1980s, Grupp was approached by the German Federal Ministry of Education and Research, with the following question: Is Germany lagging behind America and Japan in its technology? Despite a very large literature on technological change and innovation, no suitable measurement system existed to provide a concrete answer, one that could guide national policy and strategy. Grupp and Hohmeyer (1986)[2] therefore developed a framework for measuring technological sophistication, based on individual product features.

For selected knowledge-based products, five to twelve key product features or attributes were chosen, measurable in physical units (grams, millimetres, deviation from trend, and so on), and compared across product groups and across countries. Each product feature was converted into a [0,1] metric (permitting aggregation and weighted averages), with 'zero' representing the simplest available technology, and unity representing the most sophisticated. Technometric profiles of products or product groups were produced, aggregated and compared, and graphically displayed.

In this research, it was found that even very complex product technologies can be captured in no more than a dozen key attributes. This early study concluded that overall, Germany's technology did not generally lag behind America and Japan, though Germany was stronger in some areas and weaker in others.

In 1989, Grupp and Maital received a grant from the German–Israel Foundation (GIF), for a three-year research programme on technometric comparisons of German and Israeli products and industries, with emphasis on public policy implications. This project generated a number of published papers, and led to a second three-year GIF grant, in 1996, this time focusing on developing a technometric toolbox for managers of innovation. During this second project, we studied startup firms and established ones, and worked with managers to discover what types of decision tools would be of most value, as they directed the complex innovation process from idea inception to marketing and sales.

## Structure of the Book

Part I, Tools for Decisions, comprises five studies, which offer feature-based decision tools for quantitative approaches to incremental innovation (improving existing products), radical innovation (creating new products and features), measuring the feature-based sources of market value for products, and estimating brand value.

Part II, Linking Innovation and Performances, then examines the link between innovation and performance. We present evidence showing how innovation and technological excellence is linked with export success, for Israel and the European Union (EU); and extend a macroeconomic concept pioneered by Robert Solow, known as 'total factor productivity', to the firm level, to help managers better measure and understand the forces driving productivity improvements.

Part III, Quantifying Innovation in Selected Markets, applies technometric tools to the study of specific markets and products: biodiagnostics, industrial sensors, internet software, and others.

The final Chapter integrates the various microeconomic tools presented earlier, using the unifying concept of 'business design' – a model for managing idea inception, R&D, prototyping, production, logistics, supply chain management, marketing, sales and distribution.

In this book, we have pulled together both published and unpublished papers, arising out of the two GIF projects and related research. We believe that both managers and researchers will find it convenient to have these various publications in a single concentrated volume. Of the book's 16 Chapters, ten have been previously published or are in press: Chapters 1, 4, 6, 8, 9, 10, 11, 12, 14, and 15. Six Chapters are previously unpublished: Chapters 2, 3, 5, 7, 13 and the concluding Chapter.

Each Chapter is co-authored by Grupp and Maital. In some Chapters contributions of other authors are contained. We mention these colleagues in an endnote to each Chapter headline. We have chosen to print the previously published Chapters in their original forms and only updated them. This entails a cost for the reader – basic descriptions of technometrics, for instance, appear more than once in this book, and the terminology is not uniform throughout the book. For this, we apologize. There is a benefit, however, in preserving the original figures, tables, formats and equations – it enables us to employ 'the economics of speed' and get our book to market faster, avoids the inevitable errors that retyping entails, and eliminates confusion among those who are familiar with the terminology of our earlier published work. It also makes it easier to read selected Chapters only.

Our book is aimed at two different groups: scholars, teachers and advanced students of innovation, for whom the somewhat dense language of academic journals is familiar and comfortable; and managers of innovation, who might prefer a simpler, 'cookbook' style. For the latter group, interested mainly in decision tools, we suggest reading principally Chapters 1–5, Chapter 7 and Chapters 11–13. These nine Chapters will together, we hope, offer managers a consistent framework for making hard decisions under uncertainty, and for benchmarking their products and services against those of competitors, both statically at a given point in time and dynamically, over periods of time.

We conclude this introduction with a final observation. Good management is principally good common sense. The mathematics of technometrics should not be allowed to obscure its simple, common sense core message:

* Break your product or service down into its key value-creating features.
* Measure those features against your competitors.
* Determine which features need improvement by examining which features customers find truly important.
* Build visual presentations of this process, as a common language uniting all parts of your organization.
* Do this analysis frequently, to track rapidly changing technologies and market conditions.

This book on managing innovation is, appropriately, the fruit of joint research between a German, Hariolf Grupp, and an Israeli, Shlomo Maital. Germany invented the modern system of industrial research and development, the heart of innovation, in its chemical industry around the last turn of the century, still the world's strongest. Germany's precision engineering is model of organization; it made Germany for years the world's leading exporter, and Europe's second wealthiest nation (after Switzerland, and not counting Luxemburg). Today Germany seeks to increase entrepreneurial ferment (chaos), and indeed is witnessing a remarkable explosion of new knowledge-based enterprises.

Israel, in contrast, has been called the Silicon Wadi (wadi means 'valley' or 'dry river bed' in Arabic). It is said to have some 3,000 startup companies, with 118 companies listed on US stock exchanges (among foreign countries, second only to Canada). Israel's entrepreneurial energy is almost boundless. However, it is widely recognized that order and organization – managerial skills – are extremely scarce, and so far have kept Israel from generating a large truly global company like Finland's Nokia, or Switzerland's Nestlé. Many of Israel's innovative products migrate to other countries, through acquisition or technology sale (the details are in Chapter 10).

We have joined forces to study the management of innovation, and to develop tools that help bring order to chaos, and chaos to order. It is our hope that these tools will be of interest and of value to both scholars of innovation, and managers of knowledge-based companies –

in Germany, in Israel and wherever creative people seek new ways to build better lives and better products for ordinary people.

## Acknowledgements and Dedication

Our thanks and gratitude are extended to the German–Israel Foundation and its director, Dr. Amnon Barak, for supporting our research for six of the past 10 years. Dr. Amnon Frenkel has been associated with this project since its inception, co-authored several papers, and brought order to the often-chaotic research style of the Israeli principal investigator. Dr. Knut Koschatzky was a key partner in our first GIF project and was also a valued co-author and colleague. Preparation of the manuscript was placed in the capable hands of Monika Silbereis (ISI), whose skill and dedication made this book possible. The cooperation with the publisher's staff was excellent; their proofreader added value to this book.

The Samuel Neaman Institute (SNI) for Advanced Studies in Science and Technology, at Technion-Israel Institute of Technology, Haifa, provided an amicable home base for the Israeli part of this research; SNI Directors Zehev Tadmor, Daniel Weihs, and currently Arnon Bentur were always helpful and supportive of our research. The second author spent two fruitful sabbatical leaves, first at Brookings Institution in Washington and then at MIT Sloan School of Management in Cambridge, MA, and is grateful for stimulating discussions with colleagues there and for ideal conditions for thinking and writing.

The Fraunhofer Institute for Systems and Innovation Research (ISI) at Karlsruhe was the home base for the German part of this research. For very good working conditions we thank its founder Helmar Krupp, the present director, Frieder Meyer-Krahmer, and all the collaborators and helpers.

This volume is dedicated to the next two generations of innovators of whom we mention just Sebastian, Tillmann and Friedrun (Grupp's children) as well as Romema Rachel, Aharon Meir, Maya Taya and Tal Menachem (Maital's grandchildren).

Hariolf Grupp/Shlomo Maital
Karlsruhe, January 2001

# NOTES

1   See Cebon et al. (1999) for a systematic attempt to measure innovation at the firm level, across its various functional components. Their approach is organization-based, and differs from ours, which is largely product-based, focusing on product attributes.
2   Hohmeyer, after completing his dissertation in 1988, is now Professor for Energy and Environmental Management at the German–Danish university in Flensburg.

# PART I


# Tools for Decisions

# 1 Improving Existing Products: Optimal Incremental Innovation1

## Main Ideas in this Chapter

We start Part I by constructing in this Chapter new operational definitions of incremental innovation, standard innovation, and radical innovation, using a 'technometric benchmarking' model. Based on this definition, optimal incremental innovation is formulated as a linear programming problem. The model is illustrated by an actual case: reconfiguration of a gamma camera. We show how our model can contribute to improved allocation of research and development (R&D) resources, by integrating marketing and R&D in a single decision-support model. The structure of this Chapter is as follows. The Section after the introduction outlines a typology of innovation, and proposes new definitions of the three types of innovation: incremental, standard, radical. Section 1.3 outlines our model, using cost-benefit logic and building on our typology. Section 1.4 provides an empirical illustration based on reconfiguration of a gamma camera used in magnetic imaging for medical diagnostics. We conclude with some general observations on how mathematical modelling can help integrate R&D and marketing.

## 1.1 INTRODUCTION

Whether, when and how to reconfigure existing products, processes or services are standing issues facing senior managers. While much research has been conducted on managing R&D to achieve dramatic, revolutionary innovations, everyday business success probably depends more on the quality of more humdrum, incremental improvements to existing products and services. Perhaps 90 per cent or more of so-called 'new' products are in fact reworked versions of existing ones.

Yin (1994), for instance, argues that '... the mentality that seeks large breakthroughs instead of step-by-step cumulative efforts for incremental advances dominates technology strategy ... [as a result] cutting-edge companies have largely overlooked the significance of related economic returns (from incremental advances) in their planning process ...' (p. 266). Utterback (1994, p. 189, citing Gomory and Schmitt, 1988) observes, 'most products sold today were here in slightly inferior form last year, and most competition is between variants.' 'Since standard, or dominant designs, exist in most industries, one can argue that incremental innovation is a far more prevalent and common management problem – though perhaps a more tractable one – than radical innovation', Christensen et al. (1996) note.

Decision-makers facing reconfiguration dilemmas must tackle such complex questions as: When should a reconfigured 'second-generation' product, service or process be introduced to replace an existing product, service or process? How large an investment in R&D should be made in this second-generation product? Which characteristics of the product deserve priority in terms of their cost-value ratios? How can R&D resources – funds, manpower and even time – best be invested, in the most cost-effective manner, to improve the product's value-creating power?

With growing importance attached to strategic innovation, along with rising R&D costs, there is need for operational, quantitative decision-support models to guide strategic decision-making. Over a decade ago, Lee et al. (1986) asked rhetorically: 'How are managers, many of whom are not themselves technically trained, to evaluate in real time the progress – and appropriateness – of [R&D] investments?' Managers who do have the requisite technical understanding face another challenge – allocating time. Gluck and Foster (1975) observed two decades ago that top managers spend most of their time – up to 95 per cent of it – putting out fires in marketing and production even though their ability to influence their firm's outcomes is far greater in the study, design and development stages – where CEO's invest perhaps 5 per cent of their time.

How can researchers help managers best carry out R&D for product redesign? Hauser (1996a) argues persuasively for the use of mathematical models in product development, and surveys a variety of them. Following his lead, the model proposed here is an attempt to provide a quantitative tool for optimal second-generation R&D. It builds on Hauser (1996b) and Meyer et al. (1995), who have proposed a variety of 'metrics', or quantitative measures, for managing R&D.

A number of attempts have already been made to construct quantitative operational models for evaluating R&D resource allocation. Scholefield (1994) notes that 'the allocation of R&D resource in a multibusiness organisation is often based more on current operating performance than on the relative potential for technological development of the businesses.' His model seeks to link R&D allocation to business strategy. Gittins (1994) proposes a planning model he calls 'RESPRO' for new-product chemical research; Yin (1994) studies incremental improvements in petroleum refining

Our model is based on standard economic cost-benefit logic that seeks to quantify and maximize the benefits of reconfiguration, relative to resource constraints on person-hours, capital funds and time allotted to the task. Emphasis is placed on integrating technological and engineering data with the 'voice of the market' – data drawn from surveys of buyers, expressing their subjective evaluation of product attributes – and on 'benchmarking' – the continuous process of measuring products, services, and practices against the toughest competitors or industry leaders.

## 1.2   AN OPERATIONAL TYPOLOGY OF INNOVATION: SOME BASIC THEORY

### Technometric Benchmarking

Lancaster (1991) observed that 'the good, per se, does not give utility to the consumer; it possesses characteristics, and these characteristics give rise to utility' (p. 13). A product characteristic is an important feature of the product that satisfies needs or in other ways creates value for its buyers. Marketing researchers have long believed that no-one buys a 'car', but rather, buys style, glamour, comfort, convenience, economy, status, and reliability.

It follows that the development, production and marketing of goods and services can best be understood and modelled, by focusing on key product characteristics or attributes. This is the foundation of a novel approach to product benchmarking known as 'technometrics' (Grupp, 1990b, 1994, 1998; Grupp and Hohmeyer, 1986, 1988; Koschatzky et al., 1996). It is also the basis of a huge literature in marketing on what are called 'multi-attribute models' (Fishbein, 1963; Fishbein and Ajzen, 1975; Bass and Talarzyk, 1972; Wilkie and Pessemier, 1973; and Curry and Menasco, 1983).

Technometric benchmarking builds comparative metrics of product quality and competitiveness by implementing the following four stages for a given product, process or service:

1. Choose the fundamental characteristics or attributes that capture how the product, process or service creates value for customers. These attributes must be capable of being measured (though ordinal scales are acceptable), and usually number between five and twelve.
2. Measure those attributes, and do the same for competing products.
3. Normalize each of the product's attributes on a [0, 1] metric, where 0 represents the attribute's lowest value among all competing products, and 1 represents that attribute's highest value.
4. Graph, aggregate, and otherwise analyse, the product's strengths and weaknesses, across all attributes.

Here are two examples of the use of technometric benchmarking, 'laser strippers' and medical-imaging printers. Laser strippers are devices for removing photoresistive materials from silicon surfaces used in semiconductor production; while *product* features are standard, the *process* technology (laser-based, rather than chemical or mechanical) is new. Thus, while the product itself is an example of incremental innovation (existing features are improved), the process could be regarded as a radical innovation (entirely new process features are created).

Table 1.1 shows attribute values, and technometric scores for seven attributes, for the innovative laser-stripper and four competitors. The technometric scores are calculated as follows. Consider, for instance, the '0.6' value for the L-stripper's 'process performance'. This is computed as:

Technometric Score

$$= \frac{\text{(L-stripper value)} - \text{(Value for lowest-scoring competitor)}}{\text{(Value for highest-scoring competitor)} - \text{(Value for lowest-scoring competitor)}}$$

$$= (40 - 25)/(50 - 25) = 15/25 = 0.6$$

*Table 1.1: L-stripper versus four competitors. Values of key attributes: original values ('actual') and technometric [0, 1] scale ('tech')*

|  | L-stripper | | Compe-titor 1 | | Compe-titor 2 | | Compe-titor 3 | | Compe-titor 4 | |
|---|---|---|---|---|---|---|---|---|---|---|
|  | act | tech | act | tech | act | tech | act | tech | act | tech |
| Process perfor-mance | 40 | 0.6 | 50 | 1 | 25 | 0 | 30 | 0.2 | 35 | 0.4 |
| Yield | * | 1 | 77 | 0.97 | 55 | 0.6 | 19 | 0 | 79 | 1 |
| Damage | * | 1 | * | 1 | * | 1 | * | 1 | * | 1 |
| Reliabi-lity | * | 0 | * | 0.89 | * | 1 | * | 0.39 | * | 0.36 |
| therein: MTBF | * |  | 130 | 1 | 130 | 1 | 65 | 0 | 80 | 0.25 |
| therein: MTTR | * |  | 8.5 | 0.75 | 7 | 1 | 13 | 0 | 8 | 0.83 |
| therein: UPTIME | * |  | 92 | 0.93 | 95 | 1 | 85 | 0.78 | 50 | 0 |
| Through-put | 50 | 1 | 45 | 0.75 | 35 | 0.25 | 50 | 1 | 30 | 0 |
| Particles | 0.1 | 1 | 0.02 | 1 | 0.02 | 1 | 0.12 | 0 | 0.04 | 1 |
| CV | 100 | 1 | 100 | 1 | 100 | 1 | 0 | 0 | 0 | 0 |

*Notes:*
* Confidential.
Process performance — test for quality of removal of photoresistors, scale of 1 to 100 points.
Yield — per cent of total components usable, out of total number of components on the wafer.
Reliability — three characteristics: MTBF (mean time between failure), MTTR (mean time to repair),
UPTIME (per cent of time the device is operating).
Throughput — speed of operation, measured in wafers per hour.
Particles — test for presence of undesirable particles after completion of stripping process.
CV — test for presence of conductive ions (generated in the stripping process).

The new product excels in all but two characteristics: 'process performance' (rated as highly important by customers) and 'reliability', where it scores lowest. Its dismal reliability score make the product unmarketable in its current form. Further development efforts will focus on these two weak points. (See Figure 1.1.) The current version now scores 1.0 in process performance, and is much

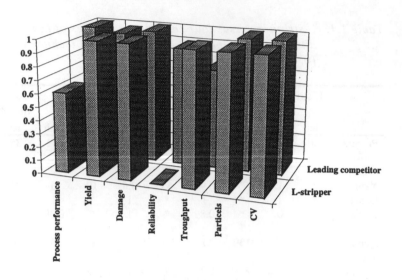

*Figure 1.1:   L-stripper versus leading competitor*

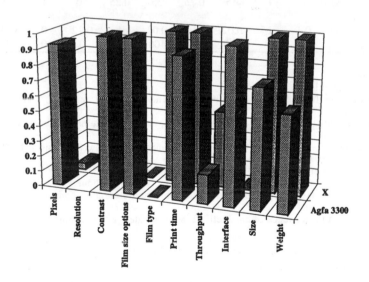

*Figure 1.2:   A graphic technometric comparison of two medical imaging printers: Agfa versus 'X'*

improved in reliability; the product is now close to commercial production.

Figure 1.2 compares a leading medical-imaging printer (Agfa) with a new challenger ('X'). The challenger excels against all models, including Agfa, in film type, print time, size and weight – but falls short in other key attributes. The new product in its existing form failed. The technometric 'silhouette' shown in Figure 1.2 helps us understand why. What appears utterly obvious, after carrying out the technometric benchmarking, is in our experience often *far from obvious* beforehand. Carrying out a characteristic-by-characteristic quantitative analysis forces the careful numerical benchmarking that decision-making demands.

## Typology of Innovation

The technometric benchmarking approach can be used to construct a typology of innovation. In our view, no satisfactory operational definition currently exists of the various types of innovation (Dewar and Dutton, 1986): incremental, standard and radical. Rosegger (1996) defines radical innovations as 'clear discontinuities in economic activity' (p. 237), for example steam engine, computers; implying that incremental innovations are innovations that are neither basic nor major, arising principally when standard or dominant designs exist as platforms on which minor improvements are made. Yin's (1994) definition for radical innovation: 'a revolutionary change that contains a high degree of new knowledge [while] incremental improvement is a renovation and adjustment of current technology with a low degree of new knowledge' (pp. 265–266).

These definitions rest on rather vague notions of 'major', and 'new knowledge'. We now proceed to build a new operational typology of innovation, based on the Lancaster attribute model (see Grupp, 1994, pp. 180–181).

We define a product, service or process as a finite collection of characteristics or attributes, all of them measurable in either physical or ordinal units (for example consumer satisfaction scales). For a given product, let those 'n' attributes be $x_i$ , where $i = 1, ..., n$ . A product, then, is simply a vector of attributes:

$$[x_1, x_2, ..., x_n]$$

## Definitions

1. An *incremental innovation* is one in which a new version of an existing product has some or all of its existing attributes improved. The new vector is:

$$[x^*_1, x^*_2, ..., x^*_n], \text{ all } x^*_i = c_i \, x_i, \text{ some } c_i \neq 1,$$

where $x^*_i$ is the new post-development value of attribute i, and $c_i$ is a vector of scalars, showing the proportion of change in each product feature.[2]

A hypothetical example of an incremental innovation is shown below in Table 1.2, for a large business jet, the Gulfstream IV. A reconfigured improved Gulfstream V may have better range, speed, payload, climb and cabin room. The new vector of attributes quantifies the degree to which the product was improved, in a way that permits easy benchmarking against competing products.

*Table 1.2: Gulfstream IV versus 'improved' gulfstream*

|     | Range | Pay-load | Speed | Climb | Take-off | Cabin room | Noise | Cost per mile |
|-----|-------|----------|-------|-------|----------|------------|-------|---------------|
| Old | 4141  | 3.66     | 459   | 4014  | 5280     | 2008       | 76.8  | 18.28         |
| New | 5000  | 3.66     | 480   | 4500  | 5280     | 2500       | 76.8  | 18.28         |

2. A *standard innovation* is one in which the vector of product attributes is:

$$[x'_1, x'_2, ..., x'_n, x'_{n+1}], \, x'_i = c_i \, x_i,$$

where $x'_{n+1}$ represents a new product attribute that did not previously exist.

The difference between a standard innovation and an incremental innovation is that one additional attribute is added to the product that did not exist before (while existing attributes may or may not be improved somewhat). An example could be the addition of CD-ROM read-only drive to PCs.

3. A *radical innovation* is an innovation such that 'k' significant new attributes are created, $k \geq 2$, which did not before exist – creating, essentially, a wholly new product:

$$[x^\circ_1, x^\circ_2, ..., x^\circ_n, x^\circ_{n+1}, x^\circ_{n+2}, x^\circ_{n+3}, ..., x^\circ_{n+k}], x^\circ_i = c_i x_i.$$

An example is a new pen-based computer that stores handwritten material in its memory, then recognizes each character and transfers the material to standard computer files. Some of its attributes: pen size, memory size, accuracy of letter recognition, and so on, are new and are thus not comparable to existing attributes of conventional computers.

Corporate decisions to launch R&D programmes for radical innovation are often crucial, and often compete with less risky, less costly – and potentially less profitable – incremental-innovation R&D. An example is Intel's decision to continue developing SISC technology for its 486-successor chip, rather than develop a RISC chip, like the Power-PC of Motorola–IBM–Apple. In retrospect, the decision was a good one, aided by clever technological improvements leading to the Pentium and Pentium Pro.

We propose here a decision tool to aid managers in optimizing their incremental innovations, based on technometric benchmarking. With slight adaptation, our model could serve decision-making for standard innovations as well, and with considerable alteration, for radical innovation.


## 1.3  A MATHEMATICAL PROGRAMMING MODEL FOR EVALUATING INCREMENTAL INNOVATION

Consider a manager with limited labour, capital and financial resources, and especially limited time, managing an R&D project to create incremental innovation for an existing product. What attributes should be improved? How can the R&D investment best be utilized? Is the project worth while at all? How can one know? Our model supplies some answers.

Managers seek the most valuable feasible combination of improvements in product (or process) specifications, that meets (a) cost; (b) skill; and (c) time constraints. 'Valuable', in our model, means: The highest possible weighted average of product attribute

improvements, where the weights reflect the value consumers attach to
the improvement of each attribute.

We believe that senior management's ultimate objective is to supply
the market with the most valuable, attractive package of attributes
possible. Products that best create value, will best create sales, market
share and profit.

### Terminology

$i$ = product, service or process characteristic, $i = 1, ..., n$,

$x_i$ = technometric specification for characteristic 'i',
based on [0,1] metric {0 is lowest performance,
1 is highest performance, among competing products},

$\Delta x_i$ = change in $x_i$ through R&D investment,[3]

$c_i$ = cost of making incremental change in $x_i$,

$t_i$ = time needed to make incremental change in $x_i$,

$l_i$ = skilled labour-hour needed to make an incremental change
in $x_i$,

$w_i$ = market value of an incremental change in technometric
specification $x_i$,

$C$ = total R&D budget ($ million),

$L$ = total number of skilled labour-hours,

$T$ = time available for completing R&D.

### Model

Objective function:
Choose $\Delta x_i$ to Max $\Sigma w_i \Delta x_i$ subject to capital, labour and time
constraints:

Capital: $\Sigma c_i \Delta x_i < C$
Labour: $\Sigma l_i \Delta x_i < L$
Time: $\Sigma t_i \Delta x_i < T$

That is: allocate labour, capital and time to R&D efforts, in order to
improve the product's attributes, in a way that generates that
highest-value 'basket' of product attributes, where 'basket' is a
weighted average of the product attributes, with weights reflecting how
the market (that is customers) values the improvements.

This is a linear programming model. Incremental improvements are
consistent with the assumption of linearity. But in many cases, the

constraints may well be non-linear in nature. This can easily be handled by implementing quadratic or other non-linear programming techniques.

Standard linear programming algorithms provide solutions that include: the optimal improvement $\Delta x_i$ for each attribute, and the way to achieve the improvement through investment of labour, capital and time.

## Voice of the Market

A vital aspect of the model is the '$w_i$' weights, which can play a crucial role in deciding which attributes of the product should be improved: How can they be determined? One approach is through conducing 'voice of the market' surveys among customers, who indicate on a questionnaire the relative importance of each of the product attributes. There are other several competing approaches to evaluating 'voice of the market', apart from the 'voice of the market' questionnaire, including the technique known as 'hedonic price indexes' (in which product price is the dependent variable of a statistical least-squares regression, with product attributes as the independent, explanatory variables; beta coefficients then become the relative 'weights' for the programming model's objective function).[4]

Finally, conjoint analysis can be used to evaluate 'tradeoffs' of consumers among competing attribute improvements. Chan Choi and DeSarbo (1994) use a technique known as conjoint analysis: 'In a typical conjoint-based product designing or concept testing procedure, estimated individual level part-worth utilities are used to simulate the potential market shares of proposed product concepts against existing competitors' brands. .... We compute equilibrium market shares and prices for each scenario of a concept profile versus existing brands' (pp. 451–454).

## 1.4   AN EXAMPLE: THE GAMMA CAMERA – 'ACU-SCAN'

**Background**

The gamma camera is an imaging system intended to assist in diagnosis of illness by doctors. It produces images of the radiation generated by radioisotopes within a patient's body, with the objective of examining organ function and anatomy and to detect abnormalities. It serves as a diagnostic tool, in the hands of the physician, for evaluation and follow-up of disease and physiological problems. Initially a radioisotope attached to a chemical mediator is injected into the human body and targeted to a specific organ. When the radiopharmaceutical accumulates in the target organ, it emits radiation, which is detected and counted by the gamma camera detectors. The data collected is then processed by a computer, and can be rendered as a graphic picture, on a computer monitor. The nuclear radiologist can then provide his interpretation and diagnosis, and report his findings.

The customers whose preferences are decisive are those of the doctors, who use the camera's output, and the technicians who operate it. The market for gamma cameras is increasingly influenced by the trend to managed health care, which focuses attention on the camera's price efficiency: cost relative to its performance.

Six basic parameters characterize the camera's appeal to customers: price; downtime; connectivity to other systems and work stations; its ability to carry out optimally a wide variety of medical applications and ease of operation (extent to which operation is automatic); ability to carry out examinations using high-energy isotops (511 keV) and thus improve resolution; and transmission/emission.

**Product**

Acu-Scan is a pseudonym for an actual multipurpose gamma camera, produced by a mid-size firm that specializes in medical instruments. Acu-Scan has two detection heads positioned opposite one another, at a fixed 180°. The heads are attached to a gantry and are placed on a large ring that rotates the heads around the patient. Patients are usually examined in a prone position, lying on a bed. The bed moves up and down, backward and forward. Acu-Scan is regarded as a highly sophisticated   system,   incorporating   cutting-edge   mechanical, electronical, and computer technologies. Its resolution is high; its automated operation provides ease of operation and reduces the need for skilled operators. Its conectivity with other systems is good, making it usable in modular form with other equipment in the clinic. However, Acu-Scan's price is regarded as above average in its market, and it lacks some attributes other cameras possess – like heads with variable, adjustable angles. Acu-Scan is unable to perform transmission of rays simultaneously with emission (of radiation), a method used to improve reliability and reduce artefacts, an attribute that now represents state of the art in nuclear medicine, specifically in nuclear cardiology (attribute no. 6).

**Management Problem**

As Acu-Scan completed its introduction and penetration of the market, a marketing need was discerned, to develop a more advanced dual-head camera, with only a twelve-month development time and a limited budget. The Acu-Scan marketing department defined a number of improvements in the camera's performance attributes that were perceived as vital to maintain market share and market leadership in the nuclear medicine marketplace.

The questions that faced management were:

- In which attributes should R&D resources be invested?
- What are the priorities?
- How much money, manpower and time should be invested?
- What will be the value of the reconfigured Acu-Scan camera compared with its predecessor, relative to the resources invested in developing it?

In other words: what is the optimal R&D programme for incremental innovation? The vital issue is, of course: *How do buyers perceive the value of improvements to the six key attributes?* Which feasible combination of such improvements would create the most attractive, marketable second-generation camera?

**Model**

The following mathematical programming model was employed. Six key product attributes were identified, together with the relative importance of each attribute, or weights. The weights were computed by consulting senior doctors and a leading professional journal; see Table 1.3.

*Table 1.3: Nuclear camera attributes and their importance*

|  | Technometric value# | Weight** |
|---|---|---|
| 1. Price | 6.2 | 9.75 |
| 2. Down time | 6.3 | 9.5 |
| 3. Connectivity | 7.6 | 9.6 |
| 4. All-purpose* | 8.5 | 9.0 |
| 5. Resolution | 6.6 | 10.0 |
| 6. Simultaneous transmission, emission | 6.0 | 8.0 |

*Notes:*
\#   For Acu-Scan camera, relative to competitors ( = 10).
\*   Ability to perform all the nuclear medicine functions.
\*\*  On a scale of 1 to 10.

The sum of up to $X million was budgeted for the development; development time was not to exceed 12 months; and up to 20 man-years of skilled labour was made available.

The model itself is shown in Table 1.4. The linear programming solution is shown in Table 1.5.

*Table 1.4:*   *Programming model: optimal incremental innovation for acu-scan camera*

| Attribute | 1 | 2 | 3 | 4 | 5 | 6 |
|---|---|---|---|---|---|---|
| Vector of weights $w_i$ | 9.75 | 9.5 | 9.6 | 9.0 | 10.0 | 8.0 |
| Cost coefficients $c_i$ | 0.9 | 0.1 | 0.1 | 1.0 | 0.6 | 0.3 |
| Labour coefficients $l_i$ | 4.0 | 2.0 | 2.0 | 10.0 | 1.0 | 1.0 |
| Time coefficients $t_i$ | 2.0 | 2.0 | 2.5 | 5.5 | 3.0 | 2.0 |

Maximize $9.75 \, \Delta x_1 + 9.5 \, \Delta x_2 + 9.6 \, \Delta x_3 + 9\Delta x_4 + 10 \, \Delta x_5 + 8 \, \Delta x_6$

subject to:
a. financial constraint:
$0.9 \, \Delta x_1 + 0.1 \, \Delta x_2 + 0.1 \, \Delta x_3 + 1 \, \Delta x_4 + 0.3 \, \Delta x_5 + 0.3 \, \Delta x_6 < \$X \, m.^5$
b. labour constraint:

$4 \Delta x_1 + 2 \Delta x_2 + 2 \Delta x_3 + 10 \Delta x_4 + 1 \Delta x_5 + 1 \Delta x_6 < 21$ man–years
c. time constraint:
$2 \Delta x_1 + 2 \Delta x_2 + 2.5 \Delta x_3 + 5.5 \Delta x_4 + 3 \Delta x_5 + 2 \Delta x_6 < 12$ months.

*Table 1.5: Optimal resource allocation for incremental innovation: by attribute*

|  | Capital | Labour | Time | Optimal value | Initial value |
|---|---|---|---|---|---|
|  | $ million | Person–years | Months |  |  |
| Price | 0.9 X | 12 | 6 | 9.2 | 6.2 |
| Downtime | 0.1 X | 2 | 6 | 9.3 | 6.3 |
| Connectivity | 0 | 2 | 0 | 7.6 | 7.6 |
| All purpose | 0 | 0 | 0 | 8.5 | 8.5 |
| Resolution | 0 | 0 | 0 | 6.6 | 6.6 |
| Transmission/ Emission | 0 | 0 | 0 | 6.0 | 6.0 |
| Total | X | 16 | 12 |  |  |

*Note:* Overall improvement in the objective function: 15 per cent.

The linearity of the model moves the solution toward improving only two of the attributes – resources are directed toward where they contribute most to the objective function, and the system does not encounter the diminishing returns present if non-linearities were taken into account. Labour is a slack variable: four person-years are unused. The identification of slack resources is an important advantage of the model – skilled workers generally work long hours, are fully occupied, and the manager's naked eye has trouble discerning that their labour may in part be superfluous.

Capital and time are 'scarce' variables, with non-zero shadow prices. From the high shadow price of time, we can see that this is the most severely binding constraint – a common situation when a two-month reduction in time-to-market may mean the difference between market success and failure.

We found that if the time constraint were relaxed, adding three months to the 12-month period, along with $100,000 in additional capital, some of the resources would then be directed to improving 'connectivity'. The sensitivity of linear programming models to small changes in parameters and coefficients make it vital to undertake sensitivity analyses – alteration of parameters to determine how the model's outcome reacts. *Another important reason for sensitivity analysis is the uncertainty that attaches to many of the underlying coefficients; it is always well to know how sensitive the solution is to possible estimation errors in key coefficients.*

The model directs managers to improve the Acu-Scan incrementally, by performing R&D that will permit a significant reduction in price (perhaps by improving the process technology used in production), and result in a significant reduction in down time. Overall, the price decline achievable is 3 technometric units, or 3 • \$20,000 = \$60,000, and raise the down time score from mediocre (6.3) to excellent (9.3). Both attribute improvements improve the cost-effectiveness of the gamma camera – an important competitive advantage in an increasingly price- and cost-sensitive market.

The optimal allocation of R&D resources leads to a 15 per cent improvement in the Acu-Scan's technometric objective-function score. About two-thirds of that improvement stems from price reduction, and one-third from improvement in down time.

**Discussion**

Management's R&D decision was not guided by the model, because it was not available to them at the time. Senior managers decided to invest R&D resources in improving the 'all purpose' attribute, and in 'transmission/emission'. This was a logical decision. The 'all purpose' attribute has a reasonably high customer-preference weight, and it is the feature in which the Acu-Scan camera scores highest. It makes good sense to further strengthen the attribute that already provides strong competitive advantage, in anticipation that competitors will work hard to close the gap in this area.

The marketplace's demand for high 'all purpose' scores is interesting. This characteristic is kind of an 'entrance exam' or 'quality test' – cameras that lack it, flunk. Yet, doctors generally do not make use of it. 'All purpose' is a buzzword that cameras must convey, or fail. Such knowledge is brought to the R&D lab from the marketplace. Knowing it can make the difference between success and failure in reconfiguration. Excess reliance on mechanical models is, for this reason, dangerous.

Resolution is a key characteristic; however, enormous investments are needed to improve it significantly enough to make a difference in the marketplace. The cost-value ratio is prohibitive.

Connectivity is driven in part by cost containment; buyers seek to purchase from suppliers their best instrument, then link them all up together, rather than buy the complete system from one supplier.

Transmission/emission was the Acu-Scan camera's weakest feature, and it made sense to work to improve it. However, the linear programming model showed that the cost-benefit ratio or return to investment in improving this attribute was dismal. In reality, a new camera that greatly improved this feature turned out to be a smash hit. We thus urge caution in using our quantitative model. While we believe it offers valuable insights, the inherent nature of the incremental innovation process require seniors managers to weigh the results of optimizing models against their own experience, intuition and intimate knowledge of their customers, needs and wants – a caveat that applies to all decision-support optimization techniques in the area of R&D.

The model, therefore, focuses R&D investment on three attributes: price, connectivity, down time. The marketplace speaks loud and clear, that cost-effectiveness is a crucial attribute in the age of managed health care and cost-cutting. It also says, for similar reasons, that in order to be competitive gamma cameras must have minimal down time – in nuclear medicine, time is literally money – and that the camera must link up seamlessly with a wide variety of peripheral equipment. These were the variables our model found gave the highest value/cost ratio for R&D investment.

In practice, considerable resources were invested in providing the camera with variable-angle capability, to make it all purpose. Managers simply believed they had no choice in this matter. All purpose capability was indeed perceived as a kind of 'entry fee' gamma cameras needed, to prove credibility in the market.

## 1.5   IMPLICATIONS AND CONCLUSION

How does this model contribute toward integrating marketing and R&D (see Griffin and Hauser, 1996)? Managing incremental innovation is a matter of balancing cost and value. The value of incremental improvements to product attributes is a crucial input to the model that can be obtained best from marketing managers in the field. The cost of those improvements is an input that the expertise of R&D managers can provide. Optimal R&D investment in incremental innovation results from obtaining the biggest bang for the buck – maximizing the value of incremental improvements, relative to their cost in terms of time, money and labour.

There is value in quantifying such decisions, even at considerable cost. It is sometimes surprising that managers who thoroughly explore investment options when engaging in financial investment, risk huge sums in R&D with very little effort to gather data or quantify and model the decision.

There will surely be occasions on which the results of a programming model deserve to be ignored – especially when high uncertainty attaches to its cost parameters. But the combination of mathematical programming, and intuition, is in almost all cases more powerful than pure intuition alone.

Incremental innovation is subject to the dangers of the 'sunk cost' fallacy – the notion that because a product exists, with considerable investment of resources and time, it is necessary to continue to improve, market and produce it.

As Phillips et al. (1994) note:

'Dassault's decision to bring out the Falcon 900 as a follow-on to the Falcon 50 illustrates a second feature of the sunk-cost risks in a market characterized by continuing technological opportunities. The need to devote resources to the development of new products does not stop after successful innovation. The learning that occurs in the first element of the process leads to ideas about improving the product. This is augmented by developments in science and technology that occur outside of the firm in question. Great pressure exists to use that knowledge in creating yet another airplane, partly because of the urges characteristic of the Schumpeterian entrepreneur' (p. 133).

We simulated the Falcon 900 investment, for instance, using our model and found only an 18 per cent incremental improvement in the objective function in return for a large investment, even when the incremental innovation is managed optimally. It is generally believed that the Falcon 900 will not be successful in challenging the market domination of the Gulfstream Series V and VI.

Two decades ago, Gluck and Foster (1975) proposed that top managers participate earlier in the R&D process, emphasizing: (1) strategic performance parameters of products in each product/market segment, how they have shifted, how they may shift in future, and the product's position in each parameter compared with that of the principal competitors; (2) the improvements that customers would value most in each parameter; (3) changes in each parameter that could lead to competitive advantage; and (4) potential moves of competitors, government, consumer groups, or work markets, that could undermine the company's advantages in each parameter (pp. 147–148).

We believe that our typology of innovation, and the mathematical programming model based on it, can provide at least partial answers to the first three issues, by bringing the key input of the marketplace to the lab bench of the R&D engineer, perhaps via the desk of the chief technology officer.

## NOTES

1   The research underlying this Chapter was supported additionally to the GIF grant by the Technion VPR Fund for the Promotion of Research, and the Y. Apter Research Fund. We thank Dr. Alexander Vaninsky for his programming assistance. A version of this Chapter was presented at a Seminar of the Tinbergen Institute, Erasmus University, where one of the authors, S. M., was Visiting Professor in Sept.–Oct. 1997. An earlier version of this Chapter was published in *Research Evaluation* 7 (2), pp. 123–131, 1998, as a co-production with Asaf Ben Arieh.

2   Note that this definition permits an incremental innovation, in which some product features are actually worsened, in order to save resources that can be directed toward improving other product features. This amounts to moving to a new point on the 'production possibilities frontier', where production possibilities are defined not in product space but in product feature space. An example: the French one-star hotel chain, Formule, dispensed with receptionists, room service and other amenities, while improving hygiene, quietness and bed quality. The incrementally innovative product has been warmly received by business travellers, who mainly want a quiet, clean room with a comfortable bed. The economic logic of worsening a product is discussed in Grupp (1998, Chapter 10).

3   Improvements are defined in terms of 'one technometric unit', which is 0.1 on the [0, 1] technometric scale (Maital and Vaninsky, 1994); for instance, an improvement of 0.1 in the product feature 'price' means development that enables a price reduction of $20,000 (from an original price of $200,000); the cost of such a price reduction, in terms of R&D investment, is $900,000, or a coefficient of 0.9. Hence, $c_i$ is equal to 0.9.

4   See, for example, Grupp and Maital (1998a).

5   The company with which we worked asked that we not disclose the R&D budget, which is noted above as $X million.

# 2 Creating New Products: Optimal Radical Innovation[1]

**Main Ideas in this Chapter**

In Chapter 1 we proposed a new operational definition of incremental, standard and radical innovation, based on a multi-attribute model known as 'technometric benchmarking'. In this Chapter, we focus on radical innovation, defined as a product such that out of 'n' product attributes, a significant subset 'k' exists, comprising product attributes that did not exist previously. We outline a mathematical programming approach to optimizing R&D investment, which provides a systematic approach to integrating R&D and marketing to provide a decision-support system for guiding R&D for radical innovation. We make use of a basic economic tool — the production possibilities curve — to examine tradeoffs between existing product attributes and radically new ones. As for the case of incremental innovation, we stress the value of the model in integrating market information ('psychology') and technological constraints and advances. Our Chapter addresses what we view as a key issue in radical innovation: how to avoid costly, unsuccessful 'technology push' products which fail to find 'demand-pull' markets. We illustrate our model with a case study from laser medicine.

## 2.1 WHAT IS RADICAL INNOVATION?

The theoretical 'innovation' or 'technical progress' construct has not been established unambiguously. Rather, literature contains a variety of partly contradictory designations and definitions of the term 'innovation'. Also, the views of economists ('world novelty') differ substantially from those of industrial and business management economists ('new potential suppliers to a market', that is, new to the

22

firm). Within the OECD, for many years work on guidelines for defining technological innovation has been proceeding for statistical purposes. The outcome is the so-called 'Oslo Manual' (OECD, 1992). According to this source, the technological innovation concept embraces both substantially new products (designated 'major innovations') and also significant technological changes to existing products and processes. An improvement in performance characteristics is termed incremental product innovation. 'Minor' technical or aesthetic modifications to products, that is, non-progress relevant product changes are not regarded as incremental innovation and excluded from the innovation concept.

The view is taken that radical innovation is a relatively coherent category within the usual spread of 'minor' versus 'major' concepts since it rarely occurs in practice, whereas the incremental innovation concept, when all is said and done, covers the vast majority of all other innovation events but is less conspicuous. Gordon (1992) contends that the 'standard innovation' falls neatly into the large gaps between the radical and the more minor forms of innovation which in bipartition of concepts is wrongly disregarded.

Yet, products differ, according to how they are made ('process technology'), the benefits they yield consumers (attributes), how they are used or perceived (consumer behaviour), or how the product is integrated with other products or systems (architecture). Thus, radical innovation can be defined by focusing on significant discontinuities or change in any or all of the above four aspects.

Henderson and Clark (1990) define radical innovation as fulfilling two necessary conditions: an 'overturned' core concept of the product, and major change in the linkage among the core components of the product. Mansfield (1968) and Nelson and Winter (1982) focus on the competitive consequences of radical, as opposed to incremental, innovation. Moore (1991) focuses on how the product is used, and defines 'discontinuous innovation' as products that require us to change our current mode of behaviour or to modify other products and services we rely on (p. 10). For the concept of discontinuity see also Ehrnberg (1995). In a simulation, Windrum and Birchenhall (1998) demonstrate that by learning effects of both producers and consumers of an innovation multiple as well as single designs configurations can occur.[2]

The one thing that all these theoretical constructs have in common is that they try qualitatively to keep the various types of innovation apart. The boundary line between them runs along verbally shaded distinctions like 'large', 'significant' or 'substantial'. The task remains to establish whether it is possible to measure all types of innovation with a formal, mathematical concept.

In Ben-Arieh et al. (1998), we put forward new definitions of incremental, standard and radical innovation. Our taxonomy was built on the premise that products are best seen as combinations of features, or attributes – an approach developed independently, and somewhat differently, in three disciplines: economics (Lancaster, 1971, 1991); management of technology and innovation (Grupp 1994; Saviotti and Metcalfe, 1984); and marketing (Fishbein, 1963; Fishbein and Ajzen, 1975; Bass and Talarzyk, 1972; Wilkie and Pessemier, 1973; Curry and Menasco, 1983). We went on to construct and illustrate a mathematical programming model for optimal incremental innovation, based on optimizing the cost-value ratios of incremental improvements in product features.

In this Chapter, we outline a new conceptual approach to optimizing radical innovation. While the core of radical innovation is generally, and rightly, viewed as a creative, inspirational process not easily adapted to quantitative models, we maintain that it is both possible and desirable to model radical innovation, in ways that aid decision-making and reduce risk.

Section 2.2 presents our concept, Section 2.3 introduces the optimizing model, Section 2.4 illustrates a case in study, laser medicine (laser scalpels), which is a knowledge-based product, and Section 2.5 demonstrates how the optimizing model works in this case.

## 2.2   A MODEL OF RADICAL INNOVATION

We choose the conventional approach and focus on product features. We define a product, service or process as a finite collection of characteristics or attributes, all of them measurable in either physical or ordinal units (for example consumer satisfaction scales). For a given product, let those 'n' attributes be $x_i$ , where i = 1, ..., n. As we need metric scales, all the attributes measured in physical or ordinal units are converted into a [0, 1] interval by the technometric algorithm (Grupp, 1994, 1998). A product X, then, is simply a vector of attributes:

$$X = \quad [x_1, x_2, ..., x_n]$$

If we now integrate Henderson and Clark's (1990) distinction between product core or component technology and peripheral systems or linkage technology, we may differentiate between 'modular' and 'architectural' attributes. Suppose our product has m modular and s systemic or architectural attributes, with m + s = n, we arrive at:

$$X = [x_1, x_2, ..., x_m, x_{m+1}, ... x_{m+s}].$$

Let us stress here that the systemic part of the attributes may, but need not in any case, be related to standardization. Thus new entrants may be forced to fulfil certain systemic features with their innovative startup products — eventually to the benefit of the incumbent market leaders by reinforcing the overall architecture of the systems.

As is well known (Swann et al., 1996), an industry standard does one or more of three things in innovation:

- it may allow products to work together (compatibility standard);
- it may define quality levels (minimum quality standard, for example for safety);
- it may reduce the number of variants in a product system (variety reduction or scale economies standard).

**Definitions**

1. An *incremental innovation* is one in which a new version of an existing product has some or all of its existing attributes improved. The new vector is:

$$X^\circ = [x^\circ_1, x^\circ_2, ..., x^\circ_n], \text{ all } x^\circ_i = c_i x_i, \text{ some } c_i \neq 1,$$

where $x^\circ_i$ is the new post-development value of attribute i.

2. A *standard innovation* is one in which the vector of product attributes is:

$$X' = [x'_1, x'_2, ..., x'_n, x'_{n+1}], x'_i = c_i x_i,$$

where $x'_{n+1}$ represents a new product attribute that did not previously exist.

The difference between a standard innovation and an incremental innovation is that one additional attribute is added to the product that did not exist before (while existing attributes may or may not be improved ot worsened somewhat in order to improve the others or fit with the new one). An example could be the addition of CD-ROM read-only drives to PCs.

| Innovation typology | Core technology reinforced | Core technology overturned |
|---|---|---|
| Pheripheral interfaces unchanged | *Incremental innovation* | *Modular (standard) innovation* $\Downarrow$ |
| Peripheral interfaces changed | *Architectural (standard) innovation* $\Rightarrow$ | *Radical innovation* |

*Figure 2.1:   Innovation typology*

If the attribute n + 1 adds to the m modular features, we speak of a modular (standard) innovation, if it adds to the s systemic proporties, we have an architectural (standard) innovation. The CD-ROM drive to a PC would certainly be a modular innovation.

3. A *radical innovation* is an innovation such that 'k' significant new attributes are created, $k \geq 2$, which did not before exist – creating, essentially, a wholly new product (thereby the 'old' $x_1$, ..., $x_n$ attributes may become obsolete):

$$X^* = [x^*_1, x^*_2, ..., x^*_n, x^*_{n+1}, x^*_{n+2}, x^*_{n+3}, ..., x^*_{n+k}], x^*_i = c_i x_i.$$

We want to emphasize that radical innovation is thus defined as a continuum which can always be decomposed in a series of $m^+$ modular standard innovations and $s^+$ systemic standard innovations, if $m^+ + s^+ = k$. However, because standardization works at least in the architectural part of innovation, and because we adopted the economic definition of innovation (new to the world market, not new to the firm), we think confidently that in most cases cores and interfaces will be overturned to a large extent in radical innovation so that we need not study the case of few standard innovations as a separate issue.

An example of a radical innovation with a strong modular component is the laser scalpel that replaces the traditional knife scalpel of surgeons affecting the periphery in the operating room to some extent. Remote surgery by micro-manipulators, whereby the doctor may be hundreds of miles away from the patient, is a radical innovation with a strong architectural component.

Another example for a modular radical innovation is a new pen based computer that stores handwritten material in its memory, then recognizes each character and transfers the material to standard computer files. Some of its attributes: pen size, memory size, accuracy of letter recognition, and so on, are new and are thus not comparable to existing attributes of conventional computers. The transition from mainframes to PCs is an architectural radical innovation.

## 2.3  OPTIMIZATION MODEL

We now alter and adapt our mathematical programming model developed for incremental innovation (Ben-Arieh et al., 1998) to provide a decision-support system for guiding R&D for radical innovation.

Terminology:
$P_a$ = price of existing product 'a'
$P_b$ = price of radically innovative product 'b'
$Q_a$ = total demand for product 'a' (units)
$Q_b$ = total demand for product 'b'
$X$ = vector of n attributes for product 'a' as defined above
$X^*$ = vector of n + k attributes for product 'b' as defined above
$FC_b$ = total fixed (R&D) costs for developing innovative product 'b'
$VC_a$ = total variable costs for producing product 'a'
$VC_b$ = total variable costs for producing radically innovative product 'b'

The price of each product is assumed to depend on two factors: the product attributes, and other factors, such as advertising, brand name, and so on,

$$P_a = A_o + A X \qquad\qquad (2.1)$$

$$P_b = B_o + B X^* \qquad\qquad (2.2)$$

where A is an (n x 1) vector of coefficients $a_1, a_2... a_n$, where $a_i$ is the subjective value of characteristic $x_i$ as reflected in the product's market price, and $A_o$ includes all factors that influence price other than product features. Similarly, B is an ((n + k) x 1) vector of coefficients $b_1, b_2, ..., b_{n+k}$ that reflect the mapping of product features into the innovative product's price.

The proposed approach has been considered sporadically in innovation literature here and there as far back as the 1960s and linked to the hedonic price concept.[3] The prime objective of the literature on hedonic pricing was certainly different from the present scenario. The method was originally developed in order to differentiate between a quality-determining price component and a quality-independent component. The question was raised as to whether price changes in an item can be viewed detached from quality changes. The use of hedonic pricing for measurement of technical change in later literature can therefore be termed 'objective-estranged' (Dorison, 1992, p. 68). As far as the neoclassical school is concerned, this approach is interesting in as much as, in so doing, demand forecasts are 'sanitized' so that the effects of technical change can disappear. With (2.1) and (2.2), the opposite is intended.

Chow (1967) constructed such hedonic price indices for computers, presenting the price (the 'net yield') of computers as a function of their memory capacity and their processing speed. He then adapted a logistic demand function to quality-sanitized units of computer production and was able to show that the actual demand could be predicted satisfactorily by these means.[4]

We assume that demand for products 'a' and 'b' depends both on the price, and on the product's features.

$$Q_a = f(Pa, X) \qquad\qquad (2.3)$$

$$Q_b = g(Pb, X^*) \qquad\qquad (2.4)$$

We assume that managers seek to maximize profit. For the existing product 'a', profit maximization is formulated as:

$$MAX\ \Pi_a = P_a Q_a - VC_a(X, Q_a) \qquad\qquad (2.5)$$

Correspondingly,

$$\text{MAX} \quad \Pi_b = P_b Q_b - VC_b(X^*, Q_b) - FC_b - rFC_b, \qquad (2.6)$$

where $FC_b$ is the fixed (R&D) costs of developing the innovative product 'b', and 'r' is the opportunity cost of the $FC_b$ capital, including a risk premium that reflects the degree of risk inherent in developing and marketing the radically innovative product 'b'.

The standard first-order conditions apply – for example, equate marginal cost and marginal price. However, a new set of conditions arise that focus on product features.

$$Q_a \, \partial P_a / \partial x_i + P_a \, \partial Q_a / \partial x_i = \partial VC_a / \partial x_i \qquad (2.7)$$

$$Q_b \partial P_b / \partial x^*_i + P_b \partial Q_b / \partial x^*_i = \partial VC_b / \partial x^*_i \qquad (2.8)$$

Equation (2.8) states: a radically innovative product should be so designed that the marginal revenue from a new product feature is equal to the marginal cost of producing that feature. This condition, of course, applies equally to existing product features, and to the conventional product 'a'.

Finally, in order for the risk and expense of radical innovation to be worth while:

$$\Pi_b \geq \Pi_a. \qquad (2.9)$$

The model of optimal incremental innovation (Ben-Arieh et al., 1998) is a special case of the above model, where production technology is assumed to be linear in time, money and labour. A key part of this model is the link between market prices P and product attributes X. *Ex post*, this link can be explored through use of hedonic price indexes, which express market prices as linear functions of attributes and use statistical regression to estimate the coefficients; see Grupp and Maital (1998).

But in making vital, difficult decisions about whether to embark on costly, risky R&D programmes to develop radically new products, product managers must estimate the link between P and X ex ante. To do this, they must in some manner gain insight into consumer preferences of existing and potential buyers. Consumers are assumed to spend their income in order to maximize utility. Assume consumers face a wide variety of products and product attributes. For a given consumer 'j' and product 'a', this implies:

$$\partial P_a / \partial x_i = \lambda\ \partial U_j / \partial x_i, \tag{2.10}$$

where U is utility and $\lambda$ is the marginal utility of one dollar. (2.10) states that 'optimized' products are such that the marginal utility value of an improvement in a product feature equals the increase in price stemming from that improvement. In competitive markets, where producers understand buyer preferences well, this condition will evolve and ultimately hold. The same condition must hold for the innovative product 'b':

$$\partial P_b / \partial x^*_i = \lambda\ \partial U_j / \partial x^*_i, \tag{2.11}$$

A 'tradeoff' optimization condition can be derived from the above. Let $X(x_1,\ x_2,\ \dots\ x_n) = $ constant be the product quality measured by the technometric concept and showing the various combinations of 'x' attributes that are feasible resp. on offer, with existing technology and resources. Profit maximization therefore implies:

$$[\partial X / \partial x_i]\ /\ [\partial X / \partial x_j]\ =\ [\partial U / \partial x_i] / [\partial U / \partial x_j],\ \text{all i, j} \tag{2.12}$$

Equation (2.12) states that the marginal rate of transformation among all pairs of product attributes must equal the marginal rate of substitution – that is, the 'cost' of improving attribute 'i', in terms of worsening attribute 'j', must equal the marginal utility of the improvement in attribute 'i', relative to the marginal utility of attribute 'j'.

Condition (2.12) is the basis of the so-called 'conjoint' model in marketing, which uses choice pairs presented to buyers to estimate marginal rates of transformation, then uses additional information to simulate market shares and profitability of existing and hypothetical combinations of product features, including those for radically innovative products, ultimately zeroing in on the optimal configuration of features.

## 2.4   A CASE STUDY FROM LASER MEDICINE

Laser medicine can be characterized by the fact that it is a comparatively new field in which physicists and engineers work alongside with doctors and which has a large and growing market potential. Thus, biomedicine and medicinal physics is subject to specific interdisciplinary interests plus the market structures differ from many other markets. So, perhaps, competition between clinics, established doctors and manufacturers of medico–technical appliances is not typified by the conventional market relationships, but by checks and balances in health care. In the place of efficiency or price competitiveness, in many countries rivalries and questions of status are cogent factors. Against this background, laser medicine appears to be a highly worthwhile sample case.

Laser applications in medicine relate to both therapeutic and also diagnostic instruments. A very important and early application of lasers in medicine relates to eye operations. Laser opthalmoscopy, for instance, is used for treating detachment of the retina particularly in diabetic patients ('spot welding of the retina'). This possibility was published in 1965. As far back as 1964, another biomedical application of lasers became known: the treatment of carcinogenic skin diseases. In 1985, that is, 20 years after description of the first capabilities, the number of annual patent applications in laser medicine was ten times greater than in 1975. Scientific publications have rocketed even faster. According to all innovation indicators, laser medicine seems to be a dynamic, comparatively new research area of substantial corporate and industrial relevance (Grupp, 1998, p. 355).

The technometric comparison between the customary surgical scalpel and the laser scalpel points to a radical or greater innovation, since virtually all properties need to be redefined. In the terminology of Section 2.2, we find $k = 9$ new attributes: maximum power, durability, tuning, beam diameter, beam divergence, mode structure, high frequency trigger, cooling requirements, power supply (Grupp et al., 1987, p. 195). The first $m^+ = 7$ attributes relate to the modular part, the last $s^+ = 2$ attributes to the operating vicinity: a knife needs neither cooling nor electricity. Most of the n old attributes are obsolete (stainless steel and so on), but some are still important (weight, overall length and so on).

What is the relationship (2.2) between product quality and price on this radically new market? In marketing literature, conventionally the start point is falling marginal yields. The main theoretical relationship is illustrated in Figure 2.2. Shoham et al. (1998), however, point out that the implications are still similar if other functional types are taken as the basis. According to Figure 2.2, supplier B can calculate his additional profit margins from higher prices P as, in accordance with the graph, his product in the attribute rating is above A but does not approach that of supplier C.

According to the technometric data for 1985, the market was characterized by 20 predominantly US products (USA: 14, Japan, France and Germany 2 each). The 20 products on the laser medical market in 1985 can be described by means of a characteristics bundle consisting of the mentioned parameters (power, beam diameter, beam divergence, and so on). If we insert in (2.2) the technometric index X*, we find a positive relation (significant at the 5 per cent level) as expected.[5]

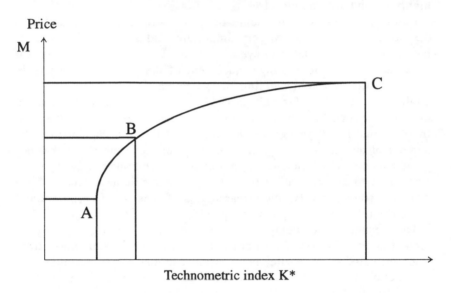

Price

M

C

B

A

Technometric index K*

*Figure 2.2:  The relationship between technometric assessment of product quality and price claimed by the marketing theory*

The hedonic prices $b_i$ can be determined with the aid of the regression calculation. On this subject, Saviotti (1985, p. 312) observes: 'Price equation coefficients ... can, therefore, be considered an approximation for users' judgement of the relative value of various characteristics.' The regression calculation (with robust errors) can account for more than two-thirds of the variance ($R^2 = 0.72$; see Table 2.1). This is open to different interpretations depending upon viewpoint. On the one hand, this means that more than two-thirds of the price variation alone is explicable in terms of the physico–technical properties of the products. On the other hand, likewise one-third is attributable to price variance which cannot be explained in terms of quality improvement but relies on the manufacturer's reputation or upon various marketing endeavours on service, maintenance, established practices or can be traced back to other preferences in certain market segments.

*Table 2.1:* *Hedonic price analysis (OLS regression of (2.2) with robust errors)*

| Attributes | $b_i$ | t (P > $|$t$|$ in brackets) | |
|---|---|---|---|
| Constant | 2746 | 0.72 | (0.489) |
| *Modular attributes:* | | | |
| Maximum power | 17558 | 3.96 | (0.003) |
| Durability | −3499 | −0.53 | (0.607) |
| Tuning | −2007 | −1.11 | (0.292) |
| Beam diameter | 5250 | 1.01 | (0.335) |
| Beam divergence | 9951 | 2.06 | (0.066) |
| Mode structure | 3251 | 1.22 | (0.251) |
| High frequence trigger | −3586 | −1.55 | (0.152) |
| *Architecture attributes:* | | | |
| Cooling requirements | −2284 | −0.69 | (0.508) |
| Power supply | −6120 | −0.78 | (0.454) |

Number of observations: 20
F = 43.3
$R^2$ = 0.72
Mean VIF = 2.6
Max VIF = 6.2
Max P = 25,000 US$ (1985)
Min P = 3,450 US$ (1985)

An investigation of individual feature profiles by the vector X* in (2.2) and multiple linear regression yields the finding (Table 2.1) that the power parameter (measured in watts) can significantly influence pricing (from heteroscedasticity robust errors, we determine the two-sided significance level at 0.3 per cent). This is shown in Figure 2.3, in isolation (without the other attributes). An exponential and a logarithmic approach is estimated. The exponential expression yields t = 3.48 at a significance level of 0.2 per cent, the logarithmic approach t = 3.58 from robust standard errors at the same level. The logarithmic approach is better than the linear one which explains only 13 per cent of the variance. The position can therefore be adopted that the other properties than maximum power play no part in price formation for this radical innovation. Why, then, do some prospective buyers prefer them?

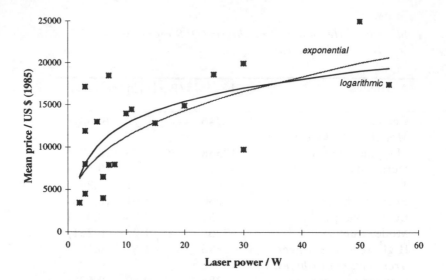

*Figure 2.3:    Relationship between one of the nine attributes of medical lasers (power) and the average price in 1985 (in US dollars)*

First of all, the constant term in (2.2) is not significant (Table 2.1). This means, that the price variation is determined by the technical attributes of this radical innovation alone. The two peripheral features are neither; their sign is negative. The price seems to be determined by the core technology. We observe no multi-collinearity (all variance of inflation factors are below 6.2), thus our features are independent of each other. Certainly, about 40 per cent of the variance between product prices is explained by the power parameter, but $R^2$ increases to 0.72 for all features. So the fact still remains that the specialists questioned consider the other technical properties important and reputable specialist journals publish these, since prospective buyers require information on the subject.

There is one more core attribute, beam divergence, which contributes weakly significantly to the price (robust significance level 6.6 per cent). If taken alone, we again find that the logarithmic fit is better than the linear or exponential one.

## 2.5 OPTIMIZING LASER SCALPELS

In order to understand this and thus optimize our radically new product, we now model product quality from our empirical observations with only these two attributes all other ones being equal. If we use subscripts p for the power and b for the beam divergence attribute, we have to look for the empirical partial relation of $x_p$ and $x_b$ with X. We checked a number of well-known functions, among them the linear, the exponential, the logarithmic, the inverse, the quadratic, the cubic and the general power ones, and also the growth, S-shape and logistic functions. In the case of the power attribute, the most significant relation turned out to be the cubic one (see Figure 2.4)[6], the best fit obtained for the beam divergence was the linear regression with a negative coefficient (see Figure 2.5).[7] Inserting the empirical relations into (2.12), we arrive at

$$\partial X / \partial x_P = p_1 + 2p_2x_p + 3p_3x^2_p \qquad (2.13)$$

and

$$\partial X / \partial x_b = b_1 \qquad (2.14)$$

with $p_i$ and $b_1$ being the estimated parameters.

At present, a conjoint analysis has not yet been performed but is planned for in order to determine the U function. However, we know from an expert survey, that customer preferences for laser light power is rated equally to beam divergence (see Grupp et al., 1987). Let us assume that the functional form of $U(x_P)$ is the same as for $U(x_b)$, and is, for simplicity, linear, then

$$\partial U / \partial x_P = \partial U / \partial x_b = a. \qquad (2.15)$$

Condition (2.12) is then an equation quadratic in $x_p$ which is roughly estimated at $x_p = 26.6$ (watts).

The innovative firm can conclude from this, if the coefficients are taken from the empirical investigation, that a laser scalpel with a light power of about 27 watts will be preferred by customers over a scalpel with more light power as beam divergence will be enlarged accordingly. Note that the 'voice of the market' asks for small beam divergence, and hence the divergences enter the technometric X function (quality function) inversely (compare Figure 2.5). So we find

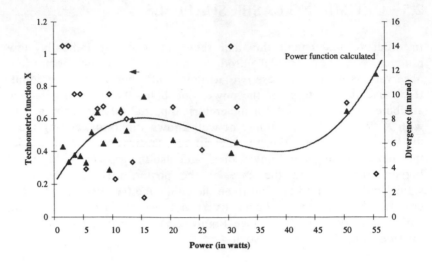

*Figure 2.4:   Empirical power characteristics and estimations*

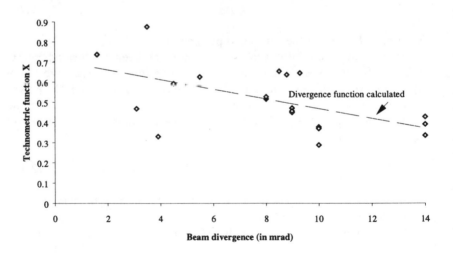

*Figure 2.5:   Empirical beam characteristics and estimations*

that in reality, that is, for technical constraints, any improvements in laser power are not easily achieved without a loss in beam quality. We have no choice. Radical innovation in this case requires breakthroughs in laser light power not enhancing beam divergence too much. If we are not good enough in the core technology there are little alternatives to compensate for by incremental innovation in the beam array.

## 2.6  CONCLUSION

We believe that our typology of innovation, and the simple models based on it, can provide useful answers for a firm facing the situation of a newly developing market. Although several if not all attributes of the new product in comparison to the substituted one change – and must be mastered – the case study tells us that profit maximization implies the goal for the management of technology to be among the advanced firms in one feature only. Peripheral or architectural innovation does not matter. This need not be the case in radical innovation generally. More case studies will be required to draw general conclusions.

Radical innovators need to move to a different, from the buyer's point of view, better position on the features tradeoff curves. This can imply to make some of the $b_i$ worse or keep them moderate. Theoretical considerations and computer simulations show that one can understand technological innovation as a complex, second-order learning system comprising a population of consumers and a population of producing firms. In some special cases just one 'dominant' design may occur, but in other cases a limited number of design configurations (Windrum and Birchenhall, 1998). This is exactly the situation modelled above: there are several 'optimal' positions on the feature tradeoff curves.

New approaches toward 'emphatic design' (Leonard and Rayport, 1997) can be embarked upon to find out by observing customers what they really want. But such types of new marketing should be complemented by optimization procedures as introduced above in order to get a systematic structure of the many possibilities which may be pursued in the laboratory.

How does this model contribute towards integrating marketing and R&D? What would be different in incremental versus radical innovation? Managing incremental innovation is a matter of balancing cost and value. In radical innovation, although many new features occur, not all of them seem to be equally important. There are limits for substitution of one achievement by another one if a core feature dominates. Even if the new market is young and may not yet be in equilibrium the model can help managers to concentrate on the most important aspects of radical innovation.

## NOTES

1   This is an original contribution to this volume not published elsewhere.
2   The latter design configurations are called 'dominant designs' in innovation theory. For a recent review see Grupp (1998, pp. 13, 100).
3   Griliches (1961, 1971) and Chow (1967). The new literature encompasses Saviotti (1985), Trajtenberg (1990) and Dorison (1992). A review of hedonics is provided by Silver (1996). Hedonism is a philosophical doctrine established in ancient times whereby the pinnacle of all endeavour is enjoyment. Such being the case, hedonic prices refer to prices arrived at by the consumer's sheer striving for enjoyment and do not represent anything but his wish. In particular, hedonic prices do not stem from the costs of capital and work input factors. Griliches (1971, p. 4) comments that the value-loaded 'hedonic' approach concept could be replaced by 'property approach'. Yet, in order to differentiate between other property approaches here, the original concept will be retained.
4   As a byproduct, it became apparent that, virtually always, one of the two technical properties was price-determining, namely memory capacity. Technological limitations at that time in regard to expansion of memory capacity, according to Chow, were an obstacle to even faster market expansion (loc. cit.).
5   We use the rather dated feature values as it is sometimes difficult to get the permission to publish complete actual data.
6   Significance level $\alpha = 0.06$ per cent, $F = 9.86$, $R2 = 0.31$. The next best fit is the logarithmic function with $\alpha = 0.5$ per cent.
7   Significance level $\alpha = 1.03$ per cent, $F = 8.21$, $R2 = 0.31$. The next best fit in this case is again the logarithmic one with $\alpha = 1.30$ per cent. The slope is $b1 = -0.02$. In Figure 2.4, for obvious reasons, not divergence vis-à-vis X can be shown but rather divergence vis-à-vis power. The pairs of data points belong to one brand each.

# 3 Innovation Investment as Doors to the Future: A Real Options Approach[1]

## Main Ideas in this Chapter

In the previous Chapter, a model for optimizing radical innovation was presented, based on a cost-benefit approach to adding new product features. That model argued that: a radically innovative product should be so designed that *the marginal revenue from a new product feature is equal to the marginal cost of producing that feature*. It can be argued that this first-order condition seriously understates the value of R&D investment in radical innovation, or provides only a lower-bound estimate, for the following reason: radically new product features may in themselves have no market value at all (and therefore, have zero marginal revenue), but may provide learning, experience and technical expertise that enables the innovator to access new technologies, new markets and new products in the future. *Without the initial investment, that door to the future could never be opened.* The 'option value' of this indirect benefit is often large, can be quantified, and must be taken into account to avoid underinvestment in promising, though risky, new technologies. We use a 'real options' model to quantify the indirect benefits of innovation, and provide a numerical illustration drawn from lasers.

## 3.1 INTRODUCTION: A REAL OPTIONS MODEL OF RADICAL INNOVATION

In the previous Chapter, a model for optimizing radical innovation was presented, based on a cost-benefit approach to adding new product features. The essence of that model was a standard microeconomic optimization model, applied in a novel way, not to entire products, but rather to individual product features, with the decision focused on optimal R&D investment in new product features. The common sense meaning of the model: *innovate so that the marginal revenue from a new product feature is equal to the marginal cost of producing that feature.*

It can, however, be argued that this first-order condition seriously understates the value of R&D investment in radical innovation, or provides only a lower-bound estimate, for the following reason: *Radically new product features may in themselves have no market value at all (and, therefore, have zero marginal revenue), but may provide technical expertise that enables the innovator to access new technologies, new markets and new products.* For example: the pharmaceutical company Pfizer invested in developing a new drug that seemed worthless, because it had 'undesirable' side effects – until it was realized that those side effects were in some contexts highly desirable. The drug became the impotency treatment Viagra.

In this Chapter, we propose a model for evaluating ex ante innovative projects, in a manner that quantifies the option value of that project. In doing so, we build on an existing literature that has used the real options framework to extend conventional net-present-value approaches to R&D project evaluation (Perlitz et al., 1999; Jaegle, 1999; Dixit and Pindyck, 1994; the standard textbook is Trigeorgis, 1996).

## 3.2   A REAL OPTIONS MODEL

Dixit and Pindyck (1994) note that investment can create opportunities which may or may not be exercised; whether they are or not, these opportunities have value that can be measured. In the context of R&D, such options could be:

- *The Option to Start R&D.* Studies help identify prospective new features. Based on these prospects the development programme can enter in the initial research phase.
- *The Option to Invest in Preliminary Development.* If a technology is discovered that might result in a promising new product or process feature, preliminary development work can begin.

- *The Option to Launch a Full-scale Development Project.* If initial work appears successful, a decision can be made to launch a full-scale development project.
- *The Option to Invest in Marketing and Production.* Following the R&D phase and test phases, it has to be decided to market the new features and start the production or to abandon operations.
- *The Abandonment Option.* At any stage, there exists the option to dump the new product features and revert to the old features or embark on R&D to develop new ones. We have found more than a few project evaluations where the 'abandonment option' has been left off the decision tree analysis, significantly biasing the result in a negative manner.

Similarly, Perlitz et al. (1999) distinguish between six kinds of real options: option to defer; time-to-build option; option to abandon; option to contract; option to switch; and growth option.

By drawing a direct parallel between 'real options' (that is, options that involve real investment, products and R&D assets) and 'financial options' (the right to buy or sell an asset for an agreed price on or before an agreed date), and by using the familiar Black–Scholes formula for pricing a financial option, the value of these real options can be determined.

In 1973, Black and Scholes published an article, unassumingly titled 'The Pricing of Options and Corporate Liabilities', in which they solved a partial differential equation in order to show that the market price of a financial option could be expressed as a simple equation, with only five variables: the stock price ('spot', or current price of the underlying asset; IBM shares, for instance); the exercise price (the price at which the asset could be acquired, or sold, under the terms of the option); the time to expiration (the time period during which the option to buy or sell can be exercised); the risk-free interest rate; and the variance of the rate of return of the underlying asset (that is, its riskiness). This single paper was largely responsible for creating an enormous market in options and related financial instruments known as derivatives, because it created an agreed standard for valuing contingent claims that until then were hard to price.

Luehrman (1998a, 1998b) offers a useful simplification of the Black–Scholes equation, distilling its five parameters down to only two. In the body of this Chapter, we will follow Luehrman's approach, while in the Appendix, we offer a more full-blown mathematical model of real options, in the context of the pharmaceutical industry, where it is necessary to use the Black–Scholes equation itself to compute option values.[2]


## 3.3   AN ILLUSTRATIVE EXAMPLE: LASERS

For our illustrative example, we chose the laser industry (for a fuller history, see Grupp, 1998, pp. 338–344).

*Laser* is an acronym for light amplification by stimulated emission of radiation. Lasers are devices that amplify light and produce coherent light beams, ranging from infrared to ultraviolet. A light beam is coherent when its waves, or photons, propagate in step with one another. Lasers harness atoms to store and emit light in a coherent fashion. The electrons in the atoms of a laser medium are first pumped, or energized, to an excited state by an energy source. They are then 'stimulated' by external photons to emit the stored energy in the form of photons, a process known as stimulated emission.

Stimulated emission, the underlying process for laser action, was first proposed by Einstein in 1917. The working principles of lasers were outlined by Schawlow and Townes in their 1958 patent application. The patent was granted, but was later challenged by the physicist and engineer Gould. In 1960 Maiman observed the first laser action in solid ruby. A year later a helium-neon gas laser was built by the Iranian-born American physicist Javan. Then in 1966 a liquid laser was constructed by Sorokin. The US Patent Office court in 1977 affirmed one of Gould's claims over the working principles of the laser.[3]

Grupp (1998) notes that while the theory-to-first technical materialization of the laser took 43 years, in the 1960s a new laser medium was being discovered practically every year. The US firm Spectra Physics launched the first laser onto the market; it became the model for a whole series of laser companies. But from 1968 on, many of those laser firms perished, finding that the original technical concepts on which commercial lasers were based were not marketable. Bankruptcies were recorded during 1973–75, as the industry went into a slump. Meanwhile, focus shifted from research to development; patent applications soared. Companies resumed their earlier laser-related development work. From $90 million in total laser sales in 1970, the market grew to about $900 million in 1977, $9 billion in 1986, and $13 billion in 1992.

Consider a hypothetical company, whom we shall call LaserWeld. LaserWeld is founded in 1972 by three creative solid-state physicists who think they can build a laser-based welder. They build a business plan, with a conventional spreadsheet, and are crestfallen to find that using a rate of discount that reflects the high risk of their venture, 18 per cent, their discounted cash flow (or net present value) is in fact negative (see Table 3.1). A $100 million initial investment in developing a laser welder (Mark I Model) generates a negative net present value of –$22 million, because the discounted cash flow during the planned five-year life of the product is insufficient to cover the $100 million total R&D investment. They reluctantly abandon their dream, because no one is willing to invest in a firm with such bleak prospects.

Then, one of the firm's founders decides to rethink the analysis. He draws a decision tree (Figure 3.1A), and realizes that the 'failure' branch of the tree is wrongly truncated. If our laser welder initially fails – sales double in years 2, 3, and 4, and triple in year 5, yet are not sufficient to pay back the initial large investment – LaserWeld will learn a lot during its R&D, sales and marketing. In year 3, the company has the option of investing another $100 million in a new generation of laser welders, building on the market experience and R&D knowledge acquired in the first two years. Will the new, improved decision tree (Figure 3.1B) give LaserWeld better financial prospects (see Table 3.2)? The answer is a resounding 'yes'! The overall net present value is now strongly positive. This project will return an economic rent above the 18 per cent risk-adjusted cost of capital.

*Table 3.1: Discounted cash flow for LaserWeld ($ million)*

| | Year | | | | | |
|---|---|---|---|---|---|---|
| | 0 | 1 | 2 | 3 | 4 | 5 |
| Cash flow | | 0 | $10 | $20 | $40 | $120 |
| R&D investment | –$100 | | | | | |
| Discount factor (18%) | | | 0.718 | 0.609 | 0.515 | 0.437 |
| Present value | –$100 | 0 | $7.180 | $12.180 | $20.600 | $52.400 |
| Net present value | | –$100 + $92.36 = –$7.64 | | | | |

*Table 3.2: Revised discounted cash flow for LaserWeld ($ million)*

| Phase 1 | | | | | | |
|---|---|---|---|---|---|---|
| | | | Year | | | |
| | 0 | 1 | 2 | 3 | 4 | 5 |
| Cash flow | | 0 | $10 | $20 | $40 | $120 |
| R&D investment | –$100 | | | | | |
| Discount factor (18%) | | | 0.718 | 0.609 | 0.515 | 0.437 |
| Present value | –$100 | 0 | $7.180 | $12.180 | $20.600 | $52.400 |
| Net present value (Phase 1) | –$100 + $92.36 = –$7.64 | | | | | |

| Phase 2 | | | | | | |
|---|---|---|---|---|---|---|
| | | | | Year | | |
| | 0 | 1 | 2 | 3 | 4 | 5 |
| Cash flow | | | | | $60 | $200 |
| R&D investment | | | | –$100 | | |
| Discount factor (18%) | | | | 0.609 | 0.515 | 0.437 |
| Present value | | 0 | | –$60.900 | +$30.900 | +$87.400 |
| Net present value (Phase 2) | –$60.9 + $118.3 = +$57.4 | | | | | |
| Total net present value, Phase 1 and Phase 2: –$7.64 + $57.4 = $49.8 | | | | | | |

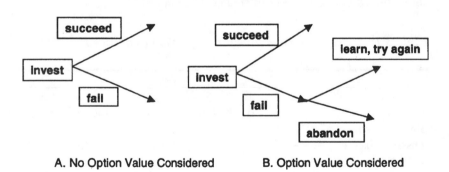

A. No Option Value Considered          B. Option Value Considered

*Figure 3.1: Decision tree analysis of investment in laser innovations*

Figure 3.1A shows a conventional decision tree analysis, typified by net present value calculations of innovation investments. Figure 3.1B shows the result of considering the value of failing, but learning, and then using that knowledge to make another attempt. The 'learn, try again' is an option – it need not be done, one can always abandon the project. But as an option, it has value; taking it into account can change an unprofitable project (3.1A) into a highly profitable one (3.1B).

## 3.4   A COUNTER-INTUITIVE RESULT

The reader may protest that this example is obvious, perhaps even trivial. We respond that the learning value of initial failures in technology-based startups is enormous (Roberts, 1994) – and is often not taken into account in conventional project evaluations.

But consider a more counter-intuitive example. Suppose that the LaserWeld project's cash flow projections look like those in Table 3.3. In this case, the initial Mark 1 Model is very profitable, with high net present value, while the Mark 2 Model is not. Using Luehrman's (1998a, b) simplification of the Black–Scholes equation, it can be shown that the option value of the Mark 2 Model is in fact large and positive, rather than – $2 million as net present value calculations indicate:

Option value of Mark 2 Model is $19.4 million. The overall net present value of the project is, therefore,[4] the net present value of Phase 1 plus the call option value on Phase 2 ($64.9 + $19.4 = $84.8 million).

Using the real options approach, the LaserWeld project appears far more attractive than using traditional net present value methods, and more attractive than the previous example, where initial learning led to later profitability. Why? What explains this counter-intuitive result? There are several reasons:

- With the passage of time, the uncertainty inherent in technology-based companies tends to decline. As lasers were perfected, and additional scientific research, patents and development work accumulated, the degree of risk inherent in the technology tended to fall. Most net present value calculations use a constant risk-adjusted rate of return. Since interest rates are composed of risk-free rates plus a risk premium, this implies that risk premia are constant over the life of the project – something which is rarely, if

ever, true. In Table 3.3, we have used a 10 per cent discount rate,
rather than 18 per cent, to compute the present value of the second
$100 million investment, precisely for this reason – when the
investment is undertaken, the degree of uncertainty associated with
it has greatly diminished.[5] For long-lived projects, lower discount
rates imply higher present value.

*Table 3.3:  Revised discounted cash flow for LaserWeld ($ million)*

| | | | | | | |
|---|---|---|---|---|---|---|
| **Phase 1** | | | | | | |
| | | | Year | | | |
| | 0 | 1 | 2 | 3 | 4 | 5 |
| Cash flow | | 0 | $60 | $200 | | |
| R&D investment | –$100 | | | | | |
| Discount factor (18%) | | | 0.718 | 0.609 | | |
| Present value | –$100 | | +$43.100 | $121.800 | | |
| Net present value (Phase 1) | | –$100 + $164.9 = +$64.9 | | | | |
| **Phase 2** | | | | | | |
| | | | Year | | | |
| | 0 | 1 | 2 | 3 | 4 | 5 |
| Cash flow | | 0 | | | $40 | $120 |
| R&D investment | | | | –$100 | | |
| Discount factor (10%) | | | | 0.751 | 0.515 | 0.437 |
| Present value | | | | –$75 | +$20.600 | +$52.400 |
| Net Present value (Phase 2) | | –$75.1 + $73 = –$2.1 | | | | |
| Total net present value: + $64.9 – $2.1 = $62.8 | | | | | | |

- As time passes, investors have the ability to exert greater control
  over their expenditures and losses. Losing projects can always be
  truncated by closing them and selling the assets. Assets can be
  shifted out of declining technologies into burgeoning ones. This
  implies that for technologies that have large underlying 'volatility'
  (very large potential profits, but also very large potential losses),
  the real options approach attaches a high value to the 'call option'
  (right to invest) aspect of such technology. The reason: as with an
  option, you have the *right* to invest in the underlying, if you
  choose, but not the *obligation*. This inherent ability to truncate a

widely spread stochastic rate of return captures the profitable part while discarding or avoiding the unprofitable part. As Perlitz et al. (1999, p. 267) explain: 'The high volatility of the value of R&D outputs positively influences the option value, because high returns can be generated, but very low return can be avoided by reacting to the changing conditions. In Net Present Value calculations, high volatility leads to a risk premium on the discount rate and so to a lower NPV.'

## 3.5  CONCLUSION

One of the most puzzling, and, for investors, anxiety-causing, phenomena is the enormous market valuations of technology-based companies. Companies, especially Internet-based ones, that have never earned a profit see their stock price soar, and their market valuation climb into the tens of billions of dollars. One camp argues that such stock prices are inflated. Another camp uses the real options approach to claim that for unprofitable but rapidly growing companies, stock prices do not reflect past or current profits but future growth. Using the real options model, Jaegle (1999) calculates that for industries like data networking, semiconductors, software and Internet businesses, the value of 'growth options' comprise a large proportion of the companies' market value.

What this implies is that capital markets may be somewhat ahead of capital budgeting techniques used for project evaluations. While capital markets understand the intrinsic value in 'growth options', project evaluators often fail to take this into account. For management of technology, there is inherent value in the passage of time; based on new learning and knowledge, losses can be avoided, while profits can be captured as new opportunities arise and old misfortunes are shut down. Variations of the Black–Scholes option pricing method enable managers to quantify this value.

A word of caution is in order, however. The real options argument can be used, misleadingly, to justify almost any investment in high-risk R&D, simply by waving at some imaginary, huge future market to emerge at some distant date.

Like all quantitative tools, real options logic demands responsibility and integrity on the part of its practitioners. They must defend their

numbers with the same rigour to which other conventional approaches
are held to.

## APPENDIX 3.1:6 MATHEMATICAL MODEL FOR EVALUATING INVESTMENT IN A NEW PHARMACEUTICAL PRODUCT

Consider a senior manager, weighing investment in a radically new technology-intensive product. At the initial phase of the investment programme, scientific uncertainties are resolved and the production profile follows a fixed pattern over its useful life. For each state of the world, the net operating cash inflow for this product equals the yearly production, $Q_t$, times the current price, $S_t$, minus the operating costs and corporate taxes.

Future cash flows are assumed to follow a stochastic process, which is modelled in discrete time by a multiplicative binomial process (for example see Cox et al., 1979). In each sub-period of one year, the project value may increase by a multiplicative factor u, or decline by a factor d. Equations (3A.1), (3A.2), and (3A.3) are used to estimate the series of future cash flows over the total life of the project (research and production phase). In the following valuation process, the hedging (risk-neutral) probability, p, is used to estimate the present value of cash inflows

$$u = e^{\sigma}, d = \frac{1}{u} \qquad (3A.1)$$

$$uV_t = V_{t+1}^{+} \qquad (3A.2)$$

$$dV_t = V_{t+1}^{-} \qquad (3A.3)$$

$$p = \frac{(1+r)V_t - V_{t+1}^{-}}{V_{t+1}^{+} - V_{t+1}^{-}} \qquad (3A.4)$$

where p is the hedging (risk-neutral) probability and r the risk-free interest rate and $\sigma$ is the standard deviation that result from commercial uncertainty.

In this fashion, commercial uncertainty results in a series of potential operating cash flows. The valuation procedure works recursively, starting at the terminal nodes of the tree and working backward in time to the beginning of the production phase. In the final production period the state project value equals the operating cash flow, $CF_S$. Equation (3A.5) summarizes the state project cash inflows when stepping backward in time.

$$V_t = CF_t + \frac{pV_{t+1}^+ + (1-p)V_{t+1}^-}{1+r} \qquad (3A.5)$$

where V = project value under continuous production.

## The Option to 'Market' or to 'Wait and See'

Now we consider the valuation of a similar programme in an earlier phase. Management must decide if and when to market the product. For production the corporation must invest in the marketing and production facilities. In pharmaceuticals, for instance, a company must typically spend $100–200 million to market the new drug. When (if at all) is it time to market in light of commercial uncertainty?

The patent on the new product, in this stage, can be viewed as similar to a call option. The underlying asset is the present value to market the product, V. In Equation (3A.6) the present value of the investment outlay in production and marketing, I, is equivalent to the exercise price. If at that time the value exceeds the investment outlay, management would invest and patent value equals: C = V − I. However, due to commercial reasons, the NPV may turn out to be negative. In this case, however, management may decide not to invest and the net value would be zero.

Besides the wait and see advantage, deferment has certain disadvantages. For example, management may receive the net operating cash inflow later on. Again the question is: what would this call option be worth if it were traded on financial markets? The investment opportunity value, NPV*, equals:

$$C^* = MAX\left[ V^* - I, \; \frac{pC^+ + (1-p)C^-}{1+r}, \; 0 \right] \qquad (3A.6)$$

where C = the option value to commercialize the patent, and I = investment necessary to market the product.

The procedure continues by working backward to the value of initial research, using the probability distributions of scientific success. During the research phase, the distribution of the quantity is updated several times: initial research can lead to the discovery of new product feature, while the test phases provide additional information about the probability of market success. Starting from the values of the market potential, the value of the testing is calculated by using Bayesian updated probability distributions.

We consider now the valuation of a radical innovation, after uncertainty in the test phases is resolved with a sufficient success to proceed with the programme. The scientific and clinical uncertainty is unrelated to the overall economy, and is therefore nonsystematic. Because this uncertainty can be fully diversified, we can estimate the value of the research programme using both the risk-free rate and the actual probabilities of the distribution.

The value of the project equals the expectation over the expected commercialisation value or zero in case of abandonment using the updated probabilities of market success after two test phases. In order to estimate this value (using Equation 3A.7), the quantity (market share) and corresponding values, including options, represent the potential values at the end of the programme. To estimate the value of the programme in case of approval the (producing and nonproducing) NPVs are multiplied by the actual probability of corresponding quantity, conditional on two successful test phases.

$$V^{FDA} = \frac{P_{reject}(0) + \sum \left\{ P_{approval}(Q) = x \mid Q > 0 \right\} NPV_Q^*}{(1+r)^{T-t}} \qquad (3A.7)$$

where $V^{FDA}$ = value of potential commercialization before approval; NPV = net present value of the commercialization phase; P is update probability of approval after successful testing $\Sigma P_{approval} = (1 - P_{reject})$; and $T - t$ = time lag of the food and drug administration (FDA) procedure.

Now we step back in time to an earlier stage in the decision process of the R&D programme, when the management has to make the expenditures for clinical testing I and II in order to acquire the proprietary option to proceed with the commercialization investment. Clinical tests maximize information on the compound and resolve the uncertainty with respect to the presence of harmful side effects. The commercial expectations must justify further investments. Since the test phases require the most outlays, the option value is most important.

The clinical test phase can be viewed as a set of two nested options. At the same time different types of uncertainty or risk are resolved in different stages. Consequently, the distribution is updated after each phase. Equation 3A.8 takes the estimation over uncertainty in the second testing phase. The option value to start the second test phase is estimated by Equation 3A.9.

$$V^{test\ II} = \frac{P_{failure}(0) + \sum\{P_{succes}(Q) = x \mid Q > 0\}NPV_Q^*}{(1+r)^{T-t}} \qquad (3A.8)$$

$$C^{test\ II} = MAX\left[V^{test\ II} - I^{test\ II}, 0\right] \qquad (3A.9)$$

In the same fashion, we can we now work backwards to valuing the first clinical test phase using equations (3.10) and (3.11).

$$V^{test\ I} = \frac{P_{failure}(0) + \sum\{P_{succes}(Q) = x \mid Q > 0\}C_Q^{test\ II}}{(1+r)^{T-t}} \qquad (3A.10)$$

$$C^{test\ I} = MAX\left[V^{test\ I} - I^{test\ I}, 0\right] \qquad (3A.11)$$

where $\{P(Q) = x \mid Q > 0\}$ is the updated probability on quantity Q after successful testing I and II respectively; $V^{test\ i}$ = value of the test programme i; $I^{test\ 1}$ = investment outlay of test phase i.

The basic logic of this model is identical to that of all dynamic optimization models: 'Think ahead backward'. We begin by valuing the final phase: sales and marketing. But of course we realize that an innovative product may well never reach this phase. So it must be treated as a 'call option' – the right, not the obligation, to invest in it. This call option, in turn, becomes part of the value of an earlier phase, say, R&D investment, which is also a call option. So, the last phase, sales and marketing, becomes nested in a series of call options. The entire project is therefore evaluated by beginning with the final phase, valuing it, inserting it into the call option value of the preceding phase, valuing that, and so on, until we reach the initial phase. This is very similar to the logic of dynamic programming.

## NOTES

1    An earlier version of this Chapter, in the context of the pharmaceutical industry, was written together with Han Smit, Department of Finance, Erasmus University, Rotterdam, Netherlands. We are grateful to Han for sharing his expertise with us.

This Chapter, in contrast with other Chapters in this book, focuses more on overall investment in new technologies, rather than on innovations in product features. Stefan Woerner, in his doctoral dissertation, seeks to substantiate or falsify our ideas.

2 This can be done using familiar software packages like Mathematica, for instance.

3 'Laser,' *Microsoft® Encarta® Encyclopedia 99.* © 1993–1998 Microsoft Corporation. All rights reserved.

4 Option value is a function of five parameters: S, 'stock price' (net present value of the project, phase 2), $73 million; X 'exercise price' (the price of the option – in this case, the $100 million investment needed to 'exercise' it, $75 million; t, the length of time the decision may be deferred (here: until year 3); r, time value of money, or the risk-free rate of return, 10 per cent; and $\sigma^2$, the variance of the returns on the project, which measures the riskiness, 10 per cent. Using Luehrman's (1998b) simplification, we get: $NPV_q = \$73/\$75 = 0.97$; and $\sigma\sqrt{3} = 0.693$. The Black–Scholes value (expressed as a per cent of S, $73 million) is (from Luehrman's table, Luehrman 1998a, p. 56) 26.6 per cent ($NPV_q/ \sigma\sqrt{3}$). In dollars, this yields an option value of 0.266 • $73 million = $19.4 million.

5 This is because this sum is associated with zero uncertainty: you know what it will cost as an 'entry free' into the Mark 2 Technology. In contrast, the cash flow numbers are still discounted at 18 per cent, because this is still highly uncertain – we do not know for sure what the Mark 2 Technology will bring in the marketplace, so the discount rate has to have a risk premium that reflects this uncertainty. This is in line with Luehrman's approach.

6 This Appendix draws heavily on an unpublished paper by Smit, and on his doctoral dissertation (Smit, 1996).

# 4 Interpreting the Sources of Market Value: A Hedonic Price Approach[1]

**Main Ideas in this Chapter**

This Chapter presents an integrated model for evaluating purchasers' perceptions of science-based products that may be useful in the management of technology. The model combines a new approach to benchmarking, known as technometrics, that provides a quantitative profile of a product's key attributes, with direct and indirect methods for measuring buyers' perceptions regarding the relative importance of product attributes as a source of value. A new measure for the demand orientation is proposed, which shows the extent to which a product's 'supply' of characteristics matches the 'demand' for them in the marketplace. The model is illustrated using several types of industrial pressure sensors. The Chapter also demonstrates how the integrated model may be made effective for quality function deployment (QFD) during the R&D phase.

## 4.1 THE SENSOR MARKET AS AN INNOVATION STRATEGY AND QUALITY ASSIGNMENT

Companies working on innovations on a particular market tend to have commonality of scientifico–technical opportunity and, because of the specific nature of the technology concerned, the resulting potentiality for appropriation of innovation rents, see, for example Cohen (1995). This Chapter tries to examine the sensor market, a 'conventional' market with monopolistic competition in which knowledge generation is largely uncoloured by state influence. It features both large and small companies, universal and special suppliers. At the same time this market for capital goods strongly depends on modern science.

The sensor market has been expanding over the last decade; characteristic growth rates for sensor submarkets are between 10 and 30 per cent. The world market for sensors is currently worth over US$5 billion[2] per annum; methods of calculation and the estimates however deviate very widely. By the year 2001, as Arnold (1991) notes, growth rates are expected to be 8 per cent per annum; the 2001 market volume could be US$43 billion. The uncertainty over sensor estimates stems directly from arbitrary drawing of sensor demarcation lines: should supply lines, decoding electronics or calibration units be included or excluded? The price of a complete sensor system can deviate from that of the sensor element contained in it by one order of magnitude.

Extension of the sensor market is to some degree the outcome of the growing plant automation market; in this area, sensors plus certain other factory integration systems definitely reflect the greatest growth. In factory automation, in value terms, sensors however only account for a few per cent. In addition, the growth in the sensor market is linked with expansion of mass consumer products (motor cars, domestic appliances), the advancing technization of medicine (biosensors) and linked with the legislation on protection of the environment (stack gas testers, probes in car catalytic converters, and so on). In all types, sensors thus play a part in capital goods marketing (product business, system business, plant business). Sensor miniaturization has led to the incorporation of microelectronics. Modern sensor technology has therefore benefited from the huge advances made in semiconductor technology which are now spilling over into measurement technology. Sensor technology, cf. Grupp (1992), is therefore science-based like semiconductor technology.

This contribution deals with the *industrial sensors* sub-market. The medical area ought to be included in the industrial. Since sensors are very small commercial and technical units, in case of doubt, it must always be assumed that the sensor has not been shown separately in economic balances but included as part of a larger unit. There is a tendency for individual in-house production of sensors in the using company that siphons off some of the sensors from the statistical data sources. Contextually, the sensor market is virtually untrammelled by state intervention; restrictions are imposed, on the one hand, by environmental protection requirements which fuel environmental measurement technology, the pricing idiosyncrasies in health care and a substantial commitment by state technology policy to microsystems engineering.

The sensor market is highly *segmented*. An overview by Grupp et al. (1987, p. 234) lists nigh on 90 measurands for which sensors are available commercially or which are in process of development. The number of types of sensors (in terms of product variants) however is clearly even larger since for each measurement parameter there are several if not many measurement processes available. Internationally, currently a total of approximately 10,000 different types of sensor are on offer; the number of brands is incalculable. In countries of the Organization for Economic Cooperation and Development (OECD), there are approximately 2,000 potential suppliers of sensors, most of whom are offering their own products.

Marked segmentation of the sensor market imposes one prime requirement on the R&D management of innovators: they must be stronger than others in *systematic early warning functions* and should set up a strategic technology management. This is a defining parameter specific to the sensor industry and common to innovation behaviour in the intersectoral comparison. It would therefore seem apposite, prior to analysing technical properties (Section 4.4) and demand preferences (Sections 4.5 and 4.6), to set out one or two general considerations for technology management. According to the above analysis of the basic structures of the sensor market, the corresponding technology management in the intersectoral comparison is problematical from both aspects: technological analysis, owing to the many technical processes and measurement parameters used for sensors is just as complex as formulating a competitive quality strategy taking segmented markets into account.

## 4.2   A NEW BENCHMARKING CONCEPT

The ability to develop and exploit new business opportunities, that is, the *economic competence*, is generally difficult to determine quantitatively. One is tempted to 'measure' economic competence by its outcomes – successful innovation. In a science-driven market, the firm's competences in various areas of activities, such as R&D, engineering, production but also general administration, have to be extended to monitor scientific achievements, coordinate learning from science and scientists outside the firm or to communicate problems to them, and to organize knowledge accumulation by appropriate risk taking, see Carlsson and Stankiewicz (1991, p. 94).

But how to measure successful science-based innovation? For measuring the tacit, embodied knowledge included in innovative products, measurement of technological characteristics is required. Here, the newly established technometric concept by Grupp (1994) may be embarked upon. It requires the consultation with technology experts and thus the handling of multidisciplinarity in the management of technology.

At.the beginning of the 1980s a series of 'metrics' for evaluating and comparing technological sophistication and quality were proposed. What was coined 'technometrics' in 1985 is a procedure designed along Lancaster's (1991) consumer theory and is based on the observation that every innovative product or process has a set of key attributes that defines its performance, value or ability to satisfy customer wants. Each of these attributes has a different unit of measurement. Problems then arise in aggregating attributes to build a single quality index. Mathematical details of the general procedure are not discussed here as they may be found in Grupp (1994). Suffice to say that the technometric indicator surmounts this difficulty by converting each measured attribute into a [0, 1] metric, enabling construction of weighted averages, and so on, and permitting comparisons across products, firms, industries and countries. The '0' point of the metric is set as the technologically standard attribute; the '1' point is set as the most technologically sophisticated attribute in existence at a given point in time.

The j-th element of the characteristics of product (or service or process) i is the specification $K(i, j)$. If monopolistic competition is assumed, one has to differentiate products k (or brands of the same firm) at time $t_0$. The measurement unit of this specification is $u(j)$. The metric measure $K^*$ (for firm $k'$) is obtained by the metric

$$K^* (i,j,k',k,t) = [(K(i,j,k',t) - K_{min}(i,j,k_{min},t_0))]/$$
$$[(K_{max}(i,j,k_{max},t_0) - K_{min}(i,j,k_{min},t_0))], \quad (4.1)$$

whereby $K_{max}$, $K_{min}$ being the maximum and minimum specifications within subset k. $k_{min}$ and $k_{max}$ denote those brands k for which K is minimum respectively maximum with respect to the total subset. By this transformation, $K^*(k')$ is no more dependent on specific physical units, but expressed as a defined point on an interval scale spanned by the specifications of all competing brands (products) in each dimension j. If the scale of the specification is inverse, that is, if the minimum value of K represents the most sophisticated technological level, then an inverse formula holds

$$K^*_{inv} (i,j,k',k,t) = 1 - K^*(i,j,k',k,t). \qquad (4.2)$$

From this micro-level, single-item definition, a technometric profile may be aggregated on the level of all j specifications per product i if functional characteristics or (revealed) preferences F are defined:

$$K^* (i,k',t) = \Sigma_j [K^*(i,j,k',k,t) \cdot F(i,j)] / \Sigma_j F(i,j). \qquad (4.3)$$

The preferences may be derived from utility functions, by introspective or market observation, from expert knowledge or via hedonic prices.

Technometric profiles may be used for measuring the economic competence through the proxy firm-specific technological performance or quality level, one of the important determinants for innovation, which includes the tacit knowledge. Yet, the compilation of technometric data is time-consuming as the specifications are not accessible in data banks. The measure also does not differentiate between the sources of know-how. It may be created within the firm by R&D, in the science system, by learning by doing or learning by using or by adoption of innovative solutions developed by other industries or firms and embodied in capital equipment and intermediate inputs.

When conducting a technology-oriented competition survey, a relative competition analysis is recommended, cf. Backhaus (1992, pp. 135 onwards) or Shillito (1994, p. 52 onwards). Usually, this is done by assessing the own position by reference to those of the relevant competitors. Owing to the lack of suitable metric data, competitor information is graphed qualitatively (for example 'low' versus 'high'). The technometric indicator is available, in competitor analysis, as a substitute for qualitative scales if the corresponding data are available from the rival company.

From competitor observation, portfolios can be compiled which just like financial business portfolios tend to be referred to in R&D management circles as *technology portfolios*. The use of portfolio procedures for technology evaluation is considered the best method in the field of corporate R&D management, see, for example EIRMA (1985, p. 27). In view of the few comments that can be made about industrial technology management, product quality measurement is still the final resort. The latest keyword of 'benchmarking' is nothing other than the systematic comparison of the quality of products and services of a company in relation to those of the leading competitors, following Camp (1989) or Shillito (1994). Interest in benchmarking has grown enormously over the last 10 years. Technometrics applied in business management is nothing more than standardization of product quality in terms of technical properties. Even now, technometric procedures still do not feature in benchmarking literature. First applications may be found in Shoham et al. (1998).

## 4.3   DATA ON TECHNICAL CHARACTERISTICS OF PRESSURE SENSORS

In this Section, the problem of pricing of technically valuable goods and the effect of technical characteristics is tackled. The sensor market is thus regarded as a market with free and floating prices dictated by supply and demand factors. The first step must be to itemize the most important technical properties of sensors and then extract a selection from the wealth of conceivable measures. Koschatzky et al. (1996) in a wide-ranging empirical survey were concerned primarily with pressure and temperature sensors (in addition to those for measuring acceleration, force and relative humidity). The inquiry related to earlier technometrics by Grupp et al. (1987) on sensors which reflected the 1986 market.

The primary data analysis thus involves large-scale gathering of exhibition material at the largest sensor fair in the world where not only exhibits, as is customary, are displayed but also specification sheets with the appropriate data.[3] Quite apart from the field survey conducted other companies were consulted so that in all 286 companies were approached in one way or another. Of these, 151 yielded comparable detailed information. Koschatzky et al. (1996) also conducted 10 personal interviews with Israeli companies so that in all data from 160 sensor firms was obtained. When considering the breakdown of companies according to country, it should be remembered that European and primarily German-speaking countries predominate since the fair in this year took place in Germany. Apart from companies from the USA and Israel, however, Japanese companies were also represented in the random sample.

The technical properties selected and compared were established by specialist discussions in the earlier investigation of the sensor market. In so doing, it became apparent that different specifications are important for different measuring principles and tasks. To illustrate the data in this Section only pressure sensor analysis is spotlighted.[4] For pressure measurement, essentially three modern processes are in use. These are the piezo-electric and piezo-resistive principle plus the use of strain gauges.

The most important technical properties of a pressure sensor are the measuring range, accuracy, that is, the maximum deviation of the instrument from the true measurand and the temperature range over which the sensor can be used (maximum and minimum working temperature). For concrete use, data on weight and diameter is important, particularly for built-in components. Apart from the accuracy of a particular measuring point, linearity is of interest, that is, the maximum deviation over the entire scale, and the so-called hysteresis effect, particularly the maximum deviation which results from the delayed response of the sensor to changes in the measurand. For the hysteresis effect, non-linear physical principles are important. Apart from maximum and minimum temperature, temperature stability is of interest, that is, the error that temperature fluctuations cause to the reading taken. Temperature stability at low and high temperatures can differ widely whence here usually two properties must be stated. Error tolerance in the event of mishandling, the overpressures which may occur without the sensor being damaged and likewise the maximum permissible electrical voltage tolerated without instrument damage are also of interest.

Among the 12 product characteristics specified are some upon which prospective customers prefer highest values (for example measuring range, maximum temperature, permissible overpressure, and so on) and also some at which preference is on low values (equipment deviation in temperature fluctuations, diameter, weight, and so on). In the technometric model, Equation (4.1) has to be used for the first group of properties; in the other case, in which technical advance progresses inversely relative to the measured variable and is expected to lead to the minimum value of characteristics, Equation (4.2).

Conceptually, if four products are deliberately chosen from the databank and the technometric indicators calculated, then a technological or characteristic profile will be obtained as per Figure 4.1. In such case, it should be noted that for certain products, isolated numerical values are missing (not divulged by the manufacturer).

Purely for the purposes of illustration, let us now refer to certain notable characteristics. The common denominator is that all four products have a comparatively small pressure measurement range. In this respect, they are similar and serve identically segmented sub-markets. The sensors compared differ little from one another in regard to hysteresis and temperature stability. Similarly, the linearity of the four products needs to be assessed and also their compactness. The maximum permissible temperature of the products is quite another matter. The UK sensor (IMO) can only be used up to 80°C, while the US sensor (Kistler) tolerates operation up to 240°C. The position is similar for low temperatures (minus 20°C for the UK one and minus 195°C for the US one).

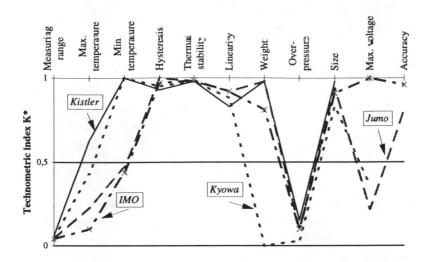

*Figure 4.1: Technometric characteristic profile of four selected pressure sensors (1991)*

The data on accuracy is fragmentary. The products differ considerably in terms of weight, the Japanese pressure sensor (Kyowa) at 530 g being substantially heavier than the German (Jumo) at 14 g. The error susceptibility at maximum permissible voltage must also be regarded as very divergent, while all four sensors react unfavourably to overpressure (in the world comparison).

Since the aggregated technometric indicator can be retained for product quality, the question arises as to what relationship exists between product quality and price. Before embarking on a systematic analysis of the relationship between technological performance and price structure, let us illustrate the problem by reference to 72 pressure sensors for which the technometric specifications are largely known. Figure 4.2 provides a comparison of the market prices of these sensors relative to the respective unweighted aggregated technometric indicators, that is, according to Formula (4.3), F(i,j) = 1 for all j. The four products illustrated in Figure 4.1 are among these products selected from eleven manufacturers from six countries. The respective prices have been converted into US dollars.

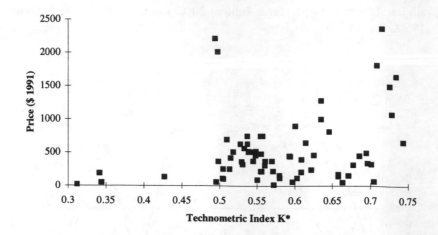

*Figure 4.2:  Comparison of market prices and aggregated*
*technometric indicators for 72 pressure sensors from six*
*countries (1991)*

With certain exceptions, Figure 4.2 shows that apparently there is a consistently monotonic relation between technical properties and price. This intimates a weakly positive connection between (unweighted) technical quality and price[5], but does not show the pattern required by marketing theory: the start point taken cannot be declining marginal yields through higher technical quality but rather according to Figure 4.2 price variation will become broader on the market under investigation. Steenkamp (1989, p. 236) generally only establishes a weak quality-price correlation. Certainly, apart from two exceptions, a high price cannot be achieved with medium to low quality. Clearly a relationship must be found linking properties to demand preferences if important price-determining specifications are to be drawn up. The unweighted technometric quality index appears to be unsuitable for this purpose on a strongly segmented market.

## 4.4 TECHNICAL QUALITY AND HEDONIC PRICES

Before embarking on an appropriate systematic analysis, an attempt can be made, using *factor analysis,* to reduce the 12 technical properties via their relationship to one another – that is, without considering price structure. For the total of 80 different pressure sensors incorporated in the sample, the following ratios emerge: a large proportion of the variance between variables is explicable by two main factors; several variables respectively having high factor loadings. The first main factor relates to product properties which concern the *area of application.* Here, the measuring range and the maximum and minimum temperature have high factor loadings. The other main factor appears to represent properties connected with *accuracy.* Apart from the variables for accuracy itself, hysteresis plus temperature stability (for high and low temperatures) and to a lesser extent linearity are involved. Weight and diameter plus error tolerance appear to be stand-alone items. Both main factors alone virtually account for half of the overall variance, thus suggesting that not all technical attributes contribute towards market price.

A systematic investigation of price structure must be extended, in the demand theory, in order to address demand for innovations in the capital goods field. Underlying the considerations is the approach developed by Lancaster (1991). According to this theory, 'consumers are not interested in goods as such, but in their properties or characteristics' (p. 5). The theory deals with the optimum mix of properties required in order to meet a prescribed set of demand preferences and the relative values which the prospective purchaser awards to each characteristic property, prompting compilation of a matrix of functions linking preference and technical property.

For the sensor market, which, according to the assessment in Section 4.1, can be construed as being functional, that is, intensively competitive and efficient, an empirical relationship should be discernible between the quantitatively measured attributes of the product and product prices. It should be possible to solve the problem by multiple linear regression (OLS), the dependent variable being market price and the independent variables being product properties. Thus, the absolute values of the coefficients show what value the market assigns to this property. The relative values of these coefficients when compared to the others can thus provide the relative weighting which the market demands and hence are interpreted as a functional characteristic per Equation (4.3).

The proposed approach has been considered sporadically in R&D management literature here and there as far back as the 1960s and linked to the hedonic price concept, see Griliches (1961, 1971) and Chow (1967). The new literature encompasses Saviotti (1985), Trajtenberg (1990) and Dorison (1992). The prime objective of the literature on hedonic pricing was certainly different from the present scenario. The method was originally developed in order to differentiate between a quality-determining price component and a quality-independent component. The question was raised as to whether price changes in an item can be viewed *detached* from quality changes.

In Saviotti's (1985) notation, product quality is modelled as follows, the variables already listed in this Chapter being retained:

$$K^*_k = \Sigma_j \, a_j \, K^*_{kj} \, . \tag{4.4}$$

Here, k denotes the compared products and j the properties. In Equation (3), the aggregated technometric indicator $K^*_k$ has been presented as a parameter deduced via a functional characteristic from the $K^*_{kj}$ property profile. $K^*_k$ is now interpreted as product quality reflecting a hypothetical market price $M_k$ together with a quality-independent factor $a_o$ ($u_k$ thus representing the random statistical error term):

$$M_k = a_0 + \Sigma_j \, a_j \, K^*_{kj} + u_k \, . \tag{4.5}$$

The hedonic prices $a_j$ can be determined with the aid of the regression calculation. On this subject, Saviotti (1985, p. 312) observes: 'Price equation coefficients ... can, therefore, be considered an approximation for users' judgement of the relative value of various characteristics.'

In the regression analysis, it was felt expedient to omit sensors with many missing data. The hedonic price determination therefore related to 68 sensors and 11 properties. The regression calculation can account for precisely half of the variance ($R^2 = 0.50$). This is open to different interpretations depending upon viewpoint. On the one hand, this means that half of the price variation alone is explicable in terms of the physico–technical properties of the products. On the other hand, likewise one half is attributable to price variance which cannot be explained in terms of quality improvement but relies on the manufacturer's reputation or upon various marketing endeavours on service, maintenance, established practices or can be traced back to other preferences.

Of the eleven variables only two are significant. They originate from application of stepwise regression in which explanatory variables are arranged (according to an F-test) in order of their ability to raise the variance explained. The maximum coefficient occurs for the variable for maximum temperature; it is almost twice as great as the next largest coefficient for the weight. It can therefore be assumed that the maximum contribution towards price elucidation is made by the *maximum temperature* and *weight* of the sensor. These are the two decisive quality variables. Interestingly, both variables, on their own, virtually account for the entire quality-dictated price variance ($R^2_{adj} =$ 0.46 in comparison to $R^2 = 0.50$ for all variables).

The hedonic price investigation for pressure sensors reveals that of the eleven technical properties two account, straight away, for the quality-determined part of sensor pricing, in all practically half of the price variation. The maximum permissible temperature has a direct bearing on the application potential in the industrial field. The supposition that lightweight versions would be among the most important consumer preferences does not hold. Higher prices are currently commanded by heavier weight sensors on the sensor market. This is presumably connected with the idea that the heavier units are more durable and can assimilate greater stress under extreme conditions.

The findings confirm the Lancaster (1991) new consumer theory according to which prospective customers are not interested in the goods as such but in their properties. From the sensor market analysis, this comment can be extended to: *'a particular handful of properties'*. It has thus been shown that for pressure sensors in 1991 questions of material saving or use of lighter materials are still not considered to be prime characteristics although this is generally postulated in literature for technical advances in sensors. Clearly, the properties associated with heavier units take precedence (durability, stability, and so on). A particularly lightweight sensor produced at high production costs which in all other respects does not differ from rival products commercially will not succeed in defraying the higher production costs. The only advice that could be given to a particular company which is bent on precisely this innovation is to 'tune into the market' and at any rate so long as the demand for dearer lightweight sensors continues to be inadequate to refrain from embarking on a corresponding innovation venture. The use of hedonic prices in connection with technometrics appears to be a valuable analytical instrument for microeconomic as well as for business management use.

Admittedly, there are more direct ways in establishing demand preferences which will be discussed in the next Section.

## 4.5 PREFERENCES VOICED BY PROSPECTIVE INDUSTRIAL CLIENTS

In Section 4.3, it has been shown that product types, measurement processes, technical characteristics (specifications), manufacturing companies, sales organizations and prices can be known to manufacturers, their rivals *and* (industrial) users – for example via exhibits and trade fair documents. Information deficits on substitute goods may originate from the wealth of information and market segmentation – but this is no leading counter-argument merely a question of adequate information processing, that is, a matter of cost.[6] It may also be that corresponding gratis information from customer–supplier relationships are available bilaterally in adequate measure to individual companies but in this case they are not recorded (formalized) in writing and hence, in principle, not accessible to *all* market participants which again leads to transaction costs.

According to current marketing literature, customer evaluations are measured with the aid of multi-attribute choice models. General articles have been written by Wilkie and Pessemier (1973) plus Curry and Menasco (1983). Attributes can, for example, be product quality, price *or* fashion externals. Attributes are therefore not identical to *technical* property profiles. Such models explain the formation of (internal) attitudes which lead to preference of one brand over another. At the same time, the tendency is for the capability of one attribute to be linearly compensated for by the other. The main disadvantage of this marketing model is the subjective nature of the evaluations. Consumers are guided by their own subjective assessments when making a choice and *in so doing assume* that a particular product *has* the relevant property. Such suppositions often provide no reliable information for the marketing division of a company on possible changes to marketing strategy. For example, it might well be that certain quality properties of a brand are regarded as poor by the users, although this is not confirmed objectively. If marketing experts want to know for sure that the customer evaluation is wrong in objective terms in comparison to the rival products, not product quality itself, but, for example, the communications strategy ought to be changed. Here, too, *technometric benchmarking* paves the way for more objective measuring processes in marketing and the management of technology.

Specifically the new consumer theory on the one hand and marketing literature on the other stress the importance of a demand-oriented corporate strategy, see Levitt (1993) or Maital (1994, ch. 8). At the same time, the missing information item relates not only to attributes such as price ranges which the prospective clients are prepared to pay (this matter can be left to market equilibrium force) or purely and simply product quality, but to detailed information about preferences for the optimal 'basket' of product properties which the demander prefers. Precisely for company secrecy reasons among competitors it is questionable whether the manufacturer of an innovative product is aware of the functions in detail which his piece of equipment has to perform for industrial users and how appropriate the profile of product technical features is for this purpose. This information can be known bilaterally in adequate measure via customer–supplier dealings; other market participants are however excluded from this information. This information deficit is vital for elucidating innovation processes, since the technical properties of innovative products must be established prior to market launch and hence before sales discussions can be conducted with potential clients. This certainly applies to innovators new to the market.

It is possible to amass information about purchasers' preferences by direct market research. This is the usual and commonest way in practice for missing blocks of information to be obtained on free markets. An entire branch of the economy makes a living from this in market research. So, in order to include 'appropriate' data on demand preferences in this context, here, too, a direct market survey has been conducted, see Frenkel et al. (1994a). This was done by asking the purchaser of industrial sensors, via a questionnaire, to rate the importance of technometrically determined properties of sensors according to their importance on a scale of between 0 and 10.[7] The same questionnaire was also handed out to sensor manufacturers (R&D personnel, production manager, sales manager) in order to establish the preference rating of their industrial clients as perceived by the manufacturer.

In such a survey, firstly the problem of missing product data does not arise; the set of technical characteristics has therefore been extended beyond the 12 considered hitherto. The inquiry also sought to check whether the technometric information available was definitely relevant in terms of demand preferences. In all, in the case of pressure sensors, 22 possible technical properties were considered part of the sensor market. Fully completed questionnaires from 50 recipients of pressure sensors were evaluated; the data likewise relate to 1991.

Having amassed this data on demand preferences, answers could be given to the following hypothesis:

Hypothesis 1:      The most important technical properties which manufacturers disclose to their customers are those which the demanders prefer.

Hypothesis 2:      Manufacturers are perfectly aware of demand preferences.

Hypothesis 3:      Potential customers on a market have identical or very similar preferences.

Hypothesis 4:      As far as the preferred properties are concerned, the technical quality of the products is higher in these characteristics than in others.

Hypothesis 5:      Products whose technical quality perfectly matches the demand preferences achieve higher market prices.

The object of this Section is to check the above five hypothesis for the pressure sensor sub-market. Table 4.1 shows that, of the 22 quality properties examined, 11 are known from the technometric investigation while a further 11 were not considered important to the inquiry. The choice of technometric characteristics was made with the help of the R&D personnel of manufacturers having coherent ideas about the important technical features of their innovative products from the dominant technical design standpoint. From these assessments, sales and marketing departments formulate the corresponding specification sheets which they offer to their customers in the context of general business relationships and supply at fairs, for example. In expert circles, the other 11 properties are to some degree contentious, as far as their importance is concerned, or only represent the individual opinions of outsiders. In some respects, they have been designated by individual prospective clients as 'unfortunately defective' in the specification sheets.

Table 4.1 shows two different things:

- in fact the preferences mentioned for technometric specifications are higher than for the rest;
- and what is perhaps even more interesting, the variances in regard to technometric characteristics are smaller than for the rest.

*Table 4.1:*  *Comparison of demand preferences for pressure sensors*
*subdivided into technometrically relevant and irrelevant*
*properties (N = 50)*

| No. | Characteristics | Average importance | Standard error |
|-----|-----------------|--------------------|----------------|
| *Technometric properties:* | | | |
| 1 | Hysteresis | 0.915 | 0.114 |
| 2 | Accuracy | 0.894 | 0.151 |
| 3 | Linearity | 0.868 | 0.157 |
| 4 | Measuring range | 0.715 | 0.370 |
| 5 | Overpressure | 0.711 | 0.312 |
| 6 | Maximum ambient temperature | 0.702 | 0.226 |
| 7 | Minimum ambient temperature | 0.692 | 0.233 |
| 8 | Thermal stability | 0.656 | 0.345 |
| 9 | Size | 0.600 | 0.272 |
| 10 | Maximum supply voltage | 0.483 | 0.288 |
| 11 | Weight | 0.417 | 0.276 |
| | Average | 0.696 ± 0.151 | 0.249 ± 0.082 |
| *Other properties:* | | | |
| 1 | Repeatability | 0.909 | 0.102 |
| 2 | Response time | 0.843 | 0.179 |
| 3 | Sensitivity | 0.764 | 0.256 |
| 4 | Output signal | 0.556 | 0.344 |
| 5 | Minimum supply voltage | 0.500 | 0.283 |
| 6 | Insulation resistance | 0.464 | 0.306 |
| 7 | Resonant frequency | 0.417 | 0.339 |
| 8 | Bridge resistance | 0.338 | 0.283 |
| 9 | Maximum storage temperature | 0.334 | 0.208 |
| 10 | Minimum storage temperature | 0.334 | 0.208 |
| 11 | Output impedance | 0.329 | 0.307 |
| | Average | 0.526 ± 0.206 | 0.256 ± 0.071 |

If this is not to be interpreted purely statistically, this means that the *notions* of the 50 industrial users of pressure sensors questioned in regard to technometric parameters are less divergent than for the rest. Consequently, it would seem to be confirmed that the technometric estimates are distinguishable from the rest in that they involve a larger consensus of the technical world. The technometrically chosen technical properties are consensual; this conceptualization is already established in theoretical design according to which specialist technical circles during their social interactions over a period of time come up with a joint picture which is important to an innovation. Hypothesis 1 has therefore been confirmed, not surprisingly, tendentially; one criticism that can be levelled against it is that the random sample could be too small to produce significant results.

The second hypothesis relates to whether the manufacturers of the sensors perceive the lists of preferences in the same way as their clients. From supplier relationships, discussions at fairs and many other contacts ideally the manufacturer should have full information about the preferred technical features of his products as perceived by the customer. If the entire set of 22 specifications according to manufacturer and customer perceptions is correlated, the result is plain: both preference scales are entirely uncorrelated. Thus, the market tends to value highly technical characteristics such as linearity, repeatability and hysteresis, while the prospective supplier sets greater store by accuracy and error tolerance (overpressure). Hypothesis 2 must clearly be discarded; not even remotely complete information can be obtained about purchaser-revealed preferences.

A further index for the non-existence of complete information about customer wishes within a comparatively limited sub-market such as pressure sensors is obtained from further observations which Frenkel et al. (1994a) have conducted. The variances in perception between individual manufacturers show considerable scatter – much more marked than with prospective purchasers. Since anonymity was promised for the field research, no data can be supplied as to what type of companies can assess relatively reliably what prospective customers prefer. We might mention with some circumspection that among sensor manufacturers whose ideas deviate flagrantly from consumer preferences are also larger concerns so that the supposition of a specific problem with medium-sized companies is unsubstantiated.

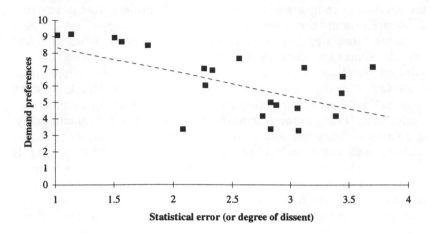

*Figure 4.3: Average consumer preferences for 22 technical properties
of pressure sensors and the degree of dissent over the
assessment (1991, N = 50)*

Hypothesis 3 takes the considerations on preference homogeneity a
step further. Table 4.1 not only includes the revealed preference
ratings of prospective purchasers but also standard deviations obtained
from the answers. They relate to the preference ratings themselves and
are not independent of them. The more important or the greater the
functionality of a technical property is considered to be, the more
convinced are the prospective purchasers as a whole of this conviction.

Figure 4.3 shows the high degree of concordance on highly preferred
technical properties. There is a greater divergence of opinion over the
generally less important quality features. The negative ratio proves to
be significant and is robust. Hypothesis 3 can undoubtedly be
considered confirmed which again points to the importance of
consensus-forming processes among economic agents in this case the
prospective purchasing group for pressure sensors.

Since Hypothesis 2 cannot be confirmed and it is to be noted that
manufacturers of science-based innovations (in this case, pressure
sensors) are not adequately informed about the wishes or functional
necessities of the user, it can be suggested that Hypothesis 4 is also
untenable. It presupposes that the anticipated requirements of the
industrial purchaser of innovative products are already considered at
the R&D, design and construction stages of the technical
specifications. Only with timely, adequate, relevant information can

the innovating company so configure its R&D projects that in so doing the desired (in the literal sense) technical designs emerge.

Taking this a step further, technological interdependencies exist and not all somewhat contrary technical design requirements can be fulfilled simultaneously. As technical modifications are differentiated from factor costs, compromises would have to be struck between technical and cost practicability and the requirement profile presented by demand. Owing to the lack of information on product functionality, it must be assumed that also the gap between the resulting compromise solution and the ideal within the context of the R&D project is unknown. This does not apply to customer-specific developments in which *a* subsequent purchaser prescribes the specifications. Even in this case, it would however be interesting for corporate technology management to know how the list of market requirements thus claimed stands in regard to all purchasers other than the one customer.

For the 72 products chosen from eleven innovative companies in six countries which were analysed in greater depth in Section 4.3 and which are incorporated in Figure 4.2, it can be tested to what extent the technical quality of these products is in accordance with the disclosed demand preferences. This is based on the assumption that an efficient company with a good database on demand requirements sets greater store by highly preferred technical features which are reflected in a correspondingly high technometric index. With a view to arriving at a compromise between factor costs and mutually exclusive technical specifications the assumption must be made that the technometric indices for the properties less prized by the prospective purchaser (or as above, the more ambiguous ratings for the entire sub-market) are not endowed with correspondingly high quality. The technometric index must then be correspondingly lower.

If the technometric profiles are compared to the requirement profiles using the numerical values in Table 4.1 (taking only the technometrically relevant part of the assessments into account), then an index can be calculated for the *demand orientation (DO)* from the mean quadratic deviation of both profiles:

$$DO_k = \Sigma_j \, (K^*_{kj} - F_j)^2. \qquad (4.6)$$

Here, F denotes the disclosed demand preferences; the other variables and indices have already been introduced. The demand orientation is large for small values of DO.

The distribution of the indices for demand orientation has the form of a continuum between good and less good orientation of the technical properties desired by the buyer. The optimum sensors from the random sample are likewise only configured in certain properties and not in all quality dimensions. By way of illustration, let us look at the best and worst sensor as oriented to demand wishes (Figure 4.4). The Kyowa

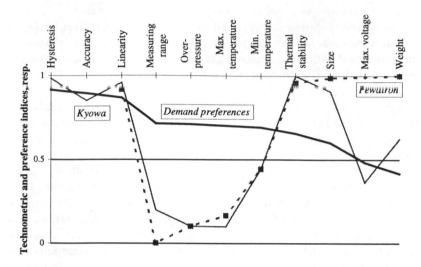

*Figure 4.4:   Revealed demand preferences and technometric profiles for two chosen pressure sensors (the technical property configuration shows preferences in decreasing order)*

(Japan) pressure sensor displays technometric specifications which in terms of the three most important properties (from the demand standpoint) are outstanding, but it is no longer appropriate for 'average' preferences. In the next ranking properties, this sensor displays moderate qualities which consumers might accept. Of the 72 products chosen, this unit was the best match to demand requirements, at least, in regard to the most important features.

The reverse applies to the Pewatron pressure sensor whose best technometric characteristics materialize in the midst of those properties which users would put at the bottom of the list. This sensor shows high quality in regard to the less important properties. Also worth noting is the fact that the corresponding specifications in regard to both most important characteristics are hardly mentioned by the would-be supplier and might therefore be unknown to the user. This does not appear to be any general corporate marketing strategy because the corresponding data on hysteresis were produced properly for sensors other than the one considered here, from the same manufacturer. Figure 4.4 gives a visual impression of the technical quality dimension of the two contrasting products in regard to demand preferences, and thus refers to a method Pugh (1990) has described earlier. Whereas in a Pugh matrix scores are being used, here metric scales are involved.

Hypothesis 4, as already suspected, is untenable. Also a satisfactorily operating market such as the sensor market, insofar as the products considered are concerned, does not lead to premature inclusion of detailed requirements from later prospective customers in the technical quality characteristics of innovative products. Therefore, the sensor market can function with correspondingly suboptimally designed products, since clearly no ideal products are available as these would otherwise drive the mismatched ones from the market. Industrial investigators choose what is for them the lesser of the various evils on offer. The marked segmentation has already been emphasized many times. To further check out hypothesis 4, the pressure sensor sub-market would have to be further segmented. Even without such segmentation it must be assumed that, essentially, attributes other than technical ones also play a part; let us cite confidential relationships, supplier relationships of long standing, incomplete awareness as to what is available on foreign markets, and so on by way of example. Also the hedonic price analysis in Section 4.4 has shown that the technical specifications can only account for half of the price variance.

## 4.6  MARKET SEGMENTATION AND IDENTIFICATION OF NICHES

The purpose of the last hypothesis is to ascertain whether a better match to customer requirements leads to higher prices. However, first of all – since more detailed information on segmentation is not available – it must be checked whether, with the help of a similarity analysis of the property spectrum, an inherent pertinent product segmentation results. According to Backhaus (1992, pp. 158 onwards), the segmentation criterion must display a determinable relationship to procurement behaviour which again can be linked to characteristic functionality, if geographical and organizational partial approaches to segmentation (not explored here) are excluded. A multidimensional scaling of the 72 sensors in terms of 11 properties yields a *technometric portfolio* per Figure 4.5.[8]

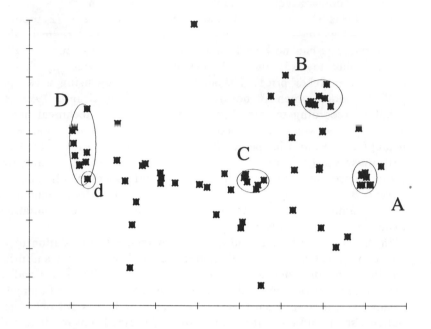

*Figure 4.5:*   *Multidimensional configuration of technical characteristics of the pressure sensor market 1991*

Figure 4.5 shows high scatter along the abscissa with certain clusters of homogeneous products. Most sensors with large measuring ranges lie in the left-hand half, low pressure precision instruments are on the right-hand side. Cluster A (deliberate visual demarcation) for example comprises eight products from three potential suppliers all with superlative accuracy and linearity but low temperature tolerance at high temperatures, light and perfect hysteresis. Manufacturers of products in Cluster B serve market segments in which moderate pressures are measured with high but not maximum accuracy, good display linearity is unimportant, but thermal stability even at higher temperatures is preferred. The Kyowa sensor from Figure 4.4, which meets customer requirements exactly in terms of top values (but not in regard to average), achieves a market price of US$444 (1991) and falls in Cluster C. The Pewatron product (d) has technical strengths in a few important properties and for which the specifications of the most important characteristics are scarcely known, achieves a market price of US$18 (1991) and falls in Cluster D. Sensor d is one of the cheapest, comparatively unreliable products, and so on.

Hypothesis 5 is likewise tested with the aid of the 72 products chosen. As we have now an empirical model of market segmentation, the hypothesis can now be formulated as follows: do sensors with a greater bias towards the technical properties desired by demand command a higher price? The answer is found by using a two-part TOBIT model which is not reported here (see Grupp, 1998, for details). According to this econometric test, higher technical quality along customer wants significantly explains whether a particular sensor belongs to the top price percentile. In the average and low price band, still, those sensors achieve a higher market price whose technological profile more closely follows the average preferences of all industrial buyers. But now manufacturing matters: with gauge strain technology, firms cannot sell expensive sensors. With these limitations, hypothesis 5 seems to be valid.

In the context of R&D and quality management, elucidation of the connections between technical change, demand preferences and prices would be out of order and inappropriate for individual cases and the pricing peculiarities. From the technical characteristics per Figure 4.4, in any case, it is apparent that the Pewatron product is not only cheap but also small and light. It is a modern miniaturized sensor whereas the products in Cluster A are many times larger.

The commercially lowly rated product appears to fit precisely into the much discussed mainstream miniaturization of sensor technology whereby information technology and microelectronics are making incursions into conventional instrument engineering. In 1991, the market was still not prepared, however, to acknowledge this price-wise and is still prepared to give preference to more conventional, larger duty units with higher accuracy and reliability. Similar findings are also obtained by the hedonic prices method (see Section 4.4).

## 4.7  CONCLUSION

In all, this Chapter results in unclear relationships and many current hypothesis do not provide confirmation of equilibrium markets. Whether the empirical findings proposed hitherto can be corroborated via further segmentation and larger random samples remains to be seen. The invalidity of the hypothesis on general information reliability is however not only supported by the empirical observations but also by the strength of theoretical considerations. Against the background of general market equilibrium, a proportion of the resource costs must be attributable to information procurement as it promotes the new microeconomics. As far as that goes, the justified hope remains that the technometric findings for the sensor market can be substantiated by further projects and are not a random event.

In the preceding Section, a temporary, rather anecdotal view of the modern sensor market supplies many informative insights into the sluggishness of this market in adopting a new scientifico–technological paradigm. Since an externally applied segmentation of this market is unknown, perhaps a bifurcation point is also available for this sub-market in which there is product differentiation between conventional products and semiconductor products or the new paradigm must reinforce the first reactions before it becomes universally established. For the moment, the miniaturized product has objective disadvantages in the highly preferred properties evaluation. Consequently, for the time being for the technically more modern product cluster only those customers who do not set great store by it (earlier non-industrial applications) are considered. Investigation of the connection between technical quality and price would then have to resolve the corresponding case differentiations before plausible results can be obtained. For QFD, starting points to improve the quality of products under the new technical paradigm can immediately be derived from the technometric portfolio.

In the *management of technology context,* the technometric benchmarking acquires additional importance in identifying niches on capital goods markets. Validation with the aid of market surveys shows that the approach is valid; the characteristics contained in the technometrics index are deemed more important to some prospective purchasers than others. In this respect, this Chapter can also be viewed as an extension of the common benchmarking literature with relevance for quality function deployment (QFD).

## NOTES

1     This Chapter was first published in *R&D Management* 28 (2), pp. 65–77, 1998.
2     In this Chapter, by 'billion' we mean 'thousand million'.

3    This is the SENSOR Fair which took place in May 1991 in Nuremberg. The authors of this article are grateful to Frenkel and Koschatzky who conducted the data inquiry on the spot, see Frenkel et al. (1994a) and Koschatzky et al. (1996).

4    According to information from Arnold (1991), pressure sensors are much sought after. Their market volume in 1991 amounted to US$3.2 billion and is expected to double to US$7.2 billion by the year 2001.

5    Official exchange rate for the randomly chosen date of December 13, 1991.

6    The costs of information procurement can be roughly estimated from the Koschatzky et al. (1996) and Frenkel et al. (1994a) research projects, and thus from the preparation of the sensor data used in this Section. Indeed, this is a R&D management research project in which the research team was no market participant but the costs of a market participant with no large internal knowledge base, for example a medium-sized enterprise, are of a similar order of magnitude. The costs of 'manufacturing' as complete a set of data as possible on the sensor market *in a particular year* must be reckoned at US$20,000 to US$35,000. In view of the size of this figure, in the mid-80s, an attempt was made to set up a permanently updated sensor databank which all market participants could search on-line. The hosts STN SENSOR databank was not however a paying proposition and after an initial public launch expired in 1987 and ceased to be updated. See Grupp et al. (1987, pp. 248–249) and Koschatzky et al. (1996).

7    If the resulting indices are divided by 10, then the results of the inquiry were referred to the same numerical interval between 0 and 1 as the techometric indicator.

8    The distance factor is calculated per the cosine measure; Figure 4.5 is unrotated, the stress at $L = 0.166$ is satisfactory, $R^2 = 0.87$ virtually explains 90 per cent of the variance, iteration was discontinued at $\Delta L < 0.001$.

# 5 Estimating the Value of Brand Names: A Data Envelopment Analysis Approach[1]

> *'What's in a name? A rose by any other name would smell as sweet'.*
>
> *William Shakespeare*

**Main Ideas in this Chapter**

This Chapter uses a variant of linear programming known as Data Envelopment Analysis to measure the contribution of brand name to the determination of market price. Strong brand names generate higher prices than the quality of their product features alone implies, hence are 'efficient' in converting features into price. Weak brand names are 'inefficient', in that they give the consumer high feature value in the absence of brand-name value. This method generates quantitative estimates of brand-name value, as well as parameters showing substitution effects among product features. The empirical part of the Chapter deals with printers and executive jet aircraft. The examination of 36 printers reveals the existence of strong brand names that in and of themselves command higher prices. In contrast, no brand-name effect is found for 18 executive jets. We interpret this finding as follows: for mass-market consumer products, amenable to brand-building techniques of marketing, there are clear, identifiable brand-name effects on price; but for investment goods (like jet aircraft) exhaustively evaluated by procurement managers, technology-based features alone drive price.

## 5.1   INTRODUCTION

With the rise of the global economy, greater importance now attaches to the establishment of strong brand names as a key element of competitive strategy. Ward et al. (1999) argue that '... it is precisely the volatile conditions (swiftly changing technology and high levels of uncertainty among buyers) that make the brand concept especially pertinent (for high-tech products). When things change quickly, and when buyers face great uncertainty, they want to deal with a company they perceive has a vision of their needs and interests that goes beyond price and performance' (p. 95).

A recent survey canvassed 106 firms in the USA and Europe (Troy, 1998). The study found that companies claiming to have a 'highly successful brand' averaged earnings growth of 33 per cent yearly, compared with 22 per cent for other firms. Between 1991 and 1995, the value of 'strong-brand' companies' stock price rose on average by 125 per cent, compared with 71 per cent for other firms. A consulting firm known as Corporate Branding Practice found that fully 5 per cent of Fortune 1000 companies' stock price was accounted for by Corporate Brand Image (Troy, 1998, p. 28) – virtually equal to the contribution of 'financial strength'.

Yet despite the clear, high return to brand names, 40 per cent of the respondents reported that 'they are minimally or not at all satisfied' (loc. cit.) with the measurement tools used to benchmark brand-building effort and investment. If indeed management begins with measurement, there is a clear need for improved methods for quantifying brand equity.

A Microsoft executive, Ann Redmond, defines brand equity as follows:

> 'If a product Microsoft offers is equal to a competitor's in every other way – in its features and capabilities – what incremental value does our product have in the eyes of the customer? That value-add is the power of the brand name – and that's what we call brand equity'.[2]

This suggests a multi-attribute approach to measuring brand equity, based on product features. Grupp and Maital (1998a) applied a multi-attribute model known as 'technometrics', commonly used to evaluate product quality, in order to measure the market value accruing to specific product features. That study showed that fully half of the variance in the market prices for industrial sensors was explained by only two key features: maximum temperature and weight. The question then arose: what factors underlie the other half of the variance in price *not* explained by product features? Is brand name a key variable in determining product price? If so – how can the 'brand-name effect' be quantified?

This Chapter uses a variant of linear-programming known as DEA (Data Envelopment Analysis) to measure the contribution of brand name to the determination of market price. We estimate an efficiency frontier, in which the 'decision-making units' are similar, competing products; 'inputs' are the objectively measured qualities of product features (measured in interval scales); and 'output' is the product price. The assumed objective of the company is to maximize price, for given product feature inputs. Companies invest in R&D that improves product features, and/or in expenditures that build brand equity. Market prices are assumed to be generated by product features and by strong brand names. Efficiency scalars measure the brand-name effect. Strong brand names generate higher prices than the quality of their product features alone implies. A high ratio of price/feature input indicates the presence of value-adding factors other product features – specifically, brand name. This method generates quantitative estimates of brand-name value, as well as parameters showing substitution effects among product features.

The structure of the Chapter is as follows. The next Section reviews the literature on multi-attribute models in economics and business administration journals. Section 5.3 surveys methods for measuring brand equity and provides an exposition of our proposed method including a numerical illustration, based on our earlier study of pressure sensors. Section 5.4 introduces the DEA relations. Section 5.5 then applies DEA to the analysis of brand equity for 36 printers. Section 5.6 uses the DEA method for measuring brand equity for executive jet aircraft. The final Section summarizes and concludes.

## 5.2   A BRIEF SURVEY OF MULTI-ATTRIBUTE PRODUCT MODELS

Multi-attribute models, which analyse products by breaking them down into measurable features or attributes, have been widely used in marketing and in the economics of consumer behaviour and technical change, with relatively little interaction among them. This Section undertakes an integrative survey of these three branches of literature, to prepare the foundations for our new approach to measuring brand equity.

In marketing, multi-attribute models date back as far as Green and Wind (1973). In economics, Lancaster reinvented the economic theory of consumer demand by adopting a multi-attribute approach (Lancaster, 1971; 1991). In the literature on the economics of innovation and technological change, Grupp pioneered in the use of multi-attribute models for quantifying technological sophistication and measuring how it changes (Grupp and Hohmeyer, 1986; Grupp, 1994, 1998). He termed his approach 'technometrics'. A natural development was to use the multi-attribute approach as the basis for optimizing investment in research and development (R&D) (Ben-Arieh et al., 1998; Grupp and Maital, 1998a, 1998b), and for integrating marketing and R&D (Horwitch et al., 2000).

## Multi-Attribute Models in Marketing

Customer value is an important positional advantage and can be a key success factor (Day and Wensley, 1988). Measuring customer value is based, in many cases, on multi-attribute models. Such models explain attitude formation, which underlies brand preference (Fishbein, 1963; Fishbein and Ajzen, 1975).

Fishbein's model (1963) arrived at attitude scores based on the multiplication of each brand's performance on an attribute and the same attribute's evaluation. Bass and Talarzyk (1972) replaced the evaluation component with an assessment of the importance of each attribute. Empirical evidence for the superiority of either model is mixed (Bettman et al., 1975; Mazis and Ahtola, 1975). Linear compensatory models have dominated (for reviews, see Curry and Menasco, 1983, and Wilkie and Pessemier, 1973; for exceptions, see Curry and Faulds, 1986, and Tversky et al., 1987).

Given the importance of attribute-level information, it is not surprising that it has been used extensively in the marketing literature. Many texts use such models and suggest a variety of strategies to improve a firm's position in a perceptual map (for example, Kotler, 1991). Most prior research concentrated on the role of product attributes in determining perceived quality. For example, Chang and Wildt (1994) manipulated product attribute information and measured the impact of the quantity of attribute information on perceived value. They found that as more attribute information was given to subjects, the importance of price as a determinant of perceived value diminished. Zeithaml (1988) also recognized the importance of attributes and suggested that intrinsic attributes underlie an abstract quality dimension, which determines perceived product quality.

Other attribute categorization schemes have also been used. Attributes can be categorized on the basis of *accessibility*. Attribute accessibility is defined as the *availability and usefulness of attribute information to potential customers* and is similar to Kotler's (1991) saliency of product attributes. Accessibility is important because it suggests which attribute information is available to and usable by potential buyers. For example, personal computer users may not know what a certain designation actually means. It may be inaccessible even to those who know what it means if they cannot assess the resulting computer performance. In a review of 42 empirical studies of multi-attribute models in marketing, Wilkie and Pessemier (1973) show that most such studies assume that their list only includes salient attributes without much substantiating evidence.

Another categorization is based on attribute *diagnosticity*. Diagnosticity is defined as *the extent to which an attribute can be used by customers to distinguish between competing alternatives*. Many product attributes lose diagnosticity with the passage of time and the maturing of an industry. This loss is explained by the three phases of product design (Watson, 1993). Innovative performance is the first phase, where there exist truly innovative features that speak to real and, at times, unspoken customer needs. Watson (1993) uses the car coffee-cup holder as an example. Prior to the launch of the Ford Taurus, such holders were unsafe add-ons. In contrast, holders were designed into the Taurus model resulting in a diagnostic attribute for some buyers. The second phase is competitive performance, during which customers compare features that are available in most brands. Many car models incorporated the cup holders during this phase. Attributes at the first and second stage can be used to compare competing brands on the basis of what Pessemier (1977) calls 'determinant attributes'. In the third phase, an attribute that was innovative is expected by all buyers and loses diagnosticity altogether. Attributes at the final phase are not used to evaluate products because they are available in most existing brands (the situation in the car market for cup holders at this time). Consumer Reports group such attributes under the heading 'All Have'. Utterback's and Abernathy's (1975) concept of the 'dominant design' refers similarly to this convergence on a common set of attributes.

Finally, some product attributes are non-monotone. They cannot be compared across consumers nor ordered on a utility function. For example, product colour is very important to some consumers (for example, clothing), but a preference for one colour over another cannot be compared across individuals. Most prior research included only monotonic product attributes for this reason.

The use of multi-attribute models in marketing has been subject to a number of critiques. Earlier critical work falls into one of three major types: choice of attributes, choice of weights, and allocation of performance scores. The first issue of choice of attributes involves their number (how many) and composition (which attributes). Wilkie and Pessemier (1973) show that the number of independent attributes assessed in previous research varied from 2 (of 9 original) to 8 (of 37 original). Consumer Reports use an average of 6.8 attributes and the similar Danish Radog Resulter uses an average of 9.3 (Hjorth-Andersen, 1984).

Second, the choice of attribute weights was the subject of much debate (Curry and Faulds, 1986; Hjorth-Andersen, 1984, 1986; Sproles, 1986). Hjorth-Andersen (1984, 1986) argued that the process used by testing firms is flawed because it is based on subjective selection of attributes and, more importantly, on non-disclosed attribute importance weights. He argues that low correlations between price and quality may have been due to the use of summary, Consumer Reports-based quality ratings. Similar concerns were voiced by Archibald et al. (1983) in their analysis of the running shoes market. Sproles (1986) uses Hjorth-Andersen's data to argue that consumer markets contain a high proportion of inefficient brands that can lead to financial losses. Curry and Faulds (1986) fault Hjorth-Andersen's summary methodology, but they agree that the proper choice of attribute weights is extremely important (see also Hjorth-Andersen, 1986).

Third, multi-attribute models in marketing are mostly subjective with regards to brand performance scores on each attribute. Subjective assessments of evaluative criteria are important since consumers act based on their beliefs regarding performance of competing products (Wilkie and Pessemier, 1973). Such beliefs can be assessed using competitive benchmarking (Bowman and Faulkner, 1994; Camp, 1989), but they sometimes fail to provide managers with the information needed to change strategy. For example, if a given brand is rated poorly by users on some attribute, say maximum speed of car, the major question is whether such ratings are justified. To the extent that objective quality is high, the firm may change its advertising strategy and attempt to convey a message of superior quality. If, on the other hand, low ratings are justified for a given product, the firm may invest in improving product quality. Another problem arises because not all users are aware of all brands and can only rate brands with which they are familiar. Their ratings are limited to known brands and evaluations are comparative only for these brands.

Furthermore, it is well known that attribute importance can vary by context (Bearden and Woodside, 1977). For example, the importance of price and quality may vary by respondents' income. This is the basis for the use of multi-attribute models as segmentation tools in many marketing contexts (Wilkie and Pessemier, 1973). Thus, it is important to either equalize the context of such studies or to divide the population into context-similar segments. Camp (1989) uses objective, benchmarked attribute measures – an approach adopted as well by Grupp (1998) in the innovation literature. Other studies deal with subjective, user-defined importance weights.

The use of objective measures at the attribute level is an important departure from most earlier research. As Hjorth-Andersen (1986) suggests, while the argument about choice of weights raged, no attention was paid to the choice of scales to measure each attribute. Hjorth-Andersen (loc. cit.) also argues that many such scales are, at best, ordinal and that the distances between points of these scales are not equal. The use of benchmarked technometrics, as discussed above, results in cardinal, interval-scaled measures of performance. Furthermore, Garvin (1983, 1987) argues that quality should be assessed on eight dimensions. Six of these dimensions (objective performance, features, reliability, conformance, durability, and serviceability) should be measured objectively. Only two incorporate subjective criteria (aesthetics and perceived quality). Technometrics result in measures that fit Garvin's criteria.

In a 'bicentennial' review of Chapters using multi-attribute models in marketing, Lutz and Bettman (1977) point out the significant impact of the existence of publicly available, objective attribute information. In their view, objective data or discrete attributes (see Hauser and Simmie, 1981) do not apply to the standard models. Availability of public information has been shown to strengthen the positive relationship between advertising and quality (Archibald et al., 1983). Thus, after ratings are published, firms adjust their advertising levels. Archibald et al. (1983) argue further that advertising levels can help consumers locate good buys. Furthermore, as shown by Katz (1995), some product attributes are not directly observable, even after trial. She suggests that dependability and complaint-handling behaviour fall into this important category. As a result of these problems, which are inherent in subjective assessments of quality, many researchers argue for the use of objective measures (for example, Adelman and Griliches,

1961; Lancaster, 1991; Lucas, 1972; Muellbauer, 1974; Rosen, 1982). Objective measures form the backbone of process benchmarking as popularized by companies such as Ford and Xerox (Zangwill, 1993).

The use of benchmarked technometrics makes it possible to measure observable and non-observable attributes on the basis of publicly available attribute information (and, at a later stage, compare them to user-based attribute assessments). This is the basis of the technometric approach, which we now briefly survey.

## Multi-Attribute Models in the Economics of Technical Change

Benchmarked technometrics is designed to measure product attributes (Grupp, 1998, Grupp and Hohmeyer, 1986; Grupp, 1994; Frenkel et al., 1994b). It is a quantitative, objective approach, which can provide profiles at brand, product line, industry, or country levels. Its output is performance data for a given brand, compared to competitors'. Benchmarked technometrics has two advantages over existing methodologies. First, product or brand attributes are measured objectively. Thus, overall product evaluations are based on a combination of objective (attribute scores) and subjective (user weights) criteria, rather than a combination of subjective attribute scores and weights as in present approaches. Second, because it is based on readily available public sources, the benchmarked data can be used by firms to improve product management relatively easily. Existing methods require users to be knowledgeable about all available brands and their performance on the various attributes. As explained below, benchmarked technometrics requires that users provide only importance weights for the various attributes.

Because of the more objective nature of benchmarked technometrics and its use of readily available data, the technique has several practical advantages. These include the generation of objective, comparative attribute profile and perceptual maps of competing brands; a menu of possible attribute improvements; and a triangulation of manufacturer-based and user-based attribute importance weights. Interestingly, the technometric technique was developed in a policy framework to improve quantitative measures of progress, following a request by the German Federal Ministry of Science and Education for an assessment of the country's competitiveness in high-technology industries. It has originally been applied in the lasers, industrial robotics, and bio-diagnostic kits' industries.

Technometrics is defined as a quantitative measurement of the quality or technological sophistication of attributes of a product, process, product line, or industry (Grupp, 1998; Grupp and Hohmeyer, 1986). Technometric measurement is based on relevant product attributes (we discuss this issue further when our empirical evidence is presented), which stabilize as products mature (Stankiewicz, 1990). Industry experts usually agree on such attributes (Grupp, 1994).

Theoretically, benchmarked technometrics builds upon the foundations laid by Lancaster (1971) in his modern consumer theory. This economic theory (Lucas, 1972; Rosen, 1974) views products as utility-generating bundles of attributes (much like the approach used in marketing). It has been used to assess the accuracy of consumer price indexes in accounting for changes in product quality from one period to another (Adelman and Griliches, 1961). Such studies utilize the hedonic price index approach (Frenkel et al., 1994a; Griliches, 1961, 1971; Saviotti, 1985).

Product attributes are typically measured in differing units of measurement, such as weight (kg) and length (cm). The technometric technique circumvents these problems by normalizing product attribute scores, say, to a [0, 1] scale, or, alternately, a [1, 10] scale (both are employed below, the latter in cases where zero values are to be omitted). The first step in assigning a technometric score is to identify the best performing and worst performing products in a product group on each attribute. These are assigned values of one (for the best) and zero (for the worst). Thus, technometric scores are normalized and become benchmarked. This normalization enables weighted and unweighted aggregation.

The approach so far yields technometric scores at the attribute level. The next step is to combine these scores to arrive at an overall technometric score. A simple summation of attribute-level scores ignores attributes' importance. A more complex approach weights attributes with their subjective importance, as perceived by buyers.

## 5.3 METHODS FOR MEASURING BRAND EQUITY: A SIMPLE ILLUSTRATION

Numerous studies in marketing have focused on the impact of brand name on price for consumer products (Leuthesser, 1988; Srivastava and Shocker, 1991; Simon and Sullivan, 1993; Sullivan, 1998). Brand equity is commonly defined as 'the added value endowed by the brand to the product' (Farquhar, 1989), or, 'the incremental cash flows which accrue to branded products over and above the cash flows which would result from unbranded products' (Simon and Sullivan, 1993, p. 29).

Simon and Sullivan (1993) list five techniques for measuring brand equity:

- changes in the market value of stock when a brand name is acquired or divested;
- the price premia that a brand name commands;
- the brand name's influence on customer evaluation;
- replacement cost: the cost of establishing a product with a new brand name;
- brand-earnings multiplier: the product of 'brand weights' multiplied by the average of the past three years' profit.

These authors themselves offer a new, sixth measure, based on financial market data, while noting serious flaws in the above existing five methods.

Troy (1998), in her survey of 106 firms, distinguishes between 'performance-based' and 'perception-based' measures, commonly used by firms. Among performance-based measures of measuring brand-building success are: market-share penetration; ability to attract a premium; customer satisfaction; market position; and brand leadership. Among perception-based measures are: brand awareness; value; and customer beliefs about brand.

While nearly all these studies focus on mass-market consumer products, it cannot be excluded that brand name plays a role for knowledge-based technology-intensive investment products as well. This Chapter proposes a new approach to measuring brand equity, one that is particularly suitable for technologically sophisticated products and services and may also be used for investment goods.

Our new method for quantifying 'brand-name' effect is suggested by a 'Lancaster' model discussed in Section 5.2.2, in which value for the buyer (based on utility) is an 'output', produced by two types of 'inputs': objective quantifiable product features, and intangible aspects, primarily brand name. This is the basic model of, for example, Hauser and Shugan (1983) and Hauser and Gaskin (1984). We estimate the price premium that brand names convey by partitioning the price into two components: that driven by product features, and that driven by the brand-name effect.

Consider the following simple example, based on Figure 5.1 in Hauser and Shugan (1983). Table 5.1(a) shows two key product features for three branded pressure sensors (data from Grupp and Maital, 1998).

Table 5.1(b) converts the basic product-feature data into 'technometric' form, as follows (for formulae see Grupp, 1998, pp. 110 onwards): First, express 'measuring range' in terms of a [1, 10] metric scale, where 1.0 is the lowest quality (that is, the 80 bars value for the Swiss Pewatron model) and 10 is the highest (the 1,379 bars range for the US Kulite); and weight similarly, as a [1, 10] scale (with the lowest weight, Kulite, as 10, and the Jumo, at 255 grams, as 1.0).[3] Finally, Table 5.1(c) computes feature score/price (multiplied by 100).

*Table 5.1:  Product attributes and prices for three pressure sensors*

| (a) Basic data | | | |
|---|---|---|---|
| Product | Measuring range | Weight | Price (1991) |
| German JUMO | 400 bar | 255 g | $373 |
| US KULITE | 1,379 bar | 13 g | $460 |
| Swiss PEWATRON | 80 bar | 170 g | $112 |
| (b) Technometric data: [1, 10] metric | | | |
| German JUMO | 3.22 | 1 | |
| US KULITE | 10 | 10 | |
| Swiss PEWATRON | 1 | 4.16 | |
| (c) Feature score/price • 100 | | | |
| German JUMO | 0.863 | 0.268 | |
| US KULITE | 2.174 | 2.174 | |
| Swiss PEWATRON | 0.893 | 3.714 | |

Now, plot these value pairs for each of the three sensors, as 'feature score/price' (see Figure 5.1). The 'isoquant' (feature per dollar of price) on which the Jumo sensor rests is far inside the isoquant for Kulite or Pewatron. This means that the Jumo brand provides far less customer value, in the form of objective product features, per dollar of price, irrespective of the subjective weights customers may put on both attributes relative to each other. There must therefore be another component of value that Jumo conveys, apart from its product features. We may call this component 'brand value'. If buyers are rational, then 0b – 0a (the radius vector distance between the Jumo isoquant and the Kulite and Pewatron isoquant) must represent brand value. From the viewpoint of the firm, JUMO is 'efficient' in generating the highest possible price for given features and a branded product; Kulite and Pewatron are inefficient.

The brand-name effect can be quantified as [PRICE (0b – 0a)/0b]. In other words: only a small part of the $373 product price derives from the product features, while most derives from the strong brand name JUMO. While this result may seem exaggerated – indeed, the example was chosen for this purpose – in fact, strong brand names like SONY, TOSHIBA, IBM, bring significant price premiums, and in mass-market consumer products like Coca-Cola, an enormous fraction of the product price stems from the brand name Coke.

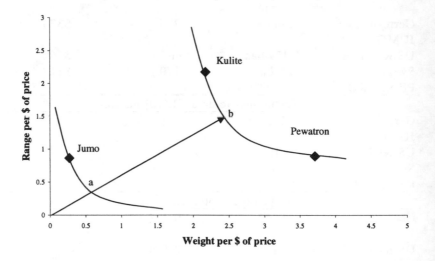

*Figure 5.1:  Efficiency frontier for three piezo-resistant pressure sensors*

This is just a simple illustration without detailing how the 'efficiency frontier' for product groups can be estimated empirically, in order to make this method operational. Any of the various methods used to estimate efficiency frontiers – some based on stochastic regressions, some based on linear programming – can be used. We now proceed to propose a method based on the Data Envelopment Analysis (DEA) model, used widely to measure operating efficiency in organizations.


## 5.4  A DEA MODEL FOR ESTIMATING BRAND EQUITY

Assume a profit-maximizing company. It seeks to maximize the price P it receives for its product, for a given amount of 'inputs', represented by product features vector $x = \{x_1, x_2, ... x_s\}$. Since features are costly to produce, and the better the feature the higher the cost, this model is simply a variation on the standard profit-maximization one. One way to achieve a higher P, apart from investing in product improvement, is by building a brand name. Another alternative is to invest in product quality by enhancing product features. Companies can therefore generate sales and profit by either building a national or global brand, while saving resources on product features per dollar, or offering value by providing high features per dollar, while saving resources in not building a national brand.

With the following terminology:
$x$ = vector of features, $\{x_1, ..., x_s\}$,
$x_i$ = feature 'i', i=1 ... s,
b = brand name variable: $0 \leq b \leq 1$ (maximal brand name),
P = price
Q = quantity
TC = total cost
z = investment in brand-building

we can formulate our model of the profit-maximizing firm which becomes then: invest resources in brand-building until the marginal revenue accruing to improving the brand-name effect equals the marginal cost of such an effect:

$$MAX [P(b(z), x) Q (b(z), x) - TC (Q, x, z)] \qquad (5.1)$$

where z, the decision parameter, comprehends the quality and quantity of marketing resources invested in brand-building. The first-order condition for optimal investment in brand-building is:

$$Q\,[(\partial P/\partial b)(\partial b/\partial z)] + P[(\partial Q/\partial b)(\partial b/\partial z)] = \partial TC/\partial z \qquad (5.2)$$

In a full-blown model − beyond the objectives of this Chapter − additional first-order conditions would exist, showing that the 'marginal profit' from the last dollar of brand-name investment equals the 'marginal profit' from the last dollar of investment in product feature enhancement. We assume that in competitive markets, all firms seek to maximize profits, hence invest optimally in brand-name building.

Following Sullivan (1998), we assume an inverse demand function for the utility maximizing consumer:

$$P = f\,\{Q,\, \mathbf{x},\, b\}, \qquad (5.3)$$

where the price of a product is determined by market quantity Q, the vector of features or attributes $\mathbf{x}$, and the brand-name parameter b.

Other things equal, better brand names will command higher prices. In general (adapting Sullivan's equation [4] ):

$$(P_1/x_{1,i})\,/\,(P_2/x_{2,i}) = b_1/b_2 \qquad (5.4)$$

where $b_j$ represents the brand-name parameter for product 'j' (j = 1, 2) and $x_{1,i}$ represents feature 'i' for product 1.

That is, ceteris paribus, better brands will command higher 'price per feature' values.

The question arises: how can $b_1/b_2$ be estimated empirically? Sullivan (1998) uses statistical regression methods, with 'Price' as the dependent variable and brand name as one of the independent variables. Here, we propose a different method, based on a well-known technique for measuring efficiency known as DEA. The basic idea is to estimate an 'efficiency frontier' for brand and non-brand products, using 'price' as the 'output' (to be maximized) and quantitatively measured 'features' (attributes) as the 'inputs', and identify 'efficient' and 'inefficient' products, as in Figure 5.1.

Data Envelopment Analysis (DEA) considers a set of agents known as decision-making units (DMU's; for example schools, bank branches, factories and so on) producing a set of outputs $\mathbf{Y} = \{Y_k\}$, k = 1, ..., r using a set of inputs $\mathbf{X} = \{X_i\}$, i = 1, ..., s; see Charnes et al. (1978); Banker (1984); Seiford and Thrall (1990). DEA floats a hyperplane on the set of inputs and outputs, and thereby separates all of the DMU's into efficient and inefficient ones (Leibenstein and Maital, 1992).

As mentioned in Seiford (1990), DEA may be viewed from two perspectives: 'envelopment' and 'multiplier'. In the envelopment form of DEA, for each DMU taken in turn the linear combination of all DMU's is defined so that

1.  minimal inputs be achieved with outputs no less than existing ones, or
2.  maximal outputs be obtained with inputs no more than actually used.

The first approach is called the input minimization DEA model, the second one, the output maximization.

Mathematically, the following problems are solved. Let r, s and n be number of outputs, inputs and DMUs respectively with $X_j = \{X_{ij}\}$, i = 1, ..., s and $Y_j = \{Y_{kj}\}$, k = 1, ..., r), j = 1, ..., n being vectors of inputs and outputs of $DMU_j$, respectively. Given some $DMU_0$, consider the following restricting inequalities defining its possible production possibilities:

$$\alpha_X \leq \sum \lambda_X; \ \beta_Y \geq \sum \lambda_Y; \ \lambda_j \geq 0; \ j = 1, ..., n; \qquad (5.5)$$

and find vector $\lambda = (\lambda_j)$ providing one of the following:

min $\alpha$ with $\beta = 1$ (input minimization problem) $\qquad (5.6)$

or

max $\beta$ with $\alpha = 1$ (output maximization problem) $\qquad (5.7)$

In both cases an additional restriction may be added:

$$\sum_j \lambda_j = 1, \qquad (5.8)$$

corresponding to variable returns to scale. If this restriction is omitted, constant returns to scale is assumed, see Banker (1984) for details. In this study, we will omit [8], and assume constant returns to scale. This statement of the DEA problem was termed by Seiford (1990) an 'envelopment DEA'.

Suppose we now treat each individual *product* as a 'DMU', characterized by one 'output' (its price), and 'inputs' (product features). By using DEA to compute the 'envelope' of 'efficient' products (those that secure the maximum price for a given level of product features), we can operationalize Hauser and Shugan's (1983) 'Defender' model and its efficiency frontier (in 'feature' space). We can identify efficient products, measure brand-name effect as an 'efficiency' scalar for non-brand products, and identify how non-brand-name products overcome brand names by strengthening certain features.

The maximization problem then becomes for a specific product labelled with subscript '0' to choose weights 'w' that maximize the 'feature efficiency' ratio:

$$P_o / \Sigma_i \, w_{io} \, x_{io} \qquad\qquad (5.9)$$

subject to the condition that for all the other 'n' products, this ratio does not exceed the value of one:

$$P_j / \Sigma_i \, w_{ij} \, x_{ij} \leq 1, \; \forall j, \; j = 1, \ldots, n$$

where the subscript 'j' represents the specific product.

Using Charnes, Cooper and Rhodes' clever transformation (1978, 1979, 1981), this non-linear programme can be translated into a linear programming one. Hence, for each DMU – in our case, specific product – the above linear programme is solved, and its brand efficiency estimated.

The essence of our model is this: non-brand-name products charge prices commensurate solely with value inherent in product features. Brand-name products charge prices higher than feature values imply. If brand-name products comprise the efficiency frontier, then the 'inefficiency' parameter – the per cent gap between the price of brand-name products and the price that would prevail in the absence of a strong brand name – measures the amount of value created by the brand, in contrast to the value created by product features.

In our model, the degree of 'efficiency' measures brand equity, because it represents value created by the printer that is not attributable to physical product features. These parameters, therefore, are directly translatable into brand equity, using the formula:

$$P/P^* = 0a/0b = e \qquad\qquad (5.10)$$

where P is the 'brand-less' price, P* is the actual price (including the brand-name effect), 0a/0b are as shown in Figure 5.1, and 'e' is the efficiency coefficient compared to the least efficient hyperplane as defined and measured by the DEA procedure noted above. Note that in

Figure 5.1 we did not specify the functional form of the efficiency frontier defining a and b. Now we specify that we mean the DEA envelope in the s-dimensional space.

Therefore the 'brand value' per product is

$$P * - P = (1-e) \, P* \tag{5.11}$$

The dollar value of brand equity – the fraction of sales accruing from the brand name, as opposed to product features – is therefore given by:

$$BE = Q \, P * \, (1-e) \tag{5.12}$$

where BE is 'operating brand equity', Q is current units sold (annual), and P* and (1–e) are as given above. We can measure Brand Equity BE as a capitalized sum, KBE, by computing the net present value of BE measured over the product's lifetime t years:

$$KBE = \Sigma_t \, (BE)/(1+R)^t \tag{5.13}$$

where R = risk-adjusted cost of capital.

Note that this concept of measuring brand effects does not assign a fixed value to an individual product, but derives the brand value from the actual competitive offer via the DEA envelope. If some non-branded products would disappear from the market, brand values of the remaining products are likely to change – this is exactly what we intended to model. Brand value is not independent from customers' preference scales with respect to an actual offer.

## 5.5   CASE STUDY OF PRINTERS

We chose to apply our method to a set of 36 printers, based on objective performance benchmarking data published in 1994 in PC Magazine (see Appendix). For each of the 36 printers (which range from inexpensive to very expensive), nine product features are measured. They are: colour (0 for no, 1 for yes); pages per minute; speed in printing text; speed in printing graphics; speed in printing Word for Windows documents; speed in printing Lotus 1-2-3 documents; speed in printing Corel Draw documents; standard RAM; and power consumption when printing (lower values indicate better performance). The DEA analysis is performed on the basis of technometric [0, 1] values as the original data (see Appendix 5.1) are quite heterogeneous.

*Table 5.2: Brand value of fully efficient printers (1994)*

| Name | Price | Brand value |
|---|---|---|
| Canon LBP 430 | 799 | 564 |
| HP L/J 4L | 849 | 599 |
| HP L/J HP | 1229 | 868 |
| Okidata OL400C | 699 | 493 |
| Okidata OL410C | 899 | 635 |
| Panasonic S/W KXP 4400 | 699 | 493 |
| Lexmark 4037 SE | 799 | 564 |
| TI Microwriter PS23 | 799 | 564 |
| TI Microwriter 600 | 999 | 705 |
| Xerox 4505 PS | 1629 | 1150 |
| Canon LBP 860 | 1839 | 1298 |
| Itoh ProWriter CI8Xtret | 2099 | 1482 |
| Itoh ProWriter CI-8XA | 2299 | 1623 |
| RMS Magicolor | 9999 | 7059 |
| Sharp JX9400H | 599 | 423 |
| TI Microlaser Pro 600 | 1599 | 1129 |
| Apple LaserWriter Select 360 | 1599 | 1129 |
| HP Color Laser Jet | 7295 | 5150 |
| QMS 1060 Print System | 2699 | 1905 |
| HP Laser Jet 4 Plus | 1829 | 1291 |
| HP Laser Jet 4M Plus | 2479 | 1750 |
| TI Microlaser Power Pro | 1899 | 1341 |
| Unisys AP 9312 Plus | 1895 | 1338 |
| Xerox 4900 Color Laser Printer | 8495 | 5997 |

Table 5.2 shows the 'brand-value' parameters for each printer, interpreted in dollar terms, that is, Equation (5.11). The efficiency measure is derived from the Iota measure of DEA programming.[4] It

represents a scalar input efficiency score, interpreted as the proximity of the data point to the facet of the piecewise linear envelopment surface and equal to the total weighted distance between observed and projected points, standardized by the inputs. In contrast to other possibilities of measuring inefficiency, Iota measures the total amounts of inefficiency, not just the proportional distance along a radius vector.

*Table 5.3: Brand value and efficiency coefficients of the remaining printers (1994)*

| Name | Price | Efficiency coefficient e | Brand value |
|------|-------|--------------------------|-------------|
| Brother HL 630 | 499 | 1.00 | 0 |
| DEC Laser 1800 | 779 | 0.43 | 440 |
| Epson A/L 1600 | 1199 | 0.34 | 792 |
| Sharp JX 9460 PS | 849 | 0.32 | 574 |
| Itoh ProWriter CI8Xtra | 1799 | 0.34 | 1195 |
| DEC Laser 5100 | 1599 | 0.37 | 1004 |
| Lexmark WinWriter 600 | 1199 | 0.31 | 831 |
| Mannesmann Tally T9008 | 1499 | 0.32 | 1020 |
| Sharp JX5460PS | 899 | 0.46 | 483 |
| Xerox 4510 PS | 2379 | 0.31 | 1632 |
| Lexmark 4039 12R Plus | 1749 | 0.33 | 1178 |
| Lexmark 4039 12L Plus | 2299 | 0.31 | 1588 |

At first glance at Table 5.2, many of the most powerful brand names being fully efficient can be found here. All models of Hewlett Packard are high-brand equity products. However, closer examination of Table 5.3 reveals that some well-known companies cannot effectively maximize brand value. They face a key strategic decision either to exploit the brand-name effect by charging premium prices or use the brand-name effect for some of their products to create value for customers by charging prices that reflect only objective 'feature value', hence increase sales and market share. Which of the two strategies is most effective may be determined only in the medium term if some brands are no longer major players in the printer business.

*Tools for Decisions*

It remains to clarify in a systematic way which features may explain the brand effect (if there are any). We have no variables for firms' strategy but only information on prices and features. This opens up the opportunity to explore whether the above key strategic decision between exploitation of brand-name effect and value for customers matters. In what follows it will not be possible to learn in detail about the general brand management strategy of the corporations producing printers. Our method simply identifies and measures a brand-name effect.

From the usual descriptive statistics it becomes clear that there are multi-collinearities between price and colour, as the colour printers are simply more expensive. Another multi-collinearity originates from the pages printed per minute and the speed in printing Word for Windows documents. After dropping these three features but keeping the price variable we find a very good mean variance of inflation factor of 3.1.

*Table 5.4: Results of a Heckman selection model for inefficiency (coefficients and t-values in brackets)*

| Variable | Selection | | Degree of inefficiency | |
|---|---|---|---|---|
| n (uncensored) | 36 | | (12) | |
| Price | – | | −0.0003 | (−4.56) *** |
| Graphics speed | – | | 0.67 | (1.62) |
| Corel Draw speed | – | | 0.45 | (2.58) * |
| Text speed | 5.16 | (2.24) * | – | |
| Lotus speed | 9.07 | (2.92) *** | – | |
| Standard RAM | – | | 0.87 | (5.16) *** |
| Power consumption | 19.29 | (3.13) *** | 1.07 | (2.80) *** |
| Constant | – | | −0.97 | (−2.13) * |
| | −21.61 | (−3.19) *** | | |
| Wald Chi² | 128.1*** | | | |

Notes
* Significant at the 5 per cent level.
** Significant at the 1 per cent level.
*** Significant at the 0.1 per cent level
    derived from heteroskedasticity-robust errors.

In a regression analysis we want to find out what makes printers inefficient, and secondly, what determines the degree of inefficiency (or brand effect). This situation resembles the classic example that explains the wages of women. Women choose whether to work and thus choose whether we observe their wages in a data set. If this decision is not made randomly the sample of observations is biased upward. A solution can be found if there are some variables that strongly affect the chances for observation (in the case of women the marital status or the number of children). In such a situation one may use a Heckman selection model (Heckman, 1976). We try to infer why some products are inefficient and which variables can explain the degree of inefficiency (that corresponds to little or no brand value). The results of a full maximum likelihood calculation are presented in Table 5.4 (heteroskedasticity-robust errors). We also tried a two-step Heckman model which did not yield better results

The above hypotheses are fully confirmed: the inefficient (no or little brand value) products offer distinct values to customers; they are highly significantly energy saving and quicker in printing (in general and in particular for printing Lotus documents). Not only the fact of being inefficient but also the degree of inefficiency is connected with energy-saving features, standard RAM and the speed of printing Corel Draw pictures. With little or no brand value, these products are offering too much customer value for low prices.

There is no doubt: in the consumer market for printers brand name is very important and the tradeoff between good features for little money (that is, good technology) and building up a brand name exists. As a complementary case study we now examine the same relations for an investment good, executive jet aircraft.


## 5.6   CASE STUDY OF EXECUTIVE JET AIRCRAFT

The market for executive airplanes has several appealing characteristics. First, the products are complexly multidimensional (Phillips et al., 1994). Customers in the marketplace, that is, corporations' procurement managers or CEOs, assess and compare performance on multiple attributes, such as range, speed, payload, maintenance costs, operation efficiency, and takeoff and landing requirements (Phillips et al., 1994). These are ideal settings for our study because the use of feature-based brand value is illustrated in a truly multi-attribute market environment.

Second, the market is extremely competitive. In a recent market analysis, Symonds and Greising (1995) estimated that the major aircraft producers are involved in fierce competition for a market that is estimated annually at 950 multinational corporations, billionaires, and heads of state. Competition is especially fierce between the two market leaders (Gulfstream and Bombardier). According to this report, the two firms have been spending an estimated \$1.1 billion on the development of new airplanes (Symonds and Greising, 1995). This high level of competition increases the likelihood that competitors will seek to differentiate their products on multiple attributes.

Third, competition in this market requires major outlays for research and development. Bombardier is spending \$800 million and Gulfstream \$300 million in their respective development projects (loc. cit.). The risks involved in these projects are immense. Failing to respond to true customer needs may result in significant losses. Therefore, information about the value of plane attributes should be very useful. Additionally, this market is entry-unstable. New entrants have been reported to displace first-movers through rapid technological improvements (Phillips et al., 1994). Thus, attribute-level information is critical even after the introduction of true innovations to the market.

Finally, as discussed earlier, attribute weights can and do vary by context (Wilkie and Pessemier, 1973). The business aircraft market provides close to ideal settings in this respect as well because such aircraft are used similarly by all customers. Executive airplanes, also termed business aircraft, can be divided into four groups: Jets, Turboprops, Pistons, and Rotorcraft (Forecast International, 1992). The world market is dominated by seven large manufacturers (Learjet, Canadair, Beech, Cessna, BAE, Gulfstream, and Dassault) with one smaller competitor (IAI). The data collection involved personal interviews with managers in a local manufacturing plant, pilots, and aeronautical engineers to identify a comprehensive list of jet attributes as they apply to business usage situations (Grupp, 1998; Wilkie and Pessemier, 1973). These discussions resulted in the deletion of a few attributes. Attributes were deleted either because they lack diagnosticity or because they may not be salient for all business jet users (Watson, 1993). Attributes such as engine options, seating arrangement, documentation, warranties, or spare parts availability are comparable across the brands and offer no diagnostic information to potential buyers. Attributes such as political considerations and product-line width were deleted because they may only be salient to users from some countries or large firms, respectively. The final list of attributes included 12 items: maximum fuel-load range, maximum useful load (the difference between non-fuelled jet and the maximum landing weight), cruise speed, mach number, rate of climb, takeoff and landing distance, cruising-speed fuel consumption, cabin volume, cargo volume, noise level, total cost per mile, and resale value.

Information on attribute scores was gathered from published sources, such as industry magazines and manufacturers' brochures. Price information for the various jets was based on a well-respected industry publishing firm (Jane's, 1993). These prices are for what Jane's terms flyaway or standard versions. Scores were benchmarked at the sub-category level into the [0, 1] range. Appendix 5.2 lists the models, attributes, attribute measures, and prices.

Earlier, it was argued that it may be useful to compare manufacturers' and users' attribute weights. Therefore, both groups were sampled. It should be noted that manufacturers may have responded to the questionnaire with a 'quality control' orientation whereas pilots may have been 'usage'-oriented. However, because of these differences, a comparison of both groups' weights may serve to identify production myopia of manufacturers. Four questionnaires were mailed to each of the manufacturers in the three sub-categories with instructions to distribute each copy to knowledgeable individuals in the firm. Additionally, each manufacturer was asked to provide a list of 20 customers for the user survey. Fifteen questionnaires from seven firms were returned. This represents a response rate of 34 per cent at the individual level and 67 per cent at the firm level. Table 5.5 lists average attribute weights for this group.

*Table 5.5: Attribute weights for jets*

|  | Manufacturers' weights | Pilots' weights |
|---|---|---|
| Range (nautical miles) | 7.786 | 8.338 |
| Payload ('000 lb) | 8.667 | 6.912 |
| Cruise speed (miles/hour) | 8.000 | 7.718 |
| Mach number | 6.667 | 6.422 |
| Climb rate | 7.500 | 6.056 |
| Takeoff distance | 7.929 | 7.549 |
| Fuel consumption (miles/gallons) | 8.286 | 8.493 |
| Cabin (feet) | 8.214 | 8.120 |
| Cargo | 7.357 | 7.408 |
| Noise (EPN dB) | 8.286 | 8.887 |
| Cost per mile | 7.500 | 7.930 |
| % Resale value | 8.000 | 7.422 |

None of the seven firms agreed to provide users' lists because such lists were trade secrets. Two groups of pilots were used to represent users since they are knowledgeable about the industry and approximate actual users' profiles. Forty pilots of a national airline and forty military pilots were asked to complete the questionnaire. Thirty-four of the former (85 per cent) and thirty-nine of the latter (98 per cent) returned completed questionnaires for an overall response rate of 91 per cent. The differences between the two groups were not statistically significant and they were combined. Table 5.5 lists their average attribute weights.

As is evident from Table 5.5, manufacturers' weights are fairly similar to users' weights. However, two weights stand out in that the differences between the two groups are large. Manufacturers assign much higher importance to payload (8.7) and climb rate (7.5) compared to pilots (6.9 and 6.1 respectively). Decisions to change performance on these two attributes should be made with caution. Improving performance on the two will do less to improve overall positioning than what manufacturers probably think. Reducing performance on the two will harm overall positioning by less.

The technometric attributes were processed by a DEA model with exactly the same specifications as for the printers. However, because we have only 18 products here, we have to be conservative and avoid using too many inputs. While DEA is relatively insensitive to model specification, it can be extremely sensitive to variable selection. This is inherent in the nature of any method that identifies envelopes of frontiers. Moreover, given enough inputs, all (or most) of the DMUs are rated efficient because there may always be one dimension where they perform best. This is a direct function of the dimension of the input–output space ($s + r = 12 + 1 = 13$ in our case) relative to n (18 in our case). In practical applications, care should therefore be taken to ensure that the condition $n \geq (s + r)$ is fulfilled (Grupp, 1998, p. 237). This is similar to preserving sufficient 'degrees of freedom' in statistical analysis.

In order to fulfil these conditions, three runs of the DEA calculation were performed, one with all attributes, one with the eight attributes ranked highest by the pilots (that is, without payload, Mach number, climb rate, cargo) and one with the eight top manufacturers' weights (that is, no Mach number, climb rate, cargo, cost per mile).[5]

*All three runs yield the same results: all jets are efficient.* Therefore no data table is given here. In fact 17 jets are fully efficient (at Iota = 1.000), one is close to being efficient (at Iota = 0.924 ... 0.935 depending on the run: it is Canadair 3A). Therefore, we cannot observe any brand effect. All jets have equal brands or no brand value. That means, in this 'rational' business market, brand effects do not matter. For mass-market consumer products, amenable to brand-building techniques of marketing, there are clear, identifiable brand-name effects on price. But for investment goods like jet aircraft exhaustively evaluated by procurement managers, technology-based features alone drive price.

## 5.7  CONCLUSION

Today's global economy can be defined in simple terms: 'In today's global economy, you can make anything, anywhere, at any time, and sell it to anyone. Sentiment plays no role.' (Thurow, 1997). With labour, capital and technology now widely available in all markets, product quality will tend to converge, as dominant designs emerge with increasing rapidity. The result is 'commoditization' – the tendency of even sophisticated products to become standard commodity-like products with product features identical across various brand names, with resulting downward pressure on prices (see Pine and Gilmour, 1999; Shapiro and Varian, 1998). This is evident, for instance, in the market for PCs, with $1,000 PCs now common and a $500 PC, with strong product features, available. Managers are rightly concerned about falling prices and the resulting shrinking profit margins (Berman, 1999). Perhaps the most effective strategy to fight 'commoditization' is that of creating a strong, widely recognized global brand name. This strategy has been successfully pursued by well-known firms. They have invested huge sums in building and supporting their brand name. They represent a handful of brand names that are recognized in virtually every country in the world. In contrast, companies with world-class products and technology that have neglected global brand-building investments have suffered enormous losses in recent years.

With growing investment in brand-name creation, managers and shareholders alike will rightly demand quantitative measures for determining the returns to investment in brand creation. We believe the approach suggested in this model can help companies both measure the presence, or lack of, a brand-name effect, and then portray visually the market position of their products relative to those of competitors, in terms of a brand-efficiency frontier. Unlike most efficiency models, the objective here, of course, is to attain the highest market price possible for given product features, by supplying consumer utility through the brand-name perception and not solely through costly product feature improvements. Ward et al. (1999) note on this issue: 'Most customers' evaluations of price and performance include multiple definitions and dimensions, and the tradeoffs individuals make in their buying decisions reflect different definitions of value and different needs. Through strong brands, high-tech companies can make it clear exactly which aspects of their offerings' price and performance benefit their customers.'

Our model suggests that brand-name equity is not a charlatan's marketing trick that extracts money from buyers without creating corresponding value. As Berthon et al. (1997) note, 'for buyers, brands reduce search costs, reduce perceived risk and provide sociopsychological rewards' (p. 21). In a sense, the DEA model proposed in this Chapter seeks to measure the value brands create, in parallel with conventional value-creating sources like technological features.

Our model could possibly find use not only in economic analysis, but also in new-product business plans, by supplying a tool that can measure the degree to which the new product's innovation and feature superiority – with zero brand name – can compete with inferior products that have the advantage of a strong, recognized brand name. It may also help indicate the magnitude of resources necessary to help an 'anonymous' non-branded new product, with superior product features, build brand recognition.

To conclude: brands help companies improve competitive positioning, battle against falling prices and shrinking profit margins. Some 38 per cent of large firms brand *all* their products and 46 per cent brand *most* of their products, while 43 per cent of companies have initiated a new corporate brand strategy since 1995 (Troy, 1998, p. 8). With new emphasis on building brand equity, growing importance attaches to developing new benchmarking methods for quantifying the return on investment in brand-building activities. In consumer markets, for many products a no-name product is nearly worthless (at least it is so for our printers being cheaper with the same utility). But, at the same time, our method has revealed that there is a class of products for which brand effects are zero. Managers seeking to create strong brands, through large investments, must know which products are amenable to creation of brand equity, and which products are inherently and solely feature-driven.

## APPENDIX 5.1

*Table 5A.1: Printers: features and prices (from PC Magazine, 1994)*

| | Name | Price | Colour | Page/ min. | Text speed | Graphics speed | Word for Win | Lotus 1-2-3 | Corel Draw | Standard RAM | When printing, power consumption (watts) |
|---|---|---|---|---|---|---|---|---|---|---|---|
| 1 | Canon LBP 430 | 799 | 0 | 4 | 3.4 | 1.2 | 3.1 | 1.1 | 1.0 | 1 | 138 |
| 2 | HP LJ 4L | 849 | 0 | 4 | 3.8 | 1.3 | 3.4 | 1.9 | 1.1 | 1 | 118 |
| 3 | HP LJ HP | 1,229 | 0 | 4 | 3.8 | 1.3 | 3.5 | 1.5 | 1.2 | 6 | 121 |
| 4 | Okidata OL400C | 699 | 0 | 4 | 4.1 | 1.6 | 3.8 | 2.2 | 1.2 | 0.512 | 127 |
| 5 | Okidata OL410C | 899 | 0 | 4 | 4.0 | 1.8 | 3.6 | 1.7 | 1.1 | 2 | 121 |
| 6 | Panasonic S/W KXP 4400 | 699 | 0 | 4 | 4.2 | 1.3 | 3.8 | 1.1 | 0.6 | 1 | 94 |
| 7 | Lexmark 4037 SE | 799 | 0 | 5 | 4.7 | 1.5 | 4.2 | 2.0 | 1.2 | 0.512 | 168 |
| 8 | TI Microwriter PS23 | 799 | 0 | 5 | 4.6 | 1.5 | 4.2 | 1.1 | 0.6 | 2 | 130 |
| 9 | TI Microwriter 600 | 999 | 0 | 5 | 4.6 | 1.1 | 3.0 | 1.3 | 1.1 | 2 | 134 |
| 10 | Xerox 4505 PS | 1,629 | 0 | 5 | 4.9 | 1.5 | 4.5 | 1.8 | 1.3 | 6 | 132 |
| 11 | Brother HL 630 | 499 | 0 | 6 | 6.0 | 2.6 | 5.1 | 3.3 | 1.3 | 5 | 132 |

Table 5A.1 continued

| | Name | Price | Colour | Page/min. | Text speed | Graphics speed | Word for Win | Lotus 1-2-3 | Corel Draw | Standard RAM | When printing, power consumption (watts) |
|---|---|---|---|---|---|---|---|---|---|---|---|
| 12 | DEC Laser 1800 | 779 | 0 | 6 | 6.2 | 2.3 | 5.5 | 2.4 | 1.5 | 1.0 | 137 |
| 13 | Epson A/L 1600 | 1,199 | 0 | 6 | 6.0 | 2.6 | 5.9 | 2.9 | 1.9 | 2.0 | 185 |
| 14 | Sharp JX 9460 PS | 849 | 0 | 6 | 6.0 | 2.5 | 6.3 | 2.6 | 0.7 | | 158 |
| 15 | Canon LBP 860 | 1,839 | 0 | 8 | 8.0 | 1.6 | 5.4 | 1.7 | 1.6 | 2.0 | 140 |
| 16 | Itoh ProWriter CI8Xtra | 1,799 | 0 | 8 | 7.1 | 2.0 | 5.3 | 1.8 | 1.4 | 4.0 | 161 |
| 17 | Itoh ProWriter CI8Xtret | 2,099 | 0 | 8 | 7.2 | 2.1 | 5.4 | 1.8 | 1.3 | 4.0 | 197 |
| 18 | Itoh ProWriter CI-8XA | 2,299 | 0 | 8 | 7.2 | 2.8 | 5.9 | 2.5 | 1.8 | 4.0 | 199 |
| 19 | DEC Laser 5100 | 1,599 | 0 | 8 | 8.1 | 2.0 | 6.6 | 2.6 | 1.6 | 6.0 | 183 |
| 20 | Lexmark WinWriter 600 | 1,199 | 0 | 8 | 9.0 | 2.3 | 5.6 | 2.1 | 1.0 | 2.0 | 158 |
| 21 | Mannesmann Tally T9008 | 1,499 | 0 | 8 | 7.9 | 2.3 | 7.1 | 2.6 | 1.6 | 2.0 | 182 |
| 22 | RMS Magicolor | 9,999 | 1 | 8 | 6.8 | 1.4 | 5.4 | 2.0 | 0.9 | 12.0 | 294 |
| 23 | Sharp JX9400H | 599 | 0 | 8 | 8.0 | 1.2 | 5.5 | 1.0 | 0.9 | 1.5 | 145 |
| 24 | Sharp JX5460PS | 899 | 0 | 8 | 8.2 | 2.5 | 7.3 | 2.0 | 1.3 | 2.0 | 167 |
| 25 | TI Microlaser Pro 600 | 1,599 | 0 | 8 | 3.6 | 3.1 | 3.1 | 2.3 | 1.6 | 6.0 | 123 |

*Table 5A.1 continued*

| | Name | Price | Colour | Page/ min. | Text speed | Graphics speed | Word for Win | Lotus 1-2-3 | Corel Draw | Standard RAM | When printing, power consumption (watts) |
|---|---|---|---|---|---|---|---|---|---|---|---|
| 26 | Apple LaserWriter Select 360 | 1,599 | 0 | 10 | 7.2 | 2.2 | 3.6 | 2.0 | 1.7 | 7 | 190 |
| 27 | HP Color Laser Jet | 7,295 | 1 | 10 | 8.6 | 0.8 | 6.8 | 2.3 | 1.3 | 8 | 440 |
| 28 | QMS 1060 Print System | 2,699 | 0 | 10 | 9.7 | 3.0 | 8.7 | 3.0 | 2.0 | 8 | 240 |
| 29 | Xerox 4510 PS | 2,379 | 0 | 10 | 9.7 | 2.7 | 8.7 | 3.4 | 1.7 | 6 | 208 |
| 30 | HP Laser Jet 4 Plus | 1,829 | 0 | 12 | 11.5 | 2.9 | 9.7 | 3.3 | 1.8 | 2 | 287 |
| 31 | HP Laser Jet 4M Plus | 2,479 | 0 | 12 | 11.3 | 2.7 | 10.0 | 3.2 | 1.9 | 6 | 273 |
| 32 | Lexmark 4039 12R Plus | 1,749 | 0 | 12 | 10.7 | 2.7 | 8.8 | 3.4 | 1.9 | 2 | 202 |
| 33 | Lexmark 4039 12L Plus | 2,299 | 0 | 12 | 10.7 | 2.7 | 9.0 | 4.0 | 1.7 | 4 | 200 |
| 34 | TI Microlaser Power Pro | 1,899 | 0 | 12 | 12.1 | 4.4 | 7.0 | 1.6 | 1.9 | 6 | 213 |
| 35 | Unisys AP 9312 Plus | 1,895 | 0 | 12 | 11.1 | 2.7 | 9.1 | 3.5 | 1.5 | 2 | 265 |
| 36 | Xerox 4900 Color Laser Printer | 8,495 | 1 | 12 | 8.2 | 1.8 | 5.7 | 1.6 | 0.9 | 12 | 130 |

# APPENDIX 5.2

Table 5A.2: *Business jets: features and prices (1993)*

| | Range | Pay-load | Cruise speed | Mach | Climb rate | Take-off dist-ance | Fuel con-sump-tion | Cabin | Cargo | Noise | Cost per mile | % Resale value | Price (mio.) |
|---|---|---|---|---|---|---|---|---|---|---|---|---|---|
| Citation 550 | 1507 | 2.45 | 335 | 0.710 | 3070 | 3450 | 0.470 | 263 | 77 | 71.6 | 4.60 | 62 | 3.47 |
| Learjet 31A | 1577 | 1.80 | 424 | 0.810 | 5100 | 3280 | 0.528 | 268 | 40 | 81.0 | 5.10 | 51 | 4.78 |
| Citation 560 | 1717 | 2.70 | 350 | 0.750 | 3684 | 3160 | 0.473 | 296 | 67 | 83.7 | 5.32 | 67 | 4.84 |
| Learjet 35A | 1924 | 2.98 | 424 | 0.810 | 4340 | 4972 | 0.428 | 268 | 40 | 83.7 | 5.31 | 52 | 4.92 |
| Learjet 36A | 2543 | 2.98 | 415 | 0.810 | 4340 | 4972 | 0.413 | 227 | 34 | 83.9 | 5.31 | 52 | 5.12 |
| Beechjet 400A | 1480 | 2.61 | 419 | 0.780 | 4020 | 4290 | 0.467 | 305 | 57 | 88.9 | 5.40 | 62 | 5.31 |
| Astra SP | 2727 | 2.77 | 412 | 0.855 | 3700 | 5250 | 0.422 | 365 | 53 | 82.3 | 7.20 | 69 | 7.54 |
| Citation VI | 1852 | 2.50 | 404 | 0.835 | 3699 | 5030 | 0.381 | 438 | 61 | 84.6 | 7.69 | 65 | 7.99 |
| Learjet 60 | 2440 | 2.19 | 420 | 0.810 | 4000 | 5560 | 0.404 | 453 | 64 | 83.0 | 7.68 | 53 | 8.30 |
| Citation VII | 1808 | 2.30 | 409 | 0.835 | 3921 | 4690 | 0.351 | 438 | 61 | 77.1 | 8.09 | 65 | 8.95 |
| Bae 800 | 2427 | 2.22 | 401 | 0.800 | 3500 | 5600 | 0.333 | 604 | 40 | 80.9 | 8.58 | 63 | 9.95 |
| Bae 100 | 3095 | 2.70 | 402 | 0.800 | 3577 | 6000 | 0.352 | 675 | 45 | 81.0 | 10.35 | 77 | 12.90 |
| Falcon 50 | 3071 | 3.64 | 410 | 0.860 | 3430 | 4700 | 0.278 | 845 | 115 | 84.3 | 12.73 | 75 | 14.75 |
| Canadair 601-3A | 3288 | 5.00 | 424 | 0.850 | 4443 | 5400 | 0.231 | 1415 | 115 | 79.4 | 12.90 | 76 | 16.95 |
| Canadair 601 RJ | 1973 | 12.20 | 424 | 0.850 | 3210 | 6125 | 0.172 | 2415 | 196 | 81.0 | 12.90 | 76 | 16.98 |

*Table 5A.2 continued*

| | Range | Pay-load | Cruise speed | Mach | Climb rate | Take-off dist-ance | Fuel con-sump-tion | Cabin | Cargo | Noise | Cost per mile | % Resale value | Price (US$ million) |
|---|---|---|---|---|---|---|---|---|---|---|---|---|---|
| Canadair 601 3AER | 3503 | 4.75 | 424 | 0.85 | 4259 | 5875 | 0.227 | 1415 | 115 | 79.8 | 12.90 | 76 | 17.39 |
| Falcon 900 | 3845 | 3.56 | 430 | 0.87 | 4000 | 4930 | 0.264 | 1862 | 127 | 79.8 | 17.58 | 78 | 22.50 |
| Gulfstream IV | 4141 | 3.66 | 459 | 0.88 | 4014 | 5280 | 0.169 | 2008 | 169 | 76.8 | 18.28 | 90 | 25.00 |

## NOTES

1   This Chapter is based on work which – in addition to the grant by GIF – was supported in part by a grant from the Technion V-P Fund for Research. We are grateful to Guy Levy and Irit Cohen, undergraduate students at Technion, for research assistance. We are indepted to Sharon Lifshitz for gathering data on executive aircraft. This Chapter was written while one of the authors, S. M., was Visiting Professor at MIT Sloan School of Management. It is an original contribution to this volume not published elsewhere.
2   Cited in Berman (1999, p. 15).
3   Note that in this case, the technometric scale is inversed as higher customer value results from lighter sensors.
4   We used two software tools (IDEAS 5.1 and Warwick DEA) which produced identical results with rounding differences in the third digit. More details on the Iota measure for innovation efficiency may be found in Grupp (1997a).
5   Again we used two different software tools; see endnote 3.

# PART II

# Linking Innovation and Performance

# 6 The Relation between Perceived Innovation and Profitability: An Empirical Study of Israel's largest Firms[1]

## Main Ideas in this Chapter

Innovation is understood as a chain-linked, non-sequential process in which research and development may be embarked upon at various stages. Therefore, there are various ways to measure innovation; there seems to be no single catch-all index. One approach is not to attempt to measure *actual* innovation but to assess the *perceived* innovativeness by trained business observers. This Chapter reports data on perceived innovativeness among the largest Israeli firms, measured by surveying a group of experienced managers. The posited links among innovativeness, sales revenue, the growth in sales revenue and profitability are examined statistically. It is found that perceived innovation is neither a cause nor an effect of growth in sales revenue, with some industries being notable exceptions. However, perceived innovation may be explained by the visibility of firms. Those firms whose shares are traded on American stock exchanges are more frequently perceived as innovative.

## 6.1 INTRODUCTION

'When you see a successful business,' Peter Drucker once wrote, 'then know that someone once made a courageous decision.' Nearly always, those decisions involve bold change and innovation. There are numerous examples.

- When Robert Haas became chief executive officer (ceo) of Levi Strauss & Co. in 1984, he found a company in crisis, with dropping sales, bloated work force and excess production capacity. He quickly moved Levi's out of the 18-to-25 age group (the 'baby bust' generation) and into the 25-and-over 'aging baby-boomers'. Between 1987 and 1990, Levi's added $1 billion in annual sales, and added $300 million in annual profit.
- In the same year Haas took over Levi's, Andy Grove met with Intel founder Gordon Moore. Together, they decided to dump Intel's DRAM (dynamic random access memory) chip business, and venture into newer products. Intel today is America's 38th largest firm, with $25 billion in sales, a staggering $7 billion in profits (second in the Fortune 500 only to Exxon and GE), and a market value of its stock equal to General Motors and Ford combined.
- John D. Rockefeller dominated the oil business in the 1860s and 1870s, by dictating to the railroads the prices they could charge for shipping his oil. But in the late 1870s, oil pipelines began replacing trains. Rockefeller saw far ahead and built his own pipeline. By 1911, his wealth – $900 million – was fully 3 per cent of the USA's entire gross domestic product.
- Sears, Roebuck head Robert Woods moved Sears out of the catalogue business into retail stores in the 1920s, moved it from the cities to the suburbs in the 1940s, then to the booming Far West from the lagging East in the 1950s. The result: Sears dominated the retail market for decades (Slywotzky, 1996; Shapiro et al., 1999).

A basic principle that has prevailed for generations (Schumpeter, 1934) is: successful innovation generates 'advances', that is, profits, market share increase and sales growth. MBA students all know that, on average, more than 25 per cent of corporate profits accrue from only 10 per cent of company products – the innovative 10 per cent. Cooper (1993; see also Cooper and Kleinschmidt, 1996) has demonstrated empirically the close link between innovation, growth and profitability.[2] Kim and Mauborgne (1997) observe that, in their five-year study of high-growth companies and low-growth ones, one key difference emerged: low-growth companies tried to stay ahead of their competition, while high-growth companies made their competition irrelevant by 'value innovation'.

How valid is the assumed link between innovation, on the one hand, and growth, market share and profitability, on the other, for an entire economy? This is not an easy issue to tackle empirically. The main difficulty lies in quantifying innovation. In principle, it is simple to measure sales revenue, sales growth, and profitability. But how can the degree of innovativeness prevailing in a company be measured?

In this Chapter, we chose to focus on Israel, a country famed for its high-tech industry and entrepreneurial energy. We decided to measure innovation subjectively, as 'perceived innovativeness', by surveying experienced managers. Before describing the data (in Section 6.3), we begin with some conceptual considerations (in Section 6.2). The results are dicussed in Section 6.4 before we conclude (Section 6.5).

## 6.2   THEORETICAL FRAMEWORK

A review of the literature[3] on the innovation process reveals the following basic characteristics (Grupp, 1998):

- the innovation stages are characterized by feedback;
- research and development (R&D) is not a unified whole but is divisible into various, specifically identifiable processes;
- the interplay between R&D and innovation processes should be regarded as functional;
- the time dimension is the key to understanding innovation; various stages (also named paradigms, cycles, phases) of innovation are an important aspect of the literature.

The functional reference scheme in Figure 6.1 meets the stated requirements and thus embodies the approaches and concepts known from the literature. The scheme can be characterized as a heuristic working model whose purpose is to structure the measurement issue. Depicted on the vertical axis are four idealized innovative stages, the premise being that the interfaces between them are not always clear cut. Under no circumstances can they always be expected to follow one another sequentially (Freeman and Soete, 1997). Arranged at right angles to it are various types of R&D processes. Their basic role is to expand the knowledge stocks which are likewise an important source for innovation. Between them and the innovation stages numerous individually intangible functions may exist that couple the random fluctuations in the knowledge base in a 'chain-linked' (Kline and Rosenberg, 1986) way to innovation.

The function of R&D may be to provide new knowledge-based technology or the production of technically operational designs. It is true that not every technical design leads to a commercially viable innovation. Often a particular project 'terminates' once certain prototypes have been constructed. While much technical design never reaches the commercial marketing stage, other designs lead to industrial product design and innovation.

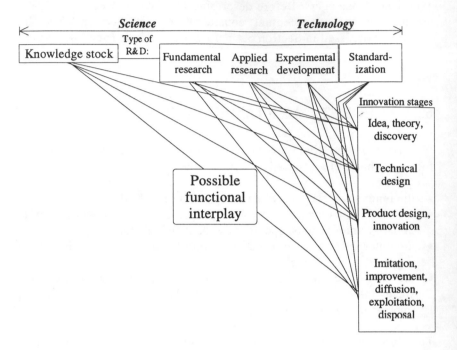

*Figure 6.1: Reference scheme for chain-linked innovative functions*

Conceptual establishment of exploitation and disposal of new products as an innovation stage requiring R&D support as in Figure 6.1 may appear unacceptable in the microeconomics and management literature of the past. So, some explanation of this stage is necessary. To economists, R&D processes only come under scrutiny if and insofar as their results are actually marketed, that is, become innovations. The economic importance of innovations is clearly greater, the more pervasive they become, which is essentially a matter of dissemination. From the macroeconomic standpoint, at any rate, the *diffusion* of innovations is thus more important than the initial innovation *process*. With all the significance supply factors have in the emergence of innovations, ultimately utilization alone, that is, utility, determines the scope for diffusion. In addition, escalating environmental problems will orient innovation processes towards the utilization and disposal areas.

Despite all the differences discussed in the innovation-oriented stages and types of R&D shown in Figure 6.1, they have much in common. All stages of knowledge-based, technological innovation are brought about by scientifically or technically trained people, and as such are inextricably linked to the supply of knowledge and hence to the education and training system. On the other hand, potentially all types of R&D are required to generate innovations whether these relate to fundamental research, applied research or experimental development. In the functional reference scheme, R&D is regarded as a kind of problem-solving in which innovation processes can become involved at any time. A company has an internal knowledge base which it scans for solutions to problems that inevitably materialize during the gestation of innovations. Some innovations can be organized from the stocks of knowledge and need no R&D input. The science and technology system tackles long-term problems which cannot be solved via the company's internal knowledge base and actually helps to broaden this knowledge base. Transactional processes are taking place between the company's internal R&D area and public institutes which are not always easily arranged.

From the structure of the theoretical reference diagram (see Figure 6.1) it becomes clear how important it is to differentiate between R&D activities and innovation stages. Input indicators are subsets of innovation indicators accounting for resources. Some resources will be wasted. It is therefore important to comprehend output-oriented indices relating to R&D processes as a specific subset and to call them 'R&D results' indicators. What is known in the literature as 'byput' or 'throughput' (Freeman and Soete, 1997) – because these measure 'attendant' or 'partial' effects of technical progress – is thus regarded as the *result* of R&D activities and not always as a prerequisite for innovation. It is also not always sufficient for this purpose. The output-oriented measurement processes, which seek to cover economically relevant innovation effects, are the 'economic' indicators and should be called 'progress' indicators. Progress indicators derive from quantity or value-related or even quality modifying effects on production, but not from achievements in R&D alone.

'Resource indicators' should be regarded as a generic term embracing every possible means for measuring personnel, monetary, investive and other expenditure on research, development and innovation. These include for instance R&D outlays, R&D personnel statistics, investment statistics, the royalties paid and many more besides. Among the R&D results indicators should be all results from research, development and standardization in the direct sense, that is, irrespective of whether or not they are important for the success of innovation, market launch, and so on. The most important result indicators come from publication, patent or standards statistics and their citations. Progress indicators relate not to detailed R&D activities but to the characteristics and micro- or macroeconomic effects of innovation. Progress indicators commonly encountered in the literature as those relating to the innovation counts recorded in corporate questionnaires, measurement of high technology markets or calculation of total factor productivities and other macro- and foreign trade indicators. A relatively new concept consists in analysing statistics on product performance and its improvement.[4]

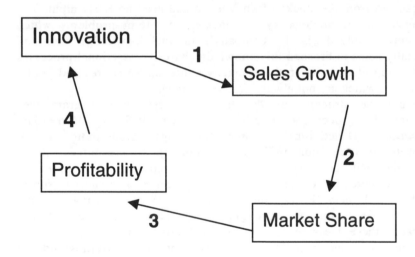

*Figure 6.2: Innovation, sales revenue, growth and profitability*

Figure 6.2 shows schematically the posited links among innovation, sales revenue growth, market share and profitability. It is widely believed, and taught, that successful innovation leads to rising sales revenue (1) and higher market share (2). Market share, in turn, is a key variable in the rate of return on investment, or in profit margins (3). Higher profitability drives or simply finances even more innovation inputs and so on (4). The link between market share and profitability is often mediated by the learning curve, which shows how average variable costs decline rapidly with higher cumulative output.

This model can easily be made more complicated, and more realistic. Innovation can generate large sales revenues, in absolute terms, which in turn affect profitability through economies of scale and monopoly effects. However, there may be negative, as well as positive, feedback loop effects. As they become larger, companies may become less innovative and less entrepreneurial. Higher profitability may encourage complacency. The positive feedback loop described in Figure 6.2 can change its direction in a remarkably short period of time – witness IBM's U-turn in profits between 1990 (record year) and 1992 (record losses). Now, in 1999, IBM again is running near-record profits.

The dynamics of Figure 6.2 could be explored through system dynamics However, we chose to examine the innovation-growth-profitability linkages empirically by quantifying each of the variables in the four boxes and examining the links among them by statistical regression. The difficult part, of course, was measuring innovation.

There have been numerous attempts to measure a company's degree of innovation. A product-based measure of innovation, known as 'technometrics' (Grupp, 1994) would be desirable. But data on product specifications are available only for rare case studies.[5] In most industrialized countries, R&D input statistics and questionnaire-based innovation output statistics for businesses are available – not so in Israel. Patent statistics as a somewhat 'hard' and established indicator would be a good choice for Israeli companies, but would cover manufacturing companies only, not banks and other service firms as in our sample.

In this study we chose to measure innovation subjectively, by surveying experienced managers and asking them to grade each of the largest firms on an innovativeness scale. The advantage of this approach is that it permits a very broad definition of innovation, which includes not only process and product innovation (traditionally the focus of empirical studies of innovation and innovation metrics) but also innovativeness in marketing, distribution, human resources management and globalization. 'Perceived' innovativeness, as we term the indicator, need not to be related significantly to actual innovation performance. The precision of this relation cannot be checked for the time being, given the poor innovation database on Israeli firms.

## 6.3  DATA

We asked participants in Technion's[6] MBA programme – mainly
engineers, aged 30–40, working in leading high-tech firms in the
greater Haifa area – to grade each of Israel's 73 largest firms,
according to their 'degree of innovativeness', where innovativeness
was explained to apply in a general sense to the firm's new products,
services and processes; improvement of existing products; marketing,
advertising and overall business strategy. Innovativeness was rated as
'high' (=3), 'moderate' (=2) or 'low' (=1). *Respondents were asked not
to grade firms with which they were not sufficiently familiar to provide
an informed estimate.* The result was a measure of 'perceived
innovativeness', according to the 47 respondents (about a 60 per cent
response rate), for 50 publicly owned industrial firms, eight non-traded
firms, five holding companies, five banks, and five real estate firms
and contractors – a total of 73 firms in all.

Data on 1997 Sales Revenues, annual per cent change in sales during
1997, Profit as per cent of Sales in 1997, and Assets were obtained, for
those 73 companies, from The Jerusalem Report's first annual ranking
of Israeli companies, compiled together with Solid Financial Markets
of Tel Aviv and New York (Sher, 1998). For 23 of the firms (mainly,
the non-industrial ones) only limited data were available. (See
Appendix 6.1 for the data.)

In addition we tried to add some 'hard' evidence; we checked which
Israeli top companies are listed on U.S. Stock Exchanges and for those
companies, gathered data on the companies' stock price (in US dollars)
for January 7th, 1999, together with the lowest and highest stock price
in 1998.

Because of the subjectivity of the 'perceived' innovation measure,
advertising strategy, visibility and information policy may influence
the innovation measure. In order to check this, we constructed two
dummy variables: No stock listed (on US exchanges) and No profit
data (in Israel) for those firms either *not listed* on US stock exchanges
or which *do not publish* their profits, respectively. Because of the close
links of Israeli firms with the USA (for historical and geopolitical
reasons), the US stock listings are a good indicator of visibility.
Generally, Israeli firms able to do so list their stocks in the USA as a
way to generate liquidity and raise new funds.

Further dummy variables are introduced to control for the various
industries: chemical firms (11 enterprises), electrical and electronics
firms (15), other manufacturing firms (17) and service firms (20). The

remaining 10 firms are pure trade houses (export–import firms) or holdings.

It must be stressed here that the firm sample is not a random sample nor representative of Israeli business firms. It is the top part of Israeli businesses as measured by size, and hence represents the majority of Israel's business activity.

## 6.4   RESULTS

We first proposed to check whether the perceived innovativeness of Israeli enterprises simply reflects what business analysts read in the newspaper: stock ratings. To test for this, we regressed the innovation index on the stock prices (in US dollars) as of January 7th, 1999, and on the 1998 minimum and the 1998 maximum prices. All three regressions are positive, but, judging from heteroskedasticity-robust errors, largely insignificant (error probability being between 22 per cent and 46 per cent). We can, thus, test for more complex explanations of perceived innovation.

Table 6.1 summarizes the results of the weighted statistical regressions using the inverse standard deviation of the innovation index as analytic weights.[7] Our main finding: while innovation may be the main driver of business success for a part of Israeli industry – technology-based firms – for the mainstream part of Israeli industry, *there is no clear link between innovation, as a cause, and economic success, as a result – nor between economic success as a cause and innovation as a result.* Here are the detailed results.

* Innovation: there is no statistical link between the degree of perceived innovativeness and the change in sales revenues (1997 versus 1996) (see Table 6.1, columns 2 and 3). Agan Industries, a chemicals firm, with $370 million in annual sales, showed 46 per cent growth in 1997, but was rated far below average in innovativeness – 62nd out of 73 firms. Scitex, in contrast, a high-tech firm that makes pre-print products, rated 7th highest in innovativeness, but its 1997 sales actually declined. Nor is there any link between innovativeness and firm size, as measured by sales revenues. The scatter appears virtually random. Among the ten largest firms in sales revenues, five scored well above average in innovativeness (Bezeq, Teva, Tadiran, ECI and Scitex), and five

scored well below average (Israel Chemicals, Blue Square, Supersol, Makhteshim, Delek).[8] This is true for those 50 out of 73 firms that publish data on sales changes. For the full sample (Table 6.1, column 3), findings are not any different.

- Significant explanations of perceived innovativeness originate from the branch structure (Table 6.1, columns 2, 3 and 4). Electrical and electronic industry is rated highly innovative, followed by chemical industry (including plastics and pharmaceuticals). Other manufacturing industry is naturally quite heterogeneous (food, drink, tobacco, metals, construction products, textiles, paper and so on) and includes some innovative firms. Service companies are definitely not innovative. The 'hierarchy' in branch innovativeness is also visible from Figure 6.3. Most electronic firms are positioned in the upper part of Figure 6.3; the chemical ones are somewhat lower, but in general are recognizable above services.

- Otherwise, Figure 6.3 represents the relation between profits and perceived innovativeness. One notes that, overall, the relation is positively significant (Table 6.1, column 1) in the multiple regression without branch structure. If we control by branches (Table 6.1, column 2), however, the profits variable loses significance as the branch disparities explain the different levels of innovativeness.

- An interesting feature is the differentiation between firms that are listed on the US stock exchanges and those that are less visible in the large US market. The listed firms are more frequently perceived as innovative than the less visible ones; this effect is highly significant, statistically. This does not mean that our respondents derive their assessment from the stock price (the respective tests are negative; see above) but it points to the central role of the information policy of firms. Firms that are visible all over the world, and disseminate easily accessible and repeated information on their business development including new products are assumed to be more aggressive and more innovative. This was recently found for a large sample of German firms (Schalk and Taeger, 1998, p. 247). If we take the stock listings as one important proxy of information available to everybody, it comes as no surprise that non-listed firms are perceived as less innovative whatever their actual innovation performance may be.

*Table 6.1:  Statistical regression results: weighted heteroskedasticity-robust ordinary least squares (t-values in brackets)*

| Dependent | (1) Inno-vativeness | (2) Inno-vativeness | (3) Inno-vativeness | (4) % change, sales | (5) Profit % |
|---|---|---|---|---|---|
| Constant | 1.484*** (14.63) | 1.757*** (9.30) | 1.930*** (10.36) | 14.649 (0.70) | 4.518 (0.86) |
| Innovative-ness | – | – | – | –1.214 (–0.12) | 1.627 (0.59) |
| Sales Revenues | 0.0002 (0.70) | 0.0001 (0.71) | –0.00004 (–0.63) | – | – |
| % change in sales | –0.001 (–0.23) | –0.002 (–0.42) | – | – | – |
| Profit % | 0.033** (2.15) | 0.009 (0.93) | – | – | – |
| Assets | 0.0001 (0.85) | –0.00001 (–1.08) | 0.000004 (1.10) | 0.00003 (1.29) | –0.0021** (–2.46) |
| Industries | | | | | |
| Electrical | – | 0.593*** (3.56) | 0.921*** (7.20) | –0.707 (–0.06) | 0.177 (0.04) |
| Chemical | – | 0.313** (2.11) | 0.335 (2.03) | 17.805* (1.74) | 4.411 (1.07) |
| Services | – | 0.008 (0.06) | 1.647 (1.65) | –0.159 (–0.02) | –0.553 (–0.15) |
| Other mfg. | – | 0.243* (1.75)* | 0.180 (1.43) | –0.974 (–0.12) | –1.624 (–0.42) |
| No stocks | – | –0.473*** (–3.00) | –0.309* (–1.822) | –12.287 (–1.51) | –3.254 (–1.58) |
| No profit data | – | – | 0.323** (2.63) | – | – |
| N | 50 | 50 | 73 | 55 | 50 |
| $R^2$ (adj.) | 0.19 | 0.73 | 0.64 | 0.24 | 0.29 |

*Notes*
\*    Weakly significant at the 10 per cent level.
\*\*    Significant at the 5 per cent level.
\*\*\*    Highly significant at the 1 per cent level.

- Profitability and growth: There seems to be a somewhat stronger link between innovativeness and the rate of profit on sales for 1997 for top firms (Table 6.2). Six of the eight most profitable firms score above average or well above average in innovativeness. ECI, the second most innovative firm, has the highest profit rate, at

19.5 per cent, with Orbotech (sixth highest in innovativeness) close behind at 18.1 per cent, and Teva, fourth in innovativeness, with a 9.1 per cent profit rate. However, Israeli Petrochemicals, Feuchtwanger, and Elco Industries all scored below average in innovativeness but had high profit rates. For the whole sample, there is no significant relation (Table 6.1, column 5). The only significant relation is the negative influence of large assets on profits. Growth of sales can neither be explained by innovation in the actual year (Table 6.1, column 4).

- Innovation and high-tech: expectedly, nine of the ten most innovative firms came from technology-driven areas: Intel, ECI, Motorola, Teva, El, Orbotech, Scitex, Elbit Systems, and Elscint. Intel leads the list of all 73 companies in innovativeness, with a remarkable score of 2.94, implying that nearly every respondent gave Intel a score of 3.0. Close behind is Motorola. The only non-high-tech firm to make it into the Top Innovative Ten was the First International Bank (see Table 6.2). The 'electronics' industry dummy as a statistically significant variable in predicting innovativeness catches this effect of the top electronic firms listed in Table 6.2.

*Table 6.2: Ten most innovative firms: Israel 1997–8*

| Company | 1998 innovation index | % rate of profit | % change in sales | Std. dev. of inno-vation | 1997 sales $ m. | Assets $ m. |
|---|---|---|---|---|---|---|
| Intel | 2.94 | – | – | 0.24 | 363 | 363 |
| ECI | 2.87 | 19.5 | 15.1 | 0.34 | 677 | 869 |
| Motorola | 2.77 | – | – | 0.50 | 946 | 946 |
| Teva | 2.64 | 9.1 | 17.1 | 0.53 | 1116 | 1188 |
| Elbit Medical | 2.64 | 1.0 | –6.1 | 0.53 | 493 | 540 |
| Orbotech | 2.57 | 18.1 | 28.7 | 0.60 | 191 | 190 |
| Scitex | 2.51 | 0.1 | –2.8 | 0.54 | 675 | 669 |
| Elbit Systems | 2.46 | 6.0 | 21.1 | 0.55 | 372 | 321 |
| First Int. Bank | 2.33 | 9.0 | 13.5 | 0.73 | 143 | 11178 |
| Elscint | 2.31 | 0.2 | –2.7 | 0.56 | 303 | 357 |

- Innovation in service firms: remarkably, all but one bank – Israel Discount – scored above average in the respondents' perception of innovativeness, although the service industry dummy points to the low or no innovation situation of this sector of the economy. The reason is that the other service firms are less innovative. Israel Electric rates below average in innovativeness – perhaps not surprising, considering that this company is a government-sanctioned monopoly. Among the Real Estate and Contractor firms only Dankner scores average in innovativeness; the remaining five firms were perceived to be at below-average innovativeness. A surprising position, ranked by innovativeness, is taken by Tnuva, once a hide-bound dinosaur that has been completely revitalized by new management. Three of the five holding companies ('other') in the sample scored below average in innovativeness: Elco, Clal and the Israel Corp. Only Koor and IDB scored slightly above average.

- Another interesting observation relates to the fact that 23 firms do not disclose their profitability data on the Tel Aviv Stock Exchange, although sales, assets, and, for five of these, sales changes are published. From this we created a 'no profit data' variable. The companies not disclosing profits are significantly perceived as more innovative than the others. How can we explain this? We are well aware that these data may be subject to the vagaries of accounting procedures (van Reenen, 1996, p. 205). On the other hand, a favourable profit–turnover ratio (or net operating margin) is always an indication of competitiveness (Hanusch and Hierl, 1992). So why not publish it? We offer two explanations: first, for the accounting systems, R&D and innovation expenditures are costs and thus directly diminish the operating result. Secondly, R&D projects are risky and some are not successful. If we assume that profits are negative or low for some highly innovative and risky high-tech firms they may decide to hide this information. Also Israeli subsidiaries of very innovative international trusts may prefer not to publish local profits in Israel which may be fed strategically into the consolidated balance sheet. The indications that for some companies a negative relation between innovation and profits may be the case may be disappointing, but we are concerned here with short-term profits – our findings contribute nothing to medium-term growth and they relate to individual firms not disclosing their profits, not to welfare effects of industry branches, spillover or the whole economy springing out of innovation. For most of the firms we confirmed a positive relation of perceived innovativeness and short-term profits (Figure 6.3).

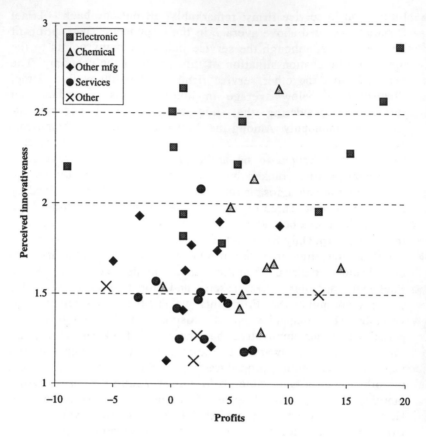

*Figure 6.3: Relation between profits and perceived innovativeness by Israeli industries*

## 6.5   CONCLUSION

While the innovative, globally competitive high-tech companies attract headlines, a large part of Israel's business sector remains strategically conservative. This will likely continue, as long as profits, sales and sales growth are not associated by senior managers with change and innovation, and as long as large parts of Israeli industry enjoy a monopoly or semi-monopoly position. This is reflected in the World

Competitiveness Index of the Swiss business school IMD, which ranks Israel only 25th (out of 47 countries), despite Israel's strong high-tech sector.

From the methodology perspective, on our agenda is research to validate and cross-check subjective measures of perceived innovation with some 'harder', that is, well-established indices. For reasons given above, this is not possible at the moment for Israeli firms. We do hope that Israel will ultimately establish a better statistical base for innovation studies, like that of the OECD countries. To study the dynamic, real growth effects, it would also be required to study time series instead of cross-section data, which are, a fortiori, not yet available.

We anticipate that when this study is done again 10 years from now, the results will show significantly tighter links between business performance and innovation. As Israeli capital, goods and labour markets become more closely integrated with world markets, and as the flow of goods, services, labour, capital and technology to and from Israel increases, the established connection between innovation and performance shown to be true in truly competitive markets abroad will become true in Israel as well. This connection clearly exists for the electronics industry. As Israel globalizes and other sectors become open to global competition (for instance, the banking sector), we should find that the feedback loop shown in Figure 6.2 will become operative and powerful.

The principle that innovation is vital for building profits and growth, taught in Israeli business schools, is only slightly ahead of its time.

## APPENDIX 6A.1

*Table 6A.1:  Data table*

| Company | Innovation index | Std. dev. of innovation | 1997 sales $ m. | % change in sales '97 vs. '96 | Profit as % of sales | Assets $ m. | Branch * |
|---|---|---|---|---|---|---|---|
| Intel | 2.94 | 0.24 | 363 | – | – | 363 | E |
| ECI | 2.87 | 0.34 | 677 | 15.1 | 19.5 | 869 | E |
| Motorola | 2.77 | 0.50 | 946 | – | – | 946 | E |
| Teva | 2.64 | 0.53 | 1116 | 17.1 | 9.1 | 1188 | C |
| Elbit Medical | 2.64 | 0.53 | 493 | –6.1 | 1.0 | 540 | E |
| Orbotech | 2.57 | 0.60 | 191 | 28.7 | 18.1 | 190 | E |
| Scitex | 2.51 | 0.54 | 675 | –2.8 | 0.1 | 669 | E |
| Elbit Systems | 2.46 | 0.55 | 372 | 21.1 | 6.0 | 321 | E |
| First Int. Bank | 2.33 | 0.73 | 143 | 13.5 | – | 11178 | S |
| Elscint | 2.31 | 0.56 | 303 | –2.7 | 0.2 | 357 | E |
| Tower Semic. | 2.28 | 0.60 | 126 | 28.6 | 15.3 | 218 | E |
| Tadiran | 2.22 | 0.59 | 1112 | –0.4 | 5.6 | 930 | E |
| Tnuva | 2.21 | 0.65 | 895 | – | – | 895 | S |
| Bezeq | 2.20 | 0.65 | 2467 | –1.6 | –9.0 | 4837 | E |
| Agis Indust. | 2.14 | 0.69 | 236 | 14.2 | 7.0 | 283 | C |
| Home Centre | 2.08 | 0.82 | 129 | 56.6 | 2.5 | 65 | S |
| Israel Aircraft | 2.04 | 0.77 | 1467 | – | – | 1466 | M |
| Tambour | 1.98 | 0.73 | 179 | -0.6 | 5.0 | 186 | C |
| Bank Leumi | 1.97 | 0.64 | 703 | 10.0 | – | 41029 | S |
| Formula Systems | 1.96 | 0.69 | 153 | 41.8 | 12.6 | 192 | E |
| Koor Indust. | 1.95 | 0.79 | 3565 | – | – | 3565 | O |

| | | | | | | |
|---|---|---|---|---|---|---|
| Tadiran Appl. | 1.94 | 0.65 | 151 | −15.4 | 1.0 | 96 | E |
| IDB Holding | 1.94 | 0.77 | 684 | − | − | 684 | S |
| Elite | 1.93 | 0.62 | 537 | −12.4 | −2.7 | 342 | M |
| Israel Military Ind. | 1.93 | 0.77 | 509 | − | − | 509 | M |
| Osem | 1.90 | 0.71 | 446 | 12.1 | 4.1 | 364 | M |
| Elco Indust. | 1.88 | 0.55 | 119 | −15.4 | 9.2 | 95 | M |
| Bank Ha-Poalim | 1.87 | 0.73 | 843 | 18.6 | − | 45312 | S |
| Bank Mizrahi | 1.84 | 0.85 | 180 | 5.2 | − | 12132 | S |
| Electra | 1.82 | 0.67 | 297 | −14.9 | 1.0 | 210 | E |
| Electra (Israel) | 1.78 | 0.71 | 240 | 10.4 | 4.3 | 160 | E |
| Tzaman-cal | 1.77 | 0.83 | 133 | 8.0 | 1.7 | 57 | M |
| Dankner | 1.77 | 0.69 | 152 | − | − | 152 | O |
| Elco Holdings | 1.75 | 0.58 | 861 | − | − | 861 | O |
| Delta-Galil | 1.74 | 0.78 | 319 | 8.0 | 3.9 | 205 | M |
| Israel Electric | 1.73 | 0.63 | 2167 | − | − | 2167 | S |
| Israel Discount Bank | 1.71 | 0.53 | 306 | 5.7 | − | 23662 | S |
| Kitan | 1.68 | 0.61 | 204 | −5.8 | −5.0 | 192 | M |
| Dead Sea Works | 1.67 | 0.75 | 453 | 26.7 | 8.7 | 984 | C |
| Malibu | 1.67 | 0.77 | 199 | − | − | 199 | M |
| Dead Sea Bromine | 1.65 | 0.78 | 493 | 7.2 | 8.1 | 604 | C |
| Israel Petro-chemical | 1.65 | 0.69 | 150 | 13.3 | 14.5 | 249 | C |
| Azorim | 1.65 | 0.81 | 323 | − | − | 323 | M |

*Table 6A.1 continued*

| Com-pany | Innova-tion index | Std. dev. of innova-tion | 1997 sales $ m. | % change in sales '97 vs. '96 | Profit as % of sales | Assets $ m. | Branch * |
|---|---|---|---|---|---|---|---|
| Clal (Israel) | 1.64 | 0.66 | 1238 | – | – | 1238 | O |
| Polgat | 1.63 | 0.62 | 181 | 0.1 | 1.2 | 144 | M |
| Maa-ariv | 1.58 | 0.65 | 125 | 4.1 | 6.3 | 161 | S |
| Dan Hotels | 1.57 | 0.73 | 131 | –.9 | –1.3 | 279 | S |
| Clal Trading | 1.54 | 0.51 | 289 | –20.0 | –5.6 | 267 | O |
| Electro-chemical Ind. | 1.54 | 0.52 | 132 | 17.8 | –0.7 | 162 | C |
| Solel Boneh | 1.52 | 0.70 | 568 | – | – | 568 | M |
| Supersol | 1.51 | 0.60 | 1269 | 21.7 | 2.5 | 784 | S |
| Israel Chemi-cals | 1.50 | 0.64 | 1685 | 3.0 | 6.0 | 3126 | C |
| Feucht-wanger | 1.50 | 0.71 | 137 | 7.4 | 12.6 | 103 | O |
| Shekem | 1.48 | 0.63 | 224 | –34.6 | –2.8 | 185 | S |
| Jaf-Ora | 1.48 | 0.65 | 127 | –1.3 | 4.3 | 86 | M |
| Blue Square | 1.47 | 0.50 | 1392 | 12.0 | 2.3 | 752 | S |
| Knafaim-Arkia | 1.45 | 0.55 | 189 | 6.1 | 4.8 | 281 | S |
| Makhte-shim | 1.42 | 0.50 | 740 | 35.3 | 5.8 | 943 | C |
| Israel Light-erage | 1.42 | 0.66 | 156 | –10.7 | 0.5 | 173 | S |
| Tempo | 1.41 | 0.59 | 157 | 10.1 | 1.0 | 120 | M |
| Tashloz | 1.36 | 0.50 | 164 | – | – | 164 | O |
| Israel Corp. | 1.33 | 0.49 | 971 | – | – | 971 | O |
| Agan | 1.29 | 0.47 | 370 | 46.0 | 7.6 | 422 | C |

| | | | | | | | |
|---|---|---|---|---|---|---|---|
| Dorban Inv. | 1.27 | 0.47 | 209 | 17.0 | 2.2 | 187 | O |
| Granite HaCar-mel | 1.25 | 0.55 | 520 | –3.4 | 2.8 | 499 | S |
| Israel Cold Storage | 1.25 | 0.45 | 155 | –10.8 | 0.7 | 174 | S |
| Amer-Israel Paper | 1.21 | 0.41 | 347 | 2.4 | 3.4 | 242 | M |
| Delek Auto | 1.19 | 0.40 | 372 | –3.4 | 6.9 | 98 | S |
| Oil Refine-ries | 1.19 | 0.51 | 2063 | – | – | 2063 | C |
| Delek | 1.18 | 0.38 | 652 | –4.9 | 6.2 | 653 | S |
| Nesher | 1.14 | 0.36 | 535 | – | – | 535 | M |
| Israel land Deve. | 1.13 | 0.35 | 228 | 0.0 | 1.9 | 761 | O |
| Israel Steel | 1.13 | 0.45 | 137 | –4.1 | –0.4 | 139 | M |

*Notes:* Branches: E = electrical and electronic, C = chemical, M = other mfg., S = service,
O = other.

# NOTES

1   This Chapter was first published in *Technovation* 20, 2000. The research outlined in this Chapter was supported in part by a grant from the Technion Vice-President's (Research) Fund in addition to the GIF support.
2   Cooper and Kleinschmidt (1996) is based on a study of 161 business units.
3   For a fuller list of references, see Grupp (1998), Kline and Rosenberg (1986) or Freeman and Soete (1997).
4   These concepts are known as 'technometrics' (Grupp, 1994).
5   See, for the example of Israel, Frenkel et al. (1994b). This article is reproduced in Chapter 11.
6   Technion – Israel Institute of Technology, Haifa, Israel.
7   The calculations were done using STATA 6 software. The reason to use weights is the subjective character of the innovation index. If standard deviation is large, we assume dissenting votes of the respondents and attribute lower weights to the respective firms.

8    Part of the reason for these results may be the focus on a single somewhat atypical year, 1997 – a year of recession for Israel. In that year, GDP grew only 2.7 per cent and unemployment rose to 7.7 per cent of the labour force.

# 7 Total Factor Productivity as a Performance Benchmark for Firms: Theory and Evidence[1]

**Main Ideas in this Chapter**

In this Chapter, we propose using Solow's macroeconomic approach and the concept of total factor productivity (TFP) as a microeconomic tool for analysing individual firms. TFP long used in analysing macroeconomic growth among countries is a useful strategic performance benchmark for individual firms. TFP calculations permit managers and investors to partition labour productivity growth between two sharply different underlying causes: capital-deepening (higher capital per worker), and exogenous technological change. The TFP benchmark can be computed from readily available information in financial statements. The structure of the Chapter is as follows. Section 7.2 presents a simple version of Solow's model, suitable for use in individual firms, and provides a numerical example. Section 7.3 gives detailed total factor productivity calculations for the 20 largest firms in the world. Section 7.4 provides three case studies of total factor productivity growth, for Intel, YPF (Argentina's largest energy company) and Merck. The final Section summarizes and concludes.

## 7.1 INTRODUCTION

It is widely accepted that productivity is a key performance benchmark for firms. Rising productivity is related to increased profitability, lower costs and sustained competitiveness. The most widely-used productivity indicator for firms is labour productivity – units of output, or value added, per employee. However, this measure has serious shortcomings. The main one: it fails to show why labour productivity has risen.

Consider, for instance, productivity among banks. Value added per worker among US banks rose by 3.5 per cent annually, in the 1990s. In contrast, overall labour productivity in the U.S. economy rose by less than half that rate. Why did labour productivity in banks outpace that in the overall economy? Was it because of massive investments in information technology, as some believe? Or because of economies of scale (in part due to mergers, downsizing and improved efficiency). The 3.5 per cent labour productivity figure itself offers no clue. Clearly, for a particular bank, benchmarking its productivity performance in a way that leads to strategic managerial interventions is vital. Labour productivity is not in itself sufficient.

A possible solution lies in the macroeconomic research of Solow. Solow (1957, 1969) found that a majority of nations' economic growth was attributable to technical change, or 'total factor productivity growth', which he proposed measuring as a 'residual', based on a so-called 'production function approach'. This 'production function approach' has been extensively used to measure the rate of return to net investment in R&D for firm or line-of-business level data (Mansfield, 1965; Clark and Griliches, 1984; Link, 1981; Griliches, 1986) and industry aggregates (Terleckyj, 1974; Griliches, 1979, 1994; Griliches and Lichtenberg, 1984; Scherer, 1982).

In this Chapter, we propose using Solow's macroeconomic approach and the concept of total factor productivity as a microeconomic tool for analysing and partitioning labour productivity change in individual firms. The result is insightful because it shows whether companies' labour productivity gains are driven principally by capital investment, or whether they are driven by technology and knowledge. For outside observers and analysts, TFP can be estimated using publicly available information contained mainly in balance sheets and pro-forma income statements. Within firms, confidential data can be used to build disaggregated measures of total factor productivity and its rate of change, for individual business units or subsidiaries.

We will argue that total factor productivity, a powerful tool in the armoury of macroeconomists, should also be added to the day-to-day toolbox of senior managers and investment analysts, keen to benchmark productivity change within the firm in an operational manner.

## 7.2 THEORY

In his classic 1957 paper, Robert Solow showed how technical progress could be measured by using a production function. In his method, the change in labour productivity was caused by two separate factors: (a) capital deepening, that is, a rise in the amount of capital per unit of labour, and (b) exogenous 'technical change', that is, improvements in knowledge, methods, and so on. While (b) could not be directly measured, it could be inferred as a residual, by subtracting the contribution of 'capital-deepening' from the overall change in labour productivity. This method was widely applied to analysis of countries and industries.

In this Chapter, we argue that Solow's method can be equally useful for benchmarking productivity change within individual firms. For countries, aggregate value added is simply gross domestic product (GDP). For firms, value added is the difference between sales revenue and the cost of material inputs.

Value added per employee for firms, as for countries, grows either because a) capital investment makes workers more productive, or b) better methods, technology, methods, incentives, motivation, and so on, makes workers more productive without additional capital investment. It is vitally important for managers, investors and for stockholders to know why labour productivity (value added per employee) has risen, or why it has not.

Solow has shown that countries grew wealthy mainly through factor (b). If this is true, it must therefore be the case that for such wealthy countries, a significant number of the firms in these countries also have significant increases in factor (b).

To adapt Solow's measure of technical progress to the individual firm, define 'total factor productivity' as total value added divided by a 'representative bundle' of labour and capital – a geometric average of labour and capital, with the exponential weights reflecting the contributions of labour and capital to overall value added:[2]

**Terminology**

TFP = total factor productivity  
VA = value added ($): Sales revenue minus cost of materials  
K = capital (generally, shareholders' equity, which is 'net assets', or gross assets, taken from the balance sheet)  
L = number of employees, or total annual labour hours

α    =  fraction of value added attributable to labour, equal to [L VMP$_L$]/VA, where VMP$_L$ is the value of the marginal product of labour

1 − α =  fraction of value added attributable to capital, equal to [K VMP$_K$]/VA, where VMP$_K$ is the value of the marginal product of capital.

**Model**

$$TFP = VA / [L^{\alpha} K^{1-\alpha}] \qquad (7.1)$$

Equation (7.1) simply states that total factor productivity is defined as value added per 'basket' of labour and capital, where the basket is the geometric mean of Labour (L) and Capital (K), weighted by their respective importance or contribution to output, as measured by α and 1 − α. Dividing by L yields

$$TFP = [VA/L] / [(K/L)^{1-\alpha}]. \qquad (7.2)$$

Total factor productivity is now seen as value added per worker, divided by an exponential function of capital per worker. The exponential function in the denominator represents the part of labour productivity (VA/L) generated by capital intensity K/L.[3] Taking logarithms of both sides provides the form

$$\log TFP = \log [VA/L] - (1 - \alpha)\log [K/L]. \qquad (7.3)$$

Derivating with respect to time (d/dt) finally gives

$$d\log TFP/dt = d\log [VA/L]/dt - (1 - \alpha)\, d\log[K/L]/dt. \qquad (7.4)$$

Since 100 dlogx/dt equals 100 [dx/dt]/x, that is, the per cent change over time in x, (7.4) can be expressed as

% change in TFP = % change in value added per employee
− (1 − α) (% change in capital per employee).    (7.5)

Equation (7.5) is the key tool for TFP benchmarking. In terms of the Solow (1957) paper, (7.5) states that whatever part of the change in labour productivity is not attributable to capital-deepening (higher capital per employee) must be caused by exogenous non-capital factors like better management, knowledge, motivation, and so on. Therefore, the change in total factor productivity, when computed for individual firms, partitions the underlying factors that drive labour productivity between expensive capital-deepening and inexpensive 'free lunch' technological change factors. It is of course understood that technological change is often embodied in capital equipment; this fierce debate, about the 'embodiedness' of technical change, is the subject of a large number of studies, and will not be addressed here.[4]

## Numerical Illustration

Consider two firms. Each has experienced a 20 per cent rise in net after tax profits in 1999 (see Table 7.1). A deeper analysis is required, to understand why profits rose. Data are collected on operating profits, value added, shareholders' equity (net capital, or assets minus liabilities) and number of employees.

*Table 7.1: A numerical illustration*

|  | Firm 1 | | Firm 2 | |
|---|---|---|---|---|
|  | 1998 | 1999 | 1998 | 1999 |
| Value added ($ m.) | 100 | 110 | 100 | 110 |
| Capital ($ m.) | 40 | 45 | 40 | 40 |
| Labour (persons) | 1,000 | 1,000 | 1,000 | 1,200 |
| NOPAT* ($ m.) | 10 | 12 | 10 | 12 |

*Note:* * NOPAT = net operating profit after tax.

These data permit calculation of standard, partial measures of productivity (see Table 7.2). Such measures reveal:

(a)  Firm 1 enjoyed a 10 per cent rise in labour productivity in 1999, while Firm 2 had an 8 per cent *drop* in labour productivity.
(b)  Firm 1 suffered a 6 per cent drop in capital productivity, while Firm 2 had a 10 per cent increase in capital productivity.

Evidently, this results from Firm 1 maintaining its labour force unchanged while increasing capital investment; while Firm 2 kept its capital investment constant, while boosting its labour force by 20 per cent.

*Table 7.2: Partial measures of productivity and profitability*

|  | Firm 1 | | | Firm 2 | | |
|---|---|---|---|---|---|---|
|  | 1998 | 1999 | % change | 1998 | 1999 | % change |
| Economic value added* | $2 m. | $3 m. |  | $2 m. | $4 m. | – |
| EVA as % of capital | 5% | 6.7% |  | 5% | 10% | – |
| Labour productivity* *($000) | 100 | 110 | +10% | 100 | 92 | –8% |
| Capital productivity* ** ($) | 2.5 | 2.44 | –6.1% | 2.5 | 2.75 | +10% |

*Notes:*   \*   Economic value added (EVA) = NOPAT minus the opportunity cost of capital. Here, we assume that shareholders can earn 20 per cent on their investment in equally risky alternatives; hence EVA = NOPAT – (0.2) (capital).
    \*\*   Labour productivity = value added per employee.
    \*\*\*   Capital productivity = value added per dollar of capital.

Moreover,

(c) Firm 1 increased its economic value added as a per cent of shareholders' equity from 5 per cent to 6.7 per cent, but Firm 2 raised the same measure to 10 per cent.

While all three of these benchmarking measures have value, what is missing is an overall summary statistic showing what part of labour productivity gains were due to what may be termed an 'economic free lunch' (not related to capital investment), and what part were due to relatively costly (though doubtless necessary) capital investments, that is, Equation (7.3). This is computed in Table 7.3.

From Table 7.3, we learn that Firm 1 experienced a 5 per cent gain in total factor productivity, while Firm 2 had a 1.67 per cent decline in this key measure. Thus, even though Firm 2 has managed to boost its economic rent to 10 per cent of shareholders' equity by avoiding additional investment, its performance in the realm of productivity has been substantially poorer than that of Firm 1. Even though the short-term profit picture may be bright, the TFP numbers raise issues related to management performance.

*Table 7.3:  Per cent change in total factor productivity*

|                                              | Firm 1           | Firm 2              |
|----------------------------------------------|------------------|---------------------|
| % change in value added per employee         | + 10%            | − 8%                |
| −(0.4) (% change in capital per employee)    | − (0.4) (12.5%)  | − (0.4) (− 16.67%)  |
| equals: % change in total factor productivity, 1998–1999* | + 5% | − 1.67% |

*Notes:*  * % change in total factor productivity = % change in value added per worker minus (capital intensity coefficient) (% change in capital per worker). See Equation (7.3).

Economic value added (EVA) – return on shareholders' equity after deducting the opportunity cost of capital – has become a widely used measure of firm performance. Strategy experts have criticized this measure, on the grounds that it narrowly measures the productivity of capital alone. The advantage of the TFP measure is that it takes into account both labour and capital in measuring productivity, as well as, of course, sales and output.

**A Macro Example**

Consider now a real-world example: two 'firms' we shall temporarily call HK Ltd. and SG Ltd. (Table 7.4). Both entities experienced similar, rapid growth in value added per worker over the two decades 1971–1990; in each, labour productivity doubled every decade. But HK Ltd. showed profitability (rates of return on capital) twice that of SG Ltd. Why? SG Ltd. attained growth in labour productivity by massive capital investments. For instance, in 1980, SG Ltd. did not produce any computer components or peripherals whatsoever. By 1983 SG Ltd. was the world's largest producer of disk drives. Such investments were profitable initially, but encountered rapidly diminishing returns. In contrast, HK Ltd. used its high quality human resources and entrepreneurial energy to drive total factor productivity growth with far less capital spending, achieving therefore higher profitability.

HK Ltd. is, of course, Hong Kong. SG Ltd. is Singapore. While Singapore's conservative economic policy has left it relatively unscathed by the Asian financial crisis, nonetheless the concomitance of massive investment, diminishing returns to capital and shrinking profitability, are seen by some as the underlying causes of Asia's 1997–98 financial crisis, in Thailand, Indonesia and Malaysia, anticipated in Young's (1992) paper. Had managers and investors been tracking total factor productivity for firms, as well as for whole countries, the impending crisis might have signalled its coming years before it happened.

*Table 7.4:  HK Ltd. and SG Ltd., 1971–1990*

| | Proportion of growth in value | | Real return on capital (%)* |
|---|---|---|---|
| | Added per worker TFP growth | Caused by: capital deepening | |
| Hong Kong | 56% | 44% | 22% – 24% |
| Singapore | –17% | +117% | 7% – 13% |

*Notes:*    *  HK: 1980–86; Sing.: 1980–89.

*Source*:    Young (1992).

## 7.3   APPLICATION OF TFP ANALYSIS TO GLOBAL FIRMS

In this Section, we provide some calculations of TFP growth for a selection of large global firms drawn from the Fortune 1000 list. Data are given in Appendix 7.1.

Rates of change in total factor productivity were computed for the largest 20 firms in Fortune magazine's Global 1,000 (see Table 7.5). They reveal several firms, like GE and WalMart, with large positive TFP gains, and several (mainly Japanese) with large declines in TFP (with Mitsubishi the exception). ATT is also notable for poor TFP performance, as is Mobil.[5]

To determine whether TFP change indeed provides new information about the firm beyond conventional measures – like the change in the price of its shares and the change in profits – we computed the Pearson correlation between per cent change in TFP and (a) per cent change in stock price during the following year, and (b) per cent change in profits in the same year. None were statistically significant, and in fact none exceeded 0.13. This suggests that TFP change does provide a new dimension of information about firm performance, largely independent of – and behaving differently from – share performance and profit. Of course, because the per cent change in revenue is a key part of the TFP

*Table 7.5:   Top 20 firms in the Fortune 1000 global list: per cent change in TFP 1997 versus 1996*

| Company | % change in TFP $1 - \alpha = 0.4$ | % change in TFP $1 - \alpha = 0.3$ | Mean % TFP change |
|---|---|---|---|
| GM | 2.51 | 3.33 | 2.92 |
| Ford | 0.98 | 1.86 | 1.42 |
| Mitsui | 0.57 | 0.03 | 0.30 |
| Mitsubishi | 12.34 | 11.25 | 11.80 |
| Itochu | –6.36 | –6.42 | –6.39 |
| Royal Dutch Shell | 4.80 | 3.60 | 4.20 |
| Marubeni | –7.38 | –8.13 | –7.76 |
| Exxon | 2.78 | 2.71 | 2.74 |
| Sumitomo | –8.94 | –10.25 | –9.59 |
| Toyota | –10.78 | –11.21 | –10.99 |
| WalMart | 14.68 | 14.11 | 14.40 |
| GE | 16.04 | 15.71 | 15.88 |
| Nissho Iwai | 7.45 | 6.54 | 6.99 |
| NTT | –1.55 | –1.58 | –1.56 |
| IBM | 3.37 | 3.38 | 3.37 |
| Hitachi | –7.05 | –7.64 | –7.34 |
| ATT | –31.38 | –30.66 | –31.02 |
| Nippon Life | –17.61 | –16.41 | –17.01 |
| Mobil | –14.81 | –15.36 | –15.08 |
| Daimler Benz | 0.27 | 0.45 | 0.36 |

*Source*: See Appendix 7.1.

formula, TFP change is highly correlated with revenue gains. This is not only a statistical artefact but also a management principle – nothing is more helpful to productivity than strong revenue gains, generated with more or less the same capital and labour resources as the year before.

An interesting, marginally significant relation was found between 'rank by firm size' and TFP change. The Pearson correlation of $-0.390$ ($p > 0.089$) was negative, indicating that smaller firms (that is, higher rank numbers) have smaller rates of growth in TFP.

## 7.4   THREE CASE STUDIES: INTEL, YPF, MERCK

The following three case studies of total factor productivity growth are drawn from publicly available data in annual financial statements. Use of such public data necessarily requires some assumptions, in order to compute TFP. Of course, when internal company data are available, no such assumptions need to be made.

### Intel Ltd.

Table 7.6 summarizes productivity data for Intel, for 1993 and 1994. They show a decline in labour productivity of 3 per cent. The TFP Equation (7.5) can help us understand why.

Applying the 'Solow equation' (7.5) yields a per cent change in TFP $= -7.8$ per cent.

Intel experienced a decline in labour productivity in 1994, despite a large increase in Intel's capital, owing to 'negative technological change'. Closer investigation would doubtless reveal Intel's massive shift from 486 microprocessors to the new 586 ('Pentium') microprocessor, and attendant loss of output and production time, as fabrication plants transitioned to new technologies and workers underwent training.

The data indicate the costliness of such transitions, in terms of lost productivity and inefficiency, but further exploration may have led investors to conclude that the productivity decline is likely temporary. Indeed, in following years, Intel's value added per worker grew impressively, driven largely by its technological change, and its stock price rose sharply. Poor TFP numbers do not in themselves prove a bleak outlook, or establish poor managerial performance, for firms. They may be temporary.

*Table 7.6: Balance sheet data for Intel*

|  | 1994 $ billion | 1993 $ billion | change |
|---|---|---|---|
| Net revenue | 11.5 | 8.8 |  |
| – Cost of goods sold | 5.6 | 3.3 |  |
| = Value added* | 5.9 | 5.5 | +7.2% |
| Labour (employees) | 32,600 | 29,500 | +10.5% |
| Value added per worker ($) | 180,982 | $186,440 | –3% |
| Capital (shareholders' equity) | 9.3 | 7.5 | +24% |
| Capital per worker ($) | 285,276 | 254,237 | +12% |

*Notes:* Assume value of $(1 - \alpha) = 0.4$.

        * Value added is not technically the difference between net revenue and cost of goods sold (as derived from the income statement), because cost of goods sold includes the cost of labour as well as materials. However, if we assume that the proportion of cost of goods sold comprised of labour costs does not appreciably change in 1994 compared to 1993, then the per cent change in value added computed by using cost of goods sold will be the same as the value computed by using the technically correct measure of value added (not computable from publicly known information).

*Source:* Intel Ltd. Annual Financial Statements, 1993, 1994.


## YPF Ltd.

YPF is Argentina's leading energy company. In 1991 the company was privatized, and slimmed its employment rolls down from over 50,000 employees to around 6,000 (although many of the 50,000 became private outsourcers for YPF). It provides one of the world's most dramatic examples of efficiency gains through privatization. YPF recorded very large gains in productivity in 1996. Was this due to gains in total factor productivity (higher value added per unit of resources), or capital investment? Solow's equation provides the answer: the per cent change in TFP equals 22.2% – (0.4) (10.5%) = 18%.

This tells us that YPF's impressive increase in value added per worker was largely due to improvements in technology, efficiency and knowledge, rather than capital investment. Indeed, the remarkable story of YPF's privatization and resulting dramatic increase in

*Table 7.7:  Balance sheet data for YPF*

|  | 1996 $ billion | 1995 $ billion | change |
|---|---|---|---|
| Revenues | 5.9 | 5.0 |  |
| Cost of sales | 3.6 | 3.2 |  |
| Value added | 2.3 | 1.8 | 27.7% |
| Labour (employees) | 9,700 | 9,300 | 4.3% |
| Value added per employee ($) | 237,000 | 194,000 | 22.16% |
| Capital | 6.7 | 5.8 | 15.32% |
| Capital per employee ($) | 694,000 | 628,000 | 10.5% |

*Note:*    Assumption: the contribution of capital to value added $(1 - \alpha)$ is 0.4, typical for a capital-intensive firm.

*Source*:   YPF Annual Financial Statements.

efficiency deserves to be more widely known and studied. As expected, YPF's higher total factor productivity found expression in the higher profitability of its capital.

## Merck Ltd.

Merck, an R&D-intensive pharmaceutical company, showed large gains in value added per worker, apparently primarily from increases in knowledge stemming from an aggressive R&D policy. It should be

*Table 7.8:  Balance sheet data for Merck*

|  | 1994 $ billion | 1993 $ billion | change |
|---|---|---|---|
| Value added | 9.0 | 8.0 | 12.5% |
| Labour (employees) | 47,700 | 47,100 | 1.3% |
| Capital | 21.9 | 19.9 | 10.1% |

noted that conventional accounting does not treat R&D expenditures as part of a company's 'intellectual capital', but rather treats them as current expenditures.

Therefrom, we get a per cent change in TFP = 11% − (0.4)(8.7%) = 7.5%.

Probably, TFP calculations should be accompanied by a recalculation of capital investment, treating R&D spending as investment and amortizing it over 3–5 years to reflect the relative short life of this asset.

From the TFP data, one can deduce that the majority of Merck's labour productivity gain stems from its technological change – probably, its successful investment in R&D for new products.


## 7.5  CONCLUSION

Analysis of total factor productivity data for countries ultimately led to a new appreciation of the key role of knowledge and technological change as drivers of economic growth in per capita output. Extension of this tool to performance benchmarking for firms has taken a surprisingly long time (Wakelin, 1998). By applying TFP to firm data, senior management and external analysts can find answers to the question: why is labour productivity growing (or not growing). Perhaps the key value of such TFP calculations is not that they provide definitive answers, but serve as a stimulus of further analytic questions that help both managers and investors better understand the firm's strengths and weaknesses.

TFP benchmarks for individual firms, or divisions within firms, are best seen as the beginning of an in-depth strategic analysis, rather than the end. A promising extension of TFP analysis for firms might be to apply the so-called 'growth accounting' analysis of Denison (1967) – which partitioned TFP growth for countries among a large array of contributing factors – to TFP data for firms, to achieve a similar goal: the answer to the question, how and why did technical change grow (or fail to grow) in the firm?

# APPENDIX 7.1

Table 7A.1:   Data for top 20 global firms (Fortune 1000)

| Company | % ch. share price 5/29/98–5/30/97 | Assets '96 | Employ-ment '96 | Assets '97 | Employment '97 | % change rev. 1997 versus 1996 | % change profits, 1997 versus 1996 |
|---|---|---|---|---|---|---|---|
| GM | 32 | 222100.00 | 647.00 | 225888.00 | 608.00 | 5.80 | 35.00 |
| Ford | 107 | 262900.00 | 372.00 | 279097.00 | 363.00 | 4.50 | 55.60 |
| Mitsui | –42 | 61144.00 | 42.00 | 55071.00 | 40.00 | –1.60 | –16.50 |
| Mitsubishi | –49 | 77872.00 | 35.00 | 71408.00 | 36.00 | 8.00 | –1.50 |
| Itochu | – | 59179.00 | 7.00 | 56308.00 | 6.70 | –6.60 | – |
| Royal Dutch Shell | 18 | 124373.00 | 101.00 | 113781.00 | 105.00 | 0.00 | –12.70 |
| Marubeni | – | 60865.00 | 65.00 | 55403.00 | 64.00 | –10.40 | –21.40 |
| Exxon | 19 | 95527.00 | 79.00 | 96064.00 | 80.00 | 2.50 | 12.60 |
| Sumitomo | –32 | 43506.00 | 26.00 | 42866.00 | 29.50 | –14.20 | 0.00 |
| Toyota | –14 | 102417.00 | 150.00 | 103893.00 | 159.00 | –12.50 | 8.00 |
| WalMart | 85 | 39501.00 | 675.00 | 45525.00 | 825.00 | 12.40 | 15.40 |
| GE | 38 | 272402.00 | 239.00 | 304012.00 | 276.00 | 14.70 | 12.70 |
| Nissho Iwai | – | 43647.00 | 17.50 | 40799.00 | 18.00 | 3.80 | –81.90 |

*Table 7A.1 continued*

| Company | % ch. share price 5/29/98–5/30/97 | Assets '96 | Employ- ment '96 | Assets '97 | Employment 97 | % change rev. 1997 versus 1996 | % change profits, 1997 versus 1996 |
|---|---|---|---|---|---|---|---|
| NTT | –14 | 115864.00 | 230.00 | 113409.00 | 226.00 | –1.70 | 77.50 |
| IBM | 36 | 81132.00 | 268.00 | 81499.00 | 269.00 | 3.40 | 12.20 |
| Hitachi | –38 | 80328.00 | 330.00 | 75837.00 | 331.00 | –9.40 | –96.40 |
| ATT | 66 | 55552.00 | 130.00 | 58635.00 | 128.00 | –28.50 | –21.50 |
| Nippon Life | – | 322759.00 | 86.70 | 316530.00 | 75.90 | –12.80 | 15.30 |
| Mobil | 12 | 46408.00 | 43.00 | 43559.00 | 42.70 | –17.00 | 10.40 |
| Daimler Benz | 31 | 72331.00 | 290.00 | 76190.00 | 300.00 | 1.00 | 161.00 |

*Source:* Fortune Global 1000: August 4, 1997; August 3, 1998; share price data is from Business Week: The Global 1000, July 13, 1998. Capital K is measured by Assets; L Labour is no. of employees; % change in value added is proxied by % change in revenue.

147

## NOTES

1   Research for this Chapter was supported by a grant from the German–Israel Foundation. This Chapter was written while the second author was a Visiting Professor at the MIT – Center for Advanced Educational Services and MIT Sloan School of Management. We also acknowledge partial support from the Technion Vice-President's Fund for Research. This Chapter is an original contribution to this volume not published elsewhere.

2   Craig and Harris (1973) develop a measure they called total productivity by using the algebraic sum of the value of factor inputs (capital, labour and materials) as the denominator. This approach, however, does not take into account differences in the relative importance, or marginal productivity, of labour and capital and treats them unrealistically as equal.

3   To see this: let $VA/L = F[(K/L, A(t)]$, where $A(t)$ is exogenous technological change, not associated with physical capital K. Assuming certain properties for F permits us to write this expression as: $VA/L = A(t) F(K/L)$. Finally, assuming a Cobb–Douglas (exponential) function form for the production function yields: $VA/L = A(t) (K/L)^{1-\alpha}$. It is therefore true that $A(t) = [VA/L] / [(K/L)^{1-\alpha}]$, which is precisely equation (7.2).

4   See Grupp and Schwitalla (1998) for a recent treatment.

5   Significantly, Mobil has since been acquired by Exxon.

# 8 Innovation Benchmarking in the Telecom Industry[1]

## Main Ideas in this Chapter

This Chapter contains a new approach to innovation benchmarking, as applied to telecom and information technology. Management always should begin with measurement. This is especially true of the difficult and risky task of managing innovation. By quantifying aspects of the innovation process, hopefully management decisions can become fact-based and hence lead to superior performance. The Chapter first explains how technological benchmarking can be done for strategic positioning of firms in global telecom markets (telecom manufacturers); second, how overall positioning of firms in the information technology market is obversed; third, how knowledge production leads to innovation and growth; fourth, how specific positioning of firms in single-product quality within the area of telecom products is examined. Finally, the Chapter provides a typology of firms based on how well product quality, measured in the proposed way, correlates with market-based preferences.

## 8.1 INNOVATION BENCHMARKING

According to Webster's dictionary, benchmarking is 'A surveyor's mark ... . of previously determined *position* ... . and used as a reference point ... . standard by which something can be measured or judged.' In business administration and management, the pioneering work of Kearns at Xerox Corporation built on the notion of measurement or judgement, when establishing the following definition: 'Benchmarking is the continuous process of measuring products, services and practices against the toughest competitors or those companies recognized as industry leaders.' (Kearns, 1986).[2] Later on, a broader understanding in terms of action-oriented concepts led to such ways of thinking: 'Benchmarking is the search for industry best practices that lead to superior performance' (Camp, 1989, p. 12).

Although benchmarking is relatively new, it is quite well established. The main problem with benchmarking is that most people use rather crude scores to carry out benchmarking comparisons. The purpose of this Chapter is to go back to the original meaning and to propose a different type of benchmarking using *quantitative measures*, in order to position a product or service in terms of its technology. That is, it concentrates on benchmarking of innovations, not of standard products or practices. This is not a critical remark toward common benchmarking – just another approach to the same goal. In general, whenever one can use quantitative data organized as a table, one is better off than when qualitative judgements are made – the conventional approach in benchmarking.

The *methodological tools* to be used for this quantitative benchmarking begin with patent statistics. But benchmarking is often not unidimensional, but rather multidimensional. So we may need to use new tools to express the multidimensional quality (strategic markets, strategic sub-technologies), such as multidimensional scaling (Section 8.2). Patent statistics are also useful to explore the knowledge production that leads to innovation and subsequent growth (Section 8.3). A technique known as technometric benchmarking is applied to give quantitative expression to the multidimensional nature of most products and services, that is, to product quality (Section 8.4).

For most people, a patent is a legal document. What interests us in patent statistics is the *knowledge output quality* that finds expression in patents. If in a company two engineers work for a year on a defined project funded from internal sources (cash flow), and if they are successful and invent something new, then we eventually have a document emerging from this lab which tells us that two engineers worked for a while on a certain invention, described very precisely. We can read from the document, as we read from scientific publications, that this company has deliberately brought about a certain inventive step, now documented and codified. So patent documents point to those areas of activity in which a company has invested R&D labour and resources. When patent examiners (in most countries civil servants at patent offices) discover that the idea is not new – but is already known – it matters to patent attorneys but little to us, because the fact remains, the company invested, say, two man-years in the R&D.

The fact that our world is still divided into national territories, and that intellectual property rights are protected by national patent offices and in national borders, means that a patent protects an idea in *one* country and *one* market. Regional coverage of patent protection must be deliberately decided by a company. So when one invention, one patent application, is filed at home, it is a sign that a company intends to market it in the domestic market only. When patents are filed in seven or eight countries, it shows the company intends to either manufacture or market the product in many countries.

Patent analysis is difficult. We must treat the data with care. Some years ago, the OECD secretariat in Paris published a *manual*, a guideline, on what one should observe in working with patent documents (OECD, 1994).[3] All the possible mistakes one can make in analysing patents are listed, so that one can prevent them if one reads this document carefully.

## 8.2 POSITIONING OF FIRMS IN GLOBAL TELECOM MARKETS – AN EXEMPLAR OF INNOVATION BENCHMARKING

Let us begin with companies in the area of telecom *manufacturing*. The companies in our analysis are listed in Table 8.1. Our objective is to examine the marketing information inherent in patent statistics.

Let us examine Siemens first. Figure 8.1 shows the number of patent documents originating with Siemens (they have a number of affiliated companies), somewhere in the world, and we first look at the domestic market. The number of patents filed is the largest in Germany. Many of them remain *only* in the domestic market. But a considerable share of all inventions originate in the UK. So out of all countries in the world, the UK is the *most preferred foreign market* for Siemens in terms of protection of their inventions. This is explained by Siemens' serious effort to enter the UK market, in part through patenting, in the late 1980s. Other large European countries are nearly equally covered with patents. For smaller countries, the patent applications declines.

The number of intellectual property rights in the domestic market is less than double those abroad – so the company is quite international in its perspective. In the USA, though it is the single largest market in the world, the number of duplicated patents remains low despite the company Rolm which was acquired there producing some inventions.

Siemens has neglected this country in comparison with Europe, and neglected Japan as well.

*Table 8.1: Analysed telecoms manufacturers and network operators*[4]

| Company | No. of European patent applications in telecom technology invented 1987–89 | Communications equipment (US $ m. resp. international communications revenue 1993) |
|---|---|---|
| Alcatel NV | 423 | 14,823 |
| AT&T | 378 | 11,801 |
| Bosch | 226 | 3,530 |
| Ericsson | 82 | 7,767 |
| Fujitsu | 288 | 4,774 |
| GEC | 181 | 1,948 |
| Hitachi | 83 | 1,555 |
| IBM | 342 | 5,299 |
| Matshushita | 100 | 2,227 |
| Motorola | 403 | 10,096 |
| NEC | 419 | 9,480 |
| Nokia | 78 | 2,355 |
| Northern Telecom | 110 | 7,860 |
| Oki | 27 | 1,590 |
| Philips | 378 | 1,868 |
| Siemens | 552 | 12,205 |
| Sony | 100 | 1,181 |
| STET/Italtel | 43 | 1,520 |
| Thomson | 132 | n.a. |
| Toshiba | 222 | 1,710 |
| Bellcore | 82 | 0 (domestic) |
| British Telecom (BT) | 121 | 3,193 |
| France Télécom (FT) | 89 | 3,693 |
| GTE-Sprint | 39 | 1,188 |
| NTT | 86 | 0 (domestic) |

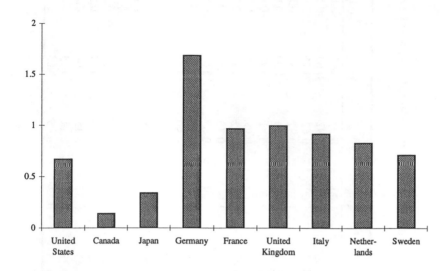

*Figure 8.1: Destination countries of telecommunications-related patent applications by Siemens (consolidated) 1987–89[5]*

We can carry out a similar analysis for other companies as well. Table 8.2 provides similar information for the other companies. In this table, the number of patents filed in the foreign country with the most patents applied for is taken as the benchmark value of 1.0.

It is evident from Table 8.2 that GEC is the mirror image of Siemens – a UK firm filing heavily in Germany; GEC and Siemens run a joint subsidiary, originating from the Plessey group. Note the behaviour of Japanese companies. This is a statistical artefact. The patent law in Japan is such that they cannot easily accumulate and combine several claims to be protected in one document. In practice, each claim requires its *own* document. Experienced patent lawyers provide a rule of thumb – divide the number of Japanese domestic patent applications by six or so to arrive at roughly comparable numbers. So we cannot surmise that the patenting activity in Japan is as fast and furious as the numbers indicate.

Table 8.2: Destination countries for telecommunications-related patent applications for selected companies 1987–896

| Corporation (consolidated) | USA | CND | JPN | DEU | FRA | GBR | ITA | NLD | SWE |
|---|---|---|---|---|---|---|---|---|---|
| Alcatel NV | 0.71 | 0.71 | 0.49 | 1.28 | 1.09 | 1.00 | 0.97 | 0.92 | 0.89 |
| Bosch | 0.40 | 0.11 | 0.39 | 1.98 | 1.00 | 0.95 | 0.92 | 0.69 | 0.58 |
| Ericsson | 0.88 | 0.37 | 0.71 | 0.92 | 0.85 | 1.00 | 0.69 | 0.76 | 1.02 |
| GEC | 0.66 | 0.37 | 0.73 | 1.00 | 0.99 | 1.30 | 0.91 | 0.81 | 0.81 |
| STET/Italtel | 0.63 | 0.34 | 0.50 | 1.00 | 1.00 | 1.00 | 0.89 | 1.00 | 0.97 |
| Nokia | 0.28 | 0.06 | 0.32 | 0.95 | 0.94 | 1.00 | 0.81 | 0.71 | 0.82 |
| Philips | 0.92 | 0.19 | 0.85 | 1.10 | 0.98 | 1.00 | 0.69 | 0.44 | 0.59 |
| Siemens | 0.67 | 0.14 | 0.34 | 1.68 | 0.97 | 1.00 | 0.92 | 0.83 | 0.71 |
| Thomson | 0.97 | 0.13 | 0.48 | 0.99 | 1.23 | 1.00 | 0.76 | 0.52 | 0.43 |
| AT&T | 1.96 | 0.84 | 0.98 | 0.93 | 0.93 | 1.00 | 0.65 | 0.54 | 0.51 |
| IBM | 1.11 | 0.10 | 0.85 | 1.00 | 1.00 | 1.00 | 0.32 | 0.10 | 0.08 |
| Motorola | 1.51 | 0.44 | 0.94 | 0.95 | 0.95 | 1.00 | 0.90 | 0.92 | 0.90 |
| NorTel | 1.00 | 0.48 | 0.38 | 0.36 | 0.36 | 0.38 | 0.20 | 0.35 | 0.34 |
| Fujitsu | 0.90 | 0.69 | 31.46 | 1.00 | 0.93 | 0.99 | 0.25 | 0.11 | 0.23 |
| Hitachi | 1.00 | 0.11 | 12.19 | 0.54 | 0.33 | 0.39 | 0.07 | 0.06 | 0.05 |
| Matsushita | 1.00 | 0.12 | 3.20 | 0.66 | 0.53 | 0.70 | 0.13 | 0.27 | 0.26 |
| NEC | 1.00 | 0.50 | 3.81 | 0.58 | 0.43 | 0.69 | 0.11 | 0.29 | 0.26 |
| NTT | 1.00 | 0.50 | 44.80 | 0.87 | 0.51 | 0.79 | 0.14 | 0.27 | 0.52 |
| OKI | 1.00 | 0.19 | 20.95 | 0.53 | 0.47 | 0.57 | 0.15 | 0.04 | 0.19 |
| Sony | 1.00 | 0.27 | 5.25 | 0.85 | 0.78 | 0.89 | 0.11 | 0.34 | 0.04 |
| Toshiba | 1.00 | 0.32 | 13.34 | 0.54 | 0.33 | 0.47 | 0.05 | 0.08 | 0.13 |

To this point, the strategic marketing aspect of innovation, as revealed in patent applications by protected national markets, has been analysed. It was seen that potential strategic initiatives of companies in foreign markets can be tracked. In analysing these data, one arrives at the conclusion that in the telecom industry there are several, very different strategic positionings of companies at the end of the 1980s (see Table 8.3). There is a group of companies from various countries, which have an average share of broad patents. We have another group of companies, selective in patenting their inventions abroad among them some Japanese manufacturers. Then we may discern a group of companies with a special focus on the US market. Finally, there are companies with a special focus on the Japanese market. And, another group of companies – among them newcomers in that market – that do little on the Japanese market.

What do we know about how these companies position themselves in the overall information technology arena, with their telecom activities? Are they broad, or narrow, in technological terms? This is a typical multidimensional problem. Here we offer a brief introduction to a statistical technique known as multidimensional scaling.

*Table 8.3:  Typical patent strategies of selected companies on foreign markets*[7]

| Feature | Examples |
| --- | --- |
| Average share of foreign patents, broad coverage | Alcatel, AT&T, Philips, Siemens |
| Generally, little foreign patenting, but broad coverage | Ericsson, GEC, Motorola, many network operators |
| Selective strategy | Hitachi, Oki, Matsushita, NorTel |
| Special focus on the US market | Matsushita, Hitachi, NEC, Thomson, Philips |
| Special focus on the Japanese market | AT&T, IBM, Motorola, NorTel, Philips |
| Low presence on the Japanese market | Bosch, Nokia, Siemens, STET, Thomson |

Suppose you were given a typical triangle of road distances between pairs of major European cities. For, say, 8 cities, there are 8 • 7/2 = 28 such distances. Now, suppose you were asked to place these cities on a two-dimensional map, such that the distance between each pair of cities precisely matches the distance noted in the table. The task: write a computer algorithm that will do so. There are such algorithms, and they position each 'city' (which in some cases is a variable, technology, or a company), state whether the 'map' is accurate or not (in terms of a coefficient of goodness of fit), and provide other types of useful information. This is multidimensional scaling (MDS), a version of which is also known as smallest space analysis (SSA). Note that there is an exact solution only in the (28-1) dimensional space, as our starting point is road distances not air distances taken from the two-dimensional surface of our globe as usual.

Let us conduct an MDS analysis of IT. We take the telecom manufacturers (including for comparison the network operator in Japan, NTT),[8] use their patent profiles over technological entities (a fine classification exists, including more than 70,000 individual items, the International Patent Classification), and define six major fields in information technology, telecom (TELCOM), electronic elements (ELTRN), multimedia technology (or audio-visual or consumer electronics, AVEL), optical technology (OPTICS), storage (STOR) and data processing (DAT). We then compare the profiles of any two companies to see whether they are similar or not. (We calculate the correlation coefficient of each pair of company technology profiles.) Two companies which each put 16.6 per cent of patenting activity in each of six fields will have a correlation of one. Two companies each of which puts 100 per cent of its patenting activity into a different field, will have a low correlation ($R^2 = 0.2$ in the example). They are thus considered dissimilar.

Figure 8.2 shows a multidimensional scaling map of companies, where distances in the diagram represent similarity – Euclidean proximity. To understand the MDS map fully, as with any map we need a convention or wind rose, a 'north' and 'south' in IT. An artificial 'north' and 'south' is created as follows. We invent an *artificial* company, one that doesn't exist and that is active in one subfield – say, multimedia or consumer electronics. For this field, we assign *all* this imaginary company's patenting activity, 100 per cent. Then this company becomes a 'pole' – one can compare all other companies to this virtual company that is the strongest possible in this field. We thus create fictitious companies to represent the 'pole' in optics, in electronics components, and so on.

This map of technological profiles, in terms of several poles, represents real findings and not artificial ones. Looking at single companies validates this method – and we have. This is the simplest

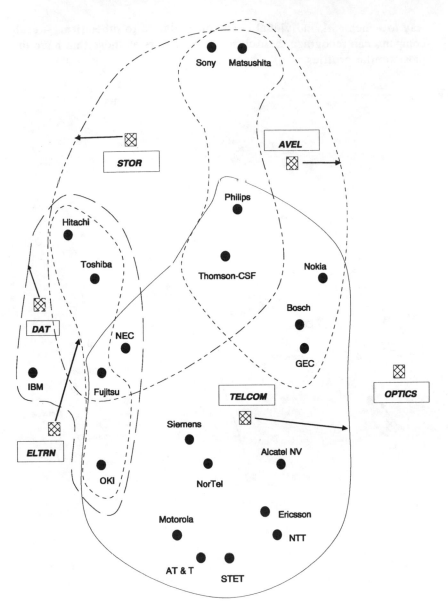

*Figure 8.2: MDS map of information technology for selected*
*companies in the period 1987–89*[9]

way to benchmark individual companies relative to other firms – each company can recognize their closest competitors as those that have the most similar profiles.

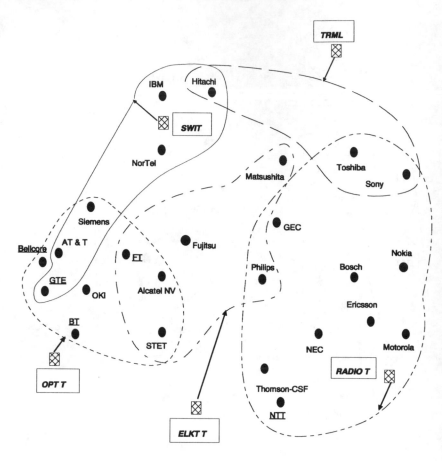

*Figure 8.3:   MDS map of communications technology for selected
companies in the period 1987–89[10]*

Now, let us zoom down to a more limited market – only telecoms. We introduce an MDS map based on a breakdown of patenting in subfields (Figure 8.3). We get in principle the same thing, but just a window of the larger map. We see groupings of companies who are strong in optical telecommunications (OPT T), switching (SWIT), mobile radio telecoms (RATIO T) and electrical transmission (ELKT T – remote measuring and sensing), and terminals technology (TRML). The map provides us with an interesting picture: we now know who are the strong innovators in optics, in transmission – Toshiba is a newcomer, so we get new information on new entrants in this field where we may not have subject information before. The network operating companies – with the exception of NTT – support the national innovation systems mainly with optical technology, an important ingredient to modern telecoms networks.

Whereas at the end of the 1980s, everyone was competing with everyone, at the beginning of the decade, there were islands of specialization, a nice partitioning of the markets. After the opening of the telecom markets through deregulation, there was fierce competition in nearly all markets. This is what a similar MDS map would show, for the beginning of the 1980s. From several snapshots of the MDS strategic positions, you can make a movie, combining them, to get a dynamic picture.

## 8.3   KNOWLEDGE PRODUCTION AND GROWTH – THE INNOVATION MODULE

Timeliness of technical results and newness of the company's technology portfolio strongly affects its innovation performance and – more specifically – new product revenues (Roberts, 1995). The lessons for clarifying the role global technology knowledge plays for the technology levels to be achieved are twofold. First of all, in general terms, the more patents with international significance a company takes out the more sophisticated its product innovations seem to be. On the other hand, some companies offer very sophisticated products on world markets with no comparable patent production (Grupp, 1998, Chapter 10).

There are three possible explanations for the latter observation. First, companies may have a very good tacit in-house knowledge base in the relevant technology, or rely on secrecy or very short market introduction times and do not care for comprehensive, international protection. Another possibility would be that companies have a strong domestic patent base but do not take out foreign duplications of their inventions, accepting all the associated international market risks. This case can be checked by an analysis of patent flows (Table 8.2) and can be ruled out. The third possibility is that the companies produce excellent products from global knowledge external to the company. By acquiring leading-edge companies, licensing, networking and other forms of technology cooperation they may produce innovative products from creative technologies of other firms (including public laboratories). This is an important element in telecommunications.[11]

From this analysis it is concluded that there are various ways to innovation. Some companies acquire technological knowledge from other, for example, global sources instead of using intramural technology generation and patent protection. But not all companies can do so in telecoms, so that for a number of companies a knowledge production relationship between in-house technology generation and innovations achieved should appear to be established. Furthermore, technology generation anticipates innovation performance levels for some years. Patent stock data for previous years should fit better to the technology levels than the most recent activities as cumulative technology acquisition by firms is so important.

The 'knowledge production function' for innovation as measured by the growth levels of innovative products can be modelled as follows (this is a further development of the knowledge production function model of Griliches):[12] It is a one-dimensional approach taking some scalar output measures as is shown below. If we, however, want to use qualitative, non-pecuniary proxy measures, that is, for product quality, we cannot use the conventional production models. A version of linear programming exists, however, that was explicitly built to measure the efficiency of decision-making units (which can be individual firms) and that does allow qualitative inputs. This approach is known as Data Envelopment Analysis (DEA). Essentially, it examines which decision-making units (DMUs) are on their production possibilities frontier, or isoquant, in the knowledge economy and which are not.[13] Here we try out how far the scalar approach holds.

The knowledge production function approach can be represented in the following way:

$$Y = A(t)K^{\beta}U$$

where Y is some measure of output of the firm, K is a measure of cumulated knowledge or research 'capital', a(t) represents other determinants which affect output and vary over time including standard economic inputs such as capital investment, labour and so forth while u reflects all other random fluctuations in output. Certainly, this is just a first approximation to a considerably more complex relationship (Griliches, loc. cit., p. 55).

From the logarithmic form we arrive at the growth equation

$$d \log Y/dt = (1/Y) \, dy/dt = a + \rho \, (R/Y) + du/dt$$

where the term $\beta$ (d log K)/dt is replaced by using the definitions $\rho = dY/dK = \beta$ (Y/K) and R = dK/dt for the net investment in knowledge capital.

We now calculate the deflated growth in communications equipment revenues 1993 in comparison to 1986[14] and approximate R by the number of patent applications following the base year 1986, that is, inventions in the priority years 1987–89. This is a 'skeletal' model of depreciation and obsolescence of (patented) knowledge, but more realistic data are difficult to obtain. It means that inventions from 1986 or earlier years do no more matter for the revenues in 1993, and inventions from 1990 and later do not yet. Patent application number always measure the increase (dK/dt) in knowledge as they add up to the already existing (and eventually patented) knowledge. The assumed lag of about four years until novel knowledge affects markets is taken from earlier empirical investigations (Grupp, 1991).

Cross-section linear regression analysis of the 19 manufacturing companies in Table 8.1 gives the results as displayed in Table 8.4. Knowledge production explains parts of the variance significantly although all the other potential inputs (labour, physical capital, tacit knowledge) are included in the residuals only. A visual impression of the relation is provided in Figure 8.4.

*Table 8.4: Regression results for the knowledge production function of telecom manufacturers (revenue growth 1993 compared to 1986)*

| Measure/Variable | Value |
| --- | --- |
| $\rho$ | $0.0053 \pm 0.0018$ |
| Constant | $0.6312 \pm 0.3700$ |
| $R^2$ adjusted | 0.298 |
| F | 8.652 |
| t | 2.941 |
| Significance | 0.91% |
| DW | 2.296 |

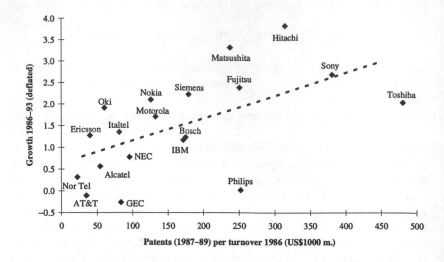

*Figure 8.4:  Delated growth of corporate revenues and knowledge
production of telecom manufacturers*

From the econometric point of view this analysis is very crude and
simplistic. For benchmarking it is however sophisticated and useful. It
tells us what a corporation gets for its technological activitites. Philips
or GEC, for instance, invested in (patented) knowledge and are
traditionally strong R&D performers. They failed to convert this into
innovations that led to average growth of revenues in this particular
market for telecoms goods. This is not to talk managers into a
reduction in R&D activities, rather, to adjust the innovation 'module'
in a more effective way to reach better yields of knowledge
investments. Newcomers in the telecoms market such as Matsushita or
Nokia grew so quickly with modest own knowledge sources[15] that one
is tempted to express a word of warning: long-term sustainable growth
may be vulnerable if you depend too much on external or tacit
knowledge sources.

## 8.4 TECHNOMETRIC BENCHMARKING FOR INDIVIDUAL PRODUCTS: THE CASE OF OPTICAL COMMUNICATIONS LASERS

After examining broader industry trends, it is possible to 'zoom down' to the product level, using a different approach. Here, patent statistics cannot help. In an invention, it is not specified what the product

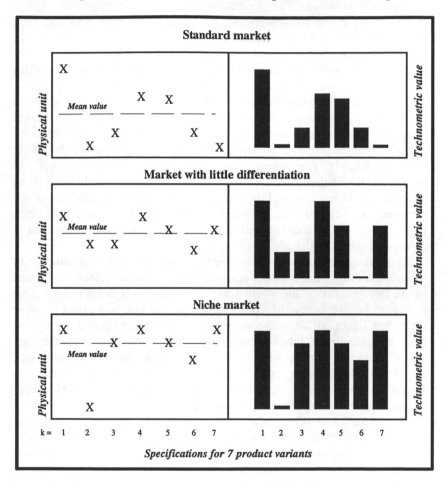

*Figure 8.5: Sketch of technometric benchmarking concept*

characteristics will be like. We need another instrument of analysis of product innovation quality – one known as technometrics.

We have the following starting point. A product is described by its characteristics. Consumers do not buy 'products', rather they purchase a combination of characteristics or attributes, that satisfy their wants and needs. For example, a laser is descibed by wavelength, power, stability, and so on. In general, experts know which are the important characteristics. But the problem is, each characteristic has a different unit of measurement. So it is not a vector – you cannot derive a comparable measure. The technometric concept converts it into a metric scale, a dimensionless one, all features between zero and one, which enables us to build a profile that can be compared one to another, one attribute to another, one product to another.[16]

Figure 8.5 provides a graphical illustration of technometric profiles for seven different products, and three different possible patterns. Technometric benchmarking makes it possible to construct a detailed profile of the product, comparing one characteristic only across products. One can also look at the entire profile of a single product, across *all* characteristics, without weights – simply draw all the [0, 1] values. Only if you want a one-dimensional scalar number, to aggregate the technometric scores, does one need weights for each product attribute. The weights are, of course, representative of the preferences of customers. They can be determined by market surveys, focus groups, or, at times, by eliciting the opinions of those engaged in direct marketing of the product.

Figure 8.6 provides a profile of product quality for laser diodes, of millimetre range, for telecom applications in optical fibres, presented in the following way: the world state-of-the-art level is set to one. This changes over the course of time, but is equal to one at a given point in time. For Japan, all Japanese manufacturers are aggregated, as if they were a single firm ('Japan Incorporated'). In some attributes, they are world class, in others, well below it. In laser power, at least one Japanese manufacturer offers world-class quality. In others, no Japanese manufacturer attains world-class sophistication. This holds for all Japanese companies taken together.

The broken line portrays a specific company, Company A. It has products, laser diodes, on a world level, in part, and below world level, in part. One can see precisely strengths and weaknesses at one glance. So this, of course, is the adequate 'zoom' for benchmarking Company A against Japanese competitors. This is a typical application of technometrics for benchmarking the products of company A for the domestic Japanese competition. Of course, in such a case, Company A can search for a remedy for this situation, if it indicates weaknesses –

by looking abroad, for those who have a technological solution. In other cases, one can search for a strategic partner in Japan.

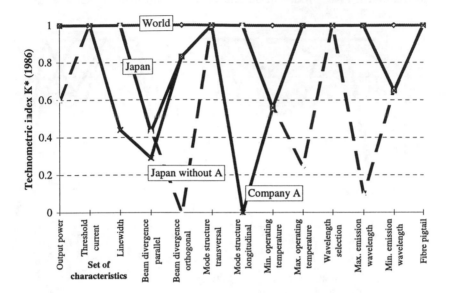

*Figure 8.6:   Example for product quality measurement for single products and domestic market aggregation: laser diodes in the μm range for optical communications*

At times, we want to have an international comparison. Figure 8.7 shows a technometric comparison of laser diodes in the micrometre range, not suitable for optical communication. There is Company A, German, and a line for Germany without Company A, and the world class – the present profile of all Japanese and all US companies. Company A will learn from this, whether there are German competitors better than itself, and whether there is expectation that one can find a partner for a strategic alliance in Germany – and if not, to which other country might one look. This is exceedingly useful for strategic innovation.

For an overall measure of product quality index, one-dimensional, we can do this only if we have preferences of customers, showing what weights they give each single characteristics. There are several methods. You can ask people, a sample of them, how they would value single characteristics. You can devise this from prices – the method of hedonic price indexes – by seeing the statistical link between product prices and their attributes, with coefficients of attributes indicating the importance of those attributes. Such information is presently not available for laser diodes in optical communications.

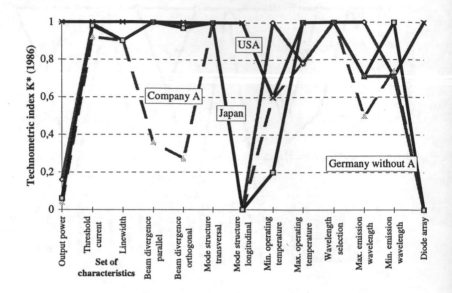

*Figure 8.7:   Example of product quality measurement for single company products and international comparison: laser diodes in the µm range*

## 8.5   A TYPOLOGY OF STRATEGIC FOCUS

One can construct a kind of typology of companies and their technological strengths or weaknesses, building on the technometric profiles. There are four basic types of firms (see Figure 8.8):

- uncompetitive;
- unfocused;
- focused;
- dominant.

One sees this by mapping firms' products in two-dimensional space, with the X axis indicating, for each attribute of a product, its technometric score (from zero to one), and the Y axis indicating, for each attribute, the weight or importance of that product in the eyes of its consumers. In other words, a product with 10 key attributes will be characterized by 10 pairs of numbers. The first number in each pair, the X value, represents the attribute's objective, technometric score, and the second number, the Y value, indicates the subjective consumer preference weight.

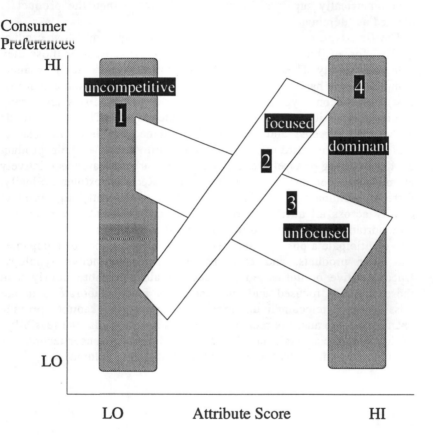

Consumer
Preferences

*Figure 8.8: Typology of firms*

The way those 10 points cluster establishes a firm's competitive position. If the firm's product is consistently weak relative to its competitors, it is 'uncompetitive'. This is shown by an essentially vertical line rising from 'LO' product quality. Its market success is highly dubious. If the firm's products are technometrically strong for attributes consumers rate as unimportant, and vice-versa – technometrically weak for attributes consumers rate as important, then the firm's product is unfocused, or rather misfocused. Its market share is unlikely to be high or growing.

If the firm's products are strong for attributes consumers rate highly, but weak for attributes consumers think unimportant – the product is focused, and market share will be strong. Finally, if the product is technometrically superior for all its attributes – then the product is defined as 'dominant'.

The first type of firm, 'uncompetitive', has uniformly low product quality, for attributes consumer value highly as well as for those they value less highly. These firms are uncompetitive, unless their products compete on the basis of very low price (and hence, are produced at low cost). The second type of firm is 'focused'. These firms are strong precisely in attributes that the market values highly. Their R&D tends to be well directed and strategically planned in line with market preferences. The third type of firm is 'unfocused' – their product quality is strong precisely for attributes the market regards as relatively unimportant, perhaps as a result of poor R&D investment. Finally, there are dominant firms. These firms have consistently high product quality across all attributes, both relatively important and relatively unimportant ones. They tend to dominate their markets.

We anticipate a positive link between the performance of companies and their products, and their placement in the above typology. Uncompetitive or unfocused products should fare more poorly than those that are focused and dominant. As more elaborate data are missing for telecommunications, we presently cannot provide examples. Such analysis remains on the research agenda; the feasibility of this strategic analysis has already been shown for sensor technology (Grupp and Maital, 1998; see also Chapter 4 in this volume).

## NOTES

1   This Chapter was published in a preliminary version as a working paper WP# No. 153–96 of the International Center for Research on the Management of Technology, Sloan School of Management, MIT, Cambridge, MA, 1996.
2   The concept dates back to c. 1979.
3   A rich bibliography on patent analysis is included in this source.
4   Data sources for patent statistics for (consolidated) company affiliations are Schmoch and Schnöring (1994) and lengthier German data annexes cited therein (from 1992). Communications equipment revenues are from *Communications Week International*, pp. 16–17, November 1995.
5   Source: Schmoch (1996).

6    Source as in footnote to Figure 8.1. The European coverage is most frequently
achieved via European patent application. Patenting in one European Union
country does not automatically confer a patent in all other countries of the
European Union, as is sometimes mistakenly believed, since the European Patent
Office (EPO) has come into being in 1978. But it works as follows: you send in
your invention to the EPO. You specify for which member countries you seek
patent protection. They make a joint examination, which is costly (compared to a
single national examination — say five times as much), but once done and when
successful, it is handed over to the national patent offices, and without further
investigation, it is accepted. If you choose this route, then count this document in
a multiple way, for all designated countries. What you save, as a company or
patent applicant, is simply the examination procedure, time and translators and
attorneys' fees. But ultimately the *national countries* grant or decline the patent
protection in their own country. This is a clear disctinction to the so-called
International Patent which has to be transferred from the international to the
national stage whereby costs accrue in each transferred system. Note that the
EPO member states are not synonymous with the European Union. They include
Switzerland, Liechtenstein and Norway — some 18 member states are involved
presently, in contrast with 15 for the EU members.
7    Source: Schmoch and Schnöring (1994).
8    This is justified as the NTT labs develop IT technology in collaboration with
Japanese manufacturers which is patent-protected by NTT; see Grupp (1993).
9    Source: Schmoch (1995).
10   Source as in footnote of Figure 8.2. Network operators underlined.
11   Compare the national R&D infrastructures in Grupp (1993, loc. cit.).
12   Summarized in Griliches (1995).
13   See, for example, Grupp (1997a) or Grupp et al. (1992b).
14   Using OECD's implicit GDP price indices.
15   The growing importance of acquiring technology from outside sources is
undeniable; see, for example, the benchmarking study by Roberts (1994).
16   Earlier concepts of technometrics, such as Grupp (1995) or Frenkel et al.
(1994b), were not turned to benchmarking. The technometric procedure in
benchmarking is best described in Grupp (1998, Chapter 11).

# 9 Relation between Scientific and Technological Excellence and Export Performance: Evidence for EU Countries[1]

**Main Ideas in this Chapter**

A two-stage model of innovation is presented, in which: (1) economic inputs (such as R&D spending) generate science and technology outputs (such as publications, citations, and patents), and (2) these science and technology outputs in turn serve as inputs, that generate knowledge-based exports. An integrated system of science and technology indicators, built on a 'stages' model of the innovation process is used as the basis for testing the model for 12 European Community countries, through statistical regression. It is shown that a systematic empirical relationship exists between inputs and outputs, for both Stage 1 and Stage 2. The structure of our Chapter is as follows. The first Section presents a 'stages' model of innovation, together with an operational, integrated network of indicators that serve to quantify each stage. In the next Section, we construct a two-stage model of comparative advantage, in which two types of efficiency are defined: Stage 1, *efficiency in translating R&D resources into technological and scientific output,* and Stage 2, *efficiency in translating scientific output into export sales of R&D-intensive products.* In Section 9.3, we define and describe our data set. Section 9.4 presents our regression results, and in Section 9.5, we conclude and summarize, and list some policy implications of our findings.

## 9.1    A 'STAGES' MODEL OF INNOVATION

The purpose of this Chapter is to utilize quantitative indicators of scientific and technology performance to examine empirically the link between scientific and technological (S&T) excellence and export performance, for 12 European Union (EU) countries. Specifically, we propose to analyse (a) whether, among these countries, investment of resources in applied and basic research – as measured by spending on research and development (R&D) – is related empirically to technological and scientific 'output', and (b) whether scientific 'output' is empirically related to generation of exports. But how to specify input and output indicators?

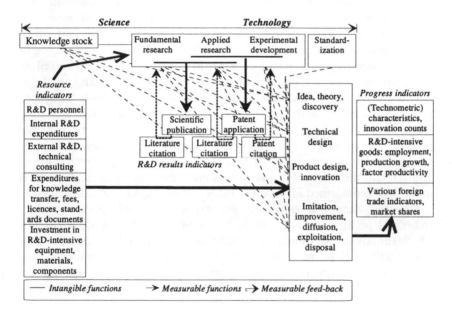

*Figure 9.1:   Stages of research, development and innovation, and corresponding science and technology indicators*

Grupp et al. (1992a)[2] have constructed a 'stages' model of the innovation process, in which six different phases or functions are defined: theory and model development, technical realization, industrial development, innovation and imitation, diffusion, and finally utilization. The model is accompanied by a comprehensive, operational set of indicators that quantify each stage and enable researchers to examine its relation with succeeding and preceding stages (see Figure 9.1 which corresponds to Figure 6.1 in Chapter 6). While, as is noted there, '... the well-known approach by indicators ... grasps only parts of the complex and cyclical (feedback) innovation-oriented processes', nonetheless, such indicators 'offer an opportunity to speak a common language in science and innovation research.'

The model takes a somewhat 'economic' perspective, in the sense that each of the stages is characterized by 'inputs' and 'outputs'. The model is highly recursive, or 'feedback', in nature, because the outputs of one stage become the inputs of succeeding stages.

The initial stage, theory and model development uses R&D spending as its inputs or resources, and generates scientific outputs: publications, and citations of publications. The field of scientometrics – the quantitative measurement of scientific output – is by now well developed, and comprehensive databases of publications and citations, by subfield, are now widely accessible. The second and third stages of the innovation process build on scientific expertise, as expressed in publications and citations, to generate patent applications and stocks of patents. Here, too, data are widely available for a wide range of products, services and processes.[3] At the innovation and imitation stage, technology – as expressed in patents – is used to generate products, processes and services, whose quality or level of sophistication can be measured by the 'technometric' approach (Grupp, 1990a). In the technological diffusion stage, product and process quality is transformed into export sales and global market share.

Detailed data are available on exports, according to standard industrial product classifications, by country of origin and by country of destination. It should be emphasized that this model is not necessarily linear or rigidly sequential; for some products and processes, some stages may be skipped, while for others, the precise sequence may differ from that in Figure 9.1 (for instance, patents may precede publications and citations).[4]

Since each stage of the innovation process is characterized by empirical indicators, the 'integrated network model' is an operational one; using it, it is possible to test hypotheses and to conduct cross-country comparisons.

The focus of this Chapter is on the extent to which inputs are used efficiently to generate outputs. In order to examine this important issue, it is first necessary to model the process through which nations acquire comparative advantage in high-technology products, and then utilize that comparative advantage in achieving high levels of exports and export market share. This is the task of the next Section.

## 9.2 A TWO-STAGE MODEL OF COMPARATIVE ADVANTAGE

A nation's export value added can be partitioned according to the sources of that value added: research and development – value added accruing from R&D spending, leading to goods and services that perform well in global markets; production of those goods and services, at minimum cost and maximum quality; and marketing and distribution. This is the so-called 'value-added chain', used effectively by Porter (1980).

It is possible to model the innovation process as a two-stage one. In the first stage, economic resources – physical and financial capital, and skilled manpower – expressed as research and development spending are invested, in order to generate scientific and technological outputs (publications, citations, patents, and so on). In the second stage, the scientific and technological outputs become inputs, that generate new products and processes, of which some are exported.

Presumably, comparative advantage in high-technology products (where science and technology play important roles) can arise either from excellence in generating scientific outputs (Stage 1), or from excellence in utilizing scientific outputs, or both.

**Stage 1**

Let X be a vector of variables $x_1$, $x_2$, ..., $1$ $x_n$, measuring the magnitude of resources invested in R&D, and let Y be a vector of variables $y_1$, $y_2$, ..., $y_n$, measuring the resulting scientific and technological outputs (citations, publications, patents, and so on). Then there exists a 'production function' F( ), that maps from R&D inputs X to scientific output Y:

$$Y = F(X) \qquad (9.1)$$

This production function can be subjected to the same types of economic analyses as conventional production functions that map from, say, labour and capital, into value added. In particular, the efficiency of translating R&D resources into scientific outputs can be measured. Grupp et al. (1992b), for example, adopt a linear programming approach to measuring efficiency in transforming scientific excellence into exports. Or, alternately, using regression analysis, the empirical relation of Y and X can be examined, and individual countries' performance compared with the trend line – an approach that we take here.

Equation (9.1) is a measure of Stage 1 efficiency – the degree to which resources invested in research are efficiently utilized to achieve scientific excellence.

**Stage 2**

The second stage in the export process involves the translation of scientific excellence into R&D-intensive, goods and services that capture export sales. This stage encompasses the production, marketing and distribution components of the value-added chain.

Let $Z$ be a measure of export performance, and $Y$ be, as above, the measure of scientific excellence. Then a production function $G(Y)$ exists that maps from scientific excellence to export performance:

$$Z = G(Y) \qquad\qquad (9.2)$$

As with $F(X)$, $G(Y)$ can also be analysed empirically, and used for comparing various countries with one another.

Availability of adequate data for $X$, $Y$ and $Z$ makes it possible to study Stages 1 and 2 efficiency for a sample of countries. Such analysis makes it possible to partition causes of superior or inferior export performance between Stages 1 and 2, and as a result, to construct policies for stimulating exports that attack the root of the problem.

We propose to test this hypothesis, using data for $X$, $Y$ and $Z$ for 12 EU countries. Before presenting our empirical results, we first describe the extensive data set itself.

## 9.3   SCIENTOMETRIC AND ECONOMIC INDICATORS

The variables used in this study are listed below, together with a description of their nature and their sources. For our purposes, 'high-technology' products are defined as those with R&D spending equal to or greater than 3.5 per cent of sales. A complete list of product groups that meet this criterion, according to the three-digit SITC code, is given in Appendix 9.2.

## 'X' variables

For our measure of R&D inputs, we simply used gross spending on research and development, expressed as a fraction of GDP data were all converted to US dollars using purchasing power parity indexes, that measure the buying power of currencies rather than existing market exchange rates.

**GERD:** gross R&D spending, annual average for 1981–85; converted to US dollars using purchasing power parity index of OECD; $ billion. Source: OECD, S&T indicators.
**GDP 81/85:** gross domestic product, average for 1981–85, $ billion, converted to US dollars using purchasing power parity index as for variable 1.
**GERD/GDP:** ratio of GERD to GDP, as per cent.

## 'Y' variables

For our measures of scientific excellence, we used indicators in three different areas: patents, citations, and publications.

### Patent indicators

For patents, we measured the number of patents granted, for the 12 EU countries, at the US Patent and Trademark Office (USPTO), as a measure of a country's aggressiveness in seeking global protection for its intellectual property. We computed the sum total of patents invented in 1977–86, as an expression of cumulative patent activity, at the USPTO, and expressed them as a fraction of GDP for each country?[5]

These indicators are based on the number of patents registered by the 12 European countries, in the US Patent and Trademark Office (USPTO). They express the willingness and desire of each country to defend their intellectual property, in proportion to GDP.

**PAT:** number of patents, matched to product groups, USPTO, 1984–86.
**PAT/GDP:** PAT, as a ratio to GDP.
**PATPOT:** cumulative number of patents, USPTO, 1977–86.
**PATPOT/GDP:** PATPOT as a fraction of GDP.

## Publications and citations

These indicators measure, for each country, the number of scientific publications by scholars who cite that country as their primary address in their publications, as listed by the databases of the Institute for Scientific Information (ISI), in Philadelphia, PA. The publications are for articles in scientific and engineering journals. Citations are similarly drawn from the ISI databases.

For publications, we used the listings of the Science Citation Index, for engineering and science journals separately, and then added the two. We also expressed this indicator as a fraction of GDP.

For citations, we used similar listings from the Science Citation Index, also divided between engineering and scientific periodicals and then summed, and also expressed as a fraction of GDP.

**PUBSCIENG:** number of publications in both scientific and engineering publications (not including Life Science publications), 1981–85.
**PUBSCIENG/GDP:** PUBSCIENG as a fraction of GDP.
**CITSCIENG:** number of citations in both scientific and engineering periodicals, 1981–85.
**CITSCIENG/GDP:** CITSCIENG as a fraction of GDP.

## 'Z' variable

**RCA**: revealed comparative advantage, for product groups; 1988, defined as:

$$RCA = 100 \{ (ES^2 - 1)/(ES^2 + 1) \},$$

where export share $\quad ES = \dfrac{EX/IM}{EXTOT/IMTOT}$

EX is a country's total exports of high-tech products, IM is that country's imports of such products, **EXTOT** is the country's total exports of manufactures, and **IMTOT** is the country's total imports of manufactures.[6]

The data based on trade figures were derived from Legler et al. (1992). It is important to note that high-tech exports are compared to total exports (and imports) of *manufactured goods* only. The trade variables therefore serve as a measure of the extent to which trade in *manufactured products* is high-tech (see Grupp, 1995, and Legler et al., 1992.) The data themselves are given in Appendix 9.1.


## 9.4   EMPIRICAL RESULTS

Regression equation estimates for the Stages 1 and 2 models are shown in Table 9.1. For purposes of this analysis, we chose to combine the 'leading-edge' (goods for which R&D spending equals 8 per cent or more of sales) and 'high-level' products (between 3.5 per cent and 8 per cent). Disaggregation does not substantively alter our conclusions. In general, the level of government intervention in leading-edge products is much greater, and hence exports of such products are less influenced by pure market forces.[7]

*Table 9.1:*  *Scientific and technological output indicators as a function of gross R&D spending/GDP (independent variable: gross R&D spending as percentage of GDP). Regression equations for 'Stage 1' model: 12 European countries*

| Dependent variable | Intercept | Coefficient of independent variable (GERD/GDP) | $R^2$ adj. | P | N |
|---|---|---|---|---|---|
| PUBSCIENG/GDP | 21.15 (5.18) | 29.02 | 0.75 | .0003 | 11 |
| CITSCIENG/GDP | 16.42 (21.82) | 115.34 | 0.73 | .0005 | 11 |
| PATH/GDP | −1.68 (0.85) | 5.07 | 0.78 | .0002 | 11 |
| PATPOT/GDP | −7.28 (2.97) | 18.59 | 0.79 | .0001 | 11 |

*Note:* * Standard error of slope coefficient in brackets.


**Stage 1: Translating R&D into scientific excellence**

Figures 9.2, 9.3, 9.4 and 9.5 show the relation between four measures of scientific output – publications, citations, patents, and cumulated patents – expressed as a fraction of GDP, and gross R&D spending, also as a fraction of GDP, for 12 European countries. The European countries chosen are: Germany, France, UK, Netherlands, Belgium/Luxemburg, Denmark, Ireland, Spain, Italy, Greece, Portugal. For each figure, the regression line for the 'Y' (dependent) variable regressed on the 'X' (independent) variable is shown.

The UK lies above the 12-country trend line both for publications and for citations, suggesting considerable Stage 1 efficiency in that country in generating scientific outputs from R&D resources, while Germany lies somewhat below the trend line (see Figures 9.2 and 9.3). It is possible that the ISI database used for publications and citations, which comprises mainly English-language periodicals, biases the results in favour of English-speaking nations (like the UK). However other studies suggest that irregardless of this bias, the UK does achieve a very high level of publications and citations, relative to other countries.

The slope of the two regression lines can be interpreted as:

$$\underline{d(PUBSCIENG/GDP)} \quad \text{and} \quad \underline{d(CITSCIENG/GDP)}$$
$$d(GERD/GDP) \qquad\qquad\qquad d(GERD/GDP)$$

meaning, the increase in publications and citations, respectively, normalized by GDP, for a 1 per cent increase in R&D spending (as a percentage of GDP). The respective slopes are, approximately, 30 and 115.

A different picture emerges for patents. Here, Germany lies well above the trend line, both for patents per GDP and for cumulative patents per GDP (see Figures 9.4 and 9.5). This suggests that German firms in large part follow an aggressive patenting policy at the US Patent Office to a greater extent than that practised by firms in other European countries.

Apart from the German 'outlier', the regression-line fit between R&D spending (as a per cent of GDP) and patents/GDP is a relatively close fit for the 12 EU countries. Here again, the slope of the regression line is a measure of the incremental rise in patents/GDP for a one percentage point increase in R&D spending/GDP.

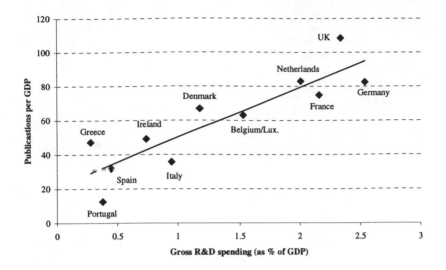

*Figure 9.2: Publications in science and engineering per GDP as a function of gross R&D spending (as per cent of GDP 1981–85) in 12 EU countries*

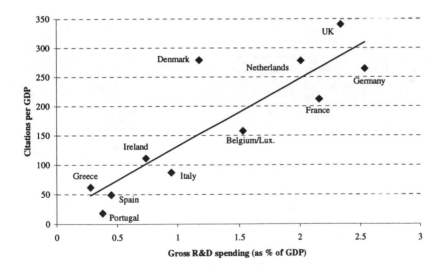

*Figure 9.3: Citations in science and engineering per GDP, as a function of gross R&D spending (as per cent of GDP 1981–85) in 12 EU countries*

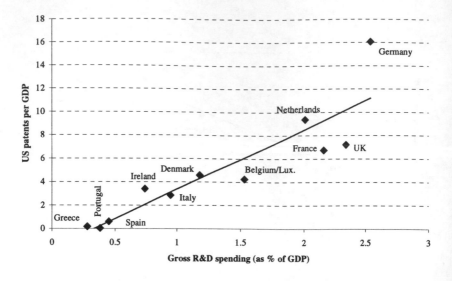

*Figure 9.4:* Patents per GDP (at USPTO 1984–86) as a function of
gross R&D spending (as per cent of GDP 1981–85) in
12 EU countries

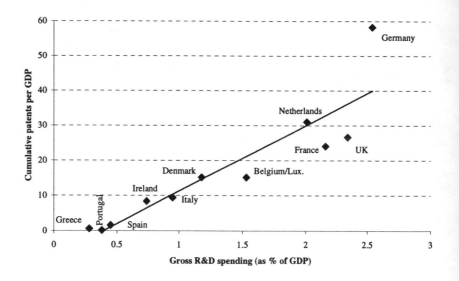

*Figure 9.5:* Cumulative patents per GDP (at USPTO 1977–86) as a
function of gross R&D spending (as per cent of GDP
1981–85) in 12 EU countries

Stage 1b: Translating publications into patents: Our empirical analysis suggested to us that Stage 1 – transforming R&D resources into scientific and technological 'intellectual property' – is really comprised of two substages: (1a) use of R&D resources to generate research results, expressed as publications and citations; and (1b) use of scientific and technological knowledge (which find expression in publications and citations) in order to generate patentable inventions.

To test this hypothesis, we computed two additional statistical regression lines, in which patents/GDP was the dependent variable, and citations/GDP and publications/GDP each served as the independent variables, respectively. The results are shown below in Table 9.2, and in Figures 9.6 and 9.7.

*Table 9.2:*   *Regression equations for stage '1b' PAT/GDP as a function of CITSCIENG/GDP and PUBSCIENG/GDP in 12 European countries*

| Dependent variable | Intercept | Slope | $R^2$ adj. | P | N |
|---|---|---|---|---|---|
| CITSCIENG/GDP | 0.76223 | 0.21577 | 0.534 | 0.0064 | 11 |
| PUBSCIENG/GDP | 0.74245 | 0.22330 | 0.501 | 0.0089 | 11 |

The results clearly indicate (a) that there is a strong trend line between patents/GDP and citations and publications; and that the two major outliers in the data are Germany, which lies well above the trend line in terms of its energetic patenting activity, and the UK, which lies well below the trend line in its patenting activity. The UK's weak patenting performance may explain in part the relative weakness of the UK's performance in knowledge-based exports, relative to its comparatively strong scientific and technological achievements.

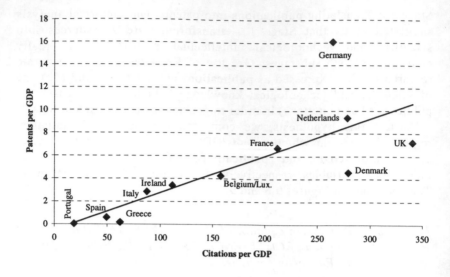

*Figure 9.6:   Patents per GDP (at USPTO 1984–86) as a function of citations in science & engineering per GDP 1981–85 in 12 EU countries*

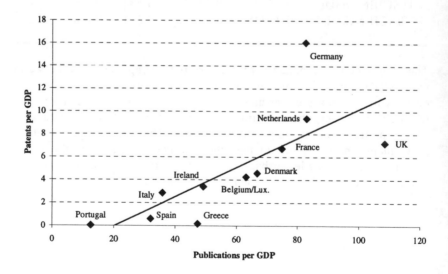

*Figure 9.7:   Patents per GDP (at USPTO 1984–86) as a function of publications in science & engineering per GDP 1981–85 in 12 EU countries*

## Stage 2

Translating scientific excellence into export sales, Figures 9.8 and 9.9 and Table 9.3 show the statistical regression lines for the Stage 2 equation, which expresses relative comparative advantage (RCA) as a function of patents and cumulative patents. Here too, the statistical fit is relatively good, confirming the close empirical link between knowledge-based export performance, in terms of an index of world market share, and patent performance.

The goodness of the regression fit is diminished because of the inclusion of Portugal and Greece. These two countries have very little patenting activity at the USPTO and are not yet really players in the global knowledge-based export market. Excluding these countries would substantially increase the value of the multiple correlation coefficient.

For Germany, success in translation of patenting activity into exporting success is not impressive. While the distance between the point signifying Germany, and the 12-country trend line, is not significantly different from zero, nonetheless Figures 9.8 and 9.9 do indicate that resources invested in Germany in activities related to patenting may not be used with full efficiency.

*Table 9.3:   Regression equation for Stage 2: revealed comparative advantage as a function of scientific inputs (dependent variable: RCA)*

| Dependent variable | Intercept | Slope* | $R^2$ adj. | P | N |
|---|---|---|---|---|---|
| PAT/GDP | −43.72 (1.75) | 5.43 | 0.46 | 0.0126 | 11 |
| PATPOT/GDP | −41.58 (0.49) | 1.45 | 0.43 | 0.0166 | 11 |

*Note:* * Standard error of slope coefficients in brackets.

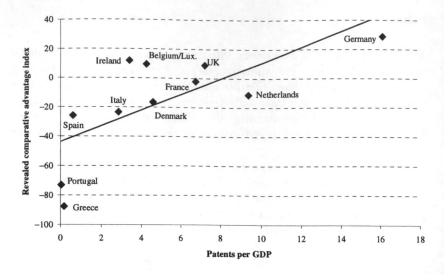

*Figure 9.8:   Revealed comparative advantage index 1988 as a function
             of patents per GDP (at USPTO 1984–86) in 12 EU
             countries*

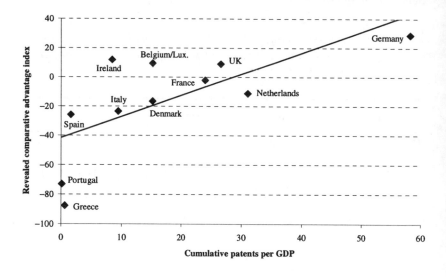

*Figure 9.9:   Revealed comparative advantage index 1988 as a function
             of cumulative patents per GDP (at USPTO 1977–86) in
             12 EU countries*

# 9.5   CONCLUSION AND IMPLICATIONS

Our empirical results have confirmed the posited link between inputs and outputs, in both stages of our two-stage innovation model: (a) between R&D resources and scientific outputs, and (b) between scientific outputs and export performance, among 12 EU countries. The Stage 1 link between R&D resources and scientific and technological outputs (publications and citations) is much stronger, in terms of the least-squares fit, than the Stage 2 link between scientific and technological output and export performance. The model's performance is somewhat improved by introducing an intermediate stage, in which patents are expressed as a function of citations and publications.

In general, the results confirm our basic hypothesis presented at the start of this Chapter that international commercial success in high-technology products exports is basically supported by R&D spending as a fraction of GDP, and by the resulting outputs of scientific and technical knowledge and patents.

One straightforward policy implication is this: there is no free lunch. Achieving larger export shares in knowledge-based products requires investment of substantial resources in research and development. At the same time, there is still considerable variation among countries in the efficiency with which they exploit scientific and technological excellence. The UK is a case in point – that country's sizeable output of publications and citations is rather inefficiently converted into high-tech exports and market share, compared to other EU countries. While the reasons for this are not clear, they may be related to passive patenting policy abroad and insufficient skill and investment in marketing.

## APPENDIX 9.1

*Table 9A.1: Data*

| STATE | GERD 81–85 | GDP 81–85 | GERD/ GDP % | PUB-SCIENG 81–85 | PUB-SCIENG/ GDP | CIT-SCIENG 81–85 | CIT-SCIENG/ GDP | PAT 84–86 | PAT/ GDP 84–86 | PAT-POT 77–86 | PAT-POT/ GDP 77–86 | PAT-RCA 1988 |
|---|---|---|---|---|---|---|---|---|---|---|---|---|
| Germany | 16.66 | 655.91 | 2.54 | 54169 | 82.59 | 173437 | 264.42 | 12461 | 16.07 | 38205 | 58.25 | 28.76 |
| France | 12.48 | 576.70 | 2.16 | 43190 | 74.89 | 122344 | 212.14 | 4370 | 6.74 | 13871 | 24.05 | –2.10 |
| UK | 12.69 | 542.17 | 2.34 | 58774 | 108.41 | 184502 | 340.30 | 4472 | 7.21 | 14443 | 26.64 | 9.07 |
| The Netherlands | 2.98 | 147.97 | 2.01 | 12276 | 82.98 | 41167 | 278.21 | 1527 | 9.37 | 4595 | 31.05 | –11.22 |
| Belgium/ Luxemb. | 1.49 | 97.48 | 1.53 | 6151 | 63.10 | 15363 | 157.60 | 461 | 4.25 | 1480 | 15.18 | 9.47 |
| Denmark | 0.65 | 55.23 | 1.18 | 3690 | 66.81 | 15418 | 279.16 | 288 | 4.58 | 838 | 15.17 | –16.55 |
| Ireland | 0.16 | 21.57 | 0.74 | 1060 | 49.14 | 2401 | 111.31 | 83 | 3.40 | 181 | 8.39 | 11.84 |
| Spain | 1.15 | 257.83 | 0.45 | 8215 | 31.86 | 12748 | 49.44 | 181 | 0.61 | 413 | 1.60 | –25.80 |
| Italy | 5.28 | 555.79 | 0.95 | 19845 | 35.71 | 48420 | 87.12 | 1777 | 2.85 | 5235 | 9.42 | –23.46 |
| Greece | 0.15 | 53.93 | 0.28 | 2550 | 47.28 | 3345 | 62.02 | 11 | 0.18 | 33 | 0.61 | –87.57 |
| Portugal | 0.19 | 49.64 | 0.38 | 622 | 12.53 | 923 | 18.59 | 2 | 0.04 | 7 | 0.14 | –73.06 |

# APPENDIX 9.2

*Table 9A.2:   List of R&D-intensive products*

| No. | SITC III | Product group (non-official terms) | R&D Intensity |
|-----|----------|-------------------------------------|---------------|
| 1   | 516      | Advanced organic chemicals          |               |
| 2   | 525      | Radioactive materials               |               |
| 3   | 541      | Pharmaceutical products             |               |
| 4   | 575      | Advanced plastics                   |               |
| 5   | 591      | Agricultural chemicals              |               |
| 6   | 714      | Turbines and reaction engines       |               |
| 7   | 718      | Nuclear, water, wind power generators |             |
| 8   | 752      | Automatic data processing machines  | Leading-      |
| 9   | 764      | Telecommunications equipment        | edge goods    |
| 10  | 774      | Medical electronics                 |               |
| 11  | 776      | Semiconductor devices               |               |
| 12  | 778      | Advanced electrical machinery       |               |
| 13  | 792      | Aircraft and spacecraft             |               |
| 14  | 871      | Advanced optical instruments        |               |
| 15  | 874      | Advanced measuring instruments      |               |
| 16  | 891      | Arms and ammunition                 |               |
|     |          |                                     |               |
| 17  | 266      | Synthetic fibres                    |               |
| 18  | 277      | Advanced industrial abrasives       |               |
| 19  | 515      | Heterocyclic chemistry              |               |
| 20  | 522      | Rare inorganic chemicals            |               |
| 21  | 524      | Other precious chemicals            |               |
| 22  | 531      | Synthetic colouring matter          |               |
| 23  | 533      | Pigments, paints, varnishes         |               |
| 24  | 542      | Medicaments                         |               |
| 25  | 551      | Essential oils, perfume, flavour    |               |
| 26  | 574      | Polyethers and resins               |               |
| 27  | 598      | Advanced chemical products          | High-level    |
| 28  | 663      | Mineral manufactures, fine ceramics | products      |
| 29  | 689      | Precious non-ferrous base metals    |               |
| 30  | 724      | Textile and leather machinery       |               |
| 31  | 725      | Paper and pulp machinery            |               |
| 32  | 726      | Printing and bookbinding machinery  |               |
| 33  | 727      | Industrial food-processing machines |               |

*Table 9A.2 continued*

| No. | SITC III | Product group (non-official terms) | R&D Intensity |
|-----|----------|-----------------------------------|---------------|
| 34 | 728 | Advanced machine-tools | |
| 35 | 731 | Machine-tools working by removing | |
| 36 | 733 | Machine-tools without removing | |
| 37 | 735 | Parts for machine-tools | |
| 38 | 737 | Advanced metalworking equipment | |
| 39 | 741 | Industrial heating and cooling goods | |
| 40 | 744 | Mechanical handling equipment | |
| 41 | 745 | Other non-electrical machinery | |
| 42 | 746 | Ball and roller bearings | |
| 43 | 751 | Office machines, word-processing | |
| 44 | 759 | Advanced parts: for computers | |
| 45 | 761 | Television and video equipment | |
| 46 | 762 | Radio-broadcast, radiotelephony goods | |
| 47 | 763 | Sound and video recorders | |
| 48 | 772 | Traditional electronics | High-level |
| 49 | 773 | Optical fibre and other cables | products |
| 50 | 781 | Motor vehicles for persons | |
| 51 | 782 | Motor vehicles for good transport | |
| 52 | 791 | Railway vehicles | |
| 53 | 872 | Medical instruments and appliances | |
| 54 | 873 | Traditional measuring equipment | |
| 55 | 881 | Photographic apparatus and equipment | |
| 56 | 882 | Photo- and cinematographic supplies | |
| 57 | 883 | Optical fibres, contact, other lenses | |

# NOTES

1   An earlier version of this Chapter, co-authored with A. Frenkel and K. Koschatzky, was published in *Science and Public Policy* 21(3), pp. 138–146, 1994.
2   Reprinted in Chapter 10 in this volume.
3   A large literature exists on the theme of productivity and efficiency in R&D activities, addressing the question, how well are R&D inputs converted into R&D outputs? Many of these studies are 'micro' in nature; see for instance Brown and Svenson (1988), Mandakovic and Souder (1987), Roll and Rosenblatt (1983), Sardana and Vrat (1989), Stahl and Steger (1977), Schainblatt (1982), Szakonyi

(1985), and Thor (1991). Our approach is aggregative and 'macro' in nature, with nation-states as our individual units.

4     '... scientific, technological and economic progress are certainly not linked in a sequential manner ... . Linear models are not at all applicable. To cope with this more general situation in science and innovation the authors ... developed cyclic or coupled models of science and innovation phases.' (Grupp et al., 1992a, p. 8). These authors go on to discuss why science, technology and innovation are often highly non-linear 'In reality improving and diffusing products and processes is seldom if ever a simple task or a replication by unimaginative imitators. From utilization of diffused innovations, that is their consumption and disposal, incentives for new research and more innovation may be triggered off at least in terms of the cyclic model suggested here. The push on science and technology from environmental problems may serve as a good example' (ibid, p. 9).

3     This variable measures not only patent activity in the US, but also the degree of willingness of firms and inventors to apply for patents at the United States Patent Office. For many reasons, the eagerness to patent inventions in the U.S. is not identical across all countries. Hence, this variable reflects not only some measure of R&D output, but also the extent to which firms and inventors are prepared to create a 'footprint' of this output in the form of patents.

6     The RCA (revealed comparative advantage) answers two questions simultaneously: (a) Do the domestic suppliers of high technology products have a solid footing in the international market compared with foreign competitors and suppliers of other domestic sectors? And (b) Do they succeed in substituting domestic production for high-technology imports, compared with suppliers in other sectors?

7     '... there are two hemispheres in the world of R&D intensity. One (the high-level consumer products with expectations of a relatively good turnover per R&D investment), in which technical performance by patents does play a role and is a decisive factor for international competitiveness alongside with R&D activities by industry. Scientific achievements are not so important here. The other hemisphere (the leading-edge technologies with moderate expectations in turnover per R&D investment) in which factors other than technology guarantee international success, is characterized by stronger government intervention both on the side of R&D and also in terms of procurement and regulation. Here, scientific excellence is indispensable' Grupp (1995). Grupp adds: 'Business-financed R&D governs the high-level commodities and thus all high technologies, whereas international success in leading edge products must be nurtured from somewhere else. ... the financial means of governments poured into the business R&D system largely explains where the position of a country in leading-edge products is. ... Governments in EU countries are the drafthorses in very R&D intensive fields and provide financial means for the pioneering of possibly less effective new leading-edge technologies.'

# 10 Linking Technological Excellence and Export Sales in Israel and the European Union: A Data Envelopment Approach[1]

**Main Ideas in this Chapter**

This Chapter addresses the question: how efficiently do countries translate scientific and technological excellence – as expressed in various measures such as patent and bibliometric indices – into export comparative advantage? The use of science and technology in generating exports is first modelled as a two-stage process. A variant of linear programming known as data envelopment analysis (DEA) is then employed to estimate empirically the relative efficiency of Israel and the European Community countries in converting scientific and technological excellence into exports of R&D-intensive products. It is found that Israel, together with Germany, are more efficient than other European nations in the production of scientific and technological outputs, but Israel is far less efficient than EU countries in utilizing its science and technology base of excellence to create high-technology exports. Among the major R&D spenders in Europe, France, Germany and Denmark together form the efficiency frontier in generating comparative advantage from these inputs.

## 10.1 INTRODUCTION

World markets for high value-added products are becoming more and more competitive. In an effort to gain competitive advantage in these markets, many countries invest costly resources, from both private and public sources, in an effort to achieve scientific and technological excellence.

Policymakers face two important questions: (a) how efficiently are the resources invested in science and technology being used, in terms of their 'output' of scientific papers and patents, for example, and in their output of high-quality products and processes? And (b) How efficiently is the scientific and technological excellence embodied in products and processes being translated into export sales and market share?

New indicators have recently been developed for measuring quantitatively each aspect of the feedback innovation, the production of knowledge, basic and applied research, industrial development, and including the innovation process (Grupp, 1991). These indicators can be regarded as 'variables' and lend themselves to the construction of optimizing economic models in which relations among the variables can be empirically estimated. Such models could be a useful guide to policymakers, by showing which innovation sources are efficiently used and which are not.

Linear and non-linear programming immediately suggest themselves as appropriate tools. However, many measures of scientific and technological excellence are non-monetary in nature – they do not represent labour-hours or capital dollars, but rather comparative metrics. This makes conventional programming models unusable.

A version of linear programming exists, however, that was explicitly built to measure the efficiency of 'decision-making units' (which could be countries, or industries, or individual firms), and that does allow qualitative inputs. This approach, devised by Charnes and Cooper in 1978, is known as Data Envelopment Analysis (DEA). Essentially, it examines which 'DMU's (decision-making units) are on their production possibilities frontier, or isoquant and which are not (Charnes et al., 1978, 1981, 1988).

In this Chapter, we propose to construct a two-stage model of the relation between technological excellence and export sales, in which monetary resources are put into relation with scientific and technological measures (such as patents, citations and publications), and then these innovation sources in turn are used to generate comparative advantage in global markets for high-technology products. The model exploits the existence of a correlated network of indicators that provide quantitative measures of innovation dynamics from the earliest to the last stage of the innovation process (Grupp, 1991). As the innovation process is not a linear, that is, not a *sequential*, one (Grupp et al., 1992a), the use of linear programming seems inappropriate. However, as will be discussed in the next Section, the DEA approach does not require explicit modelling of the relation among the variables. Hence, no assumption of a causal or sequential, 'earlier–later' relation is needed. We then illustrate this model with a DEA-based empirical study of this two-stage efficiency, for R&D-intensive products in European Union countries and in Israel: those with R&D expenditures averaging above 3.5 per cent of sales (see Appendix 9.2 in Chapter 9).

## 10.2  A MODEL OF TECHNOLOGY-BASED EXPORTS

Public goods tend to have one or both of two economic characteristics: non-rivalry in supply – consumption of them by one person does not in general leave less of them for someone else – and non-excludability – it is inefficient (because of zero or low marginal costs) and often unfeasible to exclude persons from consuming them. Examples are law and order, roads, public health and defense or national security (Bator, 1958).

In many ways, the link between knowledge, research, industrial development and innovation resembles the production of public goods. Knowledge itself is a kind of public good. In particular, when proprietary knowledge is patented, patent law forces the inventor to disclose the fruits of his or her research to the public (though the use of such knowledge for profit-making purposes is limited).

Rather than consist of a direct link between one set of inputs and another set of final outputs (exports), there is a set of chained functions linking basic inputs to intermediate inputs, to final inputs, and ultimately to final outputs and many feedback relations (Kline, 1991). Applied research may have among its inputs, basic research; industrial development, in turn, has as one of its inputs, applied research. At each stage, outputs from the previous stage become inputs of the current one.[2] On the other hand, utilization of innovative products may stimulate new development (for example, for environmental protection) and industrial development may in turn influence basic academic research. Grupp (1998) has portrayed the knowledge-innovation cycle as shown in Figure 9.1 in the previous Chapter 9, and developed a series of useful quantitative indicators to measure performance at each stage, such as: (1) theory and model development; (2) technical realization; (3) industrial development; (4) innovation and (5) production and export of products (diffusion).

In a series of research papers (Grupp, 1998; Koschatzky, 1991; Grupp and Hohmeyer, 1986, 1988) it was shown how such indicators can be used to measure and compare performance, across countries, for individual products, product groups, sub-industries or even entire industries. The existence of such quantitative indicators makes possible a further advance in the study of industrial policy – the construction of quantitative models to measure the efficiency of R&D resource use aimed at export markets. Such studies are required, because the public-good nature of innovation dynamics does not validate the assumption that competitive markets guarantee full or near-full efficiency. As Bator (1958) showed, provision of public goods is subject to market failure. Lack of competitive markets implies that allocative efficiency through the price mechanism cannot be assumed. Other systems rather than self-regulation and market forces must be employed to attain efficiency. The question then arises, how successful are such systems, in various countries, in attaining efficiency of R&D resource use? To answer this question, we begin by constructing a two-stage model of innovation.

Let X be 'monetary R&D resources', measured perhaps by the aggregate expenditure on R&D. Let Y be 'scientific and technological success variables', measured perhaps by the number of patents, publications and citations. Finally, let Z be a measure of comparative advantage in exports of high-technology products.

**Stage 1: Research and Development Efficiency**

$$Y = F(X) \qquad (10.1)$$

where Y is a vector of variables that measure R&D success, and X is a vector of variables that measure monetary resources devoted to R&D. The function F(X) measures the efficiency in converting resources into excellence in science and technology – efficiency we might term *'Y' efficiency*. We note here that innovation literature (see, for example, Dosi, 1988; Dosi et al., 1990; Grupp, 1990b, 1991; Griliches, 1990; Kline, 1991; van Raan, 1988) has often failed to detect a lag in the relationship between monetary and success variables for R&D that affirm the existence of feedback processes in innovation. Hence all these variables should be considered as partial ones that capture different aspects of innovation-related activities (Martin and Irvine, 1983; Pavitt, 1982). Y efficiency, therefore, highlights special strengths and weaknesses of national systems of innovation (be it on the expenditure, technological or scientific sides) modelled in a steady-state condition in terms of budgets, patents and papers (see Section 10.3).

## Stage 2: Export Efficiency

$$Z = G(Y) \tag{10.2}$$

where Z is a vector of measures of comparative advantage in high-tech exports. The function G(Y) measures the efficiency in translating scientific and technological excellence into exports: 'Z' efficiency.

Presumably, policymakers charged with implementing industrial policy and with wisely investing resources in basic scientific capability, with the objective of competing in global markets, need to know the level of both 'Y' and 'Z' efficiency. It has long been claimed that the US's overall lead in basic science – as exemplified by the pre-eminence of such federally funded laboratories as the National Institutes of Health – is not efficiently translated into new products. This implies high 'Y' efficiency, but because of failings in marketing (and perhaps insulation of Federal labs from industrial companies and consumers), the 'Z' efficiency is very low. This is parallel, for example, to high efficiency in converting police cars and labour hours into police patrols, but low efficiency in transforming police patrols into reductions in crime and high personal security (Bradford et al., 1969).[3]

In the remainder of this Chapter, we model both 'Z' and 'Y' efficiency through data envelopment methods, and apply it illustratively to a comparison of Israel and the major EU countries.

## A Data Envelopment Model

Let 'X' be a vector measuring monetary R&D resources, and 'Y' be a vector of variables reflecting technological excellence, in qualitative units, for a set of decision-making units (in our case, countries).[4]

Efficiency is achieved by attaining the maximum value of scientific or technological success per unit of R&D spending. Hence the problem can be framed as:

$$\text{Max } \theta_o = \sum_{r=1}^{\delta} u_r y_{ro} \Big/ \sum_{i=1}^{m} v_i x_{io} \qquad (10.3)$$

$$\text{s.t.} \sum_{r=1}^{\delta} u_r y_{ro} \Big/ \sum_{i=1}^{m} v_i x_{ij} \leq 1$$

and                         $u_r, v_i \geq 1$

where.

| | | |
|---|---|---|
| y | = | success measures (termed 'output', part of a complex phenomenon, with the reservations made above), |
| x | = | R&D budget measures (termed 'input'), |
| $y_{rj}$ | = | r-th output of DMU 'j', $x_{ij}$ = ith input of DMU 'j', |
| u | = | weights (that is, shadow prices) of outputs, |
| v | = | weights (that is, shadow prices) of inputs, |
| $u_r$ | = | coefficient of r-th ouput that maximize $q_o$, |
| $v_i$ | = | coefficients of i-th input that maximize $q_o$, |
| j | = | 1 ... n index of decision-making units, |
| i | = | 1 ... m index of inputs, |
| r | = | 1 ... s index of outputs. |

This model seeks to maximize $\theta_o$, the ratio of weighted success indicators to weighted budget indicators, for an arbitrary decision-making unit (DMU) '0', subject to the constraint that the same ratio for the other decision-making units should not exceed unity (which is by definition maximal efficiency). By solving this programming problem (n + 1) times, each time with a different DMU serving as the referent '0' unit, the efficient hyperplane can be identified and measured, and each DMU's distance from it can be measured in various ways.

*The input and output weights chosen are those that minimize the distance between each DMU and the efficient hyperplane.* They have the economic interpretation of 'shadow prices'.

The above equations are non-linear and therefore pose difficult computational problems. However, Charnes et al. (1979) proved that (10.3) can be easily converted to (n + 1) ordinary linear fractional programming problems. This ingenious transformation was the genesis of Data Envelopment Analysis (DEA).

DEA problems may be formulated in output-maximizing or input-minimizing variants, and each DEA problem, however formulated, has a 'dual'. DEA provides a set of scalar measures of inefficiency. These measures come in pairs – one set for input-oriented (that is, input-minimizing) measures, and one set for output-oriented (that is, output-maximizing) measures.

The three main scalar measures of inefficiency for input-minimizing models, are:

1. Theta: the proportional reduction in inputs possible in order to obtain the projected input values.
2. Iota: an input efficiency score, interpreted as the proximity of the data point to the facet of the piecewise linear envelopment surface, and equal to the total weighted distance between observed and projected points, standardized by inputs.
3. Sigma: summed weighted value of the output slack (difference between actual and efficient output), weighted by shadow prices, and excess input values, also weighted by the corresponding shadow prices.

Theta measures only that portion of economic inefficiency that could be eliminated by proportional reduction of inputs (that is, R&D money expenditures, in our admittedly partial picture). It is the proximity of the data point $\{Y_i, X_i\}$ to the facet of the piecewise linear envelopment surface. Even after reducing inputs by 'Theta', however, some inputs may, still exhibit slack. Iota measures the total amount of inefficiency, not just the proportional distance along a radius vector. Sigma measures the weighted Euclidean distance between the actual point ($Y_i$, $X_i$) and efficient point ($Y_i^*$, $X_i^*$).

A property of DEA that makes it particularly suitable for estimating and partitioning inefficiency is that the inputs used in DEA analysis 'may also assume a variety of forms which admit of only ordinal measurements, for example psychological tests, arithmetic scores, psychomotor skills' (Charnes et al., 1978, p. 429). In our case, this allows the use of variables that relate to factors like patent and citation performance, not solely to conventional inputs like labour hours or machine hours. The use of such variables, in turn, may permit the partitioning of inefficiency among its proximate causes, including those related to the performance of management (Leibenstein and Maital, 1992; Sengupta and Sfeir, 1988; Sherman, 1984). DEA places no restrictions on the functional form of the production relationships and makes no a priori distinction between the relative importance of any two outputs or of any two inputs. It is thus an ideal method to deal with the non-sequential, feedback-innovation processes and their partial indicators. While DEA is non-parametric, it is not free of the necessity for further modelling and theory. For example, assumptions about the underlying relationships will determine whether the efficient frontier is forced through the origin (constant returns to scale) or allowed not to pass through the origin (variable returns to scale).

While DEA is relatively insensitive to model specification (for example 'input orientation' or 'output orientation'), it can be extremely sensitive to variable selection and data errors (Ahn and Seiford, 1993). This is inherent in the nature of any method that identifies envelopes or frontiers. Moreover, given enough inputs, all (or most) of the DMUs are rated efficient. This is a direct result of the dimensionality of the input/output space (m + s) relative to n, the number of DMUs (observations).

## 10.3  DESCRIPTION OF DATA

Figure 9.1 in the previous Chapter 9 provides an overview of the various stages of research, development and innovation, along with the partial indicators and variables that serve to quantify and characterize each stage. This cognitive model (Grupp, 1998) is useful in this Chapter as well although it is certainly not sufficiently complex to fully cope with the feedback characteristics of the scientific and technological innovation process. But without entering into an extended discussion of the complexities of modelling the interrelated science and innovation processes, the model may serve to visualize available opportunities for quantifying each stage. At the same time, we note that in measuring the dynamics of science-based innovation, one faces the problem that clear-cut measurement procedures are often difficult to devise and to validate. The 'indicators' approach – construction of input and output variables – is capable of grasping only a part of the complex innovation-oriented processes and their related feedback mechanisms (Grupp et al., 1992a, p. 11).

In this Chapter, one monetary variable and four success variables are used for quantifying Stage 1 'R&D' efficiency ('Y' efficiency), and one output variable and four input, Variables, for Stage 2 'export' efficiency ('Z' efficiency). The four success variables from Stage 1 become the four input variables of Stage 2.

**X Variable**

The single input variable for Stage 1 efficiency is taken as gross R&D spending (GERD) expressed as a percentage of GDP, as defined and compiled by the OECD (OECD, 1991). These data are comparable to one another and in some cases are adjusted by the OECD staff. The GERD data, when expressed as a percentage of GDP, bypass the difficult problem of adequate conversion of national currencies. For Israel, national sources (the Central Bureau of Statistics) replace the OECD data; thus, in the case of Israel alone, there may not be full consistency with the R&D data of the remaining countries. Annual averages are taken for the period 1981–85 to overcome annual fluctuations and some missing data. This R&D series includes only the commitment of financial resources to innovation that funds formalized R&D activities, despite the fact that there are many other, complementary ways to engage in research and development activities, such as design improvement, learning by doing, and learning by using (see the review of Dosi (1988). However, at present, no better quantification of innovation resources exists. An alternate approach to using total R&D spending is to use only civilian (non-defence) R&D spending. However, for some countries (like Israel) defence-related R&D spending is confidential, and moreover, there may exist spillover effects – part of declared defence R&D may in reality be civilian in nature, though not supported by industrial policy (Roessner, 1985).

**Y Variables**

These are 'throughput' variables that serve as outputs in Stage 1 and inputs in Stage 2, and are a subset of existing, available bibliometric and patent indicators. They consist of indicators of: publications, citations, patents (single-year) and cumulative patents.

(a) Scientific publications: bibliometric indicators are a common measure of research output (van Raan, 1988). The number of scientific publications is one of those indicators, though admittedly a rather crude one. Only publications in the natural sciences and engineering during 1981–85 are counted in our PUB variable. Biomedical research and other parts of the life sciences are very important for human welfare and health; however this type of research in the 1980s was far less likely to have an impact on technology and on exports. Thus we have excluded publications and citations in the life sciences (though medical technology has been included). Publications data are derived from the Science Citation Index for the EU countries and Israel (Schubert et al., 1989). We note that Belgium and Luxemburg, which form an economic and monetary union, are treated as a single country, in bibliometric, patent and foreign trade statistics. Publication counts are normalized by dividing by gross domestic product (GDP).

(b) Citations: We do not consider the citations indicator as a measure of scientific quality, but rather as a proxy for the degree that scientific publications are exploited. If the publications of a country are frequently cited in the scientific literature, this indicates that the scientific output of this country is recognized internationally. The issue then arises, does the country itself exploit the knowledge it has created, or do scientists, engineers and firms in general in other countries? In some ways, citations are a more important throughput variable than publications, because they serve to measure the utility or impact of research, rather than its gross quantity. Again, as with publications, the natural sciences and engineering are covered, but biomedicine and life sciences are excluded (frequency of citation of papers publishing during 1981–85). The source of citations data is, as for publications, the Science Citation Index, which covers research articles, notes, letters, meeting abstracts, book reviews, and so on. In our indicator, only articles, reviews, notes and letters were counted as citable items.

(c) Patents: Private or corporate research generally produces patents, rather than academic publications (Grupp, 1990a). Patent statistics are an accepted output indicator for strategic and applied research and industrial development.[5]

However, the question arises, do publications and citations overlap, in validity, with patent data? It is true that some basic research institutions, such as universities, take out patents, and some industrial laboratories publish scientific papers. However, it has been found empirically that inventors tend not to cite their own patents in their scientific publications. Thus, the full picture of their work is revealed only when the two interrelated indicators are used together – patents and publications (Grupp, 1990b, p. 448). As patent applications are legal documents that are valid only in one country, many foreign 'duplications' of domestic priority patent applications are generated. The selection of patent data from only one patent office, therefore, does not always yield an indicator that is representative of the world output of inventions. Our study seeks to compare EU countries with

Israel. Selection of the regional European Patent Office (EPO) is inappropriate, since it would unfairly bias the data in favour of EU countries and against Israel. Therefore, for purposes of this Chapter, United States Patent and Trademark Office (USPTO) data are used. They represent the patented invention output in the world's largest market for technology, the USA, which is foreign both to EU countries and to Israel and hence has less bias than the EPO. Since patent output tends to lag behind spending on industrial research and development, we selected annual averages of granted patents for the invention years 1984 through 1986 (normalized by GDP). This patent indicator, PAT, measures the increment to the stock of patented inventions from earlier years, and thus reflects the production of recent technology.

The legal validity of a US patent is for 17 years following its granting. Thus, it is important to consider the stock of protected technology, or patent potential (PATPOT) and not just its increment as measured by PAT. We therefore compiled the number of granted patents for the period 1977 through 1986 (divided by GDP), PATPOT. We did not utilize a full 17-year period, because of the obsolescence of technology due to quick product cycles. Data sources are the same as for PAT. All patent data were supplied by the USPTO on diskettes (version as of December 31, 1990). We exclude those patents that do not reflect technology important for R&D-intensive (high-tech) exports (see description of Z variable). A patent-to-trade concordance is provided by Grupp (1998). Patents for the high-tech products we examine in this Chapter cover somewhat more than 50 per cent of all patents, with some variation across individual countries.

## Z Variable

The dynamic nature of 'high technology' presents problems in defining appropriate indicators of high-tech export sales. Many authors associate high technology with R&D intensity. In this Chapter, we utilize a list of R&D-intensive products as defined by the Standard Industrial Trade Classification (SITC revision 111) (Legler et al., 1992). Products with R&D intensities above 3.5 per cent of gross sales are included. For other purposes, we have distinguished between high-level products (those with R&D spending of between 3.5 and 8.5 per cent of sales) and leading-edge products (those with R&D spending of 8.5 per cent of sales or more). For a list of high-tech products so defined, see the Appendix 9.2 in Chapter 9. R&D intensities are based on data from seven major OECD countries, including the US, Japan and Germany (op. cit.). Details may be found in Legler et al. (1992).

We chose to measure the final Z variable not as the absolute level of high-tech exports, as defined by the SITC categories, but rather as the relation between exports and imports, which we term 'revealed comparative advantage' (RCA; see definition in the legend of Table 10.1). The RCA indicator answers two questions simultaneously: Do the domestic suppliers of a product have a solid footing in the marketplace compared with foreign competitors and suppliers of other domestic sectors? And do they succeed in substituting domestic production for imports, compared with suppliers in other sectors?

*Table 10.1:  Data*

| Countries | PAT | PUB | CIT | PATPOT | GERD | RCA |
|---|---|---|---|---|---|---|
| Germany (DEU) | 16.07 | 82.59 | 264.42 | 58.25 | 2.54 | 128.76 |
| France (FRA) | 6.74 | 74.89 | 212.14 | 24.01 | 2.16 | 97.90 |
| UK (GBR) | 7.21 | 108.40 | 340.30 | 26.63 | 2.34 | 109.07 |
| Netherl. (NDL) | 9.37 | 82.57 | 278.21 | 30.99 | 2.01 | 88.78 |
| Belg./Lux. (BEL) | 4.25 | 63.10 | 157.60 | 15.20 | 1.53 | 109.47 |
| Denmark (DNK) | 4.58 | 66.81 | 279.17 | 15.21 | 1.18 | 83.45 |
| Italy (ITA) | 2.85 | 35.71 | 87.12 | 9.42 | 0.95 | 76.54 |
| Israel (ISR) | 12.88 | 325.98 | 967.19 | 35.59 | 2.90 | 69.31 |
| Spain (ESP) | 0.61 | 31.86 | 49.44 | 1.62 | 0.45 | 74.20 |
| Greece (GRC) | 0.19 | 47.28 | 62.02 | 0.59 | 0.27 | 12.43 |
| Portugal (PRT) | 0.04 | 12.53 | 18.59 | 0.14 | 0.38 | 26.94 |
| Ireland (IRL) | 3.40 | 49.15 | 111.33 | 8.39 | 0.75 | 111.84 |

*Legend to Table 10.1:*

**PAT**: number of patents invented between 1984 and 1986 matched to HL (high-level) and LE (leading-edge) products, US Patent and Trade Office, as a ratio to GDP.

**PUB**: number of publications in both scientific and engineering publications, 1981–85 (not including life science publications), as a fraction of GDP.

**CIT**: number of citations to scientific and engineering papers published in 1981–85 periodicals, as a fraction of GDP.

**PATPOT**: cumulative number of patents, USPTO, invented during 1977–86, for both HL and LE goods, as a fraction of GDP.

**GERD**: gross R&D spending, annual average for 1981–85; converted to U.S. dollars using purchasing power parity index of OECD; $ billion. Source: OECD, Scientific Indicators. For Israel: R&D data are taken from the Central Statistical Bureau's Statistical Yearbook. Expressed as a per cent of GDP. Gross domestic product: average for 1981–85.

**RCA**: revealed comparative advantage, for HL and LE goods, for the year 1988, defined as:

$$\mathbf{RCA = 100\ \{ES^2 - 1)/(ES^2 + 1)\ \}} \qquad -100 \leq RCA \geq +100$$

where export share ES = $\dfrac{\text{EX/IM}}{\text{EXTOT/IMTOT}}$

EX is a country's total exports of HL and LE products to the outside world, IM is that country's imports of HL and LE manufactured products, EXTOT is the country's total exports of manufactures, and IMTOT is the country's total imports of manufactures.

The comparative-advantage concept dates back as far as 1817, when David Ricardo first enunciated the principle of comparative advantage in his famous wine and cloth example. The West German Federal Ministry for Research and Technology – among other actors in technology policy – adopted it years ago to regularly report on West German technological competitiveness (Legler, 1987; Grupp, 1998). Recently it was revitalized in the USA by Porter (1990). Another, recent justification of this concept is given by Dosi et al. (1990). The data are drawn from the OECD's exports and imports statistics ('trade by commodities'), and relate to the year 1988. We chose this year, because the trade effects arising from scientific and technological variables tend to lag by two to four years, in the area of high technology (Grupp, 1991). For Israel, trade data for 1987 were used, as later data (classified by the Standard International Trade Classification III) were not yet available (see Table 10.1 for the data and precise definitions of the variables.)

Note that imports from all countries are included, whereas other papers measure comparative advantage according to the country's share of the world export market only. Our approach follows Dosi et al. (1990), in taking into account a country's competitive strength in import substitution – substituting domestic production for imports of high-tech products – as well as in exports.

Country acronyms are according to the three-digit ISO convention. In later analysis, the number of countries was narrowed to eight, with Spain, Portugal, Greece and Ireland eliminated.

In order to make the RCA variable non-negative – a necessary condition for conducting linear programming analysis – we added a constant (+ 100) to each country's RCA score, so that all values should become non-negative. These shifted RCA values are shown in Table 10.1 (the lowest possible original RCA value is –100 and 0 after this transformation).

## 10.4 EMPIRICAL RESULTS[6]

### Stage 1 Efficiency in Partial Analysis

We begin our analysis of Stage 1 efficiency in converting monetary R&D resources into success measures – patents, patent potential, publications and citations – by constructing some simple two-dimensional graphs, showing each of the four 'outputs' as a function of the independent variable for Stage 1, gross R&D spending as a per cent of GDP (see Figures 10.1–10.4.) These four graphs show partial production functions – one output as a function of one input – but by their nature cannot reveal the aggregate picture that DEA portrays (see below).

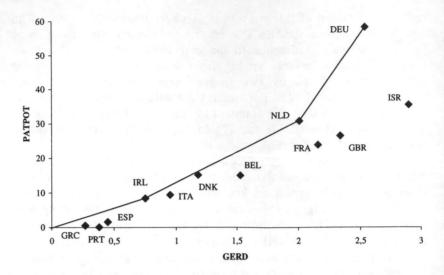

*Figure 10.1: Patents/GDP versus gross R&D spending/GDP, EU countries and Israel*

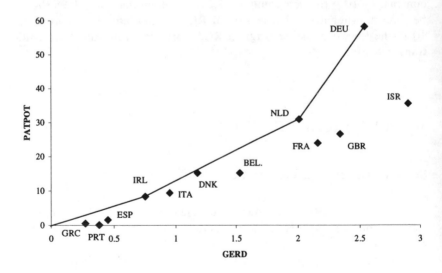

*Figure 10.2: Patent potential/GDP versus gross R&D spending/GDP, EU countries and Israel*

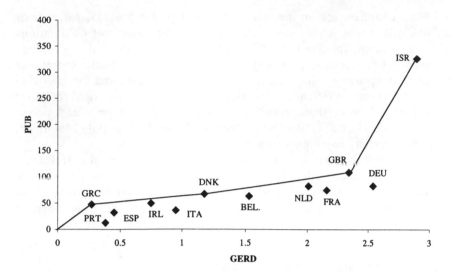

*Figure 10.3:* *Publications/GDP versus gross R&D spending/GDP, EU countries and Israel*

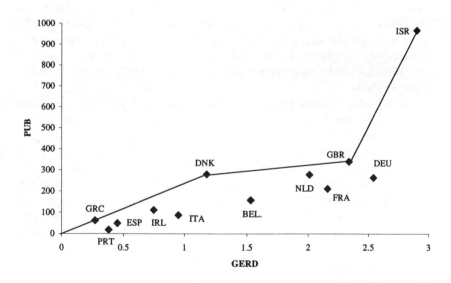

*Figure 10.4:* *Citations/GDP versus gross R&D spending/GDP, EU countries and Israel*

Most countries are on the efficiency frontier, for Stage 1, for at least one of the four R&D outputs. Israel's very high levels of publications and citations, relative to its GDP, places it very high on the efficiency frontiers for these outputs, and even skews them to indicate 'increasing marginal product', that is, a rising gradient. Denmark and the UK[7] also appear on efficiency frontiers, indicating strong scientific infrastructure in those countries. With regard to patents and patent potential, Germany, the Netherlands, Denmark and Italy dominate, with Germany enjoying a strong lead.

This initial analysis, therefore, suggests that when the full DEA study is conducted, the efficient Stage 1 countries are likely to include Israel and Germany – Israel, because of its strong performance in publications and citations, and Germany, because of its strong position in patents.

## Stage 1 Efficiency in DEA Analysis

The four 'output' indicators do not allow for two-dimensional graphical representations of the DEA results. Two of the partial indicators are valid representations of 'science' (PUB and CIT), and two are valid representations of 'industrial development' (PAT and PATPOT). It is therefore tempting to perform a DEA analysis with only two outputs, say, CIT and PATPOT, in order to represent the two dimensions 'academic R&D' and 'industrial R&D', in a preliminary analysis, and then to compare these 'reduced' DEA results to a full DEA analysis.

These reduced DEA results are shown graphically below (see Table 10.2 and Figure 10.5). As expected, Germany and Israel are seen as most efficient in Stage 1, but most of the other countries are not overall very distant, according to the SIGMA measure; that is, the weighted Euclidean distance between their actual position and the efficient 'envelope' vanishes. Only the Mediterranean EU countries Spain, Greece and Portugal are more distant from the envelope, and thus less efficient, from the two-dimensional perspective (see also Figure 10.5). As the DEA analysis was reduced to two outputs, only, there is nearly no difference between using the Iota (weighted distance) or the Theta (proportional projection) measures for assessing the efficiency of inputs.

*Table 10.2:  Reduced 'Stage 1' efficiency in converting R&D resources*
*into scientific (CIT) and technological (PATPOT) outputs*

| Country | Iota | Theta | Sigma |
|---|---|---|---|
| Germany | 1.00 | 1.00 | 0 |
| France | 0.56 | 0.56 | 0 |
| U K | 0.65 | 0.65 | 0 |
| Netherlands | 0.79 | 0.79 | 0 |
| Belg./Lux. | 0.53 | 0.53 | 0 |
| Denmark | 0.86 | 0.86 | 0 |
| Italy | 0.51 | 0.51 | 0 |
| Israel | 1.00 | 1.00 | 0 |
| Spain | 0.33 | 0.33 | 0.20 |
| Greece | 0.67 | 0.69 | 1.69 |
| Portugal | 0.14 | 0.15 | 0.54 |
| Ireland | 0.65 | 0.65 | 0 |

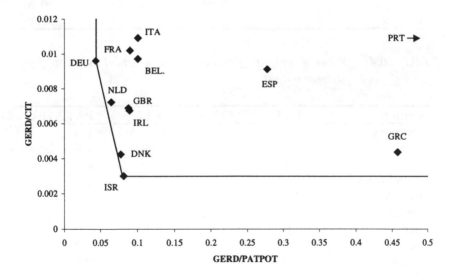

*Figure 10.5:  Schematic view of isoquants of DEA results reduced to*
*two outputs*

Tables 10.3 and 10.4 show the results of the full data envelopment analysis model, applied to the Stage 1 model of maximizing the ratio of the weighted sum of all four outputs – PAT, PATPOT, PUB and CIT – to the single input, GERD, with weights chosen to achieve the

*Table 10.3:* '*Stage V' efficiency in converting R&D resources into scientific and technological outputs*

| Country | Iota | Theta | Sigma |
|---|---|---|---|
| Germany | 1.00 | 1.00 | 0.00 |
| France | 0.57 | 0.58 | 16.63 |
| UK | 0.65 | 0.65 | 5.37 |
| Netherlands | 0.80 | 0.81 | 9.40 |
| Belg./Lux. | 0.54 | 0.57 | 33.29 |
| Denmark | 0.83 | 0.86 | 27.03 |
| Italy | 0.53 | 0.55 | 21.02 |
| Israel | 1.00 | 1.00 | 0.00 |
| Spain | 0.44 | 0.50 | 14.92 |
| Greece | 1.00 | 1.00 | 0.00 |
| Portugal | 0.20 | 0.20 | 0.20 |
| Ireland | 0.81 | 0.86 | 39.29 |

*Table 10.4:* '*Stage V' output efficiency: ratio of actual output to fully efficient output*

| Country | PAT | PUB | CIT | PATPOT |
|---|---|---|---|---|
| Germany | 1.0 | 1.0 | 1.0 | 1.0 |
| France | 0.95 | 1.0 | 0.93 | 1.0 |
| UK | 0.88 | 0.96 | 1.0 | 1.0 |
| Netherlands | 1.0 | 0.91 | 1.0 | 0.96 |
| Belg./Lux. | 0.91 | 1.0 | 0.81 | 1.0 |
| Denmark | 0.91 | 0.72 | 1.0 | 1.0 |
| Italy | 1.0 | 1.0 | 0.81 | 1.0 |
| Israel | 1.0 | 1.0 | 1.0 | 1.0 |
| Spain | 1.0 | 1.0 | 0.70 | 0.94 |
| Greece | 1.0 | 1.0 | 1.0 | 1.0 |
| Portugal | 0 | 1.0 | 1.0 | 0 |
| Ireland | 1.0 | 1.0 | 0.67 | 0.69 |

highest possible ratio. It will be recalled that Iota measures the proportional reduction in inputs needed for a DMU to achieve efficiency (that is, to be on the efficiency frontier), 'Theta' measures the total reduction in inputs for full efficiency, and Sigma is the weighted Euclidean distance of a DMU's actual point from Its fully efficient one.

The results indicate that for Stage 1, the three efficient 'facets' are Israel, Germany and Greece. Measured by Iota and Theta, Denmark is next, followed by Ireland, the Netherlands, the UK, France, Belgium/Luxemburg, and finally Italy and Spain. Portugal is last, largely because of its relatively weak patent performance.

Table 10.4 shows the comparative efficiency in each of the four output dimensions, measured by the ratio of actual output to efficient output, with 'efficient' defined by the three facets, Israel, Germany and Greece. Most countries are seen to be 'Stage 1 efficient' for at least two (and in some cases, three) of the outputs. In particular, Italy's low overall efficiency score appears to be attributable to inefficiency in the 'citations' dimension alone. This may be related in part to a language bias (as for Spain) and not solely to the low impact of Italian and Spanish science. As for Greece, which was not judged as an efficient country in the reduced DEA analysis, it must be noted that its performance in patents – comparatively low, as is R&D spending – increased only recently. Therefore, the related PATPOT output is considerably lower than the actual PAT output. By using only the potential indicator, as was done in the reduced DEA analysis (see Figure 10.5), past patent performance is emphasized.

Table 10.4 further shows that the publication output differentiates a bit less between countries than does the citation output. This is the reason we chose the citation data to represent science for the reduced DEA analysis. The PAT and PATPOT data are about the same in variation across countries. Yet, the patent potential indicator, measured over a 10-year period, seems to be a more stable measure for the inventive power of countries, and was thus chosen for the reduced analysis.

## Stage 2 Efficiency in Partial Analysis

Figures 10.6 and 10.7 show graphically the relation between the Stage 2 output, 'revealed comparative advantage', a measure of relative success in high-tech export markets, as well as in import substitution, and two of the Stage 2 inputs, publications and patents. For both of these two partial efficiency frontiers, Germany and Ireland are seen as fully efficient.

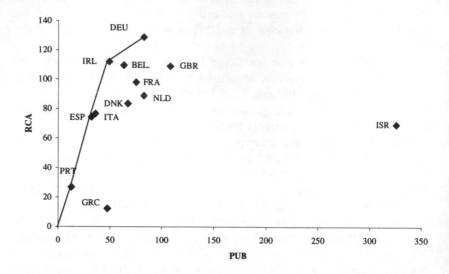

*Figure 10.6:   Revealed comparative high-tech trade advantage (RCA) versus scientific output*

**Stage 2 Efficiency in DEA Analysis**

Figure 10.8 portrays the same frontier in a different manner. Here, an 'RCA isoquant' is calculated by means of a reduced DEA analysis, with the two other inputs for science and technology only (analogous to Figure 10.5; for the reasons why we selected these two data sets, see the discussion for Stage 1 efficiency), showing the values of PATPOT and CIT needed to produce a single unit of RCA. Spain and Portugal seem to form the isoquant, with other smaller countries scattering somewhat, and all the major R&D players in Europe well beyond it. Figure 10.7 has been provided only because full DEA analysis of Stage 2 is four-dimensional, in inputs, and does not lend itself well to a graphical two-dimensional representation of isoquants. More information is certainly provided by the full DEA analysis below (without Figures). However, we wish to make the point clearly, at this stage, that the rather confusing numerical results need to be analysed

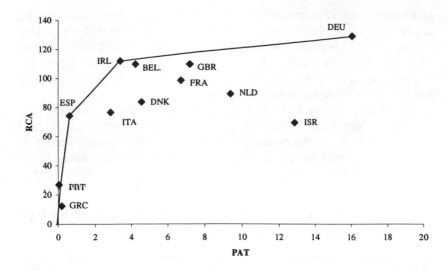

*Figure 10.7:* *Revealed comparative high-tech trade advantage (RCA) versus technological output*

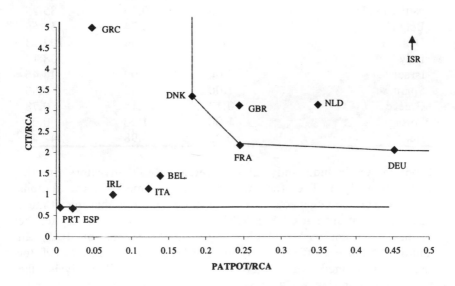

*Figure 10.8:* *Schematic view of isoquants of DEA results reduced to two inputs (Stage 2)*

carefully for their informational content, before any conclusions can be drawn from them. Such a discussion follows in Section 10.5. From this discussion, it is learned that RCA output analysis should be limited to the major R&D spenders. The reduced DEA isoquants for six major countries are also given in Figure 10.8. In this case, Denmark, France and Germany form the efficiency frontier.

Now we turn to a full DEA analysis of all four inputs, the two 'scientific' and the two 'technological' ones. As before, Portugal and Spain seem to be at the efficiency frontier, with the smaller countries following, whereas the major R&D actors in Europe including Israel drop out (Table 10.5). For reasons discussed in the next Section, it is

*Table 10.5:* *'Stage 2' efficiency in converting science and technology excellence into export advantage*

| Country | Iota | Theta | Sigma |
|---|---|---|---|
| Germany | 0.33 | 0.67 | 137.09 |
| France | 0.35 | 0.56 | 68.16 |
| UK | 0.25 | 0.43 | 85.69 |
| Netherlands | 0.25 | 0.46 | 85.25 |
| Belg./Lux. | 0.51 | 0.74 | 55.66 |
| Denmark | 0.26 | 0.54 | 102.23 |
| Italy | 0.63 | 0.92 | 38.17 |
| Israel | 0.06 | 0.09 | 44.46 |
| Spain | 1.00 | 1.00 | 0.00 |
| Greece | 0.13 | 0.14 | 0.78 |
| Portugal | 1.00 | 1.00 | 0.00 |
| Ireland | 0.73 | 0.98 | 42.41 |

tempting to include only above-average R&D investors in the high-tech analysis. Therefore, we perform the same DEA calculations with the more homogeneous sample of those countries that invest more than 1 per cent of their GDP in R&D. This threshold is arbitrary for the moment, but not without solid justification (see Section 10.5). In addition to this cut-off rule, Belgium and Luxemburg are excluded, for reasons mentioned later. Therefore, in this 'top 6' analysis, the remaining countries are: Germany, France, the UK, the Netherlands, Denmark and Israel. (The dashed envelope in Figure 10.8 includes these same top 6 countries in the reduced DEA calculation.)

The three countries (out of the top 6) that form the efficiency frontier for Stage 2 – transformation of publications, patents and citations into revealed comparative advantage – are Germany, France and Denmark. They are followed by the UK, the Netherlands, and finally Israel. The contrast between Israel's efficiency in Stage 1 – generating scientific and technological outputs from R&D resources – and its inefficiency in Stage 2 generating exports from its scientific and technological excellence is striking. It should be emphasized that this result is robust and does not depend on the number of countries compared (see Table 10.6).

*Table 10.6:*     *'Stage 2' efficiency measures for the top six R&D investors in converting science and technology excellence into export advantage*

| Country | Iota | Theta | Sigma |
|---|---|---|---|
| Germany | 1.00 | 1.00 | 0.00 |
| France | 1.00 | 1.00 | 0.00 |
| UK | 0.90 | 0.92 | 15.40 |
| Netherlands | 0.80 | 0.80 | 0.50 |
| Denmark | 1.00 | 1.00 | 0.00 |
| Israel | 0.27 | 0.35 | 172.43 |

*Table 10.7:*     *'Stage 2' input efficiency for the top six R&D investors ratio of efficient input to actual input*

| Country | PAT | PUB | CIT | PATPOT |
|---|---|---|---|---|
| Germany | 1.00 | 1.00 | 1.00 | 1.00 |
| France | 1.00 | 1.00 | 1.00 | 1.00 |
| UK | 1.00 | 0.87 | 1.00 | 0.94 |
| Netherlands | 0.95 | 1.00 | 1.00 | 1.00 |
| Denmark | 1.00 | 1.00 | 1.00 | 1.00 |
| Israel | 0.94 | 0.82 | 0.88 | 1.00 |

When the relative efficiency of utilizing each of the four inputs is analysed separately (see Table 10.7), it is seen that in approximate terms, no country lies along a radius vector that crosses the efficient hyperplane, meaning that there is no major R&D investor in our sample whose relative inefficiency in each of the four contributing inputs – publications, citations, patents and cumulative patents – is approximately the same. The UK is relatively inefficient in utilizing scientific papers, while the opposite is true for the Netherlands, which has inefficient utilization of patents for generating high-tech exports. Israel is efficient in making her patent potential pay off (that is, her older technology), but is not fully efficient in utilizing recent patents or scientific excellence.,

This concludes our presentation of the empirical results. We now turn to a discussion of our numerical findings.

## 10.5 DISCUSSION AND CONCLUSION

The conclusions reached with the aid of the Data Envelopment approach are essentially evident in the data themselves. But there are doubtless many instances in which the final result – and degrees of inefficiency – are far less obvious from simple inspection of the data. There is a significant advantage in an objective, quantitative approach that yields clear-cut numerical estimates of inefficiency and also partitions that inefficiency among the various input dimensions.

The main reservation we must discuss relates to the extent to which the input and output variables reflect R&D processes under national control. For R&D expenditures, this appears to be no problem, as the flow of funds from and to foreign sources is negligible in the sample of countries studied. EU funds overall are low, compared with national appropriations, and they are allocated in our statistics to the country where they are spent. Bibliometric data are assigned by the affiliation of the first author (university, institute, or company) and should reflect national activities quite well (with the exception of multinationally co-authored papers, like this one, and the publication output of supranational research centres).

The nature and intensity of economic – though not technological – stimuli, that stem from the abundance of particular inputs, or alternately critical scarcities, specific patterns of local demand, and levels of and changes in relative prices, generate a complex interplay between export performance and technology-gap structures among various countries (as measured, for example, by the four input variables used in the Stage 2 analysis above; van Hulst et al., 1991). As a partial reaction to this interplay, we based our answer to the difficult question, how competitive are R&D-intensive product groups in given countries, not on the level or size of export surpluses but on the relative position compared to all manufactured goods.

Inspection of the data in Table 10.1 (and also of Figures 10.1 to 10.4) reveals that of the dozen countries we analyse, five are clearly not major players in the global market for high-tech products. They are Italy, Spain, Portugal, Greece and Ireland. All spend less than 1 per cent of their GDP on R&D and have considerably lower levels of patents, citations and publications than the other countries. Ireland does have respectable high-tech exports, but much of that is done by foreign companies locating in Ireland to take advantage of sizeable tax concessions and relatively inexpensive labour and land, and does not reflect local high-tech capabilities.

For the four Mediterranean countries, it is often the case that foreign-owned multinationals pursue local high-tech production (for example in consumer electronics in Portugal, or in electric cables in Greece, Italy and Spain, or in production of German cars in Spain). Telecommunications equipment in Spain is manufactured by the French-owned Alcatel company (earlier, by the US-owned ITT). AT&T is also strong in joint ventures in these countries (Grupp and Schnoering, 1992). The 'mobile' foreign technologies do count on the output side of the Stage 2 model, but certainly not on the input side – this is our problem.

The above-mentioned countries seem to be very efficient in Stage 2 precisely because they are so weak in related inputs, where we are unable to take account of the imported and foreign-controlled technology. *Therefore, we introduce a threshold for our final analysis, excluding countries allocating below 1 per cent of their GDP to gross R&D spending.*

This cut-off rule appears arbitrary – however, there is an additional argument supporting it. Within the Commission of the European Union, there exists the concept of 'less-favoured' regions of the EU. These regions receive dedicated EU funds to foster their local R&D, and there are special subsidies for increasing cohesion within the entire EU.

As 'less-favoured', the following regions have been specified: Portugal, Ireland and Greece (the entire country); the south of Italy, Sicily, Sardinia; Spain, without Greater Madrid and the Barcelona region; in France, only Corsica; in the UK Northern Ireland. Thus, our 1 per cent threshold for R&D spending corresponds well with the less-favoured EU regions as defined above.

Also problematic is the strategic control of technology generated by patents. In most cases, inventors do not decide when, to what extent, for which markets, and for which products, their inventions are used. Nor do they have a say, in general, in licensing, selling or abandoning of patents, insofar as they are employees of commercial firms. Consider, for instance, Belgium, which spends 1.53 per cent of its GDP on gross R&D and is therefore well above the cut-off level. Belgian technology is strongly controlled by non-Belgian companies. Patel and Pavitt (1992) reported that 39.7 per cent of national patenting in the United States is due to large foreign-controlled firms, whereas for Western Europe the comparable figure is 6.2 per cent, on average. Belgium had the largest share of national patents generated by foreign capital in their sample of 11 countries. This is a different case from that reflected in the Mediterranean EU countries. Here, foreign-controlled patents are registered in our input data, but we do not know whether the owners of the patents make the related Belgian technology effective for exports from Belgium. It is known that the Dutch-speaking province of Belgium has traditionally close links with the Netherlands, and the French-speaking province is closely connected with France. The same is true for the small German-speaking part of Belgium and its ties with Germany. High-tech exports into these three neighbouring countries alone comprise half of all Belgian high-tech exports, and high-tech imports from the three countries amount to 60 per cent of total high-tech imports! We thus decided to exclude this country from our analysis, because of its foreign-controlled technology and extremely strong high-tech trade relations with a few neighbouring countries, for which large intra-firm trade exists. For these reasons, we chose to confine our final analysis to six countries: Germany, France, UK, Denmark, and Israel.

Up to now, we did not differentiate between leading-edge technology and high-level commodities (see Section 10.3). These two segments of high technology are differentiated by their R&D intensity. This may be somewhat controversial. A high percentage of sales that is spent on R&D signifies low turnover expectations. Indeed, for every million dollars spent on R&D in leading-edge technology, the average annual turnover is less than $12 million, while a typical figure for high-level consumer technology is $30 million or more (Grupp, 1991, p. 279). Leading-edge technology includes many products subject to tariff, and non-tariff protection, such as civilian aircraft and parts, aerospace, pharmaceuticals, and telecommunications. The related markets may be subject to regulation, so that a scientific and technological advantage may not easily be converted to trade advantages.

Table 10.8 provides a synopsis of Stage 1 and Stage 2 DEA results (Theta measures), along with the RCA indexes for leading-edge and high-level product groups. Our conjectures are confirmed in this table.

Those countries that emphasize the less sales-effective, often protected area of leading-edge technology do not achieve full 'Z' efficiency – the UK, the Netherlands, and Israel. On the efficiency envelope are only those countries with stronger (or at least equal) performance in the high-level markets: Germany, France and Denmark.

*Table 10.8:   Synopsis of DEA results and structural high-tech competitiveness of the top six R&D players*

| Country | Stage 1 efficiency (Theta) | Stage 2 efficiency (Theta) | Leading-edge competitiveness | Structural emphasis | High-level competitiveness |
|---|---|---|---|---|---|
| Germany | 1.0 | 1.0 | −14 | < | +49 |
| France | 0.6 | 1.0 | −2 | = | −2 |
| UK | 0.7 | 0.9 | +30 | > | +9 |
| Netherlands | 0.8 | 0.8 | −4 | > | −17 |
| Denmark | 0.9 | 1.0 | −25 | < | −11 |
| Israel | 1.0 | 0.4 | −20 | > | −36 |

Germany's high absolute performance may be related to the fact that it is fully efficient in both stages of the R&D process, while the other nations are either efficient in Stage 2 and inefficient in Stage 1 (France, more so than Denmark), or mediocre in both phases (UK and the Netherlands). As a major Mediterranean R&D nation, Israel does best in Stage 1, but is highly inefficient in Stage 2. Through her scientific and technological achievements, a relatively large amount of indigenous 'Z' inputs originate in Israel. But far too little of these inputs accrue to Israel herself, rather than to other countries. Obviously, war and unstable political relations with neighbour countries are among the unfavourable conditions that hamper the full exploitation of Israel's R&D excellence.

## NOTES

1    An earlier version of this Chapter was published in *Research Evaluation* 2(2), pp. 87–101, 1992, in co-authorship with A. Frenkel and K. Koschatzky. Thanks are also due to an anonymous referee for insightful comments.
2    Similar chained functions exist in other areas of public goods, for example, labour hours and patrol cars can produce police patrols, which in turn serve as an input for the output of public safety. This analysis is similar to that in Bradford

et al. (1969), who posit a two-stage input–output function for public goods: (a) stage one, where resource inputs produce 'intermediate' public good inputs, for example labour hours and patrol cars, as inputs, produce police patrols; and (b) stage two, where intermediate public good inputs, like police patrols, produce the public good itself, 'public safety', or 'law and order'.

Generally, because of difficulties in quantifying the public good, only Stage 1 efficiency is measured and studied. Bradford, Maital and Oates argue that because many public goods are highly labour-intensive, yet have not enjoyed rising productivity owing to new technologies, their unit costs have risen rapidly. Some of these same arguments may apply to research and development, which has also experienced rapidly rising unit costs and is in most cases highly intensive in skilled labour.

3     Lately, police have discovered, in New York City, Washington, DC, and elsewhere, that the 'old' technology of regular foot patrols has greater 'Z' efficiency in reducing crime than patrol cars.

4     We leave open the question whether 'invisible hands' exist that make decisions at the national level of aggregation. In most EU countries and Israel, the respective national governments claim to prosecute a consistent research, technology and industrial policy. In other countries, like the USA, this may not be the case (for example compare Roessner, 1985).

5     The question arises, why not use a direct measure of technical performance level, such as the 'technometric' indicator (Grupp, 1998) – a metric that quantifies the excellence of a product's characteristics or attributes on a [0, 1] scale – rather than indirect indicators such as patents? The answer is that technometric data are difficult to obtain and costly to compile, and are currently available only for a few selected countries and products. No comprehensive technometric data exist at present for all EU countries and Israel. In addition, there is an aggregation problem, in summing technometric indicators for individual products. Technometric analysis is useful in selected areas of technology, but aggregate data are often not available. Patent indicators are therefore used instead. For a discussion of the use of patent indicators to reflect the level of technology, see Griliches (1990) and Grupp (1991).

6     We are indebted to Agha Iqbal Ali, University of Massachusetts at Amherst, for providing his IDEAS DEA software – Version 3.0 (Ali, 1990). It is now available commercially.

7     This justifies our approach that includes defence R&D spending, which certainly puts the UK in a better position vis-à-vis the other European countries.

PART III


Quantifying Innovation in Selected Markets

# 11 Biodiagnostic Kits: Assessment and Comparison[1]

## Main Ideas in this Chapter

As is shown in Chapters 1 and 2, 'technometrics' is a multidimensional index of technological excellence. Technometric profiles permit objective comparisons of product and process quality between companies, industries and nations. They are applicable to services as well as goods, to low-tech as well as high-tech products, and provide basic quantitative indicators sometimes helpful in constructing technology policy. The method of constructing technometric profiles is presented for Israel's fledgling biodiagnostic industry. The conclusion emphasizes industrial policy. The structure of the Chapter is as follows. Section 11.1 provides a brief description of the technometric approach. Section 11.2 surveys Israel's biotechnology industry in general, and the biodiagnostic sub-branch in particular. Section 11.3 provides a technometric evaluation of biodiagnostic kits produced in Israel, relative to leading products in Germany, the USA and Japan, and Section 11.4 draws the main technology policy implications.

## 11.1 TECHNOMETRIC APPROACH TO PRODUCT EVALUATION

Lord Kelvin once said that 'theory begins with measurement'. While many theoretical physicists might debate that point, it is difficult to deny that policy begins with measurement. Public policy attempts to bridge the gap between what is and what ought to be – is unlikely to succeed in either framing or implementing successful policy decisions without a clear evaluation of the existing situation, what is.

In discussing industrial and technology policy for a whole nation, or for particular firms or industries, it is essential to have clear answers to the question: How good are our products and processes, compared with those of competing countries? The answers to the question 'what is our competitive situation?' must be objective, accurate and quantitative.

A series of metrics for evaluating and comparing technological sophistication have been developed.[2] These quantitative indicators have proved useful in measuring the technological level of products and processes and have served as a 'yardstick' for comparison with other firms or countries. The purpose of this Chapter is to apply technometric indicators to evaluate biodiagnostic kits produced by Israeli firms, and to draw policy implications from this analysis.

The technometric approach originated with concern at the German Ministry for Research and Technology in the early 1980s that Germany trailed Japan and the USA in important high-tech areas, concern that was aroused in particular by the influential book by Nussbaum (1984). One of the most important early links in the high-tech product-development chain is the innovation stage, where the quality of new products brought to market is evaluated, but well before market or price mechanisms provide any signals. To quantify product quality at this stage, as a means of supplying data confirming or disconfirming the Nussbaum study for the R&D Ministry, a method called 'technometrics' was developed by Grupp (1990b, 1991) and Grupp and Hohmeyer (1986, 1988).

Technometrics is the quantitative measurement of the technological quality or sophistication of a product or process, group of products or processes, or industry. This approach produces a quantitative profile of a product or process, showing graphically its performance characteristics for selected key attributes, in comparison with those of other firms or countries. Such indices can be aggregated across groups of products, to permit comparisons of the comparative technological level of subsectors or even entire industries. Technometric studies, for example, showed Nussbaum's perception that Germany lagged behind the USA and Japan was untrue, overall, but revealed important areas where Germany was at a competitive disadvantage.

Other complementary approaches to technological evaluation have been developed (Saviotti, 1985; Saviotti et al., 1982). It should be noted that a possible disadvantage of technometric studies is that they rely heavily on primary data collection and peer review and thus tend to be relatively costly and labour-intensive.

## Definition

Every product or process has a set of key specifications or attributes that define its performance or value of ability to satisfy customer wants. Almost by definition, every specification or attribute can be quantified. For instance, in the case of diagnostic kits, a key specification is 'reliability' (the proportion of tests in which accurate results are obtained). For assembly robots, 14 key specifications are axes, maximum reach, minimum reach, vertical velocity, horizontal velocity, repetitive accuracy, position accuracy, nominal load, maximum load, drive vertical reach, hand rotation, angular velocity and lifetime (Grupp et al., 1990). All are expressible in quantitative units.

It is always a subjective decision whether an item should be included or not (Grupp and Hohmeyer, 1988). However, as Stankiewicz (1990) has pointed out, as development proceeds, technological diversity gives way to standardization.[3] Particular design approaches achieve dominance and performance criteria are clearly specified. Social processes and patterns of communication between customers will influence the speed and pattern of product (or process) design and broad categorizations are broken down into related sub-categories of the characteristics which are refined through experience. Therefore, it is not surprising that (industrial) experts interviewed agree on proposed characteristics and priorities (Grupp, 1998).

Each of these attributes has its own unit of measurement: millimetres per second, years of lifetime, and so on. Problems then arise in aggregating attributes to build a single quality index. The technometric indicator surmounts this difficulty by converting each measured attribute into a [0, 1] metric, enabling construction of weighted averages, and so on, and permitting comparisons across products, firms, industries and countries. The '0' point of the metric is set as the technologically standard attribute; the '1' point is set as the most technologically sophisticated attribute in existence.

Let subscripts i, j and k represent products, product attributes or characteristics, and subgroup (company, industry or country), respectively.

Let K represent the measurement of an attribute for given i, j and k. The technometric indicator, K*, is defined as:

$$K^*_{i,j,k} = \frac{K_{max}(i,j,k) - K_{min}(i,j,k_{min})}{K_{max}(i,j,k_{max}) - K_{min}(i,j,k_{min})}. \tag{11.1}$$

where $K_{max,}(i,j,k)$ is the highest value of product characteristic 'j' for product 'i', for subgroup k; $K_{min}(i,j,k_{min})$ is the lowest value of product characteristic 'j', among all members of subgroup k; and $K_{max}(i,j,k_{max}.)$ is the highest value of product characteristic 'j', among all members of subgroup k.

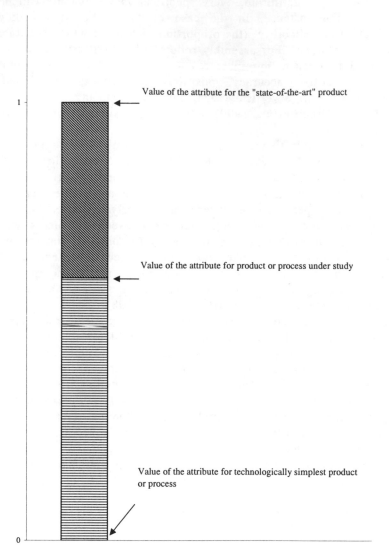

*Figure 11.1: A schematic representation of the technometric index K\**

Take, for instance, the product 'diagnostic kits'. One attribute would be 'test duration', the length of time needed to carry out the diagnostic test. The numerator of (11.1) would give the difference between the 'best' (that is, shortest) test duration for an Israeli product, compared to the 'worst' (that is, longest) test duration for any of the products under comparison, for several countries. The denominator would give the difference between the best, shortest test duration for the top state-of-the-art product, and the longest test duration for a technologically standard (and probably, relatively inexpensive) product.

What results is a metric, $K^*$, that ranges from zero to one, showing how a product stacks up for that attribute, relative to the state-of-the-art level. Note that in some cases, as in this one, lower attribute values represent higher levels of technology, requiring the values in the technometric expression to be inverted (by replacing all 'max' with 'min', and vice versa, in Equation 11.1; for a schematic presentation of $K^*$, see Figure 11.1).

Once key product attributes have been determined from interviews and $K^*$ values calculated for each, a technological 'profile' of the product can be constructed. It is possible to aggregate $K^*$ across all key attributes (for diagnostic kits, that would include sensitivity, intra-assay precision, inter-assay precision, and handling, as well as test duration) to achieve an aggregate $K^*$ measure for the product or group of products. This aggregate technometric measure can then be correlated with other variables to determine the link between technological excellence and, for instance, market success. Comparisons with economic data indicate that declines in the technometric quality of a product or process, $K^*$, occur 2–3 years before such deterioration finds expression in declining market share or export sales (Grupp and Hohmeyer, 1988). This indicates that $K^*$ can serve as a useful 'early warning indicator', ideally, one of a series of such indicators, in conjunction with other market indicators, revealing problems with product quality in sufficient time to take remedial action. Such indicators can be crucially important because, generally, by the time it is observed that market share is falling, it is too late to revamp the product and regain sales from competitors. $K^*$ can also serve a positive role, indicating products or sectors where a country has competitive advantage, technologically, hence worthy of investment to further marketing and sales efforts in foreign markets and to further improve R&D and production efficiency at home.

While the [0, 1] metric permits aggregation of widely differing product specifications (for instance, accuracy, in per cent, and sensitivity, in milligrams), it does introduce some distortion, because product quality is generally not a linear function of a physical attribute. Diminishing returns to accuracy, for example, are quite likely, implying that a technometric score of 0.9 in accuracy may be less than 50 per cent more useful or helpful than a technometric score of 0.60.

### Feasibility for Policy Analysis

Technometric measures can be used at several levels. At the national level, they can be (and have been) used to identify technology gaps in comparison with other nations, and to shape industrial and R&D policy. At the sectoral level, technometric indicators can serve to identify areas of comparative advantage. And at the firm level, they can be used to construct competitive strategy, determine the optimal 'mix' of product attributes, plan new generations of products, guide R&D investment, and form part of feasibility studies.[4] Since 1986, technometric indicators for the following products were constructed: enzymes (immobilized biocatalysts), biogenetically engineered drugs, photovoltaic cells, lasers, sensors, industrial robots, diagnostic kits, and biological waste water treatment facilities (Grupp and Hohmeyer, 1988; Koschatzky, 1991; this book adds more case studies to this list).

## 11.2  BIODIAGNOSTIC INDUSTRY IN ISRAEL

Frenkel and Maital conducted a technometric survey of eight companies in Israel that manufacture biodiagnostic kits. The objective was to evaluate product quality and to frame policy recommendations. Comparative technometric data on Germany, Japan and the USA were supplied by Reiss (1990). The results of that survey follow.

### Biotech Industry

Biotechnology is a branch of technology that seeks to harness biological processes and systems, or living organisms, in order to create useful products and processes for industry, medicine and agriculture. Using live organisms for the benefit of mankind is an old idea, used long ago for making bread, wine and cheese. In recent years, genetic engineering has permitted scientists to alter the building blocks of life itself. Advances in molecular biology have opened new horizons in influencing cellular processes and have made possible, as a result, development of entirely new products.

Scientists predict that toward the end of this century, biotechnology will be of major importance in production of food for both human beings and animals, in treatment of illness for humans and animals, in supply of new raw materials for the chemical industry, and in treatment of industrial wastes and water.

The main applications of biotechnology are medicine, agriculture, food, and environment. Within medical applications, there are three subsectors: production of drugs and hormones with genetically modified organisms; production of biosensors and biocatalysts; and production of diagnostic products for determining the nature of illnesses in humans and animals. In this Chapter, we choose to focus on the biodiagnostic industry.

## Biotech Firms in Israel

Twenty-eight biotechnology firms existed in Israel in the beginning of the 1990s. Most of them are small, and are based on products or processes developed in research done in academic institutions. A high percentage of their employees, close to one-third, are scientists and engineers.

Most of the biotechnology firms were set up as subsidiaries of research institutes or universities, and some are subsidiaries of foreign companies. Only a minority are entrepreneurial, established with venture capital. Most of them are based on technological knowledge and skills of a single academic researcher.

Most of these firms are in pharmaceuticals; nineteen are in this area, of whom ten produce diagnostic kits and two make materials used for diagnostic kits. Eight companies manufacture drugs, hormones and enzymes. In addition, three small firms produce materials used in research labs and in the biotechnology industry. Two companies are in the chemical industry and three are in agriculture.

According to the November 1988 report of the Katzir Committee (Katzir et al., 1988), set up to determine sectors in biotechnology that merit investment and development, six constraints limit development of this industry: lack of venture capital for establishing new firms; lack of venture capital and other forms of risk capital for existing companies; lack of academic research centres specializing in biotechnology; lack of trained manpower in biochemical engineering, production and management engineering; lack of technological infrastructure in existing drug and chemical companies that use traditional technology; and the small size of the local market in Israel for biogenetic products, coupled with the large distance from foreign markets.

In order to remedy some of these constraints, a National Biotechnology Programme has been established, headed by Professor Max Herzberg, President of Orgenics Ltd. (one of the companies in our survey).

In the biotechnology industry, diagnostic kits is the market 'easiest to enter, with the shortest product life and highest risks' (Stankiewicz, 1989, p. 40). Israeli firms in this industry mainly produce products for human and veterinary diagnosis, based on monoclonal antibodies. Our field survey of Israeli biodiagnostic firms was limited to companies that produce complete kits. We did not include companies that produced only components of such kits. Nor did we include companies that purchased foreign technology under licensing agreements, but only companies with proprietary technology used in developing their own unique products.

A total of twelve companies were located, of which eight complied with the above criteria. Senior managers in all of those eight firms were interviewed, and supplementary material on each firm was collected. Managers were highly cooperative and gave generously of their time. A key part of the interview was a detailed questionnaire, eliciting information on the company and on technometric details of its products.

## Nature of Biodiagnostic Companies in Israel

Analysis of the data from our field survey revealed that half of the eight firms are independent, while half are subsidiaries of foreign firms. Most of the companies are privately owned, while some are public companies whose stock is listed on stock exchanges. The companies owned by foreign firms largely began as independent firms but because of difficulties in raising capital, or the need to penetrate new markets, were bought out by larger companies abroad. These companies became subsidiaries, but retain their independence in matters of product R&D.

Seven of the eight companies were established after 1980, while one was established during the 1970s. Despite their youth, all these companies have by 1990 succeeded in producing and marketing their own products. The transition from R&D to production and marketing was remarkably swift, two years from the birth of the company. This contrasts sharply with the 7–10 years needed to develop and test new drugs, and the estimated $50–100 million cost, as noted by the Katzir Committee.[5]

Average plant size is small; the eight plants employed a total of 182 workers of all kinds, an average of 23 per firm, with size ranging from 5 workers to 45.[6] As expected, the proportion of workers in this industry comprising highly skilled and scientific manpower is very high. According to a 1987 Manpower Survey conducted by the Ministry of Industry, biodiagnostics employs a high proportion of scientific personnel, even in comparison with other high-tech industries (see Table 11.1).

*Table 11.1:*  *Manpower profile for biodiagnostic firms, high-tech firms and industrial firms in general in Israel (per cent)*

|  | Engineers and scientists | Technicians | Skilled workers | Unskilled workers | Office workers | Total |
|---|---|---|---|---|---|---|
| Biodiagnostic firms | 43.4 | 13.7 | 27.5 | 4.4 | 11.0 | 100 |
| High-tech firms | 25.1 | 20.3 | 34.8 | 9.9 | 10.8 | 100 |
| All industrial companies | 9.6 | 7.7 | 50.1 | 22.4 | 10.2 | 100 |

Our survey revealed that fully a third of employees are engaged in R&D, at least part of the time. A third of the total outlays of the eight firms goes to R&D. This proportionately heavy spending on R&D is fairly typical of young companies in science-based industries. All eight firms export at least part of their output. In aggregate, 75 per cent of the biodiagnostic firms' sales are exported. The heavy reliance on exports stems from the small size of the local market in Israel. Only two of the eight firms rely principally on the local market; in the remainder, 90 per cent of total output is exported.

## Markets, Marketing and Distribution

Europe is the main market. Two-thirds of their exports goes to that market, while one-third goes to other destinations. Half of the eight firms export diagnostic kits to Germany, which absorbs between 10 per cent and 35 per cent of their exports. The USA is not a principal market for Israel-made diagnostic kits, except for the two firms that are wholly owned subsidiaries of US companies. For the others, a maximum of 12 per cent of total exports go to the US market. For one of the companies, Japan stands second in importance as an export market, next to Europe. Two firms export to Latin America and one company has a small amount of export sales to Africa.

The survey asked managers to forecast future export sales. Most of the companies predicted a rapid expansion in exports in the next five years, between threefold and sixfold growth.

As in most high-tech products made in Israel, marketing is a major obstacle for biodiagnostic kits. Most of the firms we surveyed sell their products abroad through distributors, who acquire exclusive territorial rights. Some of those distributors belong to large foreign companies. This approach to distribution is one important way that Israeli biodiagnostic companies cooperate with foreign entities. One of the eight companies reported setting up its own marketing firm abroad, in order to achieve greater control over distribution.

All the companies responded that their products are aimed at broad market niches where some competition exists. None of the products compete on the basis of low price, but rather value added and quality. Most of the managers interviewed in our survey emphasized marketing as the main difficulty they face, rather than finance, R&D or technology.

All eight companies reported preparing for the 1992 Euromarket. Two have already set up companies in Europe, and three said they intended to do so. Two other companies reported joint-venture agreements to this end with European firms. Most of the companies felt that the main difficulties facing Israeli biodiagnostic firms, in connection with the Euromarket, would come from product standards. The present situation, in which approval by Israel's Ministry of Health is recognized in, for instance, Germany, will not continue after 1992. It is therefore vital that Israel adopt standards that are consistent with, and comply with, those prevailing in Europe.[7]

# 11.3 TECHNOMETRIC EVALUATION OF BIODIAGNOSTIC KITS

Availability of technometric data on biodiagnostic kits for Germany, the USA and Japan (Roios, 1990) makes it possible to compare the relative technological quality of Israeli kits to those abroad.

**Characteristics**

Earlier studies of biodiagnostics (loc. cit.) showed that there are six main attributes of biodiagnostic materials, which together define the quality of those materials. They are:

- Sensitivity: the minimum amount of antibodies needed to product a chemical reaction, or the 'threshold'. Units of measurement are generally thousandths of a gram per millilitre.
- Intra-assay precision: degree of internal (intra-assay) accuracy: if the same kit is used 100 times, how many times will it correctly diagnose the presence of a hormone or micro-organism; expressed as the coefficient of variation.
- Inter-assay precision: for a 100 randomly selected kits, how many of them will give precisely the same diagnostic results; expressed as the coefficient of variation.
- Measurement: range over which diagnosis is possible. Units of measurement are the same as with sensitivity.
- Test duration: length of time needed for operating diagnostic test until result is obtained, in minutes.
- Handling: number of steps required.

**Diagnostic Kits**

Data enabled comparison of diagnostic kits for the following:

- hormonal deficiencies related to the thyroid gland (lack of hormones): FT-3 (free tri-iodothyronin), FT-4 (free thyroxin), T-4 (thyroxin), TSH (thyroid-stimulating hormone), and T-3 (tri-iodothyronin);
- the sex hormone prolactin;
- infectious diseases: HIV-1 (AIDS virus), Rotavirus Ag, Chlamydia IgG and IgM.

The technometric values for hormonal deficiencies are shown in Table 11.2, and technometric profiles are drawn in Figures 11.2 and 11.3.

*Table 11.2:*   *Technometric value for hormonal diagnostic kits, Germany, the USA, Japan and Israel by type and specifications*

| Kits | Specifications | Technometric value | | | |
|------|----------------|---------|------|-------|--------|
|      |                | Germany | USA  | Japan | Israel |
| T-3  | Sensitivity    | 0.99 | 1.00 | 1.00 | 1.00 |
|      | Intra-assay precision | 0.89 | 1.00 | 0.44 | 0.00 |
|      | Inter-assay precision | 0.00 | 1.00 | m.v. | 0.43 |
|      | Measurement range | 0.00 | 1.00 | m.v. | 0.03 |
|      | Test duration  | 0.68 | 0.68 | 1.00 | 0.00 |
|      | Average        | 0.51 | 0.94 | 0.48 | 0.29 |
| T4   | Sensitivity    | 0.00 | 0.00 | 1.00 | 0.00 |
|      | Intra-assay precision | 0.25 | 1.00 | 0.75 | 0.11 |
|      | Inter-assay precision | 0.75 | 1.00 | m.v. | 0.00 |
|      | Measurement range | 0.28 | 1.00 | m.v. | 0.03 |
|      | Test duration  | 0.68 | 0.85 | 1.00 | 0.68 |
|      | Handling       | 0.00 | 1.00 | m.v. | 0.80 |
|      | Average        | 0.33 | 0.81 | 0.92 | 0.27 |
| TSH  | Sensitivity    | 1.00 | 1.00 | 1.00 | 1.00 |
|      | Intra-assay precision | 1.00 | 0.82 | 0.90 | 0.54 |
|      | Inter-assay precision | 0.89 | 0.89 | 1.00 | 0.62 |
|      | Measurement range | 0.97 | 0.42 | 0.56 | 1.00 |
|      | Test duration  | 0.70 | 1.00 | 0.90 | 0.79 |
|      | Handling       | 0.40 | 0.00 | 1.00 | 0.80 |
|      | Average        | 0.83 | 0.69 | 0.89 | 0.79 |
| FT-3 | Sensitivity    | 0.00 | 0.88 | m.v. | 1.00 |
|      | Intra-assay precision | 0.60 | 1.00 | m.v. | 0.00 |
|      | Inter-assay precision | 1.00 | 0.00 | m.v. | 1.00 |
|      | Measurement range | 1.00 | 0.00 | m.v. | 0.00 |

|  |  |  |  |  |  |
|---|---|---|---|---|---|
|  | Test duration | 0.33 | 0.00 | m.v. | 1.00 |
|  | Handling | 0.00 | 0.00 | m.v. | 1.00 |
|  | Average | 0.49 | 0.31 | m.v. | 0.67 |
| FT-4 | Sensitivity | 0.00 | 1.00 | m.v. | 0.78 |
|  | Intra-assay precision | 1.00 | 0.88 | m.v. | 0.56 |
|  | Inter-assay precision | 1.00 | 0.86 | m.v. | 0.60 |
|  | Measurement range | 0.00 | 1.00 | m.v. | 0.41 |
|  | Test duration | 0.61 | 1.00 | m.v. | 0.61 |
|  | Handling | 0.17 | 1.00 | m.v. | 0.83 |
|  | Average | 0.46 | 0.96 | m.v. | 0.63 |
| Prolactin | Sensitivity | 0.07 | 0.58 | m.v. | 1.00 |
|  | Intra-assay precision | 1.00 | 0.74 | m.v. | 0.48 |
|  | Inter-assay precision | 1.00 | 0.69 | m.v. | 0.60 |
|  | Measurement range | 1.00 | 0.00 | m.v. | 0.34 |
|  | Test duration | 1.00 | 0.62 | m.v. | 0.35 |
|  | Handling | 0.40 | 0.60 | m.v. | 1.00 |
|  | Average | 0.85 | 0.54 | m.v. | 0.63 |

*Notes:* m.v. = missing value.

What emerges is that, as expected, the USA in general holds the lead in the quality of its diagnostic kits. The USA pioneered in the field of biotechnology, and still enjoys a technological advantage. This lead is especially pronounced for T-3, T-4, and FT-4. For TSH, Japan enjoys a slight advantage over the USA and Israel, with Germany trailing. For prolactin, the German product is superior to that of Israel, with the USA in third place.

- T-3 tri-iodothyronin: the USA is far ahead of other countries in this diagnostic kit, leading substantially in all characteristics except test duration. Only for 'sensitivity' does the Israeli product equal that of the USA. When the technometric specifications are aggregated (Figure 11.3), the USA's substantial lead for T-3 kits is clear.
- T-4 thyroxin: the situation is similar to that for T-3, with the USA well ahead of Israel and Germany, but not Japan. (Data for Japan exist only for some of the six characteristics.) For TA sensitivity, the value of $K_{min}(min)$ (the global minimum of the technometric indicator) for all the kits included in the sample, and the $K_{max}$ for Germany, Israel and the USA, were all equal to one another. This indicates a weakness of the technometric approach, in cases where the '0' and 'I' points of the [0,1] metric coincide.

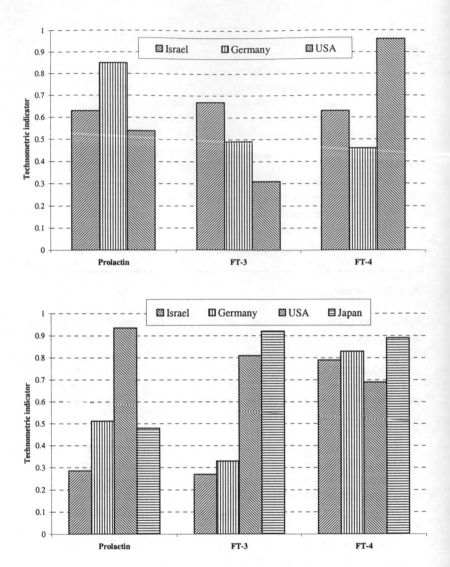

*Figure 11.2: Aggregated technometric profile for hormonal diagnostic kits in Germany, the USA, Japan and Israel, by types*

- TSH thyroid-stimulating hormone: for this kit, quality gaps among the four countries are smaller. Japan's product is superior overall, with Israel and Germany trailing slightly. The lower scores for both intra- and inter-assay precision for Israel's product, relative to the other countries, indicate a pressing need for improvement in accuracy, in order for Israel's kits to become fully competitive.
- FT-3 free tri-iodothyronin: Israel leads Germany and the USA. Israel's kit is highly automated, leading to high technometric scores for test duration and handling. Germany's strength here lies in its wide range of measurement.
- FT-4 free thyroxin: the US product has a clear technological edge, with Israel second and Germany third, trailing in sensitivity, measurement range and handling.
- Prolactin: here, Germany leads, with clear technological superiority in all characteristics except sensitivity and handling. Except for those two characteristics, in which Israel leads, the Israeli kit is mediocre compared with its rivals.

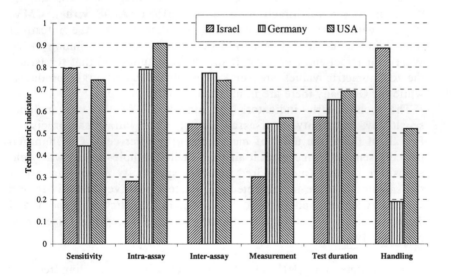

*Figure 11.3: Aggregated technometric profile for hormonal diagnostic kits including Germany, the USA, Japan and Israel, by specification*

Aggregated over the six diagnostic kits, the USA has an overall technometric lead; its 'score' is 0.72, compared with 0.58 for Germany and 0.52 for Israel. The German products trail largely because of lower scores in sensitivity and handling, characteristics that could stand improvement. Israeli kits are outstanding in sensitivity and handling.

Some statistical incoherencies might occur because data collection for the USA and Germany was completed in mid-1989, while Israeli data were collected in 1990. Nonetheless, Israel's relatively small number of biodiagnostic firms, compared with the USA, the relatively short period of time in which these firms have been active in the industry, and their short time-to-market, points to a notable, and somewhat surprising, technological achievement for that country.

The attribute most in need of improvement in the Israeli kits is intra-assay precision, and to a lesser extent inter-assay precision. Precision is apparently a characteristic that laboratories place great weight upon in their decision which diagnostic kit to buy. For this reason, we believe that if the technometric characteristics were weighted according to market preferences, the gap between Israel and the USA might be even larger than shown in Figure 11.3.

Table 11.3 presents technometric values for diagnostic kits for the detection of several infectious diseases: HIV-1 (AIDS virus), CMV, [Cytomegalovirus], Rotaviruses [a virus that attacks the intestinal tract] and Chlamydia IgG and IgM (a venereal disease common in the West), for Israel and Germany. It should be emphasized that for Israel, the technometric values are for kits produced by a single producer, while for Germany there are in most cases more than one.

The technometric indicators for almost all of the kits include: sensitivity, specificity, inter-assay precision and intra-assay precision. For all of them, the units of measurement are per cent. One hundred per cent sensitivity means that all the infected samples tested will yield a positive result.[8] One hundred per cent specificity means that all of the samples that are not infected do not test positive. Sensitivity and specificity correspond to what is known in statistics as Type 1 and Type 11 error (rejecting true hypotheses, and accepting false ones, respectively).

* AIDS detection [HIV-1]: this market amounts to hundreds of millions of dollars and is certain to grow rapidly as the illness itself spreads. Data exist for only two parameters, specificity and sensitivity. Kits made in Germany, Japan and Israel are essentially equivalent in quality.

*Table 11.3:*  *Technometric value for infectious-disease diagnostic kits,*
*Germany, the USA and Israel by type and specifications*

| Kits | Specifications | Technometric value | | |
|------|----------------|---------|------|--------|
|      |                | Germany | USA  | Israel |
| HIV-1 | Sensitivity | 1.00 | 1.00 | 1.00 |
|       | Specificity | 0.87 | 1.00 | 0.84 |
|       | Average | 0.94 | 1.00 | 0.92 |
| Chlamydia | Sensitivity | 0.76 | m.v. | 1.00 |
| Trachom. | Specificity | 0.00 | m.v. | 1.00 |
| IgG | Intra-assay precision | 1.00 | m.v. | 0.78 |
|     | Inter-assay precision | 0.59 | m.v. | 1.00 |
|     | Average | 0.59 | m.v. | 0.95 |
| Chlamydia | Sensitivity | 1.00 | m.v. | 0.67 |
| Trachom. | Specificity | 0.00 | m.v. | 1.00 |
| IgM | Intra-assay precision | 1.00 | m.v. | 0.80 |
|     | Inter-assay precision | 0.65 | m.v. | 1.00 |
|     | Average | 0.66 | m.v. | 0.87 |
| Rotavirus | Sensitivity | 1.00 | m.v. | 1.00 |
| Ag | Specificity | 0.00 | m.v. | 1.00 |
|    | Intra-assay precision | 1.00 | m.v. | 0.00 |
|    | Inter-assay precision | 0.00 | m.v. | 1.00 |
|    | Test duration | 0.00 | m.v. | 1.00 |
|    | Average | 0.40 | m.v. | 0.80 |
| CMV IgM | Sensitivity | 1.00 | m.v. | 1.00 |
|         | Specificity | 0.85 | m.v. | 1.00 |
|         | Intra-assay precision | 0.58 | m.v. | 1.00 |
|         | Inter-assay precision | 0.43 | m.v. | 1.00 |
|         | Average | 0.72 | m.v. | 1.00 |
| CMV IgG | Sensitivity | 0.50 | 0.17 | 1.00 |
|         | Specificity | 0.72 | 1.00 | 0.98 |
|         | Intra-assay precision | 1.00 | m.v. | 0.75 |
|         | Inter-assay precision | 0.83 | m.v. | 1.00 |
|         | Average | 0.76 | 0.59 | 0.93 |

*Note:* m.v. = missing value.

- Rotavirus: while Israel appears to enjoy a technological lead over
  Germany in this area, the technometric index in this case somewhat
  exaggerates the technological gap between them; the Israeli kit
  enjoys a small advantage in 'specificity' over Germany, but the

arithmetic of the [0, 1] metric makes it seem bigger. In inter-assay precision and test duration, the Israeli product does have a substantial lead.

- Chlamydia: Israeli kits lead, with demonstrable superiority in nearly all the key parameters. We note, however, that the German kit is represented in this case by a single product, and it is possible our survey failed to discover other kits of this sort made by German producers.

- CMV: Israeli kits lead those of Germany and the USA.[9] The German products trail, particularly in intra-assay and inter-assay precision. The US kit for CMV IgG led in specificity, but trailed in sensitivity.

Figure 11.4 shows the comparative aggregated technometric profile for the six infectious diseases diagnostic kits, by type.

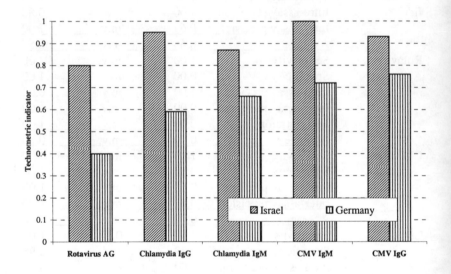

*Figure 11.4: Comparative aggregate technometric profile of selected kits connected with the diagnosis of the infections diseases, by type (CMV, Rotavirus and Chlamydia), Germany and Israel*

Figure 11.5 shows the aggregate technometric profile for all six infectious-disease diagnostic kits; it averages the technometric scores for each of four key parameters, for which data are available, sensitivity, specificity, and intra- and inter-assay precision. The profile indicates that Israel enjoys a small but notable lead. Again, we note the fact that the Israeli kits appeared on the market for the first time as late as 1988. Our interviews with top management of the Israeli firms revealed the belief that sales will expand rapidly in future years, and second-generation products are likely to appear soon.

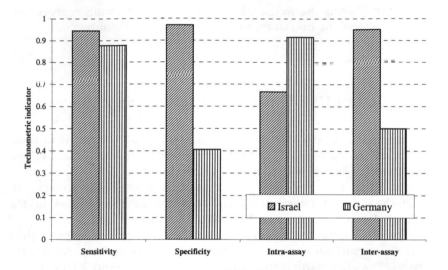

*Figure 11.5: Aggregate technometric profile for six infection-disease diagnostic kits including Germany and Israel, by specification*

## Prices and 'Voice of the Market'

Noteworthy by its absence from our analysis, and from the technometric approach in general, is data on prices and consumer preferences. Prices are not in general included as a product or process attribute in technometrics, since the objective is largely to assess data that measure product quality and relate that quality to its price; technometric specifications, thus, are in a sense one input in a study of the determinants of price. For example, in the 'hedonic price index' approach, technometric scores can be used as explanatory variables in regression equations that try to explain product prices by variables measuring, among other things, quality.[10]

Consumer preferences can play a role in providing information on the relative importance of various technometric attributes. While in this study we have simply taken the simple average of technometric scores, in aggregating, in some instances it is preferable to use weights elicited from surveys of product buyers. We note that in general, weighted averages are not very sensitive to small changes in weights; when only the most important technometric attributes are chosen from the outset, a condition inherent in the method itself, our experience has been that altering the weights of the specification, during aggregation, has not altered the overall technometric score significantly.

## 11.4 CONCLUSION AND IMPLICATIONS

These results suggest that for biodiagnostic products, Israel is in some cases at the frontier of technological excellence, according to the technometric index, and in other cases is close to it. This has occurred despite the fact that far less resources have been invested in biotechnology in Israel, compared with the other countries in the survey, Japan, Germany and the USA.

There is reason for concern that this area of proven technological excellence will not be translated into market share and export sales for Israel. The eight participating firms in our survey report a lack of risk capital, and difficulty in marketing and distributing their products. Four of the eight firms are wholly owned subsidiaries of foreign companies, suggesting that much of the benefits of excellence at the R&D stage will accrue abroad.

Moreover, Israel's industrial and R&D policy has been slow to implement many of the Katzir Committee recommendations and to support biotechnology, and biodiagnostics in particular, as a promising area of excellence.

A primary reason for the failure of government ministries to provide adequate support for this product area is that biotechnology companies are small, and the current size of their export sales is also small, relative to other industrial branches. Ministries prefer dealing with large companies, even when small science-based firms meet the key criterion of exporting a large fraction of their output.

Thus, the field of biotechnology is a particular case of a more general problem in Israel, severe constraints facing nearly all high-tech startups as they make the difficult transition from successful R&D projects to producing, marketing and distributing products and processes in distant markets. There is a danger that Israeli expertise in this area will be recognized by foreign firms, who will then purchase it, causing the employment, exports and profits to accrue outside of Israel. Israel has already experienced a sizeable export of its know-how, in the area of agricultural technology, for example, and later found its products were competing with foreign ones made with original Israeli design and technology.

Policy issues in biodiagnostics, revealed in part by the technometric indexes, have also appeared in other Israeli industries, including, for example, the plastics industry. This industrial sector, studied by Frenkel (1990), is characterized by numerous small firms, which are secretive about their products and technologies (for understandable reasons), and the firms in it are highly competitive in their business strategies. Yet ironically, in order to compete abroad it is vital for them to cooperate with their competitors, because few of them can alone mount successful marketing and distribution efforts in distant foreign markets.[11]

This is where government policy can play a major role, as mediator, initiator and peacemaker. Joint-marketing ventures could be established, in cases where technometric and other quantitative indexes reveal favourable prospects for competing abroad. Investment in such efforts are no less important than supporting research and development and providing venture capital. Yet repeatedly, fruitful public investments and support at the initial stage of the innovation cycle are frustrated by the lack of timely investments at the later stages, production and especially marketing.

There is widespread awareness in Israel of her deficiencies in marketing skill, which result in shares of world markets far below what the technological quality of Israeli products otherwise would merit. That awareness has not yet led to decisive action or sizeable allocation of resources to solve it.

# NOTES

1    An earlier version of this Chapter, co-authored with Amnon Frenkel, Thomas Reiss and Knut Koschatzky, has been published in *Research Policy* 23, pp. 281–292, 1994, and is reprinted with permission from Elsevier Science. In addition to the GIF grant, additional support for this research came from the E. Schaver and A. Meyer Research Funds at Technion. Parts of this paper were presented to the Management of Technology Seminar at MIT-Sloan School of Management, and to the 1993 conference of EARIE (European Association for Research in Industrial Economics).

2    See Chapters 1 and 2 in this volume as well as Grupp (1994).

3     Compare also Chapter 14.
4     See Grupp et al. (1990) and Chapters 1 and 2.
5     According to the US Pharmaceutical Manufacturers Association, this cost has risen to $230 million in 1990 (Moran, 1991).
6     In general, industrial firms in Israel are very small.
7     A major difficulty in doing this is that European standards in many areas have not yet been agreed upon, which some see as a deliberate European strategy to hamper imports from other countries.
8     Sensitivity is for obvious reasons a highly important attribute when the presence of infectious diseases is being tested.
9     For CMV IgG, we had only partial results for the USA.
10    See, for instance, Chapter 4 for a study of hedonic prices for sensors.
11    See Maital (1991) for a discussion of the role of joint ventures.

# 12 Sensor Technology: A Static Assessment[1]

**Main Ideas in this Chapter**

This Chapter contains a technometric benchmarking case study of Israel's sensor industry in comparison with parallel products in the USA, Europe and Japan. In distinction to the next Chapter 13, which illustrates the dynamic case, this Chapter provides a (static) cross-section analysis. It is found that even such small players as Israel – whose GDP is only 1 per cent that of the USA – are able to establish a competitive sensor industry with quality comparable to that of their much larger competitors. Technometric assessment of product performance is a useful tool for identifying market niches – customers whose needs are not met by existing products – and hence can help avoid fruitless, costly rivalry with firms who enjoy superior human and capital resources. The structure of the Chapter is as follows. The first Section provides a brief overview of the global sensor industry. Next, a description of the technometric methodology is outlined and applied to evaluating several types of industrial sensors, including sensors that measure pressure, temperature, acceleration, force and relative humidity. The final Section 12.3 draws conclusions.

## 12.1 SENSORS: AN OVERVIEW OF TECHNOLOGY AND MARKETS

Quantitative measures of technology are vital ingredients for decision-making on R&D and innovation at all levels, from the individual, firm through an entire industry or even nation (Grupp, 1995). Several different approaches for assessing technology have been suggested in the literature.[2] In this Chapter, the technometric approach is applied to a study of Israel's sensor industry, in comparison with that of Europe, the USA and Japan.

## Sensor Market Size and Growth

Sensor technology is a key technology for nearly all products in the industries of metrology, analytics, automation and transportation. It is estimated that the civil sensor market will grow annually by 7.8 per cent up to a volume of US$43 billion in the year 2001 (Arnold, 1991).

The sensor market is highly heterogeneous – many different measuring principles and types of sensors can be found. Sensors can measure temperature, pressure, acceleration, force and other physical conditions. Measurement principles range from extensometers through optical, infrared or biochemical principles.

Due to the wide variety of sensors there is no clear-cut sensor industry. Manufacturers can be found in different branches that produce different kinds of sensors. Biosensor production is more closely related to the chemical or biotechnological industry, optical sensors are closer to optics and electronics and other principles are more related to machinery and mechanics. Also the size of companies varies greatly. There are many small companies, each of which produces a very specific type of sensor (for example glucose sensor). On the other hand big international companies like Honeywell, Bosch, Siemens, ABB, Ginsbury, Fasco or Endeveco are major world-wide producers and suppliers of a wide and diversified range of sensors.

Occasionally, in the 'sensor industry', companies do not produce the sensing element (which is the measuring unit), but combine an element supplied by another company with an electronic device and put it in a box which matches the requirements for the specific measuring conditions (for example measuring water, air, or acid environment). This raises the question: what is a sensor?

Generally, distinctions are made between a sensing element, a sensor and a sensor system. A sensing element (or transducer) is the first member in the measuring chain and converts the measured value into an electric signal. The sensor often incorporates processing of the signal. The sensor system permits full information processing, that is, a computer and software for analysing the measuring values. Whether sensor systems are still sensors, or rather belong to measuring instruments, is a controversial issue. In this Chapter sensors are defined as sensing elements and sensor components including electronic devices for signal processing, microprocessors and analog-digital transformers.

According to a study made by Intechno market research institute in 1991 nearly 35 per cent of world-wide sensor demand results from process technology and mechanical engineering (Arnold, 1991). Some 14 per cent of the world's sensor production is being used in car manufacturing. Some years ago it was estimated that this sector would grow much faster. In 1991 the market volume for car sensors only reached US$2.7 billion. Demand grew slower than expected, especially in products related to car safety and car comfort. But market estimates now show an increase in demand (for example for automatic tyre, pressure control, automatic shock absorption or air bags) which will be further stimulated by new environmental laws in the USA during the 1990s.

Although car manufacturing is already the second most important application field of sensors (after process automation and machinery construction), the difference in market volume between both fields will decrease until 2001. With an average growth rate of 12.4 per cent the market volume in sensors used in car manufacturing will reach around US$9 billion in 2001 whereas process automation sensors' demand is estimated to rise to nearly US$14 billion.

The third most important application field is machinery (US$2.2 billion in 1991, US$4.5 billion in 2001). Most important are machine tools, packaging machinery, handling and robots. The most dynamic market segment is conveyor equipment with an annual growth rate of 9.8 per cent. Other important application fields are information and communication technology, building and security technology, medical engineering and environmental technology.

The world market share for the USA ranges around 34 per cent. Japan ranks second (23.6 per cent) and Germany third (13.5 per cent). Between these three countries only minor changes will occur until 2001. The market share of the USA will decrease slightly to 34.1 per cent, and Japan's and Germany's shares will increase to 24.3 per cent and 14.1 per cent, respectively. France holds a share of 7.1 per cent (2001: 7.0 per cent), the UK of 5.9 per cent, (2001: 5.5 per cent) and Italy of 5.7 per cent (2001: 5.5 per cent).

Pressure sensors are the most common type of sensor. Their market volume will reach US$7.2 billion in 2001 after US$3.2 billion in 1991. Flow and temperature sensors rank second and third. They are followed by: binary position sensors (proximity switches), filling level sensors, chemical sensors, position sensors, speed and revolution sensors, ultrasonic image sensors, and flue gas sensors. The highest annual growth rates of 10 per cent and above characterize sensors for measuring distance, acceleration, vibration, speed and revolution, as well as optical and biosensors.

## Sensor Survey and Data

Out of the above-mentioned sensor types, five were chosen for an international comparison. Selection criteria were market importance, along with data accessibility and comparability. According to these criteria, sensors measuring pressure, temperature, acceleration, force, and relative humidity, were selected. A detailed technical description of these sensor types and, also of the underlying measurement principles can be found in the technical literature (see for example Juckenack, 1990; Schanz, 1988).

A previous technometric study on sensors carried out 1986/87 was based on data supplied by the SENSOR database hosted by STN (Grupp et al., 1987). However, another method of data collection had to be chosen for this study, because, regrettably, the SENSOR database was not updated after 1986.[3] For that reason 'primary' data collection was required. During the SENSOR exhibition of May 1991 in Nuremberg, Germany, the world's largest exhibition of its kind, all exhibiting firms producing or supplying types of sensors under investigation were asked for catalogues containing descriptions and technical specifications.

Not all companies could be approached during the exhibition. Those not approached were asked afterwards to submit relevant catalogues and data sheets. Out of 286 companies from whom information was requested, 151 answered and were included in the sample. Together with 10 Israel companies interviewed directly, data from 161 sensor firms were analysed. The technical information represents the state of the art in sensor technology as of spring/summer 1991, with some supplemental updates as of autumn 1991.

The country distribution of companies reflects participation of countries in the SENSOR exhibition, since the official catalogue was used as address database. Some 86 (or 53 per cent) of the companies or suppliers are of German origin, 34, (or 21 per cent) are from the USA and 10 (or 6 per cent) are from Israel (many of which did not attend the exhibition). Other countries included are Switzerland (8 companies), the UK (5), the Netherlands (5), Japan (3), France (2), Italy (2), and Austria, Denmark, Finland, Ireland, Luxemburg, and Norway (one company each). It should be noted that this survey is biased towards Germany and Europe. Nevertheless, 21 per cent of the companies are USA in origin.

It should be emphasized that the country distribution in the survey is more dependent on the variety of the sensor principles found in the different catalogues than on the number of companies. If, for example, a German company distributes sensors from a Swiss company, these sensors were regarded as Swiss in origin. For that reason, the bias is mitigated by the different size structure of the companies and by selling sensors of parent or other companies.

## 12.2 TECHNOMETRIC ANALYSIS

### Methodology

Technometrics is the quantitative measurement of the technological quality or sophistication of a product or process, group of products or processes, or industry. This approach produces a quantitative profile of a product or process, showing graphically its performance characteristics for selected key attributes, in comparison to those of other firms or countries. Such indices can be aggregated across groups of products, to permit comparisons of the comparative technological level of subsectors or even entire industries.[4]

Every product or process has a set of key specifications or attributes that define its performance, value or ability to satisfy customer wants. Almost by definition, every specification or attribute can be quantified. Each of these attributes has its own unit of measurement: millimetres per second, years of lifetime, and so on. Problems arise in aggregating attributes to build a single quality index. The technometric indicator surmounts this difficulty by converting each measured attribute into a [0, 1] metric, enabling construction of weighted averages, and so on, and permitting comparisons across products, firms, industries and countries. The '0' point of the metric is set as the technologically standard attribute; the '1' point is set as the most technologically sophisticated attribute in existence.

According to the sensor study performed in 1986 (Grupp et al., 1987), six key technical specifications were selected for describing the performance of a sensor. These are:
• measuring range;

- lowest measurable value;
- highest measurable value;
- sensitivity;
- minimal operating temperature;
- maximal operating temperature.

This selection also reflects the accessibility of data. Although there is a group of specifications given in each catalogue or data sheet, only a few are comparable and can be found for most types of sensors.

It is obvious that the decision to buy a sensor for very specific purposes is made according to criteria other than the ones used in this study. Often it is a question of size, of linearity, of hysteresis, or of stable measuring results, under critical conditions, or just a matter of price. In an initial stage of this study more specifications were included in the analysis, but it soon emerged that international comparison was only possible by using the above-mentioned six specifications. Nevertheless, the selected specifications represent well-established characteristics of different types of sensors.

To sense a signal, different physical principles may be used. It is not only possible to measure pressure by using a strain gauge, but also piezo-resistive, piezoelectric, inductive, capacitive or mechanical principles can be found. The same is true for the other groups of sensors. Those physical or measurement principles have been included in the study where data from at least two countries were available. This makes it possible not only to compare the technological level of pressure, temperature, acceleration, force and relative humidity sensors internationally, but also the ability to use different physical principles to measure and convert the measured value into an electric signal.

For that reason the technometric analysis not only indicates the single [0, 1] metric values (K*, in technometric terminology) for six specifications, but also for different measurement principles under one measurement parameter (for example pressure). Single K* figures are shown in Tables 12.1 through 12.5. A graphical example of technometric profiles is given for pressure sensors. Here single technometric figures are linked by lines which generate a technometric plane. This plane should not suggest homogeneity but should enable the reader to have a better look at the ups and downs in the technometric profile. It was not possible to calculate values for all countries over all measurement principles because of data heterogeneity. For that reason only countries with complete or nearly complete sets of data will be reviewed.

**Pressure Sensors**

The most common principles among pressure sensors are mechanical extensometers (strain gauge), piezo-resistive (strain gauge on an electrical/electronic basis) and inductive principles. Pressure sensors are for example used in motor-management control, in air bags, airconditioning equipment and in all industrial production processes where pressure in tanks, vessels and pipes needs to be controlled. K* values for these principles are shown in Table 12.1. For Germany, Israel and Switzerland data were available for all three principles, whereas profiles for the USA, Japan and the UK could only be drawn on the basis of two principles. The Netherlands and Luxemburg were included with piezoresistive pressure sensors only. Respective data can be found in Table 12.1, which contains numbers for piezoelectric and mechanic pressure sensors as well.

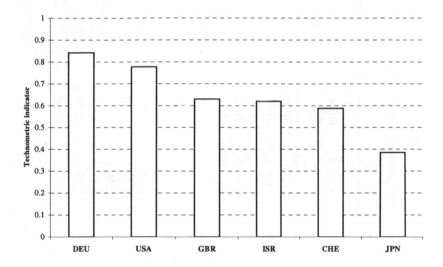

*Figure 12.1: Technometric indicator values for pressure sensors*

The profiles reveal a strong position for Germany (DEU), especially in the case of strain gauge sensors. US pressure sensor technology is also

Table 12.1:  Technometric indicator values for pressure sensors

| Principle | Country | Average K* | Measuring range K* | Lowest measuring value K* | Lightest measuring value K* | Sensitivity K* | Minimal operating temperature K* | Maximal operating temperature K* |
|---|---|---|---|---|---|---|---|---|
| Piezo-resistive | DEU | 0.90 | 0.90 | 1.00 | 0.48 | 1.00 | 1.00 | 1.00 |
| | ISR | 0.65 | 0.90 | 0.00 | 0.48 | 0.99 | 0.73 | 0.80 |
| | JPN | 0.27 | 0.23 | 0.00 | 0.00 | 0.89 | 0.36 | 0.12 |
| | NLD | 0.31 | 0.76 | 0.00 | 0.19 | 0.81 | 0.00 | 0.08 |
| | LUX | 0.24 | 0.18 | 0.00 | 0.00 | 0.20 | 0.55 | 0.48 |
| | NOR | 0.36 | 0.49 | 0.00 | 0.03 | m.v. | 1.00 | 0.30 |
| | CHE | 0.62 | 0.90 | 0.00 | 0.48 | 0.97 | 1.00 | 0.40 |
| | USA | 0.80 | 1.00 | 0.00 | 1.00 | 0.97 | 1.00 | 0.84 |
| | GBR | 0.64 | 0.84 | m.v. | m.v. | 0.81 | 0.36 | 0.55 |
| Strain gague | DEU | 1.00 | 1.00 | 1.00 | 1.00 | 0.98 | 1.00 | 1.00 |
| | GBR | 0.62 | 0.66 | 1.00 | 0.12 | 0.98 | 0.74 | 0.19 |
| | ISR | 0.26 | 0.00 | 1.00 | 0.00 | 0.54 | 0.00 | 0.03 |
| | ITA | 0.67 | 0.83 | 1.00 | 0.33 | 0.82 | 0.75 | 0.26 |
| | FRA | 0.66 | 0.72 | 1.00 | 0.17 | 0.98 | 0.82 | 0.26 |
| | JPN | 0.50 | 0.83 | 1.00 | 0.33 | 0.54 | 0.27 | 0.03 |

Table 12.1 continued

| Principle | Country | Average K* | Measuring range K* | Lowest measuring value K* | Lightest measuring value K* | Sensitivity K* | Minimal operating temperature K* | Maximal operating temperature K* |
|---|---|---|---|---|---|---|---|---|
| | CHE | 0.65 | 0.72 | 1.00 | 0.17 | 1.00 | 0.75 | 0.26 |
| | USA | 0.66 | 0.83 | 1.00 | 0.33 | 0.82 | 0.78 | 0.19 |
| Inductive | DEU | 0.70 | 0.85 | 1.00 | 0.25 | 1.00 | 0.73 | 0.40 |
| | ISR | 0.95 | 1.00 | 1.00 | 1.00 | 0.97 | 1.00 | 0.73 |
| | CHE | 0.73 | 0.83 | 1.00 | 0.20 | 0.60 | 0.73 | 1.00 |
| Piezoelectric | DEU | 0.61 | 0.78 | 0.00 | 0.14 | 1.00 | 0.81 | 0.91 |
| | USA | 0.87 | 1.00 | 1.00 | 1.00 | 0.22 | 1.00 | 1.00 |
| Mechanic | DEU | 1.00 | 1.00 | 1.00 | 1.00 | 1.00 | 1.00 | 1.00 |
| | CHE | 0.35 | 0.76 | 0.00 | 0.16 | 0.95 | 0.22 | 0.00 |

*Note:* m.v. = missing value.

251

well advanced although there are some weaknesses in strain gauge sensors (highest measurable value and maximal operating temperature). Israel (ISR) does well in inductive pressure sensors and to a lesser extent also in piezo-resistive pressure sensors. Switzerland's (CHE) performance over all specifications is diverse with some strong positions in piezo-resistive and strain gauge sensors.

When all pressure sensor principles are combined into a single aggregate index – made possible by the [0, 1] technometric index – Germany attains an overall technometric indicator of 0.84, which emphasizes her leading international position in pressure sensors (Figure 12.1). The United States (USA) ranks second at 0.78, followed by the United Kingdom (GBR) with 0.63. Israel is in fourth position (0.62), ahead of Switzerland (0.59). Since only a few Japanese (JPN) companies were included in the survey the technometric indicator for Japan (0.38) should be regarded only as a rough indicator.

**Temperature Sensors**

Temperature sensors are mainly based on thermoelectric, resistive and infrared principles. Thermoelectric and resistive sensors measure temperature through an electric or resistive change induced by temperature variation. Thermoelectric sensors can be found in temperature measurement in gases or liquids and can also be utilized for calibrating measurement equipment. Resistive sensors are used for several industrial applications where temperature needs to be measured under different conditions concerning pressure or flow. Infrared sensors belong to the group of contactless measuring equipment. Their application field is high temperature measurement for example in metallurgical engineering. Beside these major principles fibre-optic, electro-optic and mechanical temperature sensors can also be found.

Table 12.2 presents technometric data for five major principles. Again, Germany reaches the highest scores in nearly all specifications. Compared to Israel and the USA there are only a few weak points in thermoelectric sensors (that is, highest measurable value and maximal operating temperature). Israel's temperature sensor technology is also quite strong, with some slight weaknesses in lowest and highest measurable value (both for thermoelectric and resistive sensors). Data for the USA and Switzerland reveal a standard performance only in some specifications of infrared and thermoelectric sensors, but show high K* figures otherwise.

*Table 12.2:    Technometric indicator values for temperature sensors*

| Principle | Country | Average K* | Measuring range K* | Lowest measuring value K* | Lightest measuring value K* | Sersitivity K* | Minimal operating temperature K* | Maximal operating temperature K* |
|---|---|---|---|---|---|---|---|---|
| Thermoelectric | DEU | 0.94 | 0.95 | 1.00 | 0.86 | 1.00 | 1.00 | 0.85 |
| | ISR | 0.96 | 0.96 | 0.89 | 0.90 | 1.00 | 1.00 | 1.00 |
| | CHE | 0.58 | 0.89 | 0.89 | 0.77 | 0.95 | 0.00 | 0.00 |
| | USA | 0.81 | 1.00 | 0.80 | 0.99 | 0.99 | 0.25 | 0.84 |
| | FRA | 0.75 | 0.65 | 0.89 | 0.44 | 0.97 | 1.00 | 0.51 |
| | ITL | 0.63 | 0.98 | 0.53 | 1.00 | 0.00 | m.v. | m.v. |
| Resistive | DEU | 0.99 | 1.00 | 1.00 | 1.00 | .00 | 1.00 | 0.94 |
| | GBR | 0.58 | 0.72 | 0.28 | 0.57 | 0.90 | 0.32 | 0.69 |
| | ISR | 0.91 | 0.90 | 0.80 | 0.84 | 1.00 | 0.91 | 1.00 |
| | JPN | 0.52 | 0.71 | 0.20 | 0.57 | 0.60 | m.v. | m.v. |
| | CHE | 0.75 | 0.92 | 0.80 | 0.84 | 0.80 | 0.91 | 0.20 |
| | USA | 0.91 | 0.92 | 0.80 | 0.84 | 1.00 | 0.91 | 1.00 |
| Infrared | DEU | 1.00 | 1.00 | 1.00 | 1.00 | 0.99 | 1.00 | 1.00 |
| | CHE | 0.49 | 0.92 | 0.09 | 0.84 | 1.00 | 1.00 | 0.08 |
| | USA | 0.64 | 0.98 | 0.00 | 1.00 | 0.92 | 0.72 | 0.23 |

*Table 12.2 continued*

| Principle | Country | Average K* | Measuring range K* | Lowest measuring value K* | Lightest measuring value K* | Sensitivity K* | Minimal operating temperature K* | Maximal operating temperature K* |
|-----------|---------|-----------|--------------------|--------------------------|----------------------------|----------------|----------------------------------|----------------------------------|
| Mechanic | DEU | 0.92 | 1.00 | 1.00 | 1.00 | 1.00 | 0.50 | 1.00 |
| | ISR | 0.42 | 0.23 | 0.36 | 0.00 | 0.95 | 1.00 | 0.00 |
| Fibre-optic | JPN | 0.08 | 0.00 | 0.25 | 0.00 | m.v. | m.v. | m.v. |
| | USA | 0.50 | 1.00 | 1.00 | 1.00 | 0.00 | 0.00 | 0.00 |

*Note:* m.v. = missing value.

Combining individual K* figures for all analysed temperature sensors, Germany reaches again the highest technometric indicator (0.96). Israel takes the second position (0.76) slightly ahead of the USA (0.72). Switzerland ranks fourth (0.61) whereas Japan's rather low figure is due to technological weaknesses in fibre-optic temperature sensors (and in addition, the low number of companies included in this study).

## Acceleration Sensors

Acceleration sensors are needed for motor car development (crash analysis) and are used in aircraft and space technology. Two major physical principles can be found: piezoelectric and inductive sensors. Other types of acceleration sensors are based on piezo-resistive, capacitive, fibre-optic and strain gauge principles.

As the measurement of acceleration is closely linked with aircraft and space technology, the USA reaches the highest scores in the technometric analysis, although the K* figures for sensitivity and the lowest measurable value in piezoelectric sensors represent only standard technology (Table 12.3).

Switzerland, as well as Israel, is strong in some specifications of piezoelectric sensors. Here sensors from Israel are internationally ahead in sensitivity. Acceleration sensors from Germany only represent standard technology. Only one high score is reached for the minimal operating temperature at inductive sensors. No figures could be found for lowest and highest measurable value for these sensors in the catalogues. For that reason no technometric figures have been calculated. Norway also shows some strong positions in the field of inductive acceleration sensors.

The combined technometric indicator values underscore the advanced position of the USA, which could already be seen from the previous figures. The USA reaches a K* figure of 0.89, far ahead of Switzerland (0.40) and Israel (0.38). Compared to these three countries German acceleration sensor technology is not very well advanced. Combining all available single K* figures Germany reaches an overall indicator of only 0.35.

*Table 12.3: Technometric indicator values for acceleration sensors*

| Principle | Country | Average K* | Measuring range K* | Lowest measuring value K* | Highest measuring value K* | Sensitivity K* | Minimal operating temperature K* | Maximal operating temperature K* |
|---|---|---|---|---|---|---|---|---|
| Piezoelectric | DEU | 0.27 | 0.65 | 0.00 | 0.05 | 0.00 | 0.60 | 0.30 |
|  | USA | 0.80 | 1.00 | 0.00 | 1.00 | m.v. | 1.00 | 1.00 |
|  | ISR | 0.26 | 0.00 | 0.00 | 0.00 | 1.00 | 0.54 | 0.00 |
|  | CHE | 0.61 | 0.97 | 1.00 | 0.50 | 0.00 | 0.59 | m.v. |
| Inductive | CHE | 0.09 | 0.53 | 0.00 | 0.00 | 0.00 | 0.00 | 0.00 |
|  | USA | 0.89 | 1.00 | 0.34 | 1.00 | 1.00 | 1.00 | 1.00 |
|  | NOR | 0.69 | 0.90 | 1.00 | 0.26 | m.v. | 1.00 | 0.27 |
|  | DEU | 0.42 | 0.00 | m.v. | m.v. | m.v. | 1.00 | 0.27 |
| Piezo-resistive | USA | 0.98 | 1.00 | m.v. | m.v. | m.v. | 1.00 | 0.93 |
|  | GBR | 0.75 | 0.00 | m.v. | m.v. | 1.00 | 1.00 | 1.00 |
| Capacitive | ISR | 0.50 | 0.00 | m.v. | m.v. | 0.00 | 1.00 | 1.00 |
|  | CHE | 0.50 | 1.00 | m.v. | m.v. | 1.00 | 0.00 | 0.00 |

*Note:* m.v. = missing value.

*Table 12.4:  Technometric indicator values for force sensors*

| Principle | Country | Average K* | Measuring range K* | Lowest measuring value K* | Highest measuring value K* | Sensitivity K* | Minimal operating temperature K* | Maximal operating temperature K* |
|---|---|---|---|---|---|---|---|---|
| Inductive | DEU | 0.70 | 1.00 | 1.00 | 1.00 | 0.53 | 0.29 | 0.40 |
| | ISR | 0.83 | 0.85 | 1.00 | 0.40 | 1.00 | 0.74 | 1.00 |
| | USA | 0.60 | 0.13 | 1.00 | 0.00 | 0.95 | 1.00 | 0.52 |
| Strain gauge | DEU | 0.93 | 0.94 | 1.00 | 0.61 | 0.99 | 1.00 | 1.00 |
| | FRA | 0.47 | 0.73 | 1.00 | 0.10 | 1.00 | 0.00 | 0.00 |
| | ISR | 0.53 | 0.81 | 1.00 | 0.20 | 0.99 | 0.00 | 0.16 |
| | JPN | 0.73 | 1.00 | 1.00 | 1.00 | 0.98 | 0.18 | 0.21 |
| | USA | 0.47 | 0.30 | 1.00 | 0.00 | 0.93 | 0.31 | 0.28 |

257

**Force Sensors**

Force sensors can measure traction and pressure forces and are used in control equipment as well as in tool machinery, feed presses or robots. Sensors included in this study are based on inductive and strain gauge principles. Piezoelectric and mechanic force sensors can also be found but, due to missing figures for certain specifications, they were not included in the technometric analysis.

Inductive sensors are supplied by German, US and Israeli companies, whereas force sensors based on strain gauge principle are also produced by French (FRA) and Japanese companies (Table 12.4). German force sensors never reach a low K* figure but show some weaknesses in sensitivity and operating temperatures (inductive principle). Inductive force sensors are a competitive Israeli product, although the highest measurable value is higher among German sensors. In strain gauge technology, where German products always show good performance, Japanese sensors rank second despite their comparatively low figures for operating temperatures. France, the USA and Israel follow in the third to fifth positions.

Germany's advantages in strain gauge technology are responsible for an overall technometric indicator of 0.81. Israel's strong position in inductive force sensors put her on a second rank at 0.68 whereas the USA reaches 0.53. Japan is not included in this ranking because data were available for inductive sensors only. For these only, Japan reaches an indicator value of 0.73.

**Relative Humidity Sensors**

Relative humidity can be measured by capacitive, resistive and also optic principles. Only in German catalogues, both capacitive and resistive relative humidity sensors were offered. From other countries mentioned in Table 12.5, either capacitive or resistive sensors were found. For this reason no overall indicator values were calculated for relative humidity sensors.

As with many other measurement parameters, German technology is also well advanced in relative humidity sensors. For all but one specification (maximal operating temperature) Germany reaches K* figures of 1 for both sensor types. Nearly the same state of technology can be observed for Finnish (FIN) capacitive sensors. The only weak point is the low sensitivity. France, Switzerland and Austria (AUT)

Table 12.5:  *Technometric indicator values for relative humidity sensors*

| Principle | Country | Average K* | Measuring range K* | Lowest measuring value K* | Highest measuring value K* | Sensitivity K= | Minimal operating temperature K* | Maximal operating temperature K* |
|---|---|---|---|---|---|---|---|---|
| Capacitive | DEU | 0.97 | 1.00 | 1.00 | 1.00 | 1.00 | 1.00 | 0.81 |
| | AUT | 0.75 | 1.00 | 1.00 | 1.00 | 0.00 | 1.00 | 0.52 |
| | FIN | 0.92 | 1.00 | 1.00 | 1.00 | 0.51 | 1.00 | 1.00 |
| | FRA | 0.86 | 1.00 | 1.00 | 1.00 | 0.6 | 0.75 | 0.81 |
| | CHE | 0.79 | 1.00 | 1.00 | 1.00 | 0.9 | 0.50 | 0.33 |
| Resistive | DEU | 0.93 | 1.00 | 1.00 | 1.00 | 1.00 | 1.00 | 0.60 |
| | GBR | 0.93 | 0.92 | 0.93 | 0.80 | 0.92 | 1.00 | 1.00 |
| | ISR | 0.61 | 0.56 | 0.50 | 0.50 | 0.71 | 1.00 | 0.40 |
| | JPN | 0.20 | 0.00 | 0.00 | 0.00 | 0.00 | 1.00 | 0.20 |

also reach quite high K* figures with 0.75 for Austria as the lowest for capacitive sensors. In the case of resistive sensors the UK ranks second behind Germany, followed by Israel. Here no specification was recorded for maximum K* figures. Japan does not reach the forefront of technology in this technical area, as can clearly be seen from the low scores in the table.

## Technometric Principles According to Measurement Principles

It was mentioned above that it is possible to compare the technological level of countries in sensor technology, not solely by measurement parameters, but also by measurement principles. According to Table 12.6, Germany takes the lead in six out of nine analysed physical principles employed in sensors – strain gauge, resistive, piezo-resistive, capacitive, mechanical and infrared. For the last three principles data for only three countries are available, which makes the results less significant than for the first three principles, for which five countries can be compared. Israel performs surprisingly well in thermoelectric and inductive sensors, reaching the top position for each. The USA ranks first in piezoelectric principles, mainly because of her good performance in acceleration sensors.

As was noted earlier, the method of data collection produced a bias towards those countries represented by sensor producers at the Nuremberg SENSOR exhibition. For that reason it is not possible to compare directly the results of the 1986 technometric study with the results derived in this one. Not only is the database different, but also the variety of measurement principles is different.[5] Three of the six principles analysed in 1986, piezoelectric, resistive and strain gauge (extensometers) sensors can only be compared roughly. For piezoelectric sensors Germany lost considerable ground compared to the USA. Both countries reached an indicator value of around 0.8 in 1986. In this study the USA retained this value. Germany reached only 0.44, mainly because only a few companies still offer this type of sensor.

In resistive sensor technology Germany improved her position significantly from 0.55 in 1986 to 0.96 in 1991. The USA is stable at around 0.9 for both years. Japan's K* figure decreased from 0.55 to 0.36 in 1991; this might be a statistical artifact because of lack of data, hence we offer no analysis or interpretation of these data.

In strain gauge sensors Germany already ranked first in 1986 at 0.85 and still holds this position in 1991 (0.96). The USA reached 0.65 in

1986 and 0.56 in 1991. Israel was not included in the 1986 study so no comparison with recent results can be made.

This short comparison reveals a quite advanced but also quite stable position for US sensor technology and a technological push in resistive sensors for Germany. During the five years after 1986 Germany was able to extend her solid position in strain gauge sensors, not only because Germany's competitors lagged but also due to improvements in German technology.

## Technometric Position of Countries

The aggregation of all average K* figures per country according to sensor types makes it possible to calculate an overall K* figure for each country (Figure 12.2). What can be observed is a very small advantage of Germany over the USA (0.74 and 0.73 respectively). Nearly close figures were obtained in 1986 when Germany reached 0.75 and the USA 0.74. Although Germany improved her sensor technology in selected areas (for example resistive sensors), the small distance between the two countries nearly diminished. As these overall figures are based on different sets of data they can only indicate that both Germany and the USA were, and still are, the international pacemakers in sensor technology. This technometric-based result is also supported by the Intechno market study. According to that survey the USA produce leading-edge sensor technology for application in car and aircraft manufacturing, building and security technology, medical engineering and environmental technology. Germany is especially

*Table 12.6: Technometric indicators for sensors according to measurement principles*

| Principle | DEU | USA | ISR | CHE | JPN | GBR | FRA |
|---|---|---|---|---|---|---|---|
| Strain gauge | 0.96 | 0.56 | 0.39 | 0.65 | 0.61 | 0.61 | 0.56 |
| Resistive | 0.96 | 0.91 | 0.76 | 0.74 | 0.37 | 0.75 | |
| Piezo-resistive | 0.90 | 0.89 | 0.65 | 0.62 | 0.27 | 0.64 | |
| Thermoelectric | 0.94 | 0.81 | 0.96 | 0.58 | | 0.74 | |
| Inductive | 0.61 | 0.74 | 0.89 | 0.41 | | | |
| Piezoelectric | 0.44 | 0.83 | 0.26 | 0.61 | | | |
| Capacitive | | 0.97 | | | 0.65 | | 0.86 |
| Mechanic | 0.96 | | 0.42 | 0.35 | | | |
| Infrared | 1.00 | 0.64 | | 0.49 | | | |

strong in applying sensors to machinery. Taking all European countries together, they hold the technological lead in machinery ahead of Japan and the USA. The same is true for process technology and mechanical engineering.

Although Japan reached relatively low technometric scores in this analysis, it seems justifiable to put Japan in the third position behind Germany and the USA, because of its strong international market position. According to Intechno (Arnold, 1991), Japan holds the world's strongest position in sensors for household appliances and electronic products, as well as in information and communication technology. This is a mass market for cheap sensors where Japan and the USA have strong advantages over Europe.

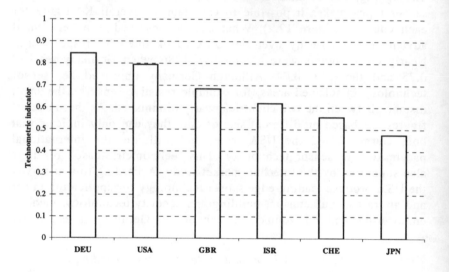

*Figure 12.2: Technometric indicators for sensor technology according to countries*

Compared to Switzerland (K* 0.53) where some well-established sensor producers are located, Israel's overall indicator of 0.61 is unexpectedly high. It can be concluded that Israel possesses an advanced sensor industry, although not much of its activities are known abroad. In contrast to Switzerland, Israel's sensor variety is smaller which makes it possible to concentrate technological know-how in specific fields.

## 12.3 CONCLUSION

We have applied the technometric technology assessment approach in order to evaluate relative performance levels of sensors, across different types, physical principles, and countries. Overall, technometric indicators provide an in-depth portrait of the relative levels of the major players' sensor technologies.

An important result of this study is that nipping at the heels of the 'Big Three' (USA, Germany, Japan) are not only such well-known players like the UK, France, Switzerland and Italy, but also smaller countries like Israel, who proved herself able to establish a competitive sensor industry, at least in certain parts of the market. Israel – and some other smaller countries as well – not only produce high-performing competitive sensors, but in some cases sensors that represent the most advanced technology which can be purchased internationally at the present time. The market performance of these countries – including Israel – often falls short of what the performance of their products could justify, because of shortcomings in their marketing skills.

By collecting readily accessible data on product specifications, often obtainable in large part from material distributed at major trade fairs, and by organizing that data in a coherent and systematic fashion, using technometric methods, it is possible to generate an up-to-date audit of the state of technology in a given industry. The results of that audit can provide highly valuable data for plotting both corporate-level innovation strategy (such as R&D plans for second- or third-generation products) and country-level science, innovation and industrial policy.

## NOTES

1   An earlier version of this Chapter, co-authored with Knut Koschatzky and Amnon Frenkel, was published in *Int. J. Technology Management, Special Issue on Technology Assessment, Vol. 11*, Nos. 5/6, pp. 667–687 (1996).
2   See, for instance, Grupp (1991), Koschatzky (1991), Saviotti (1985), Saviotti et al. (1982); as well as Part I of this book.
3   Market reports could be an alternative source although they are mostly biased towards national manufacturers and suppliers, are quite expensive and have the same updating problem as electronic databases.
4   See Chapters 1 and 2 and also Frenkel et al. (1994b), Grupp (1994, 1998), Grupp and Hohmeyer (1986, 1988).
5   For a true dynamic comparison, see the following Chapter 13.

# 13 Sensor Technology: A Dynamic Assessment[1]

**Main Ideas in this Chapter**

This Chapter proposes an extension of the microeconomic benchmarking approach known as 'technometrics'. We offer a novel approach to measuring technical change at the product level, based on intertemporal comparison of product characteristics, using objective performance measures. Our goal is to provide a straightforward tool for benchmarking technological sophistication, susceptible of clear graphical portrayal; one that shows how technological capabilities have changed between two points in time. In a way, the Chapter continues the analysis of the previous Chapter 12, as it again deals with sensors. The structure of this Chapter is as follows. The first part presents our methodology, outlining the static and dynamic versions of technometrics. Next, we describe our database. Section 13.3 analyses the data and presents our results. Finally, we summarize and conclude.

## 13.1 THE TECHNOMETRIC APPROACH TO MEASURING QUALITY AND TECHNICAL CHANGE: MATHEMATICAL MODEL

One of the most complex problems facing managers is how to benchmark their firms' technological capability relative to competitors, in order to identify points of strength and weakness, as part of strategic planning. It is no accident that the best-selling Harvard Business Review article of all time is C.K. Prahalad and Gary Hamel's (1990) famous piece on the core competence of the firm. Today managers understand how vital it is to identify core competencies – but face major difficulties when seeking to quantify and benchmark capabilities in technology.

Industrial sensors are used as our example. To measure technical change at the individual product level, a technometric feature-by-feature comparison was undertaken twice, once in 1990 and again in 1998. By comparing benchmarking scores for each product feature between 1991 and 1998, the quality improvement for each firm's sensors was measured. To our knowledge, this is one of the first attempts to measure technical change, for individual products, in a direct manner, by focusing on improvements in key product features.[2]

Data on product features were initially collected from pamphlets distributed at the industry's key trade fair for measurement instruments, held every two years in Nuremberg, Germany, in 1991. Using the technometric approach, we compared the quality of industrial sensors for the USA, Japan, Germany, Israel and other countries at that point in time (Koschatzky et al., 1996; see also Chapter 12).

In 1998, we again collected data on firms exhibiting their sensors at the Nuremberg Trade Fair held in 1997. This time, rather than focus on comparing product quality at the country level, we chose to examine product quality at the firm level, and individual product level. To this end, we chose several firms included in the 1991 survey that also took part in the 1997 Trade Fair. We selected from these firms' catalogues products shown both in 1991 and 1997. By benchmarking each of several product features, and comparing their improvements over time, we developed a measure of dynamic technical change at the micro-micro level. This enabled us to measure in concrete terms the technology strategy chosen by each firm in seeking to strengthen its sales and market share.

In this Section, we outline the technometric approach to technology benchmarking, which was introduced in the 1980s (Grupp and Hohmeyer, 1988) in a revised terminology:

$i$ = product, $i$ = 1, ... , n
$j$ = feature, $j$ = 1, ... , m
$K$ = vector of product features
$k$ = firm, 1 = 1, ... , r
$t$ = time index, $t$ = $t_o$, $t_1$
$u$ = units of measurement for feature 'j'

$$\begin{pmatrix} K(i,1,k',t) \\ K(i,2,k',t) \\ .... \\ .... \\ K(i,r,k',t) \end{pmatrix} \bullet \begin{pmatrix} u(1) \\ u(2) \\ ... \\ ... \\ u(r) \end{pmatrix} \Rightarrow \begin{pmatrix} K^*(i,1,k',k,t) \\ K^*(i,2,k',k,t) \\ .... \\ .... \\ K^*(i,r,k',k,t) \end{pmatrix} \qquad (13.1)$$

Equation (13.1) simply uses the u vector to eliminate the units of measurement (for example degrees, pounds, inches) in which technical product features or specifications are measured.

$$K^*(i,j,k',k,t) = \frac{[(K(i,j,k',t) - K(i,j,k_{min},t))]}{[(K(i,j,k_{max},t) - K(i,j,k_{min},t))]} \qquad (13.2)$$

Equation (13.2) converts the K values to [0,1] metrics, by expressing the $j^{th}$ attribute of brand k' in relation to a minimum value, set as zero (the value of the simplest, or least sophisticated, feature available on the market), and a maximum value, set as one (the value of the most sophisticated feature available on the market).

$$K^*_{inv}(i,j,k',k,t) = \frac{[(K(i,j,k',t) - K(i,j,k_{max},t))]}{[(K(i,j,k_{min},t) - K(i,j,k_{max},t))]} = 1 - K^*(i,j,k',k,t). \qquad (13.3)$$

For some features, a higher feature score (for example weight) means lower product quality. Hence, equation (13.3) is used in such cases, where the need arises to invert feature scores.

$$K^*(i,j,k',k,t_1) = \frac{[(K(i,j,k',t_1) - K(i,j,k_{min},t_o))]}{[(K(i,j,k_{max},t_o) - K(i,j,k_{min},t_o))]} \qquad (13.4)$$

Equation (13.4) introduces change over time. It measures the $j^{th}$ feature score at time $t_1$ in relation to feature scores in period $t_o$ (compare Grupp, 1998, pp. 112 onwards).

The essence of the technometric method is the use of physical units for measuring feature sophistication and quality, while the [0, 1] metric enables (a) aggregation of feature scores into an overall score for the entire product, or (b) comparison across features, and across products.

Figure 13.1 provides an example in which a temperature sensor can measure up to a maximum temperature of 50°, at time $t_0$, while the least sophisticated sensor on the market measures up to 20° and the most sophisticated, up to 80°. This product's technometric feature score is therefore 0.5: (80–50)/(80–20). This sensor is 'halfway' from the least to the best.

If this feature remains constant during time $t_1$, while the most sophisticated sensor improves its maximum temperature to 110°, then the benchmark score remains at 0.5 on a 'progress scale' that is extended to 1.5; the sensor is now one-third of the way to the progress frontier. In this simple manner, managers can benchmark their products and track how they measure up relative to competitors, over time.

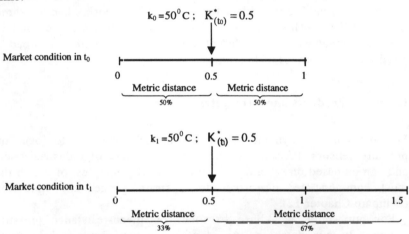

*Figure 13.1: Schematic diagram of the technometric change over time in product k*

## 13.2 DATA SPECIFICATIONS

In Koschatzky et al. (1996), we use the technometric benchmarking approach to compare industrial sensors for a given point in time, the year 1991. This study was based on a mail survey of some 268 firms producing sensors that measured pressure, temperature, acceleration, force and humidity. We chose this sample after visiting the large sensor trade fair in Nuremberg at which over 400 firms had exhibits. Of those 268 firms who made sensors appropriate for our study and to whom we wrote, 150 firms responded. A detailed database was constructed, benchmarking individual product features for specific brand names. We later used this database to identify those product features that generate inferred customer value by examining (through regression analysis) those features that appeared most closely related to product price (Grupp and Maital, 1998a; see also Chapter 4).

In 1998, we repeated our 1991 survey with a view to measuring, for individual products, the technological improvements that had occurred since our earlier study. To this end, we identified the 663 participating firms at the Nuremburg Trade Fair held in 1997 and wrote to each one. Of these, some 100 firms responded and sent us detailed data on their product features. We then identified firms whose sensors had appeared in the earlier 1991 study, as well as in the 1998 one. We tried to choose companies from different countries to provide as broad a possible a spectrum of technologies.

## Choice of Products and Attributes

For this study of dynamic technical change, we chose to focus on pressure sensors. Pressure sensors serve a variety of industrial uses, and can be based on several different physical principles, of which the most common are: piezo-resistance; strain gauge; and induction (compare Chapter 12).

For our study, we chose to focus on piezo-resistance pressure sensors. In our database, we identified seven firms making such sensors [Jumo, Eurosensor, Kulite, Pewatron, Philips, Keller, Bourdon]. Of these, five were included in the 1991 study [Jumo, Eurosensor, Kulite, Pewatron, Philips]; three of those five also supplied data for the 1998 study [Jumo, Eurosensor, Kulite], permitting a comparison between 1991 and 1998. Two companies in the 1991 data did not respond to our 1998 survey; in contrast, two firms provided data in 1998 who were not represented in the 1991 study [Keller and Bourdon].

We selected six key physical sensor attributes as dimensions on which technical change would be measured and compared:

• Measuring range: maximum range of pressures the sensor could measure, in bars.

- Maximal operating temperature: the highest temperature at which the pressure sensor could operate efficiently (degrees).
- Minimal operating temperature: the lowest temperature at which the pressure sensor could operate efficiently (degrees).
- Sensor weight: weight of the sensor (grams); measures miniaturization; many sensors are used in products where size and weight are important.
- Non-linearity: maximal measuring error, measured as the deviation from a linear response line (per cent).
- Hysteresis: maximal measuring error, caused by fluctuations in measuring various pressures, measured as deviation from the initial measured pressure (per cent), and reflecting the tendency of a system to remain in its initial state even when subject to change.

Table 13.1 shows the value of these six attributes for piezo-resistant pressure sensors for the seven companies in our sample: Jumo, Keller and Bourdon (Germany); Kulite (USA); Eurosensor (UK), Philips (Netherlands), and Pewatron (Switzerland). Since each firm makes a wide range of pressure sensors, we recorded the maximum and minimum values for each attribute, intra-firm. This then enabled us to conduct cross-firm comparisons, searching for the maximum and minimum values for the entire seven-firm sample, on the way to calculating our technometric benchmark scores according to equations (13.2) to (13.4). It will be recalled that the highest feature value gets the score of [1] in 1991 and the lowest, the score of [0]. Table 13.1 shows technometric scores for each of the seven firms, and for each of the six features, for 1991 and 1997. *Since our study aims to examine the technology envelope, we picked the best-performing sensor for each firm, in order to measure the extremes of technology, but considered the most sophisticated, and least sophisticated, attributes on the market.*

## 13.3 PRESSURE SENSORS REVISITED: A CASE STUDY

Figures 13.2 and 13.3 show the technometric profile of piezo-resistance sensors for 1991 and for 1997, respectively. These profiles

*Table 13.1: Value of physical characteristics for piezo-resistant pressure sensors for seven firms: 1991 and 1997; and technometric scores for each firm*

| Name of firm | Parameter | Specifications 1991 | | | | | |
| --- | --- | --- | --- | --- | --- | --- | --- |
| | | Measuring range (bar) | Temperature operating Maximum °C | Minimum | Sensor weight (g) | Linearity (%) | Hysteresis (%) |
| Jumo (Germany) | Maximum | 400 | 120 | -30 | 14 | 0.3 | 0.1 |
| | Minimum | 1 | 50 | 0 | 310 | 0.6 | 0.1 |
| | K* | 0.29 | 0.33 | 0.67 | 0.96 | 0.55 | 0.98 |
| Eurosensor (UK) | Maximum | 345 | 125 | -40 | 0.3 | 0.05 | 0.01 |
| | Minimum | 0.14 | 80 | -20 | 3 | 0.5 | 0.15 |
| | K* | 0.25 | 0.36 | 0.80 | 1.0 | 1.0 | 1.0 |
| Kulite (USA) | Maximum | 1379 | 260 | -55 | 13 | 0.2 | 0.1 |
| | Minimum | 69 | 120 | -20 | 150 | 0.2 | 0.3 |
| | K* | 1.0 | 1.0 | 1.0 | 0.96 | 0.73 | 0.98 |
| Pewatron (Switzerland) | Maximum | 100 | 100 | -30 | 1 | 0.3 | 0.2 |
| | Minimum | 1 | 80 | -20 | 170 | 0.5 | 6 |
| | K* | 0.07 | 0.24 | 0.67 | 0.99 | 0.55 | 0.97 |
| Philips (Netherlands) | Maximum | 400 | 180 | -30 | 2.8 | 0.5 | 0.1 |
| | Minimum | 0.4 | 80 | 20 | 200 | 0.5 | 0.1 |
| | K* | 0.29 | 0.62 | 0.67 | 0.99 | 0.18 | 0.98 |

Table 13.1 continued

| Name of firm | Parameter | Specifications 1997 | | | | | |
|---|---|---|---|---|---|---|---|
| | | Measuring range (bar) | Temperature operating °C Maximum | Minimum | Sensor weight (g) | Linearity (%) | Hysteresis (%) |
| Jumo (Germany) | Maximum | 1000 | 200 | −50 | 14 | 0.3 | 0.1 |
| | Minimum | 0.25 | 90 | −30 | 320 | 0.35 | 0.2 |
| | K* | 0.73 | 0.71 | 0.93 | 0.96 | 0.55 | 0.98 |
| Eurosensor (UK) | Maximum | 34.5 | 125 | −40 | 3 | 0.02 | 0.01 |
| | Minimum | 0.07 | 125 | −40 | 27 | 0.1 | 0.1 |
| | K* | 0.03 | 0.36 | 0.80 | 0.99 | 1.06 | 1.0 |
| Kulite (USA) | Maximum | 2100 | 273 | −195.5 | 3 | 0.1 | 0.1 |
| | Minimum | 0.35 | 37.5 | −30 | 270 | 0.1 | 1 |
| | K* | 1.52 | 1.06 | 2.87 | 0.99 | 0.91 | 0.99 |
| Keller (Germany) | Maximum | 1000 | 150 | −45 | 8 | 0.2 | 0.1 |
| | Minimum | 0.1 | 40 | 10 | 440 | 0.5 | 0.5 |
| | K* | 0.73 | 0.48 | 0.87 | 0.98 | 0.73 | 0.99 |
| Bourdon (Germany) | Maximum | 5000 | 150 | −55 | 15 | 0.2 | 0.2 |
| | Minimum | 0.25 | 40 | −25 | 1200 | 0.8 | 0.8 |
| | K* | 3.63 | 0.48 | 1.00 | 0.95 | 0.73 | 0.97 |

are a graphic way of visualizing product quality, feature by feature, within a corporate brand name. They also permit a clear, visual view of how relative product quality changed between 1991 and 1997, feature by feature. In comparison, one may derive the extent of technical change in these six years.

From Figure 13.2 we learn that four firms except Kulite offer about the same quality in terms of measuring range, maximum and minimum operational temperature. In these features, Kulite is the world leader. In terms of weight all five brands are about equal as it is the case for hysteresis. In linearity (accuracy) the product of Eurosensor performs best, that is, it is the most accurate product among the five products compared.

In the three features concerning weight, linearity and hysteresis, little has changed over the six years from 1991 to 1997. Some more detailed observations may be found on the next pages. Obviously, the sensor of Bourdon leads the measuring range now with an outstanding attribute, but also the Kulite sensor has improved in this respect. The same is true for minimum temperature of operation, which may be much lower for the newer products of Kulite.

An aggregate measure of technical quality can be computed by simply taking the arithmetic average of the six feature scores for each company. These scores are shown in Table 13.2. In reality, some consumer preferences are required here but are not available for 1997 (compare Chapter 4).

*Table 13.2:*   *Aggregate technometric score for firms producing piezo-resistant sensors, 1991 and 1997*

| Firms' name | 1991 | 1997 |
|---|---|---|
| Jumo (Germany) | 0.63 | 0.81 |
| Eurosensor (UK) | 0.73 | 0.71 |
| Kulite (USA) | 0.95 | 1.39 |
| Pewatron (Switzerland) | 0.58 | n.d. |
| Philips (Netherlands) | 0.62 | n.d. |
| Keller (Germany) | n.d. | 0.80 |
| Bourdon (Germany) | n.d. | 1.29 |

*Note:* n.d. = no data.

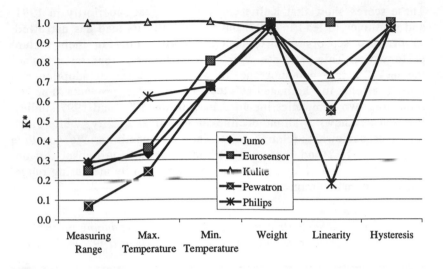

*Figure 13.2: Technometric profile of piezo-resistive sensors – comparison between five firms in 1991*

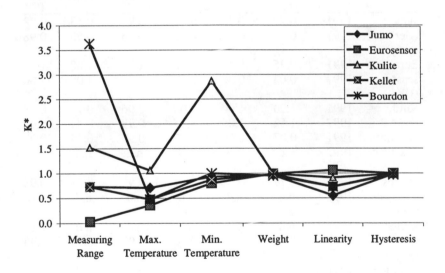

*Figure 13.3: Technometric profile of piezo-resistive sensors – comparison between five firms in 1997*

These scores show that Kulite enjoyed technical superiority in 1991, and continues to lead in 1997, but numerically its lead has narrowed, as pressure sensors tend to become more similar in their feature performance. This pattern – which we could term 'regression toward the mean' – is a common one, in which processes of adoption and imitation tend to 'homogenize' technology-based products. For the remaining two companies included in both the 1991 and 1997 studies, Eurosensor shows a slight decline in technical quality, while Jumo improves somewhat, relative to its (new) competitors. We conclude from Table 13.2 and Figures 13.2 and 13.3 that Eurosensor did not take vigorous action to remedy the weaknesses in its measuring range, and maximum and minimum temperatures.

*Table 13.3:*     *Technometric score for seven firms producing piezo-resistive sensors: dynamic comparison, 1991 versus 1997*

| Name of firm | Year | Specifications | | | | | |
|---|---|---|---|---|---|---|---|
| | | Measuring range (bar) | Temperature operating Max. Min. °C | | Sensor weight (g) | Linearity (%) | Hysteresis (%) |
| Jumo | 1991 | 0.29 | 0.33 | 0.67 | 0.96 | 0.55 | 0.98 |
| (Germany) | 1997 | 0.73 | 0.71 | 0.93 | 0.96 | 0.55 | 0.98 |
| Euro-sensor (UK) | 1991 | 0.25 | 0.36 | 0.80 | 1.00 | 1.00 | 1.00 |
| | 1997 | 0.03 | 0.36 | 0.78 | 0.99 | 1.05 | 1.00 |
| Kulite | 1991 | 1.00 | 1.00 | 1.00 | 0.96 | 0.73 | 0.98 |
| (USA) | 1997 | 1.52 | 1.06 | 2.87 | 0.99 | 0.91 | 0.98 |
| Pewatron | 1991 | 0.07 | 0.24 | 0.67 | 0.99 | 0.55 | 0.97 |
| (Switzerland) | 1997 | n.d. | n.d. | n.d. | n.d. | n.d. | n.d. |
| Philips | 1991 | 0.29 | 0.62 | 0.67 | 0.99 | 0.18 | 0.98 |
| (Netherlands) | 1997 | n.d. | n.d. | n.d. | n.d. | n.d. | n.d. |
| Keller | 1991 | n.d. | n.d. | n.d. | n.d. | n.d. | n.d. |
| (Germany) | 1997 | 0.73 | 0.48 | 0.86 | 0.98 | 0.73 | 0.98 |
| Bourdon | 1991 | n.d. | n.d. | n.d. | n.d. | n.d. | n.d. |
| (Germany) | 1997 | 3.63 | 0.48 | 1.00 | 0.95 | 0.73 | 0.97 |

*Note:* n.d. = no data.

One of the advantages of our method is that we are able to benchmark the two firms – Bourdon and Keller – in 1997 relative to 1991, even without firm-specific data for them for 1991, using market-best scores for 1991 as our base benchmark measures.

### Feature-by-feature Analysis

Dynamic technometric analysis can focus on individual features, and analyse changes in each over time. Table 13.3 shows dynamic technometric scores for each feature, using the 1991 values as the base values In this way, the technometric score can of course exceed 1.0, if the highest feature value in 1997 exceeds that in 1991 (which was in fact the case for Kulite's measuring range, for instance, scoring 1.52 in 1997, and scoring 2.87 for minimum temperature in 1997 compared with 1991).

### Firm Analysis

For three firms, a comparison of their quality strategy is possible, since they are represented in the data base in both years. Starting with Jumo (Figure 13.4), a clear technology management strategy seems to be the case. While the three features, weight, linearity and hysteresis which were not bad in the 1991 comparison were kept as they are, Jumo improved the three specifications which were farther behind the market leader in 1992, Kulite. Jumo technology managers improved specifications nearly up to the level Kulite offered to the markets in 1991. Of course, for the 1997 comparison, this is not the leading-edge, but still Jumo is following the technological frontier.

In Figure 13.5 we observe that the features' profile of the best brand of Eurosensor did not change much. In fact some features deteriorated (meaning that some brands with superior specifications were taken off the market, probably because of non-competitive high prices). This is true for the measuring range (not visible in Figure 13.5, where only improvements are marked in black). A little step forward is observed in terms of accuracy (linearity).

Clearly, Kulite (Figure 13.6) enjoyed technological superiority in 1991, scoring highest in all but one feature, 'linearity' (accuracy). While Kulite's sensors improved relatively in linearity in 1997, they remained where they are in another accuracy measure, hysteresis, and

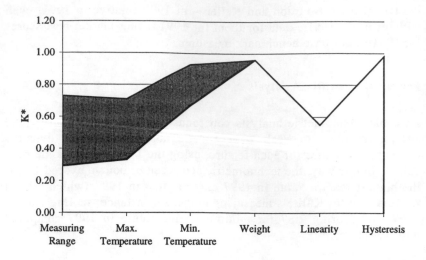

*Figure 13.4: Dynamic comparison of Jumo piezo-resistant sensors, 1991 (white) and 1997 (shaded), for each feature*

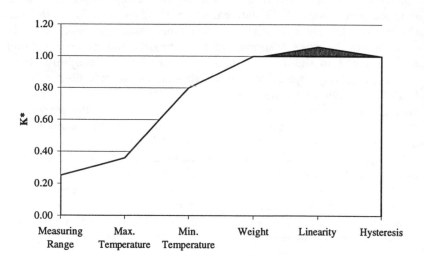

*Figure 13.5: Dynamic comparison of Eurosensor piezo-resistant sensors, 1991 (white) and 1997 (shaded), for each feature*

improved somewhat their measuring range, while Bourdon sensors took top place here. The marketplace implications of this relative change depend, of course, on the relative importance the customers for sensors attach to the various features. With extreme low operating temperatures they are now far ahead of their competitors.

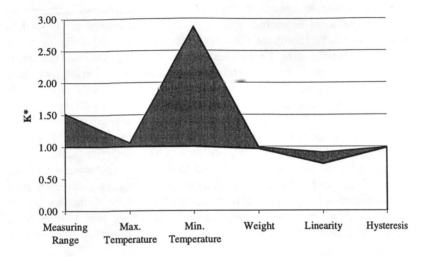

*Figure 13.6: Dynamic comparison of Kulite piezo-resistant sensors, 1991 (white) and 1997 (shaded), for each feature*

## 13.4 CONCLUSION

In this Chapter we attempt to demonstrate the usefulness of technometrics for dynamic analysis. Yet, our sensor study has several severe shortcomings. First of all, the data are limited to few companies, and for some of them data are not present in both years 1991 and 1997. For a direct comparison of company performance we are left with only three firms. A real analysis of the dynamics in sensor technology certainly has to be founded on a more representative sample of firms.

Despite this limitation, it was possible to show that technical progress in these six years did not develop uniformly over the sensor products, as only some specifications were improved considerably.

Many other features remained about the same. Thus, the theoretical notion of a 'linear trend' or else in technical progress is certainly not justified. Firms observe a technology strategy; they know of customer preferences and improve their products *selectively*. Sometimes they take advanced products off the market, probably because of high prices and low customer preparedness to pay them.

On the research agenda more such dynamic studies remain. In particular we want to include real customer preferences as we did in the hedonic study (compare Chapter 4 for sensors and Chapter 5 for aircraft). It would also be interesting to include, next to the most advanced product of major producers of sensors, a variety of their brands and compare them relative to each other. Such analysis is possible as has been shown for photovoltaic products (Grupp, 1998, pp. 402 onwards). For strategic management of technology, our novel approach to measuring technical change at the product level in intertemporal comparison of product characteristics and using objective performance measures seems to be a straightforward tool for benchmarking technological sophistication. Managers can learn how their own technological capabilities have changed between two points in time in relation to their respective competitors which may have changed significantly over time.

## NOTES

1    This Chapter was originally written for this book. First author is Amnon Frenkel who was also responsible for data handling and the survey. We are grateful to the companies who participated in the survey reported in this Chapter for their cooperation in supplying data. A later version has been submitted to the *International Journal of Technology Management* and is likely to be published there in volume 20, nos. 3–4, 2000 (note added in proofs).

2    Another such example is on solar cells; compare Grupp (1997b).

# 14 Twelve Product Groups: Complexity and Diversity[1]

## Main Ideas in this Chapter

What is the relation between the average level of complexity that characterizes a product's technology, and the degree of diversity of that technology across rival firms? Evolutionary theories of innovation and technical advance are consistent with either a direct or an inverse relation. The issue thus becomes an empirical one. This Chapter uses a unique database containing detailed quantitative data on the specifications of 12 high-tech product groups for the USA, Japan and selected European countries, for 1982, for both products and processes. It is found that the more complex the technology, the less diverse is the technology of rival firms that produce the product. This is consistent with the following evolutionary process: economies of scale and scope inherent in high-level technologies require firms who adopt them to dispose entirely of older technologies, in order to remain competitive; at the same time, older, simpler technologies continue to exist and permit wide diversities among firms who pursue 'niche' market strategies. The structure of this Chapter is as follows. Section 14.1 surveys the relevant evolutionary theories of innovation. Section 14.2 defines the technometric indexes that are used to measure the level and diversity of technology. Section 14.3 describes the database that permits us to generate empirical estimates of those indexes for the USA, Japan and some European countries. Section 14.4 presents the main empirical results and examines their implications. The concluding Section suggests some directions for future research.

## 14.1 EVOLUTIONARY THEORIES OF INNOVATION

For rival firms within a given industry or product group, are product and process technologies uniform in their level of complexity? Or in contrast, are such technologies highly diverse? Evolutionary theories of innovation are consistent both with models in which variations in technological quality diminish as the technology ages – through a kind of competitive 'natural selection' – or with models in which such variations increase, as conservative firms manage to coexist with more innovative ones. The issue thus becomes an empirical one.

This study proposes a new measure for the diversity of technology, based on the technometric indexes (Grupp, 1991, 1994; Grupp and Hohmeyer, 1986, 1988), and applies that measure to the estimation and comparison of the relation between the average level of complexity in technology, and its diversity across firms, principally those in the USA and Japan. Use is made of a unique Japanese database that provides detailed cross-country quantitative data on product and process specifications for 12 high-tech product groups.

One of the most powerful paradigms for technological advance is Schumpeter's model of the evolutionary process (Schumpeter, 1939, 1950, 1961) and the related interpretations and extensions of the model (Freeman, 1982; Nelson and Winter, 1982). According to this model, ideas, innovations and technologies compete for resources in a market environment. Basic and applied research, like mutations, generate variations within 'species' of products and processes. These variations are then sorted by a process of 'natural selection' – in economics, competitive rivalry for profits and market share. Ultimately, the technology of products and processes most suited to the existing market conditions triumphs. This evolutionary process may be long, time-consuming and somewhat inefficient in the short run.

Schumpeter perceived this dynamic process as the very essence of capitalism. He wrote:

> 'In dealing with capitalism, we are dealing with an evolutionary process ... The fundamental impulse that sets and keeps the capitalist engine in motion comes from the new consumers' goods, the new methods of production or transportation, the new markets, the new forms of industrial organization that capitalist enterprise creates. ... The opening up of new markets, foreign or domestic, and the organizational development from the craft shop and factory to such concerns as U.S. Steel illustrate the same process of industrial mutation – if I may use that biological term – that incessantly revolutionizes the economic structure from within, incessantly destroying the old one, incessantly creating a new one. This process of Creative Destruction is the essential fact about capitalism. It is what capitalism consists in and what every capitalist concern has got to live in' (Schumpeter, 1950, pp. 82–83).

In his books and articles, Schumpeter repeatedly cautioned against embracing biological evolution and natural selection in its entirety as a model for innovation. Nelson, too, has noted that there are major differences between the biology of evolution and the evolution of technology:

'... the feature that most sharply distinguishes the evolutionary process through which technology advances, from biological evolution, is that new findings, understandings, generally useful ways of doing things, do not adhere strictly to their finder or creator but are shared, at least to some extent. In many cases, the sharing is intentional, in others despite efforts to keep findings privy' (Nelson, 1990, p. 1941).

One major difference between biological and economic evolution, as Nelson observes, lies in learning and imitation. Economies, unlike ecologies, evolve in part when 'firms watch other firms and try to learn from their experience', Nelson wrote (1990, p. 211).

A somewhat different evolutionary theory, associated with Utterback, suggests that a wide range of technological innovations ultimately leads to a *dominant product design* a new product with a fairly standard, common set of features – that enforces or encourages standardization, and narrows the variety of possible new products down to a few 'species' or standard products (Utterback and Abernathy, 1975).

Some of these Schumpeterian 'learning' models posit that as a technology design configuration ages, more and more firms gain the opportunity to learn and use it, as they observe other firms and adapt and acquire their technology. This suggests the following hypothesis:

'Firms learn with time': *the older (and presumably, less complex) a technology is. the smaller should be the degree of diversity in the level of technology across rival firms.*

However, while learning, diffusion and market forces operate to narrow technological diversity over time, a different and opposing evolutionary force – one that works to *broaden* diversity in technological complexity and leads to product differentiation. In order to meet customer wants, product differentiation often presents a do-or-die decision – either adopt costly new technologies and replace existing plants with new ones (because the new technology is optimally efficient at such high levels of output that it does not pay to run old product variants and new ones in parallel) or remain solely with the old plant and equipment. Once firms do begin adopting the new level of quality and complexity, it is often so cost-effective or high-quality that competing firms face another fateful either-or choice:

Either adopt the new technologies that competitors have implemented, or leave the industry entirely.

In his book *Scale and Scope*, business historian Chandler (1991) notes two examples in which powerful economies of scale and scope led major companies to dominate their industries through new technologies in a very short space of time. In the USA in the 1880s, the Standard Oil trust built a massive new kerosene plant, whose economies of scale slashed production costs by an order of magnitude and generated large profits. In Germany, at the same time, Bayer, Hoechst and BASF built huge new chemical plants capable of producing a large number of different dyes on the same chemical base. The resulting economies of scope reduce production costs dramatically and gave the three above-mentioned firms a dominant position in the market.

This particular evolutionary process, in which dramatic economies of scale and scope make it imperative to adopt new technologies, implies a do-or-die decision: *the newer and more complex the technology, the smaller the degree of diversity across different firms*. Firms must either adopt the new technology quickly, or 'die' (leave the industry). Over time, diversity in technology increases, as firms find 'niche' strategies and exploit market segments that larger, more technologically advanced firms ignore.

The two contradictory hypotheses cannot in fairness be labelled 'Schumpeter versus Chandler', because Schumpeter's views themselves were somewhat ambiguous, and changed and evolved over time.

As Heertje (1992) points out, Schumpeter's earlier writings emphasize the key role played by small, new firms who act as technology pioneers. Thus, Schumpeter wrote in 1939 that 'even in the world of giant firms, new ones rise and others fall into the background. Innovations still emerge primarily with the "young" ones, and the "old" ones display as a rule symptoms of what is euphemistically called conservatism .... [our model] explains why innovations are not carried into effect simultaneously and as a matter of course ... by all firms' (1939, p. 97). This is 'firms learn with time'.

But in *Capitalism, Socialism and Democracy*, Heertje notes that Schumpeter 'seems to have lost sight of the relative importance of new, often small firms as the carriers of minor and sometimes major innovations, not to speak of their role in the process of invention' (Heertje, 1992, p. 10). There, the emphasis is on scale, and on 'do-or-die'.

In this sense, both hypotheses may be viewed as Schumpeterian. The evolutionary model of innovation in capitalist development is thus consistent with either: (a) diminishing diversity in technological quality, as the technology ages; or (b) increasing diversity. The issue then becomes an empirical one – appealing to data and facts to determine which hypothesis is valid.

It is possible to point to specific technologies that fit either the 'firms learn with time' or the 'do-or-die' hypothesis. For instance, Ray (1989) describes four process technologies for which the equipment incorporating them 'is usually of large capacity, often large enough to make the older technique wholly redundant ,. when built, the new plant takes over huge quantities of output, in large indivisible chunks, from the earlier technology. Thus diffusion is swift.'

These four technologies are: oxygen steelmaking, continuous casting, the tunnel kiln and the float glass process. Two newer technologies also belong in this category, he believes: robots and automatic flexible manufacturing systems.

Here, firms face all-or-nothing decisions. Those that adopt the technologies must replace older ones completely. Those that will not, or cannot afford to, may quickly disappear. This type of new technology does not leave much room or much time for differentiation in technology or for 'varieties of species'.

But not all technologies are of this sort. There are some more 'divisible' technologies. Ray cites as examples shuttle looms and numerically controlled machine tools. In Europe, about two-thirds of all cotton-type looms are shuttle looms of older vintage and shuttleless looms, Ray observes; and the share of numerically controlled machine tools is far lower. Here, new and old technologies coexist, leaving a wide variance or range across firms in the level of technological advance.

The precise nature of the process through which technology diffuses through an economy and from one economy to another – and through which one firm learns from another – is very important, because it is a crucial determinant of competitive advantage. It has been widely claimed and believed that the Japanese efficiency in exploiting and diffusing existing technology gives that country an advantage over slower-moving competitors. Nelson has argued that 'the Japanese system is not of fundamentally different design from the American but rather is a different and perhaps more effective model in the same broad class' (1990, p. 211). Attaining a better understanding of the technology diffusion process, in general, and empirically testing which of the above two hypotheses is correct, may have important policy implications.

Empirical studies of evolutionary models in general, and the diffusion of technology in particular, face severe measurement problems. Ray's studies of the life-cycle of several technologies (1989) measure diffusion by 'the proportion of the new machines [embodying a new technology] in the total stock of productive equipment.' Ray notes that 'lack of data prevents measuring diffusion in another, perhaps more informative manner, namely *the contribution of the new technology to total production*'.

The next Section suggests a new operational technique for measuring both the level of best-practice technology and its degree of diversity across firms.

## 14.2  THE TECHNOMETRIC APPROACH TO MEASURING TECHNOLOGICAL QUALITY AND COMPLEXITY

A technometric index of product and process quality has been developed by Grupp and Hohmeyer (1986, 1988).[2] Technometrics begins by observing that every product or process has a set of key attributes that define its performance, value or ability to satisfy customer wants. Most of these attributes can be quantified – for instance, in the case of solar cells, such attributes as intrinsic cell efficiency, flash current, standard power, voltage, bulk factor, module efficiency, power per unit of area, power per unit of weight, and warranty time can all be defined and measured in physical units.

Each of these attributes has a different unit of measurement. Problems then arise in aggregating attributes to build a single quality index. The technometric indicator surmounts this difficulty by converting each measured attribute into a [0, 1] metric, enabling construction of weighted averages, and so on, and permitting comparisons across products, firms, industries and countries.

Formally, let subscripts f, i, j and k represent firms, products, product attributes or characteristics, and subgroup (industry or country), respectively.[3] Let $K_f(i, j, k)$ represent the measurement of an attribute for given f, i, j and k.

The technometric indicator, $K^*$, is defined, on the [0, 1] metric, as the maximum national performance of attribute j in product group i:

$$K^*i,j,k = \frac{K_{\max}(i, j, k) - K_{\min}(i, j, k_{\min})}{K_{\max}(i, j, k_{\max}) - K_{\min}(i, j, k_{\min})} \tag{14.1}$$

where:

| | |
|---|---|
| $K_{\max}(i, j, k) =$ | the highest value of product characteristic 'j' for product 'i', for country k, achieved by some firm in that country. |
| $K_{\min}(i, j, k_{\min}) =$ | the *lowest* value of product characteristic 'j', among *all* countries k, produced by some firm in country $k_{\min}$. |
| $K_{\max}(i, j, k_{\max}) =$ | the *highest* value of product characteristic 'j' among *all* members of country k, produced by some firm in country $k_{\max}$. |

It is possible to aggregate K* across all key attributes of a product or process in order to achieve an aggregate K* measure for the product or group of products. This aggregate technometric measure can then be correlated with other variables to determine the link between technological excellence and, for instance, market success. K* can also contribute to policymaking, indicating products or sectors where a country has a competitive advantage, technologically, and hence worthy of investment to advance marketing and sales efforts in foreign markets and to further improve R&D and production efficiency at home.

Constructing technometric indexes, especially for cross-country comparisons, is costly and highly data-intensive. Fortunately, a database exists containing technometric specifications for some 42 different product groups and processes. The data were compiled in 1982 in Japan (Agency for Industrial Science and Technology, 1982). We shall now describe these data and then use them to test our two hypotheses.[4]


## 14.3 DATABASE AND SPECIFICATIONS

In a survey sponsored and funded by the Japanese Agency for Industrial Science and Technology, Japanese experts were asked in 1982 to evaluate specifications for 42 different product groups for the USA, Japan, and selected European countries.[5] These product groups included high-technology, medium-technology and low-technology products. The data include 984 specification items and 5,584 data points – experts were asked to estimate maximum, minimum, and model values for each specification, for Japan and the USA, and for some foreign countries as well.

Of the 42 product groups, 12 were in the high-tech realm. High-tech was defined as a product group within a three-digit industry (according to the Standard Industrial Classification) characterized by research and development expenditures amounting to at least 3.5 per cent of sales turnover. The 12 high-tech product groups selected for study were: (1) optic fibres; (2) industrial assembly robots; (3) ultra high-tension transformers; (4) video tape recorders; (5) large computers; (6) digital X-ray equipment; (7) LSI memory; (8) semiconductor lasers; (9) passenger cars; (10) general ships; (11) civilian aircraft; (12) LSI probers (large-scale integrated circuit probers, or sensors, designed to determine whether LSI microchips are defective).

The experts provided their quantitative estimates of technical specifications $K_f(i, j, k)$, including, for each, $K_{max}$, $K_{min}$, and $K_{mode}$ (the modal value of $K_{i,j,k}$ for each specification, for firms in each country). They also indicated whether the specification was 'standard' (coded S, in column D of Table 14.1), or 'key' (coded K, in column D), meaning of major future importance.

Detailed descriptions of a sample of the raw data (for optic fibres), and the manner in which $K^*_{range}$ and $K^*_{mode}$ were computed, are shown in Table 14.1. All told, we extracted and analysed 844 data points.

$K_{mode}$ was converted to the [0,1] technometric index $K^*_{mode}$ through:

$$K^*_{mode} (i, j, k) = \qquad\qquad\qquad\qquad\qquad\qquad (14.2)$$

$$[K_{mode}(i, j, k) - K_{min}(i, j, k_{min})]/[K_{max}(i, j, k_{max}) - K_{min}(i, j, k_{min})]$$

That is, $K^*_{mode}$ was put into the [0,1] metric for each country by expressing it as a fraction of the difference between the global state-of-the-art value (the highest value of the specification available anywhere) and the value for the lowest-performing (and presumably, least costly) specification anywhere.

*Table 14.1: Data on product and process specifications for optic fibres for the USA, Japan and the UK, 1982*

| Specifications | Units | Type | Pro-duct key | Expert weight | Agg-regate weight | Max Japan | Min Japan | Mode Japan | Max USA | Min USA | Mode USA |
|---|---|---|---|---|---|---|---|---|---|---|---|
| A | B | C | D | E | F | G | H | I | J | K | L |
| Attenuation (0.85 μm) | db/km | product | S* | 0.505 | 0.039 | 3.00 | 2.40 | 2.50 | 3.50 | 2.50 | 3.00 |
| Attenuation (1.3 μm) | db/km | product | S | 0.693 | 0.053 | 1.00 | 0.40 | 0.70 | 1.00 | 0.50 | 0.70 |
| Attenuation (1.3 μm) | db/km | product | S | 0.815 | 0.063 | 0.50 | 0.40 | 0.50 | 0.70 | 0.60 | 0.40 |
| Bandwidth (6 db. 0.85 μm) | MHz/km | product | S | 0.725 | 0.056 | 1000.00 | 500.00 | 1000.00 | 1000.00 | 500.00 | 800.00 |
| Bandwidth (6 db. 1.3 μm) | MHz/km | product | S | 0.845 | 0.065 | 2000.00 | 100.00 | 1500.00 | 1300.00 | 80.00 | 1000.00 |
| Transmission range (100 mbits) | km | product | S | 0.690 | 0.053 | 300.00 | 15.00 | 15.00 | 25.00 | 10.00 | 15.00 |
| Transmission range (400 mbits) | km | product | S | 0.690 | 0.053 | 40.00 | 20.00 | 20.00 | 30.00 | 20.00 | 20.00 |
| Power loss (0.85 μm) | db/km | product | S | 0.560 | 0.043 | 0.20 | 0.10 | 0.10 | 0.20 | 0.10 | 0.10 |
| Breakdown force (50%, 1.25 μm) | kg/mm$^2$ | product | S | 0.715 | 0.055 | 600.00 | 500.00 | 550.00 | 600.00 | 500.00 | 500.00 |
| Lifetime (standard conditions) | years | product | S | 0.690 | 0.053 | 100.00 | 30.00 | 50.00 | 100.00 | 50.00 | 50.00 |
| De-OH process (water quantity) | ppb* | process | K | 0.930 | 0.072 | 20.00 | 0.20 | 1.00 | 15.00 | 1.00 | 10.00 |

*Table 14.1 continued*

| Specifications | Units | Type | Product key | Expert weight | Aggregate weight | Max Japan | Min Japan | Mode Japan | Max USA | Min USA | Mode USA |
|---|---|---|---|---|---|---|---|---|---|---|---|
| A | B | C | D | E | F | G | H | I | J | K | L |
| Purity | ppb*** | process | K** | 0.435 | 0.034 | 3.00 | 0.00 | 1.00 | 1.00 | 0.00 | 0.20 |
| Control of refraction | 0.01% | process | K | 1.000 | 0.077 | 13.30 | 0.10 | 1.00 | 1.00 | 1.00 | 1.00 |
| Control of diameter (1.25 μm) | μm | process | K | 0.505 | 0.039 | 2.00 | 0.50 | 1.00 | 2.00 | 0.50 | 1.00 |
| Control of diameter (50 μm) | μm | process | K | 0.505 | 0.039 | 2.00 | 1.00 | 1.00 | 2.00 | 1.00 | 2.00 |
| Loss from nonhomogeneity | db/km | process | K | 0.780 | 0.060 | 0.20 | 0.05 | 0.10 | 0.10 | 0.10 | 0.10 |
| Control of temp. gradients | indexed | process | K | 0.780 | 0.060 | 100.00 | 100.00 | 100.00 | 100.00 | 90.00 | 90.00 |
| Control of impurities | indexed | process | K | 0.430 | 0.033 | 100.00 | 100.00 | 100.00 | 100.00 | 90.00 | 100.00 |
| Flame Method | indexed | process | K | 0.360 | 0.028 | 100.00 | 100.00 | 100.00 | 100.00 | 100.00 | 100.00 |
| Etching | indexed | process | K | 0.215 | 0.017 | 100.00 | 100.00 | 100.00 | 100.00 | 100.00 | 100.00 |
| Colour coating | indexed | process | K | 0.360 | 0.028 | 100.00 | 100.00 | 100.00 | 100.00 | 80.00 | 100.00 |
| Control of micro-marginal losses | indexed | process | K | 0.425 | 0.033 | 100.00 | 90.00 | 100.00 | 100.00 | 80.00 | 90.00 |

Table 14.1 continued

| Specifications A | Max GBR M | Min GBR N | Mode GBR O | Max world P | Min world Q | Range Japan R | Range USA S | Range GBR T |
|---|---|---|---|---|---|---|---|---|
| Attenuation (0.85 μm) | 4.00 | 2.50 | 3.00 | 4.00 | 2.40 | 0.60 | 1.00 | 1.50 |
| Attenuation (1.3 μm) | 1.00 | 0.70 | 1.00 | 1.00 | 0.40 | 0.60 | 0.50 | 0.30 |
| Attenuation (1.3 μm) | 0.60 | 0.40 | 0.50 | 0.70 | 0.40 | 0.10 | 0.10 | 0.20 |
| Bandwidth (6 db. 0.85 μm) | 1000.00 | 400.00 | 500.00 | 1000.00 | 400.00 | 500.00 | 500.00 | 600.00 |
| Bandwidth (6 db. 1.3 μm) | 1300.00 | 1000.00 | 1000.00 | 2000.00 | 800.00 | 1900.00 | 1220.00 | 300.00 |
| Transmission range (100 mbits) | 30.00 | 15.00 | 20.00 | 30.00 | 1.00 | 15.00 | 10.00 | 15.00 |
| Transmission range (400 mbits) | 30.00 | 20.00 | 20.00 | 40.00 | 20.00 | 20.00 | 10.00 | 10.00 |
| Power loss (0.85 μm) | 0.20 | 0.10 | 0.10 | 0.20 | 0.10 | 0.10 | 0.10 | 0.10 |
| Breakdown force (50 %, 1.25 μm) | 550.00 | 500.00 | 500.00 | 600.00 | 500.00 | 100.00 | 100.00 | 50.00 |
| Lifetime (standard conditions) | 100.00 | 50.00 | 50.00 | 100.00 | 30.00 | 70.00 | 50.00 | 50.00 |
| Purity | 1.00 | 0.00 | 0.20 | 3.00 | 0.30 | 3.00 | 1.00 | 1.00 |
| De-OH process (water quantity) | 18.00 | 1.00 | 10.00 | 20.00 | 0.20 | 19.80 | 14.00 | 17.00 |
| Control of refraction | 1.00 | 1.00 | 1.00 | 13.30 | 0.10 | 13.20 | 0.00 | 0.00 |
| Control of diameter (1.25 μm) | 2.00 | 0.50 | 2.00 | 2.00 | 0.50 | 1.50 | 1.50 | 1.50 |
| Control of diameter (50 μm) | 2.00 | 1.00 | 2.00 | 2.00 | 1.00 | 1.00 | 1.00 | 1.00 |
| Loss from nonhomogeneity | 0.10 | 0.10 | 0.10 | 0.20 | 0.05 | 0.15 | 0.00 | 0.00 |
| Control of temp. gradients | 100.00 | 90.00 | 100.00 | 100.00 | 90.00 | 0.00 | 10.00 | 10.00 |
| Control of impurities | 100.00 | 90.00 | 100.00 | 100.00 | 90.00 | 0.00 | 10.00 | 10.00 |
| Flame Method | 100.00 | 100.00 | 100.00 | 100.00 | 100.00 | 0.00 | 0.00 | 0.00 |

*Table 14.1 continued*

| Specifications | Max GBR | Min GBR | Mode GBR | Max world | Min world | Range Japan | Range USA | Range GBR |
|---|---|---|---|---|---|---|---|---|
| A | M | N | O | P | Q | R | S | T |
| Etching | 100.00 | 100.00 | 100.00 | 100.00 | 100.00 | 0.00 | 0.00 | 0.00 |
| Colour coating | 100.00 | 80.00 | 90.00 | 100.00 | 80.00 | 10.00 | 20.00 | 10.00 |
| Control of micro-marginal losses | 90.00 | 80.00 | 90.00 | 100.00 | 80.00 | 10.00 | 20.00 | 10.00 |

*Notes:* \*S = standard \*\*K = key \*\*\*parts per billion.
P = MAX(G, J, M); Q = MIN(H, K, N); R = G–H; S = J–K; T = M–N

*Source:* Agency for Industrial Science and Technology (1982).

290

The measure of the degree of diversity in technological specifications across firms in the same product group and country, $K_{range}$, was taken as the difference in the K value across firms in the same country, $K_{max}(i, j, k) - K_{min}(i, j, k)$, expressed as a fraction of the global range in the K value for all countries, within the given product specification:

$$K^*_{range}(i, j, k) = \frac{K_{max}(i, j, k) - K_{min}(i, j, k)}{K_{max}(i, j, k_{max}) - K_{min}(i, j, k_{min})} \qquad (14.3)$$

The two competing hypotheses could then be tested statistically by examining whether the relation between $K^*_{range}$ and $K^*_{mode}$ is direct or inverse for the 12 product groups, for the USA, Japan, and such European countries as the UK and Germany.

*If 'firms learn with time' is valid, then $K^*_{range}$ should vary inversely with $K^*_{mode}$. If 'do-or-die' is valid, then $K^*_{range}$ should vary directly with $K^*_{mode}$.*

All told, the part of the database we extracted, for the 12 high-tech products, comprised data points including a value for $K^*_{range}$ and $K^*_{mode}$, for each particular specification, for the 12 above-mentioned product groups. Thus, for each product group, and each country, a value of $K^*_{range}$ and $K^*_{mode}$ was computed, by taking the simple average of $K^*_{range}$ and $K^*_{mode}$ values for all of the specifications given for the specific product group.[6]

The data for $K^*_{range}$ and $K^*_{mode}$ are shown below in Table 14.2.

In addition to $K^*_{range}$ and $K^*_{mode}$, we extracted from the database five additional variables that characterized each specification:

1. *the product group*, described with a two-digit code, from 1 to 12;
2. *product or process* specification;
3. *future importance of the specification*: yes, if judged by experts to be of likely future importance, coded K; no, coded S;
4. *the relative importance of the specification*: a weight, given by the experts, normalized to add to one.[7]

Table 14.2: Values of $K^*_{range}$ and $K^*_{mode}$, 12 technology-intensive product groups, the USA, Japan and other countries, 1982

| Product | All range | All mode | Japan range | Japan mode | US range | US mode | Other range | Other mode | No. of experts | No. of Specs |
|---|---|---|---|---|---|---|---|---|---|---|
| Optic fibres | 0.638 | 0.553 | 0.668 | 0.575 | 0.644 | 0.534 | 0.603 | 0.550 | 9 | 22 |
| Indust. robots | 0.284 | 0.560 | 0.669 | 0.521 | 0.095 | 0.739 | 0.089 | 0.422 | 5 | 8 |
| Ultra High-tension transformers | 0.288 | 0.788 | 0.232 | 0.855 | 0.250 | 0.743 | 0.381 | 0.766 | 8 | 15 |
| Video tape recorders | 0.517 | 0.517 | 0.537 | 0.697 | | | 0.497 | 0.338 | 7 | 19 |
| Large computers | 0.443 | 0.527 | 0.514 | 0.573 | 0.372 | 0.481 | | | 5 | 16 |
| Digital radiography | 0.259 | 0.644 | 0.234 | 0.522 | 0.264 | 0.825 | 0.277 | 0.584 | 3 | 20 |
| LSI memory | 0.566 | 0.464 | 0.668 | 0.460 | 0.463 | 0.469 | 0.460 | | 5 | 44 |
| Semiconductor lasers | 0.457 | 0.530 | 0.537 | 0.666 | 0.457 | 0.530 | 0.460 | 0.450 | 5 | 46 |
| Cars | 0.444 | 0.577 | 0.453 | 0.717 | 0.429 | 0.513 | 0.453 | 0.500 | 6 | 35 |
| Ships | 0.352 | 0.712 | 0.401 | 0.857 | 0.356 | 0.746 | 0.298 | 0.534 | 7 | 23 |
| Civ. aircraft | 0.449 | 0.627 | 0.59 | 0.366 | 0.221 | 0.883 | 0.534 | 0.631 | 11 | 36 |
| LSI probers | 0.383 | 0.580 | 0.638 | 0.456 | 0.128 | 0.703 | | | 6 | 21 |

Source: Agency for Industrial Science and Technology (1982) and own calculations (see Table 14.1)

292

## 14.4 EMPIRICAL RESULTS

Figures 14.1, 14.2 and 14.3 plot $K^*_{range}$ against $K^*_{mode}$ for the USA, Japan and selected European countries; Japan alone; and the USA alone, respectively. Figure 14.1 shows a statistically significant negative relation between the level of technology and its range or variance for all of the countries in the database taken together. This result is replicated when Japan (Figure 14.2) and the USA (Figure 14.3) are examined in isolation. The regression equations are also given with the Figures.

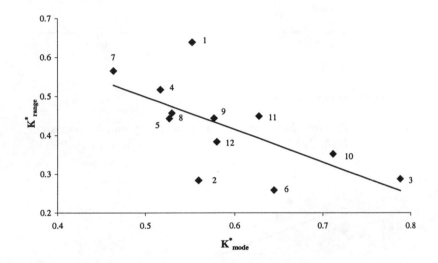

1. optic fibres
2. industrial assembly robots
3. ultra high-tension transformers
4. video tape recorders
5. large computers
6. digital radiography

7. LSI memory
8. semiconductor lasers
9. passenger cars
10. general ships
11. civilian aircraft
12. LSI probers

*Figure 14.1: Relation between average complexity of technology and its diversity, USA, Japan and European countries, 1982*

This suggests that the 'do-or-die' (economies of scale and scope) hypothesis is more compatible with the data than the 'firms-learn-

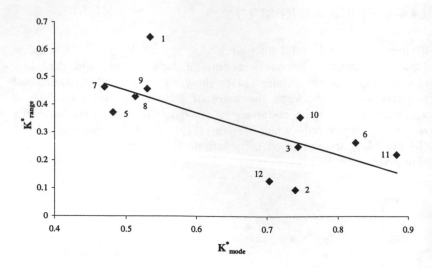

Code numbers as in Figure 14.1.

*Figure 14.2: Relation between average complexity and its diversity,
            USA, 1982*

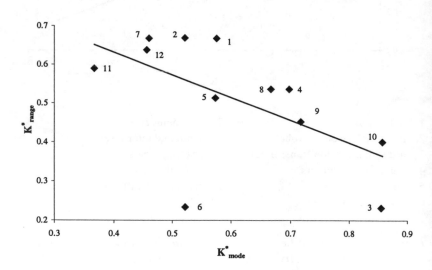

Code numbers as in Figure 14.1.

*Figure 14.3: Relation between average complexity and its diversity,
            Japan, 1982*

over-time' hypothesis. That is, the higher the modal level of technological excellence across firms, the less likely it is that firms will differ widely. This appears to be the case in all the countries included in the database.

## Process versus Product

We performed a t-test on the average values of both $K^*_{range}$ and $K^*_{mode}$, for *product* specifications vis-à-vis *process* specifications, to see whether there were significant differences across the whole database (that is, all 844 data points, divided into 657 product specifications and 187 process specifications):

### MEAN VALUES of $K^*_{mode}$ and $K^*_{range}$

|  | $K^*_{mode}$ | | $K^*_{range}$ | |
|---|---|---|---|---|
|  | *product* | *process* | *product* | *process* |
|  | 0.585 | 0.618 | 0.410 | 0.500* |
| N = | 657 | 187 | 657 | 187 |

* significant at $p<0.01$

For the whole sample, while the modal *level* of technologies did not differ significantly for products compared with processes, the technometric range across firms did differ significantly, with substantially higher variation existing for processes than for products.

Interestingly, the inverse relation between $K^*_{mode}$ and $K^*_{range}$ noted above in Figures 14.1–14.3 held well for *product* specifications, but not for *process* specifications, as shown in the two regression equations below (the t-values of slope coefficients are shown in brackets below the coefficient):

PRODUCTS (N = 657 specifications):

$$K^*_{range} = 0.497 - (0.150) K^*_{mode}, \qquad R^2 \text{ adj.} = 0.021$$
$$(3.88)$$

PROCESSES (187 specifications)

$$K^*_{range} = 0.550 - (0.077) K^*_{mode} \qquad R^2 \text{ adj.} = 0.006$$
$$(1.05)$$

While the coefficient of $K^*_{mode}$ was statistically significant for the 'product' regression, it was not statistically significant for the 'process' regression. This implies that the 'either-or' hypothesis holds more strongly for product technology than for process technology, where presumably 'firms-learn-with-time' dominates.

## Future Importance

Another t-test comparison was conducted for specifications judged to be of future importance, against those which the experts thought would *not* be important in the future. The difference in $K^*_{range}$ between the two groups was *not* statistically significant – implying the experts foresaw no substantial rise in the degree of variation across firms.

However, expectedly, there *was* a statistically significant difference in $K^*_{mode}$, with specifications perceived to have future importance being technologically more advanced than those thought important now but less important in future:

*MEAN VALUES* of $K^*_{mode}$ and $K^*_{range}$

|  | $K_{mode}$ | | $K_{range}$ | |
|---|---|---|---|---|
| Future importance: | NO | YES | NO | YES |
|  | 0.454 | 0.687* | 0.403 | 0.448 |

* significant at p<0.01

We then chose to regress $K^*_{range}$ on $K^*_{mode}$, first for the 344 specifications adjudged 'important now but not likely to be important in future', and then on the 500 specifications adjusted 'important now and in future'.

For the first 'unimportant in future' group, there was no significant correlation between $K^*_{range}$ and $K^*_{mode}$. But for the second, 'important in future' group, the slope coefficient was negative and strongly significant statistically (t-value in brackets):

$$K^*_{range} = 0.60753 - (0.20576) K^*_{mode}, \quad R^2(adj.) = 0.040;$$
$$(4.69) \qquad\qquad N = 500$$

This result suggests that much of the inverse relation between the range and modal value of technological quality stems from 'forward-looking' specifications – those which are likely to be newer, more technologically advanced, and hence have had less time for evolutionary processes to work themselves out.

In a sense, then, the data support *both* seemingly contradictory hypotheses. The 'do-or-die' hypothesis is supported by the inverse relation between $K^*_{range}$ and $K^*_{mode}$; but the 'firms learn with time' hypothesis is supported by the fact that the inverse relation holds only for 'future-important' specifications, not for those unlikely to be important in the future.

## Japan versus the USA

An interesting result is obtained when the diagram for Japan is overlaid on the diagram for the USA (see Figure 14.4). This indicates that:

(a) in 1982, for the dozen high-tech product groups, the USA appears to enjoy technological parity with Japan, in the sense that the values of $K^*_{mode}$ for the USA and Japan seem roughly equal; and
(b) the values of $K^*_{range}$ in technological specifications across firms appeared to be significantly *higher* for Japan than for the USA.

To test this statistically, a t-test comparison was done for Japan and the USA, for the whole sample of 844 specifications. $K^*_{mode}$ did not differ significantly for Japan versus the USA. However, $K^*_{range}$ (technometric range) for Japan was significantly greater than that for the USA – which runs counter to impressions of Japan's allegedly ubiquitous high-quality technology:

*MEAN VALUES* of $K^*_{mode}$ and $K^*_{range}$

| $K_{mode}$ | | $K_{range}$ | |
|-------|-------|-------|-------|
| Japan | USA | Japan | USA |
| 0.600 | 0.624 | 0.529 | 0.356* |

* significant at $p < 0.01$

Between 1982 and 1990, Japan experienced rapidly growing trade surpluses with the USA. Though it is likely that Japan's technological deficit with respect to the USA narrowed during this period – for instance, in industrial robots – nonetheless the data appear to confirm the well-known conclusion that Japanese skill in marketing and distribution explains more of that country's export success than underlying technological excellence.

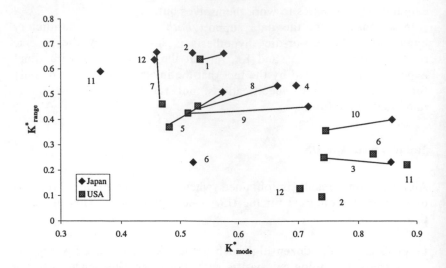

1. optic fibres
2. industrial robots
3. ultra high-tension transformers
4. video tape recorders
5. large computers
6. digital radiography

7. LSI memory
8. semiconductor lasers
9. passenger cars
10. general ships
11. civilian aircraft
12. LSI probers

*Figure 14.4: Relation between level of technology and its diversity,
USA versus Japan, 1982, 12 high-tech groups*[8]

At the same time, Figure 14.4 reveals an interesting fact about the structure of Japanese industry. Many large Japanese manufacturing firms – especially those in the automobile industry – rely on a large network of small-scale parts suppliers. While these suppliers are held to rigorous quality standards, they are often not technologically advanced. This may in part explain the larger across-firm range of technological excellence in Japan than in the USA, even though the US economy is more than twice the size of Japan's, and has more than twice the number of firms.

**Spurious Correlation?**

The Japanese database was constructed by canvassing experts, and asking each to supply values for specifications, for each product group, including their modal values, and maximum and minimum levels. The number of experts varied across the 12 different product groups, from 5 for product groups 2, 5, 7 and 8, to 11 for product group 13 (see Table 14.1). It could be argued that a product group with a larger number of experts supplying data would naturally have a larger range or variance in those estimates – the more persons supplying responses, the greater the likelihood of extreme values.

To test for this source of bias, we correlated the $K^*_{range}$ with the number of experts, for all countries, for the USA and for Japan. In each case, the correlation was very close to zero and, of course, statistically insignificant. This implies that there was no systematic relation between the number of experts for each product group and the size of diversity for that group.

## 14.5 CONCLUSION

Our main finding is this: for a dozen high-tech product groups, there is a consistent, inverse relation between the *level* of technological quality – measured quantitatively by product attributes – and its *diversity*, measured by the range of values those attributes take on, across firms. This relation exists both in Japan and in the USA. The degree of diversity of technology in Japan is as great as, or greater than, that of the USA.

This inverse relation is consistent with the evolutionary view of technical change that emphasizes the economies of scale and scope inherent in new, costly technology, and which downplays the importance of learning effects through which firms become more homogeneous in their technologies over time, at least with regard to significant future technologies. Thus, our results support the variant of the evolutionary model of technical progress that is based on the 'do-or-die' notion of technology adoption.

The policy implications of this result are unclear. One might conjecture that in some sense, a larger 'variety of species' in technology may be preferable to a larger degree of uniformity among firms. The market is thus provided with a greater degree of choice between costly state-of-the-art products and simpler, cheaper ones.

The marketplace itself can then 'vote' for different technologies, as they compete for survival, and work efficiently to ensure the 'survival of the fittest'. What becomes significant, then, for industrial policy, is not that there exist plants that are relatively backward, technologically, but whether there are at the same time plants that are at the global, state-of-the-art frontier. Encouragement of technological excellence may work to increase the range of technological excellence across firms, because many firms may choose not to strive for the frontier but rather remain in the relatively cheap and safe hinterland. This heterogeneity may in fact be desirable, just as the wide variety of species serves a function in biology by efficiently filling all the available biological spaces and niches.

## NOTES

1   Besides the grant from the German–Israel Foundation, we gratefully acknowledge the Y. After Fund for Research, administered by the Vice-President (Research), Technion-Israel Institute of Technology, for additional financial support. An earlier version of this Chapter – co-authored with A. Frenkel and K. Koschatzky – was presented at the 10th World Congress of the International Economics Association, in Moscow, Aug. 1992, in the session chaired by professor A. Heertje, in honour of the 50th anniversary of the publication of Joseph Schumpeter's landmark book, *Capitalism, Socialism and Democracy*. The authors are grateful to the chairperson and participants at this session for insightful comments, as well as to three anonymous referees for their detailed and painstaking critiques of our Chapter. The before-mentioned earlier version was published in the Journal of *Evolutionary Economics* 4, pp. 273–288, 1994.
2   Compare also Chapters 1 and 2 in this volume.
3   For our purposes here, the subscript 'k' will represent different countries – namely, the USA, Japan, or selected European countries.
4   Unfortunately, like so many costly databases, this one was not updated; like an unsuccessful mutation, its brief but useful lifetime begins and ends with 1982.
5   For an early analysis of these data, see Grupp and Hohmeyer (1986).
6   It was found that weighting each specification by a coefficient indicating its relative importance did not affect the results, but simply added more complexity; we therefore used a simple average.
7   As noted above, these weights were found to have virtually no effect on the empirical results, and hence were not used for the final computations as presented here; aggregation was done by taking simple arithmetic averages.
8   Dotted lines join data points for the same product group in the USA and Japan.

# 15 An Internet Software Product: Integrating Marketing and R&D[1]

### Main Ideas in this Chapter

How can companies best integrate their marketing function with research and development (R&D)? As product life-cycles and development cycles become ever shorter, and as increasing proportions of R&D are outsourced, linking the marketplace with the laboratory becomes both crucially important and increasingly difficult – especially for transnational companies whose R&D sites are distant from markets and marketing operations. The case study in this Chapter examines integration of marketing and R&D in the context of free IBM Internet software, 'Mapuccino'[TM] (available at IBM's corporate Web site[2] and known internally as 'WebCutter'), developed at IBM's Haifa Research Laboratory in Israel.

## 15.1 INTRODUCTION

### Fall and Rise of IBM

'I'm amazed at how much more respect IBM has in the technology world than in the investing world' (Daniel Mandresh, Merrill Lynch, 1993).[3]

Fifty-one-year-old Louis V. Gerstner, a former McKinsey & Co. consultant, took over as chief executive officer (CEO) of IBM in the spring of 1991. At the time, IBM's stock had slid to $95 from its late-1988 peak of $125. In 1993, losses were mounting, totalling $16.6 billion in the four quarters ending September 1993, amounting to five-sixths of total shareholder equity; total return to investors was a dismal minus15 per cent. In late 1993, IBM's stock dropped to nearly $35.

At the time the PowerPC microprocessor was the centrepiece of IBM's technology strategy. 'PowerPC appears to be the only architecture that can compete with the Pentium,' said Gordon Bell, architect of Digital Equipment's VAX system.[4] But despite the PowerPC's technological advantages – smaller in size, lower heat generation, smaller silicon use, faster speed – the Pentium triumphed. Intel's marketing muscle triumphed. In 1995 Gerstner disbanded the business unit that sought to build an alternative to Intel-based PCs using the Power PC chip.

Aggressive cost-cutting brought IBM back to profitability. The number of IBM employees was pared from close to 400,000 to about 250,000. By second-quarter 1995, IBM's earnings were $1.5 billion (annual rate) and its stock was back to $110. In 1996 IBM's earnings were $5.4 billion on sales of $76 billion, making it the 15th largest company in the world, measured by sales.[5] Its market capitalization on May 30, 1997, was $86 billion, 13th largest in the world.[6]

The turnaround CEO Gerstner had engineered was impressive. But many fundamental problems remained. Perhaps the key one: IBM's lack of innovative alacrity, which kept it from translating superior technological capability into dominant market share. In comparison, Intel – IBM once owned some 30 per cent of its stock – had earnings nearly as large as IBM's, with one-fifth the number of employees and about one-fourth IBM's sales. As a result, as of May 30, 1997, Intel's market capitalization exceeded IBM's by almost one-half.

Despite its high stock price, IBM *still* commanded more respect in the technology world than in the investment world. For example, IBM sought to be a major Internet player. Yet new Internet-based firms' total market value soared from near-zero in April 1995 to $10 billion in April 1997, while, according to strategy expert Gary Hamel, IBM's share of total computer industry market capitalization dipped from 46 per cent in 1988 to only 14 per cent in 1997.[7] As Hamel noted, cost-cutting and down-sizing may succeed in raising share prices, but they 'do not create new wealth, do not yield new revenue streams, do not take the company into new markets, and do not create fundamentally new value for customers.'

Despite Gerstner's widely quoted – and misinterpreted – statement in the summer of 1993 that the last thing IBM needed was a grand vision, IBM *does* have a new value-creating strategy. That strategy is based on a network-centric model, in which IBM builds and sells networking software and hardware as an integrated systems provider. The marketplace itself helped IBM shape this strategy – IBM revenues from the sale of services grew by a third in 1995, to $12.6 billion, while other divisions stagnated or grew slowly.

Gerstner now sees IBM as a 'business process outsourcer', licensing software as it once rented its mainframes.8 IBM is arraying its global resources for an assault on the wired world. The objective: 'to use [IBM's] global reach, its expertise in dozens of technologies and its knowledge of how major customers conduct their businesses to offer all sorts of computing resources across networks – either public or private ones.' In a way, this strategy returns IBM to its original winning formula – leasing computer services together with superior maintenance, software and related services.

Will IBM succeed? A major determinant will be IBM's ability to integrate its marketing and R&D functions. Chief executive officer Gerstner stated this in a November 1993 interview:

'Increasingly, the value for our customers is going to come in designing applications that will help them restructure their businesses. Those involve a combination of hardware, software, and services, and we've got to be able to put those together to build solutions.' ....

'What we bring in our services strategy is our laboratories, right there working with customers, thinking through how technology will evolve. When the cycle of technological evolution gets more rapid, the closer you are to laboratory work, the more you will be able to give clients a solution that achieves competitive advantage. .... The issue of whose workstation or PC it is becomes less and less of an issue, as opposed to who knows how to bring about the change. ... IBM will continue to be the primary source, the dominant source, of technology in this field. I'm absolutely convinced of that because of the almost impossible task for anybody in the next five years to duplicate our R&D function. What we have got to do is convert our technology into products faster – higher-quality products that respond to our customer needs quicker. I'm driving IBM to serve our customers. What customers are telling me is stop giving me all this stuff about what might happen. Help me solve my problems.'9

The challenge to management is enormous. For instance, a far-flung global operation exists, in which IBM software programmers in China, India, Latvia, the USA and Israel write programmes based on Sun Microsystems' Java language, for companies to use to create their own in-house software. The total R&D investment in this programme amounts of hundreds of millions of dollars. And there are numerous others like it.

*How well will IBM succeed in leveraging its technological capability to create value and rebuild its market share?* IBM's Haifa (Israel) Research Laboratory is one of only three such IBM laboratories outside the USA. Its history and evolution are instructive in examining

IBM's technology-marketing interface. Before analysing its WebCutter product, we first review HRL's history.

## 15.2 IBM (ISRAEL) AND THE HAIFA RESEARCH LABORATORY

'What we bring in our services strategy is our laboratories, right there working with customers, thinking through how technology will evolve'.[10] IBM established its Israeli branch in 1949, just one year after the country was born. IBM's Scientific Centre (now Haifa Research Laboratory) was established In Haifa in 1972, and was founded and headed by Dr. Josef Raviv, a leading IBM scientist. Raviv chose at that time to return to his home country, Israel, from the USA, and corporate IBM recognized his value to the company in part by providing resources for him to build a scientific centre there.

Sweeping changes have occurred in the focus, character and organizational structure of HRL, changes that are reflective of IBM's new directions and its approach to integrating marketing and R&D. Many of those changes were implemented or guided by IBM Israel's current chairperson, and previous managing director, Joshua Maor.

Maor, trained as an electrical engineer, worked for a decade with the Israel Defence Force's computer installation, becoming deputy director. He developed expertise in software, a new field at that time, through the need to develop diagnostic tools for hardware. Maor then joined IBM Israel's marketing department, working with universities and research institutions in Israel. In the mid-1970s, he was transferred to IBM's European division headquarters in Paris, where he was part of a team that sought solutions to the division's growing business problems. Maor notes that his stint in Paris helped him understand the links between 'corporate' IBM and branches in individual countries.

In 1980 Maor returned to IBM Israel as head of marketing, and became managing director in 1984. Shortly after, in July 1985, the Israeli government implemented a sweeping plan to halt the runaway inflation that afflicted the country. The result was a serious, prolonged economic slowdown. IBM Israel, structured for 18–20 per cent annual growth in sales, was forced to restructure and refocus its business strategy.[11] At the same time, PCs, accounting for about a quarter of IBM Israel's business, were becoming a commodity-like product with sharp downward pressure on prices from IBM clones.

'We had the high cost levels of 1976,' Maor noted, 'and the lower growth rates of 1986. The two were inconsistent. We decided to cut costs, and at the same time shift our focus toward the service part of our business. During the period when we focused on hardware sales, we lost some of our capability as solutions providers, while other such providers in Israel grew stronger. So at the same time, we had to slash expenses while building up the systems part of IBM Israel.'

The key to this strategy – which preceded a similar strategic shift in IBM's global operations – was, according to Maor, IBM's Scientific Centre in Haifa. The Centre's objectives, and its very name, were radically changed. Until then, a typical IBM Scientific Centre engaged in research together with other research bodies, to contribute to scientific knowledge and to the community.

'We changed its name to the Science and Technology Division,' Maor recalls. 'Two major changes followed. First, the division began to do more contract development work for corporate IBM in the U.S. Second, we created an Advanced Solutions Centre unit in Haifa whose mandate was not only to develop new technologies, but to build business solutions based on those technologies.'

As an example, Maor cites a new system announced in late 1996, developed in Haifa, in which X-ray, MRI and other medical images are digitalized, stored, analysed and transmitted to distant sites to facilitate medical diagnosis and treatment in a cost-effective manner. The system is based on sophisticated integration of software and hardware and is now in place in Israel and several European sites. It took eight years to perfect.

In the late 1980s, IBM branches in other countries experienced the same growth slowdown that IBM Israel encountered in 1985. IBM Israel, having had the 'good fortune' to grapple with the local downturn, unrelated to global industry or IBM problems, was as a result better prepared for the slowdown than IBM branches in other countries.

In Israel and elsewhere, IBM shifted its focus from research to development. IBM scientific centres, where once scholars pursued research independently, based on their own interests, not unlike academic departments, became much more focused and directed. IBM's Scientific Centre in Haifa, as the core of IBM Israel's Science and Technology Branch, grew from 20–30 researchers to over 350 employees. Hiring policies increasingly sought talented engineers and scientists with market-based interests.

As managing director, Maor personally sought out scientists at the Haifa lab who were keenly interested in seeing their ideas applied in the marketplace, rather than simply published in academic journals. The profile of researchers at the Scientific Centre greatly changed. This process of change was neither simple nor easy nor rapid, and was one that many IBM research installations in other countries underwent.

The basic management change was to separate the research and the development functions. IBM continues to engage in research, but is more strongly focused on development. At IBM Israel, this shift occurred as much as a decade earlier than it was implemented throughout the global IBM operation.

In January 1997, a major organizational change occurred. HRL was transferred from IBM (Israel) to IBM's world-wide R&D organization. While administration of HRL is still done by IBM Israel, HRL now actively seeks internal customers and projects in other IBM branches and divisions.

## 15.3  INTEGRATING MARKETING AND R&D AT IBM: DEVELOPING 'WEBCUTTER'

### Technology

'WebCutter' is a Java-based Internet tool that builds and maintains visual maps for Internet sites.[12] It does not utilize search engines at all, but rather uses its own built-in dynamic search instead of the slow static search services. IBM regards WebCutter not as a 'product' but rather as a tool/system/solution/service. It is fully compatible with all Java-enabled browsers. It forms part of an overall strategic initiative to develop a broad range of Java products for Internet servers. WebCutter's development began at IBM's Haifa Research Laboratory in June 1996; the WebCutter technology was announced in June 1997. It is available as freeware at IBM's corporate Web site, and is known there as Mapuccino (trademark[TM]).

WebCutter provides a detailed, organized visual 'street map' of Internet sites, capable of leading users quickly and efficiently to their desired destination. It offers several different types of maps, including a 'star-shaped' map, showing various parts of the site and how they are linked (see Figure 15.1) and a 'fish-eye' map, which magnifies those parts of the site relevant to the user, and minimizes other parts less relevant.

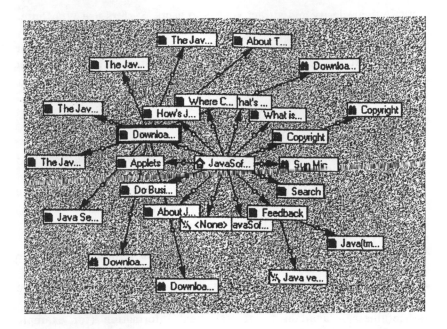

*Figure 15.1: WebCutter map of Sun Microsystem's Java internet site*

WebCutter uses IBM's proprietary 'conceptual search' text-analysis technology. Users indicate their interests in plain language, and WebCutter maps relevant sites in ways adapted to, and meaningful for, users. Colour coding directs the eye of the user to important areas in the site. WebCutter is capable of integrating several sites into a single map. It is compatible with all browsers now in use, and can be used on both Unix and NT servers.

## Market

Who are the potential customers/users for WebCutter? There are two separate markets, which differ considerably:

- Websurfers – those who surf the Internet, seeking information, and
- Webmasters – those who build Internet sites.

Surfers' needs and wants differ greatly from Webmasters (site managers). The latter use WebCutter to optimize design of sites, and increase their clarity and attractiveness to users. Surfers use WebCutter to facilitate browsing. While Webmasters are likely willing to pay significant sums for tools that improve their capabilities, surfers for the most part are accustomed to acquiring Internet software without charge.

## Competing Products

WebCutter has competition: Microsoft's NetCarta webmapper; MAPA; and NetScope. (NetCarta was an Internet acquisition of Microsoft).

Five key technological features of the four competing products were identified:

- display – quality and variety of display options;
- achieves its objectives – degree to which product maps site information;
- user-friendliness and documentation – degree of assistance available to users;
- usefulness – availability of statistical information (for example number of 'hits'), integration of several sites, use of filters, search options, and so on;
- performance and stability – time it takes to construct a visual map, compatibility with Internet protocols.

These features were aggregated from 15 individual product features. Table 15.1 compares the key features of the four products, quantifying each on a scale of 0 to 3.

We assembled a panel of four potential WebCutter users, including a Web site developer, a Website manager, and two Internet users. It was not our intention, of course, to conduct serious market research. The objective was to elicit perceptions of the product on the part of a small number of knowledgeable users, and match those perceptions against the beliefs of the developers. We sought to show that even a small sample of users could generate useful, important information for developers.

We asked them to rate the importance of each of the five product features on a scale of one to three. The average scores are shown in column 2 of Table 15.1. We discovered from conversations with our panel that *the quality of the display was the most important feature, both for browsers and for Web site developers and managers.*

*Table 15.1:* *Comparison of WebCutter with competing products*

| Feature | Weight | Web-Cutter | NetCarta | MAPA | Net-Scope |
|---|---|---|---|---|---|
| Display | 3 | 2 | 3 | 1 | 3 |
| Achieves Objectives | 2.5 | 3 | 3 | 1 | 3 |
| User-friendly | 2 | 3 | 2 | 1 | 2 |
| Usefulness | 1 | 2.5 | 2 | 1 | 1.5 |
| Performance | 1 | 1.5 | 2 | 1 | 1 |
| Average | – | 2.4 | 2.4 | 1 | 2.1 |
| Weighted Average | – | 2.47 | 2.58 | 1 | 2.42 |

*Note:* Features are scored on a scale of one to three by a panel of potential users. Weight reflects the relative importance of each feature, as stated by the user panel. Simple average is the average of the five feature scores; weighted average is the feature score weighted by the feature's relative importance.[13]

Clearly, WebCutter's main competitor is Microsoft's NetCarta. NetCarta's display scores higher, according to our panel; this is the principal reason that the weighted average score of WebCutter's features falls slightly below that of NetCarta.

How closely did the market perceptions of WebCutter's developers match those of the market itself? To check this, we asked the developers to rate the importance of the five product features, and compared the results to the ratings of our user panel (see Table 15.2).

*Table 15.2:* *Importance of the five product features: perceptions of developers versus users*

| Feature | Developers | Users |
|---|---|---|
| Display | 2.5 | 3 |
| Achieves its objectives | 3 | 2.5 |
| User-friendliness | 1.5 | 2 |
| Usefulness | 2 | 1 |
| Performance and stability | 1 | 1 |

*Note:* Importance is scaled from 1 (least important) to 3 (most important).

Developers rated usefulness, and 'achieving its objectives' more highly than users, but rated display and user-friendliness less highly. This is quite typical of product development, where the technical skills of developers are highly refined and often lead product developers to misperceive the crucial importance of making products simple, clear, friendly and easy to view, for users whose computer skills are often minimal.

### Psychology versus Technology

A key measure of how well marketing and R&D functions are integrated is this: How well do product features (technology) match market preferences (psychology)? In general, where marketing inputs have a significant voice in R&D decisions, product features will reflect buyer preferences strongly.

To examine this in the context of WebCutter, we applied a model developed in Grupp and Maital (1996) and Ben-Arieh et al. (1998).[14] This model plots the scores of product features against the weights or importance of those features. Four types of products are identified:

a. *Focused products:* where highly valued product features are also those in which the product scores high, and low-valued features are those where the product scores low.
b. *Unfocused products:* where highly valued product features are precisely those in which the product scores low.
c. *Dominant products:* where all product features score high, including those not highly valued by customers.
d. *Inferior products:* where all product features score low, relative to competitors.

Figure 15.2 shows this diagram for the WebCutter. It was significant, in our view that the exceptionally talented, creative developers at HRL did not have significant, ongoing direct contact with users or the marketplace. We felt that the distribution of WebCutter to beta-sites, for instance, was not optimally exploited to bring significant information, feedback or benefit to product developers.

Based on our interactions with potential users, and the above analysis, a number of suggestions were made to the developers, several of which were accepted and implemented.

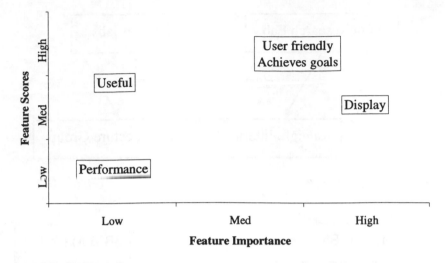

*Figure 15.2:  WebCutter: psychology versus technology*

## 15.4  INTEGRATING MARKETING AND R&D: IBM'S ORGANIZATION

Figure 15.3 diagrams the organizational structure linking marketing and development for WebCutter.

A variety of Internet products are currently under development by IBM's Internet Division. A large set of Java-based applications is currently in process. The Internet Server Architecture Group, based in Raleigh, North Carolina, spearheads applications, prototyping, product development and business planning. This group monitors relevant research carried out at IBM's labs and research centres. Members of the group spend time at these various labs, in order to 'get in synch with them'.

The general pattern is one of *prototyping to productizing to localizing*, that is – developing prototypes of products based on research and development, then turning prototypes into products, then adapting those products to local market needs. Part of the group's mission involves product benchmarking. Its expertise, according to key members, is in 'harvesting' the research developed in IBM labs (like that in Haifa) and in building prototypes.

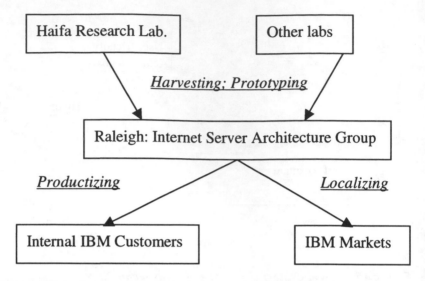

*Figure 15.3: Integration of marketing and R&D in IBM's Internet*
*server architecture group*

The group's mandate is to 'look around the corporation' and 'to play a coordinating role'. The general development pattern is for the group to discern market-based requirements for a product, and then develop and deliver products that meet those requirements.

## 15.5 STRATEGIC ISSUES

1. Is IBM's current organizational structure – specifically, the links among its research labs (including HRL) and marketing and business planning units in the USA - capable of optimally and rapidly translating the needs and wants of both internal IBM units and external IBM customers into winning innovative products? How might it be modified?
2. Is the process whereby new product ideas are 'harvested' from IBM's R&D units world-wide conducted optimally? What measures could improve this process?
3. Is the new organizational structure through which HRL reports directly to IBM US preferable to one in which HRL is an integral part of IBM Israel? How does that change impact the integration of marketing and R&D at HRL?

4. What does the WebCutter case indicate regarding IBM's ability to speed up its product development process, and better exploit its high-level scientific and technological capabilities?
5. What can be learned from WebCutter regarding IBM's ability to engage in 'concurrent engineering' – the simultaneous development, prototyping, production and marketing of new products?
6. How could key market-based information better be brought to HRL developers?
7. IBM has chosen to provide Mapuccino TM as freeware through its Internet site. Were there other marketing options? Was this the correct one? How could other options be explored?

## 15.6 CONCLUSION

Hasso Plattner, founder and vice-chairman of SAP, a global leader in business-application software, once said:

> 'I'm not interested in whether in whether we are better than the competition. The real test is, will most buyers still seek out our products even if we don't market them'.[15]

In other words – by far the most effective marketing tool is from the outset to develop products so desirable in the marketplace that marketing becomes almost unnecessary. While this may seem to be a far-fetched ideal for most companies, it is in fact achieved by high-growth innovative companies. Only by effectively, seamlessly integrating the knowledge and experience of a company's marketing function – market psychology – with the capabilities and creativity of the developers and researchers – technology – can this ideal be attained. As the case of WebCutter indicates, integrating marketing and R&D remains one of senior management's most difficult and challenging tasks.

### Postscript

After this case was completed, Microsoft announced it was changing the focus of its NetCarta product from 'end-user site mapping' (that is, for use by Web browsers) to part of its site management tools. Its new product name: Site Analyst.

## NOTES

1   This Chapter is co-authored with Mel Horwitch (I.T.E., Polytechnic University, New York), based in part on research conducted by Galit Dopelt and Galit Sobel, (then) undergraduate students in the Davidson Faculty of Industrial Engineering and Management, Technion. We are indebted to Dr. Yoelle S. Maarek, manager, information retrieval and organization group, IBM Haifa Research Lab, and the WebCutter development team; to Joshua Maor, Chairman of the Board of Directors, IBM Israel; and to Mary-Ellen Rosen and Jeff Reiser, Manager, Internet Server Architecture Group, IBM Internet Division, Raleigh, NC, for their kind cooperation. Views expressed in this case study are solely those of the authors. This case was presented at the Round Table on 'New Dimensions in Global Technology Strategy: High-Tech U.S. Investment and Collaboration in Israel', Institute for Technology and Enterprise, New York, Sept. 25, 1997. We are grateful to the participants for their comments and criticism. In addition to the GIF grant partial support was provided by the Technion Vice-President's Fund for Research – Smoler Research Fund. An earlier version of this Chapter was published in the *Advances in Business Marketing and Purchasing* 9 (A. G. Woodside, ed.), Stamford, JAI Press, pp. 203–214 (2000).
2   See: http://www.ibm.com/java/mapuccino.
3   Quoted in Kirkpatrick (1993), p. 32.
4   Ibid., p. 30 (see footnote 3).
5   Fortune Global 500, Aug. 4, 1997, p. F–2.
6   Business Week, Global 1000, July 7, 1997, p. 53.
7   Hamel (1997), p. 24.
8   Business Week, Oct. 30, 1995, p. 49.
9   Fortune, Nov. 15, 1993, p. 28.
10  Gerstner in op. cit. (footnote 9).
11  This occurred somewhat before IBM world-wide underwent a similar wrenching process, revising its near-term sales projections sharply downward from the $100 billion level.
12  See: Maarek et al. (1997), pp. 1269–1279.
13  For scores and weights definition and treatment see Grupp and Maital (1998a); or Chapter 4 in this book.
14  Compare also Chapters 8 and 1 in this volume.
15  Cited in Kim and Mauborgne (1997), p. 106.

# Conclusion: How to Build a Successful Business Model

## Main Ideas in this Chapter

This concluding Chapter focuses on the importance of building a complete, integrated and well-conceived business design around a new product or process idea: including production, marketing, finance, design, advertising, sales, distribution, human resource management, and so on. Success at innovation is comprised of a large number of necessary conditions – which together are jointly sufficient for market success, but failing even one component, generate a high probability of failure. The 'direct business model' is used as a unifying example. We also cite examples drawn from knowledge-based startups whom we interviewed and studied during our research. We indicate how the microeconomic tools described in this book can help build a successful business model, and alter it when and where necessary. We start with a definition of a business model and then present the direct business model of Dell. After introducing the elements of business design and transition problems we explain the writing of a winning business plan.

## WHAT IS A BUSINESS MODEL?

### Introduction

Conceiving a new product or process and then bringing it to the marketplace is comparable to the 3,000-metre steeplechase event in an Olympic track competition – a medium-distance race interspersed with hurdles. In new product development and innovation many things must come together: the idea; R&D and prototyping; raising financial resources; hiring staff; organizing production; developing marketing,

315

sales and advertising plans; building distribution channels; and setting up and managing supply chains. In new product development, as in the steeplechase, each hurdle must be successfully surmounted in turn, in order to reach the finish line victorious, and win the gold medal. In both activities, though in theory you can stumble once and still win – each time this happens, the odds of succeeding are greatly reduced. To win, you need to have the short-term stamina to leap over each hurdle – and also the long-term endurance to last the full course, while running at near-top speed.

So, consider for a moment a set of 11 obstacles or hurdles, each of which must be successfully surmounted, in order to complete the innovation course successfully. Imagine yourself as a hurdler. Suppose the odds of leaping each obstacle are very high – 80 per cent. What are your chances of finishing the entire obstacle course, by surmounting every single one of the 11 hurdles?

The answer: 0.8 multiplied by itself 11 times, or only 8.6 per cent. Even when the odds are very high for succeeding at each stage, overall the chances for a successful new product launch – even when the initial idea is very well conceived – are about one in twelve. The reason: every aspect of the new product's business design must be successful, from start to finish. The overall probability of success is multiplicative, meaning that failure at any stage brings the entire innovation process crashing down. A great many entrepreneurs, especially those with little business experience, fail to grasp this fundamental point, believing that the brilliance of their initial conception is sufficient to generate momentum that will create a winning product in the marketplace. By short-changing the business design, and failing to devote to it sufficient resources and thought, many great new product ideas are doomed to failure.

The reader may wonder why precisely 11 obstacles or hurdles were chosen. The reason: the business design checklist includes 11 stages or aspects – see the Section on the elements of a business design below.

This chapter examines in depth the detailed aspects of a complete business design. In addition to the technology underlying the creative process, there must be considerable management skill to build a winning business design. It must be clearly understood: *the amount of creativity invested in the design of the business model that brings the product to market must be no less than the creativity that spawns the new product itself.* Often, a creative business design applied to a humdrum product generates enormous business success, while a faulty business design applied to a phenomenal creative idea leads to massive failure.

## Definition

A *business model is a comprehensive integrated plan covering every aspect of conceiving, developing, prototyping, producing, selling, marketing, advertising and financing a new product, process or service.* Business design is the process that creates the business model. Good business design is as essential for achieving competitive advantage as strong product innovation.

---

**Example 1: First Alert**

The second author, his wife and two of his children awoke one morning, all with splitting headaches. The cause turned out to be a gas heater, whose chimney had been blocked by wind-blown debris, causing incomplete combustion and generating dangerously high levels of carbon monoxide. Death could not have been very far away.

A technological breakthrough has now created a small platinum-based CO sensor, now comfortingly on the Maital household's wall. One might think that this innovation would lead to instant marketplace success. Yet despite the clear need, the lifesaving value of the product, and its reasonable cost (about $40), a faulty business model could easily lead to rapid bankruptcy. Rather than build costly independent retail sales and distribution systems, the First Alert product was cleverly sold through gas utilities, who have a very strong interest in preventing disasters and near-disasters of the sort described above. Some US states, and countries, now mandate such detectors wherever gas heaters are used. The combination of legislation, and gas utilities, brought this product to far more households than would have been the case had the company built a conventional retail-type model. In this case, creativity was as evident in the business model as in the product's core technology.

---

**Example 2: 'Kind of Blue'**

One of the most famous jazz albums of all time, 'Kind of Blue', was based on music sketched out by trumpeter Miles Davis only hours before the recording session. Jimmy Cobb (drums), Miles Davis (trumpet), Bill Evans (piano), John Coltrane (tenor sax), and Cannonball Adderly were among the performers. None of the musicians had seen the music before, or rehearsed it. This album innovated modal improvization – jazz inventions based on changing scales, rather than changing chords. Over a period of two days, what many regard as the greatest, most innovative jazz album ever recorded was completed. It remains one of the perennial top-selling jazz albums.

This album illustrates a key point in new product development. The spontaneity, serendipity and creative spark are all vital elements; often, they emerge out of controlled chaos, like that prevailing in the 'Kind of Blue' recording session. Once that chaos has created an innovative product, order takes over. The album has to be produced, advertised, marketed and distributed, in a rapid, orderly fashion. *It is this combination of chaos and order, so difficult to create and even more difficult to manage, that is the basic requirement for a successful business design for innovation.*

### A Metaphor

A second metaphor is useful for understanding the link between new product development and business design – that of the human cell. The nucleus of the cell contains key genetic material, and is the cell's most important part, just as the product or service is at the centre of the business design. But the nucleus cannot survive without the cell wall, cytoplasm, and so on – all of which support it and enable the cell to thrive and to reproduce, just as the various components of the business design – logistics, supply chain, marketing, production, assembly, advertising, human resources, finance – enable the core product idea to reach the right people, at the right time, at the right cost and price. Roberts has shown clearly that 'companies that historically show product strategic focus perform substantially better over extended periods than companies that implement multiple technologies and/or seek market diversity' (1991, p. 306; see also Meyer and Roberts, 1986, 1988). With innovative products at the core of the business design, and with the design focused on creating marketplace success for the product, performance and success are substantially enhanced.

## DIRECT BUSINESS MODEL OF DELL

Perhaps the most dramatic example of a winning business design is Dell's 'direct business model' – sale of computers direct to consumers and businesses – an example that will serve as a unifying theme in this Chapter. We will also make reference to a number of high-tech startups whom we studied and interviewed, while researching the implementation of our technometric approach in innovative companies.

Consider now perhaps the most successful business model of the past two decades: Dell's direct sale of computers, through Internet, phone and fax, to consumers and businesses. Michael Dell, founder and principal owner of Dell Computers, is only 34 years old and his personal worth is more than $16 billion dollars.[1] Measured by sales, Dell was the 78th largest firm in the USA in 1998, up from 125th in 1997; its 1998 revenue was $18.2 billion, with profits of $1.46 billion. Dell's stock was worth $111.3 billion on March 15, 1999; and its rate of return on shareholders' equity (operating profit as a per cent of shareholders' equity) was a startling 63 per cent, implying that Dell earned its shareholders a billion dollars in economic rent in 1998 (profits over and above the opportunity cost of its capital).[2] Clearly, the 'direct business' model pioneered by Michael Dell is worth close study. Here is an account of the nature and origin of Dell's business design, with his own words in italics.[3]

As a young student at the University of Texas, Dell found computers more interesting than biology. His parents wanted him to be a doctor. But when he went off to college as a freshman, he had three computers in his trunk and was making supplemental income by reselling used PCs. His parents actually made him stop selling computers because they noticed he was not concentrating on his school work. He quit selling them, but only for a month and then realized computing was what he really wanted to do. He saw this as his major opportunity. In 1982-3, he realized that IBM was selling PCs for $3,000, when the components cost only $1,000. The difference was accounted for by retailers' margins, cost of inventory, shipping, distribution, and so on. Dell realized that he could buy those same components, assemble PCs and sell them directly to customers, saving the high costs of retailing. This was his basic business model. The key advantage of the direct model, apart from cost savings: it facilitates direct contact with the consumer, enabling Dell to learn about changes in market demand and consumer preferences, and bring to market winning new models long before competitors learn of such changes through indirect channels.

The success of this business model is remarkable. Dell is growing at an incredible rate. There are only 82 companies in the world that have had revenue growth for the last 10 years of at least 10 per cent per year. There are only 11 companies that have had revenue growth for the last 3 years of 30 per cent per year. Dell is one of them. And there is only one company (Dell) that has had revenue growth for the last 3 years of greater than 50 per cent per year (they actually had 55 per cent growth). They have no distribution channel conflicts because they have no distribution channels! Dell designs, manufactures and distributes their own computers and the combination of all these factors into one firm has created tremendous value for the customer and his company. Though they didn't get into the consumer market until several years ago, their consumer business is operating in 35 countries via direct distribution without problems. Dell built 2 million PCs in the third quarter of 1998 alone, and *they only maintain 7 days of inventory stock.*

A significant differentiation that they provide is customer software image preloads, of the 7 million machines they will sell this year, 2.5 million of them have custom software from the énd-user preloaded. The fact that they only have 7 days of inventory on hand provides a direct financial payback because PC supplies typically depreciate at a rate of 1 per cent per week.

## Integrating Marketing and R&D

They also mentioned that unlike other PC manufacturers and distributers who are forced to 'guess' what customer demand will be and 'guess' what the right product mix is to send to their distributors, Dell is intimately involved with their customers and knows exactly what their customers want and the guessing is removed; they build exactly what the customers are ordering/buying and this is a competitive advantage.

The Dell theme is lower overall cost for sales and support. They first started out in direct personal selling, then added phone, and now Internet sales. They are now booking over $10 million a day in Internet sales (20 per cent of their sales are currently online) and they are looking for that to grow to at least 50 per cent online in the 'near' future. Two million visitors go to their Web sites a week.

> 'Because we're direct and can see who is buying what, we noticed ... the industry's average selling price was going down, but ours was going up. Consumers who wanted the most powerful machines were coming to us ... and without focusing on it in a significant way, we had a billion-dollar consumer business that was profitable!'

Dell introduced the concept of Premier pages where they dedicate a specific set of Web pages to a particular company that has preselected configurations, prices and so on which a company can direct their employees to choose their work PC from these pages. They have over

8,500 of these Premier Web pages. Eighty per cent of their online business is to large business and institutional customers.

## Supply Chain Management

Eighty per cent of Dell's components are purchased from only 20 suppliers; with this they have a very tight link with their suppliers. They are convinced *you can replace physical assets in the distribution channel with information assets* and this strategy has worked all over the world. They started with desktops, then added laptops, now servers and they will continue to add more offerings as it makes sense.

Dell currently owns only 9 per cent of the world's PC market and he sees a huge opportunity to own much more of it. Dell went from 2 per cent to 20 per cent market share in two-and-a-half years in the USA, surpassing HP and IBM without any specialized service and support infrastructure of their own. They contract out service and support with companies like Unisys, Wang, EDS and so on to do this job. PC standards have really allowed the Dell model to work and as standards settled in, cost became a greater factor and they have capitalized on this.

Dell predicts the next phase of expanding their business will depend on improving the quality of the total product including service and support – the total customer experience. Dell thinks the overall PC industry is currently very bad with quality and overall support and sees this as an opportunity for him to differentiate himself and his company.

## What Can Be Learned?

What other industries will this Dell model work? Dell mentioned the automotive industry as having potential. There are a tremendous amount of assets in car production, start to finish. The only reason it's this way is because history dictated this. The problems IBM and some of their other competitors are having is exactly this history, or legacy, of distribution channels that is weighing them down (see the Section on 'Transition Problems' below).

'We concluded we'd be better off leveraging the investments others have made and focusing on delivering solutions and systems to customers. ... We said ... shouldn't we be more selective and put our capital into activities where we can add value for our customers (by not creating every piece of the value chain, and by using outsourcers and suppliers)? ... It's fair to think of our companies as being virtually integrated. That allows us to focus on where we add value ...'.

# ELEMENTS OF BUSINESS DESIGN

Business design is a process that can be perceived as running down a list of key questions that need concrete answers (Slywotzky, 1996) right from the moment that a new product, process or service is conceived (see Table). It was this process that Dell followed, whether explicitly or intuitively.

## Basic Assumptions

The essence of every business model is a clear brief statement about how the product or service creates value for customers, beyond what is currently (or in the near future) available. For example: here is the value statement of the USA Coast Guard, as provided by a Coast Guard officer and MBA student: 'The Coast Guard is a multimission force that seeks to: (a) eliminate death, injury and property damage, and eliminate environmental damage and natural resource degradation, in the maritime environment; (b) protect maritime borders from all intrusions; (c) facilitate maritime commerce; and (d) defend the nation as one of the five armed forces.'

Value statements must be constantly evaluated, in response to changes in basic assumptions:

- How are customers changing? How do their lifestyles, preferences, values, goals, family life, and so on change? And how must our products change in response?
- What are customers' priorities? For instance: the baby-boomer generation appeared to some focused on acquisition of wealth and goods; the baby-bust generation seems more interested in quality of life. Product innovation must reflect this.
- What are the profit drivers? New products should be profitable. What factors drive profitability? And how can this profitability be sustained, in the face of inevitable competition and imitation? Success, if it comes, will almost certainly draw imitators. A good business design considers long in advance how this competition will be met.

*Table C1:   Business design – a checklist*

| | |
|---|---|
| 1. | **Basic Assumptions**<br>How are customers changing?<br>What are customers' priorities?<br>What are the profit drivers? |
| 2. | **Customer Selection**<br>Which customers do we want to serve?<br>Which customers will drive value growth? |
| 3. | **Scope**<br>Which products do we want to sell?<br>Which support activities should be in-house?<br>Which ones should we subcontract or outsource? |
| 4. | **Differentiation**<br>What is my basis for differentiation?<br>What is my unique value proposition?<br>Why should the customer want to buy from me?<br>Who are my key competitors?<br>Who will be my key competitors in 1 to 5 years?<br>How convincing is my differentiation relative to that of my competitors? |
| 5. | **Value Recapture**<br>How does the customer pay for the value we create?<br>How are my shareholders compensated for the value we create? |
| 6. | **Purchasing System**<br>How do we buy, transactional or long term, antagonistic or partner? |
| 7. | **Manufacturing and Operations**<br>How much do we manufacture versus subcontract?<br>Are my manufacturing/service delivery economies based primarily on fixed or on variable costs?<br>Do we need state-of-the-art or 90th percentile technology? |
| 8. | **Capital Intensity**<br>Do we use capital-intensive (high fixed cost) systems or flexible less-capital-intensive systems? |
| 9. | **R&D and New Product Development**<br>Internal or outsourced, focused on process, or on product?<br>Focused on astute project selection or on speed of development? |
| 10. | **Organizational Configuration**<br>Centralized or decentralized?<br>Pyramid or network?<br>Functional or business or matrix? |

Internal promotion or external hiring?
11. Go to Market Mechanism
    Direct sales force?
    Low cost distribution?
    Sales representatives (multi-brand)?
    Account management? Licensing?
    Direct business model?
    Hybrid system?

*Source: Adapted from Slywotzky (1996).*

Some of the greatest new innovations arise from the direct needs of inventors. For instance:

---

**Example 3: Surgery?**
An Israeli engineer was found to have a brain tumour. He was dissatisfied with the accuracy of existing imaging techniques, and was unwilling to undergo the surgeon's knife facing such inaccuracy. Using his engineering skills, he found an innovation that achieved what was to him the required imaging precision – and underwent the surgery. The innovation became a fast-growing startup. Few value statements – or 'needs assessments' – are more meaningful than one involving personal need or distress experienced by the entrepreneurs themselves.

---

**Example 4: 'Please sign here'**
In 1990, many entrepreneurs worked on pen-based computing. Most of the uses of this new technology focused on drawing, highlighting, or correcting text – all done reasonably well with keyboards.

A basic assumption was that individual signatures would, for legal and other reasons, remain handwritten. A British entrepreneur named Jeremy Newman refused to accept this assumption, and created software designed to get a legally binding signature without paper, by signing on a pressure-sensitive pad. His company, PenOp, based in New York, shipped 30,000 copies in a short time. His product creates value for field agents of insurance companies, police officers and financial services firms.[4]

**Customer Selection**

Business design begins with an analysis of the nature and size of the potential market, including the 'demographics' – basic data on income, education and age of potential buyers. These data help provide answers to these questions:

- Which customers do we want to serve?
- Which customers will drive value growth?

Good business models have a sharply defined image of who potential customers are – their needs, preferences, and goals. They include a brief statement about who these customers are. For example: We plan to sell our line of upscale T-shirts to males aged 30–40 with above-average incomes and college education. Demographic analysis should also consider the rate at which targeted customers are growing in numbers, and in resources. For instance: the fastest-growing demographic group in the USA in the next two decades will be those over age 65.

---

**Example 5: 'Now Johnny – eat your fork like a good boy'**

A startup company we studied invented remarkable technology for producing edible straws – straws stiff enough to drink through, yet made of tasty food-like matter that could be eaten. The technology was patented. The same material could produce edible plates and utensils. The company's senior management tended to waiver between focusing on 'edible utensils' (stressing the functionality of the utensil) and on 'tasty snacks' (stressing the value of the material as a crunchy food).

The 'utensil' product had the following key features: functionality, hardness, elasticity, weight, price, appearance, storability, shelf life. The 'snack' product had the following features: taste, texture, colour, sweetness, appearance, aftertaste, natural food content. The company had difficulty defining whether it would sell the product as a utensil or as a snack. Its business model never did solve the basic problem of production: existing food companies were unwilling to rent production capacity, yet the startup itself could not afford to build its own production line. The product has yet to reach the market.

---

## Scope

There is perpetual tension between the desire to reach the largest possible market – a key factor that attracts venture capital is market size – and the need to focus sharply on high-likelihood customers. This requires hard decisions about:

- Which products do we want to sell?
- Which support activities should be in-house?
- Which ones should we subcontract or outsource?

Pioneering new business models sometimes eschew actual production of products, preferring to subcontract or outsource such production to plants in, say, Southeast Asia, while investing scarce capital in R&D and in marketing – a model followed with huge success by Nike. It should not be assumed from the outset that to bring a new product to market, it is necessary to produce it. In today's global deflation, widespread excess productive capacity often means that subcontractors can be found, who are happy to produce to order and who already have the factory capacity in place. This can save large amounts of capital – though it runs the risk of facing shortages in booming markets, when excess capacity suddenly changes into production delays and excess demand.

A winning business design often perceives innovation as creation of product platforms – a whole series of new products – rather than single new products. For example: Intel's n86 series of microprocessors. Like other aspects of business design, platforms must be planned from the outset (Clark and Wheelwright, 1993; Tabrizi and Walleigh, 1997).

---

**Example 6: 'Six workers, three products'**

We spoke with a startup company, a wholly owned subsidiary of a large US medical products firm, that was engaged in R&D on three wonderful products: (a) a medical laser printer; (b) a precise calorimeter for measuring caloric intake; and (c) software for creating images from ultrasound data. The company had three employees with Ph.D.'s and three technicians. Each product was among the best of its kind, or even unique – but each lacked a winning business design. In the cost-cutting environment of US health care, the company's high-priced products met stiff market resistance; inferior products with cheaper price tags sold much better. The company seemed to us to lack product focus. Its printer was best in size and weight, but scored low in interface flexibility, contrast and resolution – key features for its specific market. The founder eventually joined another medical startup as its chief executive officer.

## Differentiation

Business design always follows a popular version of Einstein's relativity theory: value creation is always relative to some alternative, and new products require strong 'differentiators', showing how they differ from what can already be bought. 'Me-too' is not a winning innovation philosophy. Product differentiation requires answers to these questions:

- What is my basis for differentiation?
- What is my unique value proposition?
- Why should the customer want to buy from me?
- Who are my key competitors?
- Who will be my key competitors in 1 to 5 years?
- How convincing is my differentiation relative to that of my competitors?

Dell's business model 'differentiator' is the ability to offer customers computers precisely tailored and customized to their needs, based on their choice of a wide range of options, rather than forcing them to buy computers 'off-the-shelf'. Dell's defence against imitators is the huge difficulty of making the transition from conventional retailing to the direct model. This example shows why building the appropriate business model from the outset is so crucial. It is extremely difficult to migrate from one business model to another, once the design is set in concrete (see below the Section on 'Transition Problems').

---

### Example 7: 'Pen to computer'

A string of companies tried to launch pens that recognized handwriting and stored handwritten material, for transfer to computers later. They included GO; IBM's Thinkpad-plus pen (cancelled); EO; and Apple's Newton. None succeeded. All were based on OCR (optical character recognition) software. An Israeli entrepreneur chose a different approach. His computer-pen, instead of recognizing characters pixel by pixel, had motion sensors that recognized the *motion* of handwriting, and recognized, for example, the letter 'a' according to the kinetics of how the writer wrote it. The pen achieved a 5 per cent error rate – good or better than the prevailing optical technology. The product was

---

superb – but faced the obstacle that virtually no Israeli company had successfully pioneered and sold a mass-market product in the USA and Europe. The enormous marketing and advertising resources needed to launch a revolutionary product were not forthcoming. Again, a great core idea stumbled when the surrounding business design fell short.

## Value Recapture

Business designs consider carefully how value creation can, through pricing policies, be turned into profit. Value creation is a sufficient, but not necessary, condition for profit, and the issue of how to capture value is a vital one. The key questions:

- How does the customer pay for the value we create?
- How are my shareholders compensated for the value we create?

Internet businesses provide an example. The Internet grew extremely rapidly, in part through its open nature and in part because it offered information and services without charge. Internet users became accustomed to this. When Internet businesses sprang up, they faced the key dilemma: how can value be captured by charging non-zero prices, for things users had been accustomed to getting for nothing. This required innovative pricing policies.

In an age when shareholders are increasingly militant, return to shareholders is crucial. A business model must carefully conserve shareholders' capital, in order to ensure the highest possible return on capital investment. For example: a leading spreadsheet software firm invested excessively in a splendid new headquarters building, rather than in R&D for its new-generation product, and soon found itself acquired and out of business.

### Example 8: 'Expensive means good'

We met with a company that had developed a radically new method for cleaning silicon wafers electronically (the existing process was chemical-based, and hence, costly, and environmentally unfriendly). This product matched the market leader in every product feature but two: price (it was very expensive) and reliability (it had significantly greater downtime).

The company's business design called for maintaining the high price, since the product created high value for its users, and investing heavily to resolve the reliability problem. The company's initial public offering was successful; investors saw high profit potential in the product, and hence placed a high market value of the company's stock.

## Purchasing System

Managing relationships with suppliers has become increasingly important, as growing numbers of firms choose to outsource. The issues that must be addressed are:

- How do we buy: transactional or long term; antagonistic or partner?
- What part of our operation do we outsource: components, service and maintenance, information technology, data processing, R&D?
- How can we integrate our suppliers seamlessly into our own operations? (A good model for supplier management is Dell Computers.)
- How can effective use be made of enterprise resource planning (ERP) software, to manage our purchasing operations?

## Manufacturing and Operations

Here, a key issue is: Do we need to build our own production facility? A business model growing in popularity is one where production is subcontracted to producers elsewhere; in the Dell model, computers are assembled, customized to each customer's preferences, using components made by other firms.

- How much do we manufacture versus subcontract?
- Are my manufacturing/service delivery economies based primarily on fixed or on variable costs?
- Do we need state-of-the-art or 90th percentile technology?

## Capital Intensity

Production and assembly may be either labour-intensive or capital-intensive. In low-wage countries, it makes sense to use labour-intensive methods. The issues here are:

- Do we use capital-intensive (high fixed cost) systems or flexible less-capital-intensive systems?

- Is replacement of labour with capital, using robotic systems, a wise short-term and long-term investment?

## R&D and New Product Development

Management of research and development is a vital part of every business design. The issues that arise here are:

- Should R&D be internal or outsourced, focused on process, or on product? How much of our R&D resources should be devoted to research, and how much to focused development?
- How can R&D personnel best learn about marketplace needs?
- How can R&D teams work effectively with marketing, production, advertising and sales functions, to accelerate time-to-market?
- What mechanisms ensure that R&D projects will be completed on schedule? This is especially important – missing a 'window of opportunity' by even a month or two can be damaging or even fatal to a company, at a time when the pace of innovation is rapid and competition is fierce.

A key principle widely embraced in knowledge-based businesses is: outsource capacity (that is, production, assembly, and so on), not knowledge. Competitive advantage generally resides in a company's proprietary knowledge; outsourcing knowledge creation gives up this advantage from the outset.

## Organizational Configuration

The organizational structure of a company has much to do with whether the company achieves its goals. Just as in architecture, where form follows function, so in innovation does structure follow the organization's objectives. A company focused on being innovative, and on creating new products and bringing them rapidly to market, needs a flat, flexible organization in which individual workers and managers are empowered and are able and willing to accept responsibility and make decisions. The issues are:

- Should the organization be centralized or decentralized, hierarchical or flat, inverted tree or pyramid, or network, functional or business or matrix?

- Should managers be developed through internal promotion or external hiring?
- How can learning within the organization be facilitated? How can the organizational structure be so organized, as to smooth internal communication and transfer of knowledge and experience from one part of the organization to another?

**Go to Market Mechanism**

From the outset, the way in which the product is delivered to the customer must be carefully thought through. Too often, product innovators adopt an implicit 'Field of Dreams' approach – if we build it, then, they will come. The issues are:

- Use a direct sales force or low cost distribution, employing non-salaried sales representatives (multi-brand)?
- How will account management be handled? Licensing of the product?
- Is the direct business model applicable? If so: in what form?
- How will the Internet be used as a sales channel?

---

**Example 9: 'Value to consumers'**

A business consultant worked with a chip manufacturer, who had developed a chip for digital cameras. The product did not sell well. His recommendation: enhance the value of digital cameras by enhancing the ability of users to print out digital photographs with home printers. The result was a new chip, designed for PC printers, that made digital photography more worth while. The result: more direct sales, and more sales to digital-camera producers, because their product was made more worth while to consumers.

---

All these questions, and many more, must be carefully considered, even at the stage of inception, when the product is only an idea. The reason: the business design will be as an important a part of the product's marketplace success as the quality and features of the product itself. Moreover, it is vital to design a winning business model from the outset. Changing an existing business model leads to 'transition' problems that can be exceptionally difficult; a business model creates agents who have a vested interest in preserving it, even when it is inimicable to the company's continued success.

## TRANSITION PROBLEMS: GETTING TO THE RIGHT BUSINESS MODEL FROM THE WRONG ONE

Two innovative new business models now dominate their industries.

- Dell's 'direct business model' for selling computers directly to businesses and individuals through telephone, fax and Web sites;
- ETrade's 'Internet Web-based stock trading', where customers pay $14.95 per trade implemented through ETrade's Web site.

Some 30 per cent of all computers are now sold through the direct business model, and Dell expects this to rise to above 50 per cent within two years. Some 15 per cent of all stock trades are now done through online trading, and this percentage too is rising rapidly.

Now, consider the management problem facing, say, IBM and Merrill Lynch, leading companies in their industries. IBM's chief executive officer clearly recognizes the power of the direct business model. Why not embrace it immediately? Surely IBM has organizational skills at least close to those of Dell. Merrill Lynch's chairman also cannot fail to have noticed the tidal wave of online trading. Why, then, can you do nearly everything with Merrill Lynch online – except buy and sell stocks?

The problem is one of transition. If IBM, or Compaq, were to announce tomorrow that their sales would henceforth be 'direct' – or largely, direct – how would their resellers react? How would Sears, Circuit City and other retailers respond? They would instantly regard IBM as a competitor, rather than supplier, and stop selling IBM products. During the transition period from resellers to the direct model, IBM or Compaq sales would suffer grievously.

What constituency keeps Merrill Lynch from moving rapidly to online trading? Their own stockbrokers, of course, who profit handsomely from commissions and related bonuses. Those stakeholders are at least as powerful as the shareholders.

Often, the power of a new business model – and the ability of an innovator to sustain it – is in the difficulty established incumbents have in abandoning their existing business model. Large organizations, when faced with a new business model, have to grapple with the issue: How do we get there from here? For Merrill Lynch, IBM, Compaq, and many other established incumbents – there seems to be no trustworthy road map.

# WRITING A WINNING BUSINESS PLAN[5]

Business design is similar to architectural design. Conceptions must be turned into blueprints that show builders what must be erected and how. The blueprint of a business model is known as a business plan. Strong business plans are essential for success at innovation. The business plan provides a common language for all those involved with the new product, gives them a clear focus and objective, and sets goals. It also conveys to insiders – senior management within the company, or members of other divisions – and to outsiders – venture capitalists or other investors, suppliers, and strategic allies – what the innovators' intentions are.

Good business plans deal with four elements, and how they interact: people (human resources; those starting the venture, plus those outside the company who will assist); context (the industry, marketplace, and economy; factors beyond the entrepreneurs' control); risk-reward (profitability and the risk entailed in gaining it; what can go wrong, what can go right, and how to respond); and opportunity (the value-creation formula and how and whether it can be sustained; what will be sold, to whom, when, how, and why).

A common misconception is that the most important element of a business plan is the spreadsheet showing projections of costs and revenues. This is not the case. It is precisely the ease of creating such spreadsheets that makes them suspect. As Sahlman (1997, p. 98) notes: 'Most [business plans] waste too much ink on numbers and devote too little information that really matters to the intelligent investors. ... Numbers should appear mainly in the form of a business model that shows the entrepreneurial team has thought *through the key drivers of the venture's success or failure*' (our italics).

Every innovation project, whether involving a new business startup or an R&D project within an established firm, needs a detailed business design, blueprinted in a business plan. One purpose of a business plan is to convey the project's intentions to others (investors, suppliers, customers, and so on). Another purpose, no less important, is to define to the entrepreneurs or project managers *themselves* what the ends and means for achieving them are. A good business plan is like a clear, easy-to-read road map – you can navigate without it, but navigating with it is far easier and improves the chances of reaching your destination speedily.

## UTILIZING THE TOOLBOX IN BUILDING A BUSINESS MODEL

In this concluding Section, we conclude and summarize our book by indicating how our microeconomic tools can help build a business model.

### Incremental Improvements

The introduction to this book began with a rudimentary business model built around improving a single feature: taking a pharmaceutical product (Fosamax) weekly, rather than daily. Significantly improving one key feature can often create winning new products.

Philosopher Isaiah Berlin spoke of thinkers who were either 'foxes', who knew many little things, or 'hedgehogs', who knew one big thing. Consider, for instance, the Palm Pilot. Previous PDAs (personal digital assistants) like Apple's Newton tried hard to do too much. Palm Pilot, like the hedgehog, knew one basic thing – keeping track of our meetings, addresses and phone numbers – and did it very well. Identifying a key feature, or features, and improving them, can generate successful products. Chapter 1's tool, for optimizing incremental innovation, can help guide this process, using basic economic cost-benefit logic.

Feature improvement must be market-driven. Chapter 15 shows how key information from the marketing department can be used to match 'psychology' – the benefits buyers derive from features – with 'technology' – the relative cost and feasibility of feature-based innovations. Ways to integrate value knowledge residing in marketing and research and development departments, when those groups are often separated by geographical distance and always by cultural distance, is an issue that business models must address.

### Radical Innovation

Akio Morita's Walkman had a radically new feature: its size, and earphones, enabled Walkman owners to hear music wherever they happened to be. The cellular phone, invented only 16 years ago, offered the same radically new feature – the ability to communicate from almost anywhere. Both these radical innovations encountered stiff internal resistance within the companies developing them. Why would anyone *want* to hear music while walking around – or talk to their wives or friends or colleagues on the phone?

Alfred North Whitehead once said that we live in the concrete, but think in the abstract. We tend to disagree. Most of us *think* in the concrete as well. Radically new innovations demand a leap of insight, and a courageous managerial decision to take that leap, precisely because people think in the concrete, and, lacking concrete examples, find it hard to image a radically new feature and the benefits it conveys. This is why market research can often be radical innovations' nemesis. Chapter 2 offers a quantitative tool for analysing and optimizing radical innovation, while at the same time recognizing that many of the inputs and data needed for this model are highly uncertain. Often, the need to quantify something inherently resistant to quantification helps clarify our thinking, even if the method itself is too demanding of data to be fully workable.

Frequently, R&D investment in new, pioneering technologies proves fruitless. This was the case with the first companies to produce commercial lasers. Conventional approaches to quantifying the economic returns on such investments – discounted cash flow, or net present value – often cause bottom-line-conscious managers to avoid such projects. A new approach to valuing risky R&D investment in radical innovations, explained in Chapter 3, takes into account the 'option value' of such investments – the fact that while first-generation lasers were clumsy and flawed, second- and third-generation ones created an enormous market, benefiting humankind greatly; and obviously, the success of second-generation products build on the (often expensive) learning process experienced in the failure of first-generation ones. The metaphor of R&D investment as a 'real option' can sometimes turn what appears to be an unprofitable innovation into a profitable one – and point to a correct decision.

## Creating Value

The essence of every business model is the creation of value for customers. Value creation is often a rather mysterious process, with customers themselves finding it difficult to articulate precisely what they need, or why, or why they value a particular product or service. In Chapter 4, we offer a tool for using market-based information to help answer the question: *Which product features drive value, and hence price?* By helping innovators determine which features 'explain' (in a statistical sense) market price, the 'hedonic price' tool can often identify the nature and direction of innovation activity. In our experience, generally a small number of key features explain most of the variance in market price. Innovative products that fail to excel in those key features will not likely succeed.

One way products create value is by reducing uncertainty and offering assurance of quality and consistency – features inherent in globally known brand names. Chapter 5 offers a new feature-based approach to measuring the market value of brand names, by measuring separately the contribution of brands to market price, and the contribution of product features. This approach can help business-model builders quantify the potential value of the large (and often vital) investments required for brand-building.

## How Important Is Innovation?

Adam Smith, in *The Wealth of Nations* (1776), asked why some countries grow wealthy, while others remain poor. His answer focused on the availability of land and resources relative to population. Seven years earlier, in 1769, fellow Scot James Watt had invented the steam engine, which made physical and financial capital, rather than resources, the key growth-generating resource and led to the First Industrial Revolution (caused by steam power) and the Second, powered by electricity. Today, the world is experiencing a new Industrial Revolution, the Third (see Moss, 1996). This revolution is powered by global markets and knowledge-based products and services generated by innovative companies and nations. The posited link between science, technology, innovation and economic performance is examined in depth in Part II of this volume. Chapter 6 focuses on the microeconomic link between firm-level profitability and innovation in Israel, while Chapters 9 and 10 look at the link between scientific excellence and export performance at the country level for the European Union and Israel. Chapter 7 proposes applying a tool widely used for measuring technical change at the country level (total factor productivity) to individual firms, and shows how; while Chapter 8 offers some benchmarking tools for one of the world's most innovative and fastest growing industries, telecommunications.

**Tracking Product Quality**

Good business models try to create sustainable competitive advantage. They are inevitably based on careful assessments of competing products. Part III offered a series of product and industry studies showing how our feature-based technometric approach can be used to benchmark and compare product quality at a given point in time (for biodiagnosic kits, in Chapter 11, and for industrial sensors, in Chapter 12), and to measure changes in product quality across two points in time (Chapter 13), also for sensors. Chapter 14 studies a variety of knowledge-based products, and discovers that new and old technologies tend to coexist, offering a range of potentially successful business models from 'create the radically new' to 'perfect the old and reliable'.

# EPILOGUE

Joseph Schumpeter characterized innovation as 'creative destruction'. Lester Thurow has observed that a better characterization of the innovative process might be 'destructive creation'. The process of innovation destroys markets for old products in the course of bringing new and better ones to consumers. In this process, there are winners and losers, as in nearly all dynamic change. Those who lose belong to products and industries that are on their way out. Those who win are linked with innovative products and industries.

We began this book with an observation about innovation being a delicate balance between chaos and order. It is our hope that achieving this balance, with the aid of some or all of the microeconomic tools we describe, can place managers and workers together in the ranks of the winners. Recently, a leading US toymaker announced that at the height of the Christmas toy-buying peak, it was laying off thousands of workers – its senior managers had failed to anticipate the shift away from conventional toys and into video games and electronic toys, a shift evident years earlier. A systematic effort to quantify innovation and benchmark it might have prevented a bleak Christmas for laid-off workers.

Ultimately, innovation is about improving people's lives. We hope this book makes a small but noticeable contribution.

## NOTES

1   According to Forbes magazine (1999), he is the sixth wealthiest billionaire in the world, behind Bill Gates, Warren Buffett, Paul Allen, Steve Ballmer and Philip Anschutz, and the youngest (by one year, over Amazon.com founder Jeff Bezos, 35).
2   Fortune Magazine (1999, pp. F1–F20). Also: Business Week (1999, p. 64).
3   Michael Dell Speech at MIT, in Wong Auditorium, November 19, 1998; and Magretta (1998, pp. 73–84).
4   Fry (1998, p. B7).
5   This Section is based in part on Sahlman (1997, pp. 98–108).

# References

Adelman, I. and Z. Griliches (1961), 'On an index of quality change,' *American Statistical Association Journal*, **56**, pp. 535–548.

Agency for Industrial Science and Technology (1982), (Wagakuni sangyogijutsu, nokoku saihikaku). Japanese Industrial Technology in International Comparison (compiled by Japan Techno-economic Society), Tokyo.

Ahn, T. and L. M. Seiford (1993), 'Sensitivity of DEA to models and variable sets in a hypothesis test setting: the efficiency of university operations,' in Y. Ijiri (ed.), *Creative and Innovative Approaches to the Science of Management*, New York: Quorum Books.

Ali, A. I. (1990), *IDEAS, Version 3.0.0 – Integrated Data Envelopment Analysis System*, University of Massachusetts: Amherst, MA., Available commercially as: Available as IDEAS Version 5.0.1, 1 Consulting, P.O. Box 2453, Amherst MA., 01004–2453.

Archibald, R. B., C. A. Haulman and C. E. Moody (1983), 'Quality, price, advertising, and published quality ratings,' *Journal of Consumer Research*, **9**, pp. 347–356.

Arnold, H. (1991), 'Wachstumsmarkt Sensorik', *Markt und Technik*, **26**, pp. 78–79.

Backhaus, K. (1992), *Investitionsgütermarketing*, München: Verlag Franz Vahlen, 3rd edition.

Banker, R. D. (1984), 'Estimating most productive scale size using data envelopment analysis,' *European Journal of Operation Research*, **17**, pp. 35–44.

Bass, F. M. and W. W. Talarzyk (1972), 'An attitude model for the study of brand preference,' *Journal of Marketing Research*, **9**, pp. 93–96.

Bator, F. M. (1958), 'The anatomy of market failure', *Quarterly Journal of Economics*, **72**, 351–379.

Bearden, W. O. and A. G. Woodside (1977), 'Situational influences on consumer purchase intentions,' In A. G. Woodside et al. (eds), *Consumer and Industrial Buyer Behaviour*, New York: North Holland, pp. 167–177.

Ben-Arieh, A., H. Grupp and S. Maital (1998), 'Optimal incremental innovation: an evaluative approach for Integrating Marketing & R&D,' *Research Evaluation*, **7** (2), pp. 121–132.

Berman, M. (1999), 'Survey of CEOs,' *The Conference Board*.

Berthon, P., J. M. Hulbert and L. F. Pitt (1997), *Brands, Brand Managers and the Management of Brands: Where to Next?* Marketing Science Institute: Cambridge, MA., Report 97–122.

Bettman, J. R., N. Capon and J. R. Lutz (1975), *An Information Processing Theory of Consumer Choice*, Reading, MA.: Addison-Wesley.

Black, F. and M. Scholes (1973), 'The pricing of options and corporate liabilities,' *Journal of Political Economy*, **81**, May/June, 637–659.

Bowman, C. and D. Faulkner (1994), 'Measuring product advantage using competitive benchmarking and customer perceptions,' *Long Range Planning*, **27** (1), pp. 119–132.

Bradford, D., S. Maital and W. Oates (1969), 'The rising cost of local public services: some evidence and reflections,' *National Tax Journal*, **22**, 185–202.

Brown, M. G. and R. A. Svenson (1988), 'Measuring R&D productivity' *Research Technology Management*, **31** (4), pp. 11–15.

Business Week, Global 1000, July 12, 1999.

Camp, R. C. (1989), *Benchmarking: the Search for Industry Best Practices that Lead to Superior Performance*, Milwaukee: ASQC Quality Press.

Carlsson, B. and R. Stankiewicz (1991), 'On the nature function and composition of technological systems,' *Journal of Evolutionary Economics*, **1** (2), 93–118.

Cebon, P., P. Newton and P. Noble (1999), 'Innovation in firms: towards a model for indicator development,' Working Paper No. 99–9, Melbourne Business School.

Chan Choi, S. and W. S. DeSarbo (1994), 'A conjoint-based product designing procedure incorporating price competition,' *Journal of Product Innovation Management*, **11**, pp. 451–459.

Chandler, A. (1991), *Scale and Scope*, Cambridge, MA.: Harvard University Press.

Chang, T. and A. R. Wildt (1994), 'Price, product information, and purchase intention: An Empirical Study,' *Journal of the Academy of Marketing Science*, **22** (1), pp. 16–27.

Charnes, A., W. W. Cooper and E. Rhodes (1978), 'Measuring the efficiency of decision making units,' *European Journal of Operational Research*, **2** (4), pp. 429–444.

Charnes, A., W. W. Cooper and E. Rhodes (1981), 'Evaluating programme and managerial efficiency: an application of data envelopment analysis to programme follow through.' *Management Science*, **27** (6), pp. 668–697.

Charnes, A., W. W. Cooper and R. L. Clarke (1988), 'An approach to testing for organizational slack via banker's game theoretic DEA formulations,' Research Report CCS 613, Center for Cybernetic Studies, University of Texas at Austin.

Chow, G. (1967), 'Technological change and the demand for computers,' *American Economic Review*, **57**, pp. 1117–1130.

Christensen, C. M., F. F. Suarez and J. M. Utterback (1996), 'Strategies for survival in fast-changing industries', Working Paper, ICRMOT, MIT Sloan School of Management, July 16.

Clark, K. B. and S. C. Wheelwright (1993), *Managing New Product and Process Development*, New York: The Free Press.

Clark, K. B. and Z. Griliches (1984), 'Productivity growth and R&D at the business level: results from the PIMS data base,' in Z. Griliches (ed.), *R&D, Patents and Productivity*, Chicago: University of Chicago Press, pp. 393–416.

Cohen, W. (1995), 'Empirical studies of innovative activity,' in P. Stoneman, (ed.) (1995), *Handbook of the Economics of Innovation and Technological Change*, Oxford and Cambridge, MA.: Blackwell, pp. 182–264.

Cooper, R. G. (1993), *Winning at New Products: Accelerating the Process from Idea to Launch*, Reading, MA.: Addison-Wesley.

Cooper, R. G. and E. J. Kleinschmidt (1996), 'Winning businesses in product development: the critical success factors', *Research Technology Management*, **39**.

Cox, J. C., S. A. Ross and M. Rubinstein (1979), 'Option pricing: a simplified approach,' *Journal of Financial Economics*, **7**, pp. 229–263.

Craig, C. E. and R. C. Harris (1973), 'Total productivity measurement at the firm level,' *Sloan Management Review*, Spring, pp. 12–29.

Curry, D. J. and D. J. Faulds (1986), 'Indexing product quality: issues, theory and results,' *Journal of Consumer Research*, **13**, pp. 134–145.

Curry, D. J. and M. B. Menasco (1983), 'On the separability of weights and brand values: issues and empirical results,' *Journal of Consumer Research*, **10**, June, pp. 83–95.

Day, G. S. and R. Wensley (1988), 'Assessing advantage: a framework for diagnosing competitive superiority,' *Journal of Marketing*, **52**, pp. 1–20.

Denison, E. (1967), *Why Growth Rates Differ*, Washington, DC: Brookings Institution.

Dewar, R. L. and J. E. Dutton (1986), 'The adoption of radical and incremental innovation: an empirical analysis,' *Management Science*, **32**, pp. 1422–33.

Dixit, A. and R. Pindyck (1994), *Investment under Uncertainty*, Princeton: Princeton University Press.

Dorison, F. (1992), *Produktbezogener technischer Fortschritt*, Ludwigsburg: Verlag Wissenschaft & Praxis.

Dosi, G. (1988), 'Sources, procedures and microeconomic effects of innovation,' *Journal of Economic Literature*, **26**, pp. 1120–1171.

Dosi, G., K. Pavitt, and L. Soete (1990), *The Economics of Technical Change and International Trade*, New York, London: Harvester Wheatsheaf.

Ehrnberg, E. (1995), 'On the definition and measurement of technological discontinuities,' *Technovation*, **15** (7), pp. 437–53.

EIRMA (ed.) (1985), 'Evaluation of R&D output,' Working Group Report No. 29 of the European Industrial Research Management Association, Paris.

Farquhar, P. (1989), 'Managing brand equity,' *Marketing Research*, pp. 24–34.

Fine, C. (1999), *Clockspeed: Supply Chain Management*, New York: Perseus.

Fishbein, M. (1963), 'An investigation of relationship between beliefs about an object and the attitude toward the object,' *Human Relations*, **16**, pp. 233–40.

Fishbein, M. and L. Ajzen (1975), *Belief, Attitude, Intention, and Behaviour*, Reading, MA.: Addison-Wesley.

Forbes magazine (1999), 'The world's working rich,' July 5, p. 204.

Forecast International (1992), 'Civil aircraft forecast,' a report.

Fortune (1999a), 'America's 500 largest companies,' p. F–1.

Fortune (1999b), 'America's wealth creators', p. 277.

Fortune magazine (1999), 'Fortune 500 largest U.S. corporations,' April 26.

Freeman, C. (1982), *The Economics of Innovation*, London: Francis Pinter.

Freeman, C. and L. Soete (1997), *The Economics of Industrial Innovation*, 3rd edition, Pinter: London.

Frenkel, A., E. Harel, K. Koschatzky, H. Grupp and S. Maital (1994a), 'Identifying the sources of market value for science-based products: the case of industrial sensors,' Working Paper No. 111–94, The International

Center for Research on the Management of Technology, Sloan School of Management, MIT, Cambridge, MA.

Frenkel, A., Th. Reiss, S. Maital, K. Koschatzky and H. Grupp (1994b), 'Technometric evaluation and technology policy: the case of biodiagnostic kits in Israel,' *Research Policy*, **23**, pp. 281–292.

Frenkel, H. D. (1990), 'The polymer industry in Israel and the world: present status and future prospects,' Samuel Neaman Institute for Advanced Studies in Science and Technology, Haifa, November 1990.

Fry, J. (1998), 'When the pen may be mightier than the keyboard,' *Wall Street Journal*, August 6.

Garvin, D. A. (1983), 'Quality on the line,' *Harvard Business Review*, **61**, pp. 65–75.

Garvin, D. A. (1987), 'Competing on the eight dimensions of quality,' *Harvard Business Review*, **65**, pp. 101–109.

Gittins, J. C. (1994), 'A planning procedure for new-product chemical research', *R&D Management*, **24** (3), pp. 219–227.

Gluck, F. W. and R. N. Foster (1975), 'Managing technological change: a box of cigars for Brad', *Harvard Business Review*, Sept.–Oct., pp. 139–50.

Gomory, R. and R. W. Schmitt (1988), 'Science and product', Science, **240**, May 27, pp. 1131–1132 and pp. 1203–1204.

Gordon, R. (1992), 'Alternative logics of innovation and global competition in the U.S. electronics industry: a comparative assessment,' in S. Okamura, F. Sakauchi, I. Nonaka (eds), *New Perspectives on Global Science and Technology Policy*, Tokyo: Mita Press, pp. 329–357.

Green, J. and Y. Wind (1973), *Multi-attribute Models in Marketing*.

Griffin, A. and J. Hauser (1996), 'Integrating R&D and marketing: a review and analysis of the literature', *Journal of Product Innovation Management*, **13**, pp. 191–215.

Griliches, Z. (1961), 'Hedonic price indexes for automobiles: an econometric analysis of quality change,' in NBER – National Bureau of Economic Research (ed.) (1961), *The Price Statistics of the Federal Government*, No. 173, New York, pp. 137–196.

Griliches, Z. (ed.) (1971), *Price Indexes and Quality Change, Studies in New Methods of Measurement*, Price Statistic Committee Federal Reserve Board, Cambridge, MA.: Harvard University Press.

Griliches, Z. (1979), 'Issues in assessing the contribution of R&D to productivity growth,' *Bell Journal of Economics*, **10** (1), pp. 92–116.

Griliches, Z. (1986), 'Productivity puzzles and R&D: another nonexplanation,' *Journal of Economic Perspectives*, **2** (4), pp. 9–21.

Griliches, Z. (1990), 'Patent statistics as economic indicators: a survey', *Journal of Economic Literature*, **28**, pp. 1661–1707.

Griliches, Z. (1994), 'Explanations of productivity growth: is the glass half-empty?' *American Economic Review*, **84** (1), pp. 1–25.

Griliches, Z. (1995), 'R&D and productivity: econometric results and measurement issues, in P. Stoneman, (ed.), *Handbook of the Economics of Innovation and Technological Change*, Oxford: Basil Blackwell, pp. 52–89.

Griliches, Z. and F. Lichtenberg (1984), 'Interindustry technology flows and productivity growth: a re-examination,' *Review of Economics and Statistics*, **66** (2), pp. 325–29.

Grupp, H. (1990a), 'On the supplementary functions of science and technology indicators', *Scientometrics*, **19**, pp. 447–472.

Grupp, H. (1990b), 'Technometrics as a missing link in science and technology indicators', in J. Sigurdson (ed.), *Measuring the Dynamics of Technological Change*, London: Pinter, pp. 57–76.

Grupp, H. (1991), 'Innovation dynamics in OECD countries: towards a correlated network of R&D-intensity, trade, patent and technometric indicators,' in OECD (ed.), *Technology and Productivity: the Challenge for Economic Policy*, Paris: OECD, pp. 275–295.

Grupp, H. (ed.) (1992), *Dynamics of Science Based Innovation*, Berlin and New York: Springer-Verlag.

Grupp, H. (1993), 'Efficiency of government intervention in technical change in telecommunications: ten national economies compared,' *Technovation*, **13** (4), pp. 187–220.

Grupp, H. (1994), 'The measurement of technical performance of innovations by technometrics and its impact on established technology indicators,' *Research Policy*, **23**, pp. 175–193.

Grupp, H. (1995), 'Science, high technology and the competitiveness of EC countries, *Cambridge Journal of Economics*, **19** (1), pp. 209–223.

Grupp, H. (1997a), 'External effects as a microeconomic determinant of innovation efficiency,' *International Journal of the Economics of Business*, **4** (2), pp. 173–187.

Grupp, H. (1997b), 'Technical change on a global market: competition in solar cell development', in J. Howells and J. Michie (eds), *Technology, Innovation and Competitiveness*, Cheltenham: Edward Elgar, pp. 177–202.

Grupp, H. (1998), *Foundations of Innovation Economics: Theory, Measurement and Practise*, Cheltenham: Edward Elgar.

Grupp, H. and O. Hohmeyer (1986), 'A technometric model for the assessment of technological standards,' *Technological Forecasting and Social Change*, **30**, pp. 123–137.

Grupp, H. and O. Hohmeyer (1988), 'Technological standards for research-intensive product groups,' in A.F.J. van Raan (ed.), *Handbook of Quantitative Studies of Science and Technology*, Amsterdam: Elsevier, pp. 611–673.

Grupp, H. and S. Maital (1996), 'Innovation benchmarking in the telecom industry,' Working Paper No. 153–96, MIT Sloan School of Management.

Grupp, H. and S. Maital (1998a), 'Interpreting the sources of market value in a capital goods market: R&D management in industrial sensors,' *R&D Management*, **28** (2), pp. 65–77.

Grupp, H. and S. Maital (1998b), 'Optimal radical innovation,' Working Paper, Samuel Neaman Institute, Technion, Haifa.

Grupp, H. and Th. Schnoering (1992), 'Research and development in telecommunications: national systems under pressure,' *Telecommunications Policy*, January–February, pp. 46–66.

Grupp, H. and B. Schwitalla (1998), 'Embodied and disembodied technical change: a multi-factorial analysis of German firms,' *METU Studies in Development*, **25** (1), pp. 75–105.

Grupp, H., O. Hohmeyer, R. Kollert and H. Legler (1987), *Technometrie. Die Bemessung des technisch-wirtschaftlichen Leistungsstandes*, Köln: Verlag TUEV Rheinland.

Grupp, H., U. Schmoch, B. Schwitalla and A. Granberg (1990), 'Developing industrial robot technology in Sweden, West Germany, Japan and the U.S.A.,' in J. Sigurdson (ed.), *Measuring the Dynamics of Technological Change*, London: Pinter, pp. 106–129.

Grupp, H., E. Albrecht and K. Koschatzky (1992a), 'Alliances between science research and innovation research,' in H. Grupp (ed.), *Dynamics of Science-Based Innovation*, Heidelberg: Springer Publishers, pp. 3–18.

Grupp, H., S. Maital, A. Frenkel and K. Koschatzky (1992b), 'The relation between technological excellence and export sales: a data envelopment model and comparison of Israel to EC countries,' *Research Evaluation*, **2** (2), pp. 87–101.

Hamel, G. (1997), 'How Killers Count', *Fortune*, June 23, p. 24.

Hanusch, H. and M. Hierl (1992), 'Productivity, profitability and innovative behaviour', in F. M. Scherer and M. Perlman (eds), *Entrepreneurship, Technological Innovation and Economic Growth*, Ann Arbor: The University of Michigan Press, pp. 237–250.

Hauser, J. and S. M. Shugan (1983), 'Defensive marketing strategies,' *Marketing Science*, **2** (4), pp. 319–360.

Hauser, J. and S. P. Gaskin (1984), 'Application of the "defender" consumer model', *Marketing Science*, **3** (4), pp. 327–351.

Hauser, J. R. (1996a), 'The role of mathematical models in the study of product development', Working Paper No. 149–96, ICRMOT, MIT Sloan School of Management.

Hauser, J. R. (1996b), 'Metrics to value R&D: an annotated bibliography,' Working Paper No. 143–96, ICRMOT, MIT Sloan School of Management, 143–96, March.

Hauser, J. R. and P. Simmie (1981), 'Profit maximizing perceptual positions: an integrated theory for the selection of product features and price,' *Management Science*, **27** (1), pp. 33–56.

Heckman, J. (1976), 'The common structure of statistical models of truncation, sample selection, and limited dependent variables and a single estimator for such models,' *The Annuals of Economic and Social Measurement*, **5**, pp. 457–492.

Heertje, A. (1992), 'Capitalism, socialism and democracy after 50 years,' invited lecture, Tenth World Congress, International Economics Association, Moscow.

Henderson, R. and K. Clark (1990), 'Architectural innovation: the reconfiguration of existing product technologies and the failure of established firms,' *Administrative Science Quarterly*, **35**, 9–30.

Hjorth-Andersen, C. (1984), 'The concept of quality and the efficiency of markets for consumer products,' *Journal of Consumer Research*, **11**, pp. 708–718.

Hjorth-Andersen, C. (1986), 'More on multidimensional quality: a reply,' *Journal of Consumer Research*, **13**, pp. 149–154.

Horwitch, M., H. Grupp, S. Maital, G. Dopelt and G. Sobel (2000), 'Global integration of marketing & R&D Maital: IBM's Haifa Research Laboratory and its "WebCutter" technology,' in A. Woodside (ed.), *Getting Better at Sensemaking*, JAI Press, Stamford: pp. 203–214.

Hulst, N. van, R. Mulder and L. L. G. Soete (1991), 'Export and technology in manufacturing industry,' *Weltwirtschaftliches Archiv*, **127**, pp. 246–264.

Jaegle, A. J. (1999), 'Shareholder value, real options and innovation in technology-intensive companies,' *R&D Management*, **29** (3), pp. 271–287.

Jane's All the World's Aircraft 1993–1994 (1993), Alexandria, VA: Jane's Information Group.

Juckenack, D. (ed.) (1990), *Handbuch der Sensortechnik – Messen mechanischer Groessen*, 2nd edition, Landsberg/Lech: Verlag Moderne Industrie.

Katz, J. H. (1995), 'The impact of brand attitude and new information on product evaluation,' paper presented at the Conference of the European Association for Consumer Research, Copenhagen, pp. 15–17.

Katzir E. et al. (1988), 'Policies for advancing research and development in biotechnology in Israel,' report presented to the Minister of Science and Development and to the Minister of Industry and Trade, Jerusalem.

Kearns, D. T. (1986), 'Quality improvement begins at the top,' in Bowles (ed.), *World*, **20** (5), p. 21.

Kim, W. C. and R. Mauborgne (1997), 'Value innovation: the strategic logic of high growth,' *Harvard Business Review*, Jan.–Feb., p. 106.

Kirkpatrick, D. (1993), 'Gerstner's new vision for IBM', *Fortune*, November 15, p. 32.

Kline, S. J. (1991), 'Models of innovation and their policy consequences,' in H. Inose, M. Kawasaki, F. Kodama (eds), *Science and Technology Policy Research*, Tokyo: MITA, pp. 125–140.

Kline, S. J. and N. Rosenberg (1986), 'An overview of innovation,' in R. Landau and N. Rosenberg (eds), *The Positive Sum Strategy. Harnessing Technology for Economic Growth*, Washington, DC: National Academy Press, pp. 275–306.

Koschatzky, K. (1991), 'New concepts of measuring technological change,' in U. Blum and J. Schmid (eds), *Demographic Processes, Occupation and Technological Change*, Heidelberg: Physica-Springer, pp. 104–121.

Koschatzky, K., A. Frenkel, H. Grupp and S. Maital (1996), 'A technometric assessment of sensor technology in Israel vs. Europe, the United States and Japan, *International Journal of Technology Management*, **11** (5/6), pp. 667–687.

Kotler, P. (1991), *Marketing Management*, Englewood Cliffs, NJ: Prentice-Hall.

Lancaster, K. (1971), *Consumer Demand: A New Approach*, New York, NY: Columbia University Press.

Lancaster, K. (1991), *Modern Consumer Theory*, Aldershot, UK: Edward Elgar.

Lee, T. H., J. C. Fisher and T. S. Yau (1986), 'Getting things done: is your R&D on track?' *Harvard Business Review*, Jan.–Feb.

Legler, H. (1987), 'West German competitiveness of technology-intensive products,' in H. Grupp, (ed.), *Problems of Measuring Technological Change*, Cologne: Verlag TUEV Rhineland, pp. 171–190.

Legler, H., H. Grupp, B. Gehrke and U. Schasse (1992), *Innovationspotential und Hochtechnologie*, Heidelberg, New York: Physica-Springer.

Leibenstein, H. and S. Maital (1992), 'Empirical estimation and partitioning of x-inefficiency: a data envelopment approach,' *American Economic Association Papers and Proceedings*, **82**, pp. 428–433.

Leonard, D. and J. F. Rayport (1997), Spark innovation through empathic design, *Harvard Business Review*, **6**, November/December.

Leuthesser, L. (1988), 'Defining, measuring and managing brand equity,' report 88–104, Marketing Science Institute, Cambridge, MA.

Levitt, T. (1993), *The Marketing Imagination*, New York: Free Press.

Link, A. N. (1981), 'Basic research and productivity increase in manufacturing: additional evidence,' *American Economic Review*, **71**, pp. 1111–12.

Lucas, R. E. B. (1972), 'Working conditions, wage-rates, and human capital: a hedonic study,' an unpublished doctoral dissertation, Massachusetts Institute of Technology.

Luehrman, T. (1998a), 'Investment Opportunities as real options: getting started on the numbers,' *Harvard Business Review*, July–August, pp. 51–67.

Luehrman, T. (1998b), 'Strategy as a portfolio of real options,' *Harvard Business Review*, Sept.–Oct., pp. 89–99.

Lutz, R. J. and J. R. Bettman (1977), 'Multi-attribute models in marketing: a bicentennial review,' in A. Woodside (ed.), *Consumer and Industrial Buyer Behaviour*, New York: North Holland, pp. 137–150.

Maarek, Y., M. Jacovi, M. Shtalhaim, S. Ur, D. Zernik and I. B. Shaul (1997), 'WebCutter: a system for dynamic and tailorable site mapping,' *Journal of Computer Networks and ISDN Systems*, **29**, pp. 1269–1279. An earlier version appeared in the Proceedings of the WWW6, Santa Clara, CA, April 1997.

Magretta, J (1998), 'The power of virtual integration: an interview with Dell Computer's Michael Dell,' *Harvard Business Review*, March–April.

Maital, S. (1991), Competing by Cooperating – How to Woo Your Rival, *Across the Board*, July–August.

Maital, S. (1994), *Executive Economics*, New York: The Free Press/Macmillan.

Maital, S. and A. Vaninsky (1994), 'Reconfiguring existing products: a benchmarking model for optimal strategic innovation,' Working Paper, S. Neaman Institute for Advanced Studies in Science and Technology.

Mandakovic, T. and W. E. Souder (1987), 'A model for measuring R&D productivity,' *Productivity Management Frontiers – I*, pp. 139–146.

Mansfield, E. (1965), 'Rates of return from industrial R&D,' *American Economic Review*, **55**, pp. 863–73.

Mansfield, E. (1968), *Industrial Research and Technical Innovation*, New York: Norton.

Martin, B. R. and J. Irvine (1983), 'Assessing basic research: some partial indicators of scientific progress in radio astronomy,' *Research Policy*, **12**, pp. 61–90.

Mazis, M. B. and O. T. Ahtola (1975), 'A comparison of four multi-attribute models in the prediction of consumer attitudes,' *Journal of Consumer Research*, **2**, pp. 38–52.

Meyer, M. H. and E. B. Roberts (1986), 'New product strategy in small technology-based firms: a pilot study,' *Management Science*, **32** (7), July 1986, pp. 806–821.

Meyer, M. H. and E. B. Roberts (1988), 'Focusing product technology for corporate growth,' *Sloan Management Review*, **29** (4), Summer 1988, pp. 7–16.

Meyer, M., P. Tertzakian and J. M. Utterback (1995), 'Metrics for managing R&D,' Working Paper No. 124–95, ICRMOT – MIT Sloan School.

Moore, G. (1991), *Crossing the Chasm: Marketing and Selling High-tech Products to Mainstream Customers*, New York: Harper Business.

Moran, N. (1991), 'Prescriptions for Pharmaceutical Research,' *Nature*, **353**, pp. 873–874.

Moss, D. (1996), 'Confronting the Third Industrial Revolution,' *Harvard Business School*, Case No. 9–796–161, April 29.

Muellbauer, J. (1974), 'Household production theory, quality, and the "hedonic technique",' *American Economic Review*, **64**, pp. 977–994.

Nelson, R. and S. Winter (1982), *An Evolutionary Theory of Economic Change*, Cambridge, MA.: Harvard University Press.

Nelson, R. R. (1990), 'Capitalism as an engine of progress,' *Research Policy*, **19**, pp. 193–214.

Nussbaum, B. (1984), *Das Ende unserer Zukunft: Revolutionaere Technologien draengen die Europaeische Wirtschaft ins Abseits*, Munich: Kindler.

OECD, *Main Science and Technology Indicators*, various years, Paris: OECD.

OECD (1991), *Basic Science and Technology Statistics*, Paris: OECD.

OECD (ed.) (1992), *OECD Proposed Guidelines for Collecting and Interpreting Technological Innovation Data (Oslo Manual)*, Paris: OECD.

OECD (ed.) (1994), *The Measurement of Scientific and Technological Activities: Using Patent Data as Science and Technology Indicators*, Patent Manual 1994, OECD/GD (94) 114, Paris: OECD.

Patel, P. and K. Pavitt (1992), 'Large firms in the production of the world's technology: an important case of 'non-globalization,' *Journal of International Business Studies*, **22**.

Pavitt, K. (1982), 'R&D, patenting and innovative activities,' *Research Policy*, **11**, pp. 33–51.

PC Magazine (1994), 'Buyers Guide', PC Magazine, **13**, supplement.

Perlitz, M., T. Peske and R. Schrank (1999), 'Real options valuation: the new frontier in R&D project evaluation,' *R&D Management*, **29** (3), pp. 255–269.

Pessemier, E. A. (1977), *Product Management*, New York: John Wiley and Sons.

Phillips, A., A. P. Phillips and T. R. Phillips (1994), *Biz Jets: Technology and Market Structure in the Corporate Jet Aircraft Industry*, Dordrecht, Netherlands: Kluwer Academic.

Pine, B. J. II and J. Gilmour (1999), *The Experience Economy*, Boston, MA.: Harvard Business School Press.

Porter, M. E. (1980), *Competitive Strategy: Techniques for Analyzing Industries and Competitors*, New York: Free Press.

Porter, M. E. (1990), *The Competitive Advantage of Nations*, London: Macmillan.

Prahalad, C. K. and G. Hamel (1990), 'The core competence of the corporation', *Harvard Business Review*, **68** (3), pp. 485–502.

Pugh, S. (1990), *Total Design*, Reading, MA.: Addison-Wesley.

Raan, A. F. J. van (ed.) (1988), *Handbook of Quantitative Studies of Science and Technology*, Amsterdam: Elsevier.

Ray, G. F. (1989), 'Full circle: the diffusion of technology,' *Research Policy*, **18**, pp. 1–18.

Reenen, J. van (1996), 'The creation and capture of rents: wages and innovation in a panel of U.K. companies', *Quarterly Journal of Economics*, **CXI**, pp. 194–226.

Reiss, Th. (1990), *Perspektiven der Biotechnologie*, Cologne: Verlag TUEV Rheinland.

Roberts, E. B. (1991), *Entrepreneurs in High Technology: Lessons from MIT and Beyond*, New York: Oxford University Press.

Roberts, E. B. (1994), 'Benchmarking the strategic management of technology – I,' Working Paper No. 115–94, Massachusetts Institute of Technology (MIT), Sloan School of Management, International Center for Research on the Management of Technology, Cambridge, MA.

Roberts, E. B. (1995), 'Benchmarking the strategic management of technology – II,' R&D Performance, Working Paper No. 119–95, Massachusetts Institute of Technology (MIT), Sloan School of Management, International Center for Research on the Management of Technology, Cambridge, MA.

Roessner, J. D. (1985), 'Prospects for a U.S. national innovation policy,' *Futures*, **17**, pp. 224–231.

Roll, Y. and M. J. Rosenblatt (1983), 'Project productivity measurement,' *International Journal of Productivity Measurement*, **21** (5), pp. 787–794.

Rosegger, G. (1996), *The Economics of Production and Innovation*, 3rd edition, Oxford, UK: Butterworth-Heinemann.

Rosen, S. (1974), 'Hedonic prices and implicit markets: product differentiation in pure competition,' *Journal of Political Economy*, **82** (1), pp. 34–55.

Sahlman, W. A. (1997), How to write a great business plan, *Harvard Business Review*, July–August 1997, pp. 98–108.

Sardana, G. D. and P. Vrat (1989), 'Productivity measurement of applied industrial research in an organization: a conceptual framework', *Productivity Management Frontiers*, **II**, pp. 47–54.

Saviotti, P. P. (1985), 'An approach to the measurement of technology based on the hedonic price method and related methods,' *Technological Forecasting and Social Change*, **29**, pp. 309–334.

Saviotti, P. P. and J. S. Metcalfe (1984), 'A theoretical approach to the construction of technological output indicators, *Research Policy*, **13**, pp. 141–151.

Saviotti, P. P., P. C. Stubbs, R. W. Coombs and M. Gibbons (1982), 'An approach to the construction of indexes of technological change and technological sophistication', *Technological Forecasting and Social Change*, **21**, pp. 133–147.

Schainblatt, A. H. (1982), 'How companies measure the productivity of engineers and scientists,' *Research Management*, **25**, p. 3.

Schalk, H. J. and U. C. Taeger (1998), 'Wissensverbreitung and Diffusionsdynamik im Spannungsfeld zwischen innovierenden und imitierenden Unternehmen', Munich: ifo report.

Schanz, G. W. (1988), *Sensoren. Fuehler der Messtechnik*, 2nd edition, Heidelberg: Huethig Verlag.

Scherer, F. (1982), 'Interindustry technology flows and productivity growth,' *Review of Economics and Statistics*, pp. 627–34.

Schmoch, U. (1995), Evaluation of technological strategies of companies by means of MDS maps, *International Journal of Technology Management*, **10** (4–6), pp. 426–440.

Schmoch, U. (1996), 'International Patenting Strategies of Multinational Concerns: The Example of Telecommunications Manufacturers,' in OECD (ed.), *Innovations, Patents and Technological Strategies*, Paris, pp. 223–237.

Schmoch, U. and Th. Schnöring (1994), 'Technological strategies of telecommunications equipment manufacturers,' *Telecommunications Policy*, **18** (5), pp. 397–414.

Scholefield, J. H. (1994), 'The allocation of the R&D resource,' *R&D Management*, **24**, pp. 91–97.

Schubert, A., W. Glanzel and T. Braun (1989), 'Scientometric data files,' *Scientometrics*, **16**, pp. 3–478.

Schumpeter, J. (1934), *The Theory of Economic Development*, New York: Oxford University Press; the German original dates from 1911.

Schumpeter, J. (1939), *Business Cycles*, vols. I, II, New York: McGraw-Hill.

Schumpeter, J. (1950), *Capitalism, Socialism and Democracy*, 3rd edition, New York: Harper and Bros.

Seiford, L. M. (1990), *A Bibliography of Data Envelopment Analysis* (1978–1990), version 5.0, Technical Report, Department of Industrial Engineering, University of Massachusetts, Amherst, MA.

Seiford, L. and R. M. Thrall (1990), 'Recent developments in DEA: the mathematical programming approach to frontier analysis,' *Journal of Econometrics*, **46**, pp. 7–38.

Sengupta, J. K. and R. E. Sfeir (1988), 'Efficiency measurement by data envelopment analysis with econometric applications,' *Applied Economics*, **20**, pp. 285–293.

Shapiro, B. P., A. J. Slywotzky and R. S. Tedlow (1999), 'How to stop bad things from happening to good companies,' See Web site: http://www.strategy-business.com/ strategy/97104/page13.htm.

Shapiro, C. and H. Varian (1998), *Information Rules*, Boston, MA.: Harvard Business School Press.

Sher, H. (1998), 'A year of painful adjustment', *The Jerusalem Report*, p. 38.

Sherman, H. D. (1984), 'Improving the productivity of service businesses,' *Sloan Management Review*, **25** (3), pp. 11–23.

Shillito, M. L. (1994), *Advanced Quality Function Development: Linking Technology to Market and Company Needs*, New York: Wiley.

Shoham, A., S. Lifshitz and S. Maital (1998), 'Technometric benchmarking: identifying sources of superior customer value,' unpublished manuscript, Technion – Technical University of Haifa.

Silver, M. (1996), 'Quality, Prices and Hedonics', *International Journal of the Economics of Business*, **3** (3), 351–366.

Simon, C. J. and M. W. Sullivan (1993), 'The measurement and determinants of brand equity: a financial approach,' *Marketing Science*, **12** (1), pp. 28–52.

Slywotzky, A. (1996), *Value Migration*, Boston, MA.: Harvard Business School Press.

Smit, H. T. J. (1996), 'Growth options and strategy analysis,' unpublished doctoral dissertation, University of Amsterdam.

Smith, A. (1776), *An Inquiry into the Nature and Causes of the Wealth of Nations*, Dent edition of 1910.

Solow, R. (1957), 'Technical progress and the aggregate production function,' *Review of Economics and Statistics*, **39**, pp. 312–320.

Solow, R. (1969), *Growth Theory: An Exposition*, Oxford, UK: Clarendon Press.

Sproles, G. B. (1986), 'The concept of quality and the efficiency of markets: issues and comments,' *Journal of Consumer Research*, **13**, pp. 146–148.

Srivastava, R. K. and A. D. Shocker (1991), 'Brand equity: A perspective on its meaning and measurement', report 91–124, Marketing Science Institute, Cambridge, MA.

Stahl, M. J. and J. Steger (1977), 'Measuring innovation and productivity,' *Research Management*, **20**, p. 1.

Stankiewicz, R. (1989), 'An overview of Israel's biotechnology industry,' *Biotech Europe*, pp. 39–43.

Stankiewicz, R. (1990), 'Basic Technologies and the Innovation Process,' in J. Sigurdson (ed.), *Measuring the Dynamics of Technological Change*, London, UK: Pinter, pp. 13–38.

Steenkamp, J.-B.E.M. (1989), *Product Quality*, Assen: Van Gorcum.

Sullivan, M. W. (1998), 'How brand names affect the demand for twin automobiles,' *Journal of Marketing Research*, **35**, pp. 154–165.

Swann, P., D. Temple and M. Shurmer (1996), Standards and trade performance: the UK experience, *The Economic Journal*, **106**, pp. 1297–1313.

Symonds, W. C. and D. Greising (1995), 'A dogfight over 950 customers,' *Business Week*, p. 39.

Szakonyi, R. (1985), 'To improve R&D productivity,' *Research Management*, **28**, p. 3.

Tabrizi, B. and R. Walleigh (1997), 'Defining next-generation products: an inside look.' *Harvard Business Review*, Nov.–Dec., pp. 116–124.

Terleckyj, N. (1974), *Effects of R&D on the Productivity Growth of Industries: An Exploratory Study*, Washington, DC: National Planning Association.

Thor, C. G. (1991), 'Performance measurement in a research organization,' *Productivity and Quality Management Frontiers*, **III**, pp. 29–35.

Thurow, L. (1997), *The Future of Capitalism*, New York: William Morrow.

Thurow, L. (1999), *Building Wealth. The New Rules for Individuals, Companies and Nations in a Knowledge-based Economy*, New York, NY: Harper Collins.

Trajtenberg, M. (1990), *Economic Analysis of Product Innovation – The Case of CT Scanners*, Cambridge, MA.: Harvard University Press.

Trigeorgis, L. (1996), *Real Options. Managerial Flexibility and Strategy in Resource Allocation*, Cambridge and London: MIT Press.

Troy, K. (1998), *Managing the Corporate Brand*, The Conference Board: New York, NY, Research report 1214–98–RR.

Tversky, A., S. Sattah and P. Slovic (1987), 'Contingent weighting in judgement and choice,' *Psychological Review*, **95**, pp. 371–384.

Utterback, J. M. (1994), *Mastering the Dynamics of Innovation*, Boston, MA.: Harvard Business School Press.

Utterback, J. M. and W. J. Abernathy (1975), 'A dynamic model of process and product innovation,' *Omega*, **3**, pp. 639–656.

Wakelin, K. (1998), 'Productivity growth and R&D expenditure in UK manufacturing firms,' Working Paper, University of Nottingham, May.

Ward, S., L. Light and J. Goldstine (1999), 'What high-tech managers need to know about brands,' *Harvard Business Review*, pp. 85–95.

Watson, G. H. (1993), *Strategic Benchmarking*, New York, NY: John Wiley & Sons.

Wilkie, W. L. and E. A. Pessemier (1973), 'Issues in marketing's use of multi-attribute models,' *Journal of Marketing Research*, **10**, pp. 428–441.

Windrum, P. and C. Birchenhall (1998), 'Is product life cycle theory a special case? Dominant designs and the emergence of market niches through coevolutionary-learning,' *Structural Change and Economic Dynamics*, **9**, pp. 109–134.

World Bank (1999), *World Development Indicators* (on CD-ROM), World Bank: Washington, DC.

Yin, J. (1994), 'Managing process innovation through incremental improvements: empirical evidence in the petroleum refining industry,' *Technological Forecasting and Social Change*, **47**, pp. 265–276.

Young, A. (1992), 'A tale of two cities: factor accumulation and technical change in Hong Kong and Singapore,' O. J. Blanchard and S. Fischer (ed.), NBER Macroeconomics Annual, Cambridge, MA.: MIT Press, pp. 13–63.

Zangwill, W. I. (1993), *Lightning Strategies for Innovation*, New York, NY: Lexington.

Zeithaml, V. A. (1988), 'Consumer perceptions of price, quality, and value: a means-end model and synthesis of evidence,' *Journal of Marketing*, **52** (3), pp. 2–22.

# Subject Index

353